THE SPOKEN ARABIC OF IRAQ

BY

JOHN VAN ESS, M.A.
AMERICAN MISSION, BASRAH

SECOND EDITION
With Revised and Additional Vocabulary

OXFORD UNIVERSITY PRESS

Oxford University Press, Walton Street, Oxford OX2 6DP
Oxford New York Toronto
Delhi Bombay Calcutta Madras Karachi
Petaling Jaya Singapore Hong Kong Tokyo
Nairobi Dar es Salaam Cape Town
Melbourne Auckland
and associated companies in
Berlin Ibadan

Oxford is a trade mark of Oxford University Press

Published in the United States
by Oxford University Press, New York

ISBN 0-19-815145-4

First edition 1917
Reprinted 1918, 1920, 1930
Second edition 1938
Reprinted 1941, 1942, 1944, 1946, 1953, 1961, 1971, 1975, 1976, 1978
First issued in paperback 1975
Reprinted 1976, 1978, 1989

Printed in Great Britain by Biddles Ltd
Guildford and King's Lynn

PREFACE TO SECOND EDITION

SINCE this book was first published extensive changes have occurred, especially in the vocabulary in everyday use. Persian, Turkish, and English words have largely disappeared and their place has been taken, even on the lips of the common people, by pure Arabic words. Due to the spread of education, the general literary level is also higher. In view of the fact that this book was originally set up in plate form, it has been found impracticable to introduce changes into the text itself. Indeed, except for new or different words which are introduced into the revised vocabulary, few changes are necessary. Such changes concern only those who study the character and involve a few corrections, chiefly in vowelling.[1]

It is admitted that there are a few inconsistencies in the transliteration, particularly in the use of *y* and *ow*. On account of the extreme fluidity of the sounds on the lips of the people, the forms used have been an attempt to approximate the sounds as closely as possible.

The student is urged to observe and practise the use of participles. I would almost say that one's proficiency in the spoken language is measured by his command of their extraordinary variety.

J. V. E.

BASRAH, IRAQ,

September, 1937

[1] In order not to confuse the beginner, I would now omit the *hemza qaṭ'* with the definite article in pause, the simple imperative, the VII Measure, &c., though such use is current among modern Arabic grammarians.

PREFACE TO FIRST EDITION

The object of this book is to assist the reader in acquiring a knowledge of the Spoken Arabic of Iraq. Only so much of the literary language has been inserted as is required by those who prefer thus to approach the colloquial. For further means of obtaining a knowledge of literary Arabic the student is referred to the bibliography at the end of Part I.

It is important to remember that in this manual the colloquial must not be regarded as a transliteration of that in the character. For while the written language retains the forms and grammar of an earlier age, the Arabic spoken in Iraq to-day, though its direct descendant, is much simplified in structure and has acquired many dialectical peculiarities. It may be urged that transliteration is a concession to weakness; but its justification lies in the fact that this book has been written to meet the special needs of those to whom the element of time is of prime importance. and who desire chiefly a working knowledge of the colloquial. The words used are universally understood in Iraq.

CONTENTS

	PAGE
PREFACE	iii
Note on Transliteration	vii
INTRODUCTION	1
The Alphabet	1
Vowels and Diphthongs	3
Other Signs in Arabic Script	4
PART I	
GRAMMAR AND EXERCISES	7
The Plural	8
Elision and Assimilation	8
Salutations	10
Arab Etiquette	11
'To have'	13
The Regular Verb	25
Active Voice: Past Tense	25
Active Voice: Present Tense	27
The Imperative	28
The Active Participle	30
The Passive Participle	31
Nouns of Place or Time	31
Nouns of Instrument	32
Nouns of Action	32
The Irregular Verb	32
Class I	33
Class II	37
Class III	40
Possession	48
The Verb *jà*, 'he came'	52

PAGE
Genders 54
Numerals 56
Ordinal Numbers 64
Pronominal Suffixes of the Verb 69
The Relative Pronoun 72
The Measures of the Verb 73
The Measures of the Verb illustrated . . . 76
Summary of the Strong Verb 80
Summary of Irregular Verbs 84
Adjectives for colours and bodily defects . . . 95
Fractions and Arithmetic 99
Time of Day 101
Conditional Sentences 106
Comparison of Adjectives 106
Idiomatic Expressions 108
Days and Months 113
The Diminutive 118
The Literary Passive 119
Bibliography 120

PART II

VOCABULARY 121
REVISED AND ADDITIONAL VOCABULARY . . 257

NOTE ON TRANSLITERATION

The following table gives the values of the letters and symbols sed in the transliteration ; only the colloquial is transliterated.

a	as in *along*
à	as in *fat*, but lengthened
â	as in *father*
e	as in *let*
ê	as in *obey*
i	as in *pin*
î	as in *ravine*
o	as in *forest*
ô	as in *hope*
u	as *oo* in *good*
û	as in *true*
ai	as in *aisle*
aw	as in *howl*
g	as in *gum*
gh	a gargling sound
ḥ	a dry, sharp *h*
kh	as in *loch*, as pronounced by the Scotch
j	as in *join*
q	as in *stuck*, a heavy *k*
r	with a roll
ṣ	a heavy *s*, as in *buzz-saw*
ṭ	a heavy *t*, as in *but then*
ch	as in *chat*
th	as in *thin*
dh	as *th* in *father*
ʿ	indicates the heavy consonant *ain* and is pronounced with a choking sound.

The consonants b, d, f, h, k, l, m, n, p (rarely), s, t, w, y, and z are employed with their English values in the transliteration.

INTRODUCTION

(Need not be studied for colloquial.)

THE ALPHABET

Ordinarily only the consonants are written. There are twenty-eight of these. They are written and read from right to left. The vowels will be explained later. In the case of twenty-two of the consonants, each has four special forms, depending on whether it stands alone, or is connected with adjacent consonants at the beginning, in the middle, or at the end of a word; the remaining six consonants have only one additional form each, when connected with the preceding consonant in the middle or at the end of a word.

Name	*End*	*Middle*	*Beg.*	*Alone*	*Eng. Equiv.*
Alif	ـا	ـا	ا	ا	See Vowels, Hemza
Ba	ـب	ـبـ	بـ	ب	*b*
Ta	ـت	ـتـ	تـ	ت	*t*
Tha	ـث	ـثـ	ثـ	ث	*th* as in *thin*
Jim	ـج	ـجـ	جـ	ج	*j* as in *join*
Ha	ـح	ـحـ	حـ	ح	*ḥ*; a dry, sharp *h*
Kha	ـخ	ـخـ	خـ	خ	*kh* as *ch* in *loch*
Dal	ـد	ـد	د	د	*d*
Dhal	ـذ	ـذ	ذ	ذ	*dh* as *th* in *father*
Ra	ـر	ـر	ر	ر	*r* with a roll
Zen	ـز	ـز	ز	ز	*z*
Sin	ـس	ـسـ	سـ	س	*s*
Shin	ـش	ـشـ	شـ	ش	*sh*

Name	*End*	*Middle*	*Beg.*	*Alone*	*Eng. Equiv.*
Sad	ـص	ـصـ	صـ	ص	ṣ; s as in *buzz-saw*
Dhad	ـض	ـضـ	ضـ	ض	heavy *dh* as in *and the*
Ta	ـط	ـطـ	طـ	ط	ṭ; heavy *t* as in *but then*
Tha	ـظ	ـظـ	ظـ	ظ	*th* (or *dh*) as in *this*
Ain	ـع	ـعـ	عـ	ع	ʻ; a choking sound
Ghain	ـغ	ـغـ	غـ	غ	*gh*; a gargling sound; *h*, somewhat like the French *r* in grasseyé or the Dutch *g*
Fa	ـف	ـفـ	فـ	ف	*f*
Qaf	ـق	ـقـ	قـ	ق	*q*; a heavy *k* as in *stuck*; sometimes hard *g*
Kaf	ـك	ـكـ	كـ	ك	*k*
Lam	ـل	ـلـ	لـ	ل	*l*
Mim	ـم	ـمـ	مـ	م	*m*
Nun	ـن	ـنـ	نـ	ن	*n*
Ha	ـه	ـهـ	هـ	ه	*h*
Waw	ـو	ـو	و	و	*w*
Ya	ـي	ـيـ	يـ	ي	*y*

Exercise i.

ذهب زيد الى السّوق ليشتري اللحم فتخاصم هو والقصاب لنقصان في
الوزن ثم ترافعا بيد الشرطي الى الحاكم فالقاهما في السجن شهرا وزيادة على
ذلك لتأديبهما اخذ من كل واحد منهما مقدارا من الدراهم ثم اطلقهما
فبعد ذلك لم يقع لاحدهما مخاصمة مع احد ابدا ولزم كلّ منهما طريق ما
يتعيش به من بيع وتجارة ونحوهما ٭

VOWELS

The short vowels in Arabic are normally not written at all. When written they are placed above or below the consonant which in pronunciation they follow, as it were: p^{o}t^{a}t^{o}. There are only three short vowels recognized in Arabic writing.

1. *a* is indicated by a stroke ـَ called Fet-ḥa, written above the consonant; e.g. بَ ba.

The *a* becomes long by the addition of Alif to the consonant; e.g. بَا bâ. The alif here is only a sign of prolongation, and is called the cognate of fet-ḥa. The fet-ḥa then frequently takes the form of a vertical stroke.

2. *i* is indicated by a stroke ـِ called Kesra, written below the consonant; e.g. بِ bi.

The *i* becomes long by the addition of Ya to the consonant with kesra; e.g. بِي bî. The ya here is only a sign of prolongation, and is called the cognate of kesra.

3. *u* is indicated by a sign ـُ called Dhumma, written above the consonant; e.g. بُ bu.

The *u* becomes long by the addition of Waw to the consonant with dhumma; e.g. بُو bu. The waw here is only a sign of prolongation, and is called the cognate of dhumma.

DIPHTHONGS

When waw and ya are preceded by heterogeneous vowels, that is, by vowels of which they are not cognate, diphthongs result.

E.g. a + waw yields أَوْ aw (in colloquial often *ô*)

a + ya yields أَيْ ai (in colloquial often *ê*).

Note on Vowel Variation.

As in all languages which have a strong stress accent, a short vowel in an unstressed syllable in Arabic, whether it be theoretically fet-ḥa, kesra, or dhumma, becomes practically colourless, as e.g. in English *along*, *holiday*, *moustache*. Even in stressed syllables the short vowels are extraordinarily fluid and subject to variation. The chief influence at work to modify them is the presence of heavy or light consonants. Thus the thin or light consonants tend to produce the thinner vowels, as *i* or *e*, while the heavy consonants, as *dh*, and the gutturals, as *kh*, tend to produce the heavier vowels, as *a* or *u*, regardless of the fact that in Arabic script they are the same vowels.

E.g. كَتَبَ keteb, ضَرَبَ dharab, which in Arabic script have precisely the same vowel signs. Even the long vowel *â* is subject to such influence. E.g. كَاتِبْ kàtib, غَافِلْ ghâfil.

OTHER SIGNS IN ARABIC SCRIPT

Hemza: When to a European ear a short vowel sound occurs initially in a word or syllable, the Arab professes to detect a light consonant in the slight contraction of the throat. This light consonant is indicated by a sign ـٔ called Hemza. The hemza is usually accompanied by an alif, which serves as its carrier, but which has no value in itself. When the vowel which follows this light consonant is fet-ḥa, the hemza is written over the alif, and when the vowel is kesra the hemza is written under the alif. When the word begins with a hemza which has dhumma, the alif is also the carrier, but when hemza with dhumma occur in the middle of a word, beginning a syllable, the carrier is usually waw; or, if likewise in the middle of a word hemza occurs with kesra, the carrier is ya without dots; e.g. أَكتب إسلام أُصور رُؤُوس تائل.

Wasl: Arabs cannot pronounce a word which begins with two consonants. E.g. *skin* with an Arab becomes *iskin*. Hence, when a word would in the course of inflexion begin with two consonants, they place an alif before it, over which is written the sign ـٱ called Wasl. This is a bridge which links the final vowel of the preceding word to the first consonant of the second word. Here again the alif is only a carrier, and has no value in itself. The wasl occurs in the definite article ال el, in parts of the verb, and in a few nouns to be explained later. When the wasl would occur after a pause, the hemza is usually retained, and the words are not connected.

Shedda: the Shedda ـّ, written over a consonant, indicates that the consonant must be doubled; e.g. محمّد Muhammad. The Arabs are very particular about pronouncing doubled consonants. Cf. pen-knife, book-case.

Medda: when أ is followed by ا, as e.g. أأكل, a very long *a* results, which is indicated by a mark ـٓ called Medda, which is really an alif prostrate; e.g. آكل âkul, I eat. When alif is followed by hemza, medda may likewise be written; e.g. امرآء. Thus the medda comprises in one sign an alif, a hemza, and a fet-ḥa.

Nunation: There is no indefinite article in Arabic. Indefiniteness in literary Arabic is indicated by the ending of the noun, as follows:

Nominative *un* represented by a sign ـٌ called Dhummatên, e.g. كِتَابٌ.

Genitive, Dative *in* represented by a sign ـٍ called Kesratên, e.g. كِتَابٍ.

Accusative *an* represented by a sign ـً called Fet-ḥatên. When in the accusative the noun has a masculine ending, explained later, the fet-ḥatên is followed by alif, which, however, is not pronounced; e.g. كِتَابًا.

Certain nouns in literary Arabic are without nunation; they then have only two case-endings, *u* for the Nominative and *a* for the other cases.

Nunation is not observed in ordinary conversation, save in rare instances. In colloquial, indefiniteness is rendered by the simple noun without the article.

Sukun: When a consonant has no vowel of its own following it, a mark ـْ called Sukun is placed over that consonant, e.g. بَصْرَةُ Baṣrah. Likewise a sukun is placed over the waw or ya which go to form a diphthong. Arab grammarians also place the sukun over any vowelless letter, even though it be a cognate alif, or waw or ya.

Stress: Counting from the end of the word, the stress generally falls on the first long syllable, or the first closed syllable encountered. If none such occurs the stress falls on the first syllable of the word, except when such begins with a wasl, in which case the stress falls on the second syllable.

Exercise ii.

Explain all the marks and signs in the following:

إِقْدِمْ أَيُّهَا ٱلتِّلْمِيذُ عَلَى ٱكْتِسَابِ رُتْبَةِ ٱلْعِلْمِ مَا دُمْتَ صَغِيرَ ٱلسِّنِّ
فَإِنَّ ٱلْحَوَاسَّ ٱلظَّاهِرَةَ وَٱلْبَاطِنَةَ فِي هٰذَا ٱلْحَالِ قَوِيَّةٌ فَإِذَا ضَعُفَتْ ضَعُفَ
ٱلْكَسْبُ وَحَصَلَ ٱلْأَسَفُ عَلَى مَا فَاتَ وَلَا يُمْكِنُ عَوْدُهُ وَإِعْلَمْ أَنَّهُ لَا يَكُونُ
أَعْلَى لَقَبٍ وَأَلْطَفُ شَرَفٍ وَأَسْنَى رُتْبَةٍ مِنَ ٱلْعِلْمِ فَإجْتَهِدْ تُصِبْ ◊

PART I

GRAMMAR AND EXERCISES

(The first column of each Word List and the last section of each Exercise give equivalents, in the written language, of the colloquial forms and expressions; see Preface, p. iii.)

WORD LIST

Arabic	*English*	*Colloquial*
تَعَالَ (*pl.*) ج تَعَالُوا	come	ta'âl, *pl.* ta'âlû (used only in imp.)
رُحْ ج رُوحُوا	go	rûḥ, *pl.* rûḥû
هُنَا	here	hina
هُنَاكَ	there	hinàk
اُجْلُبْ ج اُجْلُبُوا	bring	jîb, *pl.* jîbû
وَدِّ ج وَدُّوا	take away	waddi, *pl.* waddû
اُنْقُلْ ج اُنْقُلُوا	remove	shîl, *pl.* shîlû
مَاءٌ	water	mai
خُبْزٌ	bread	khubz
وَ	and	wa
مَا هٰذَا	what is this ?	shinû hàdha ?
أُرِيدُ	I want	arîd
قَلِيلٌ	a little	shwêya
حُطَّ ج حُطُّوا	put	ḥaṭṭ, *pl.* ḥaṭṭû

Exercise 1.

1. Come here. 2. Bring the bread and the water. 3. What is this ? 4. I want a little bread. 5. Remove the water.

6. Bring the bread here. 7. Put the water there. 8. Come here and go there.

1. Ta'âl hina. 2. Jîb el khubz wa el mai. 3. Shinû hàdha? 4. Arîd shwêya khubz. 5. Shîl el mai. 6. Jîb el khubz hina. 7. Ḥaṭṭ el mai hina. 8. Ta'âl hina wa ruḥ hinàk.

١ تعال هنا. ٢ اجلب الخبز والماء. ٣ ما هذا. ٤ اريد قليلاً من الخبز. ٥ أنقل الماء. ٦ اجلب الخبز هنا. ٧ حط الماء هناك. ٨ تعال هنا ورح هناك ❖

THE PLURAL

No definite rule can be given for the formation of the plural. The plurals of nouns can only be learned individually, a task which is not so formidable as would at first appear. The student is urged to learn the plural as soon as he meets the noun. A regular plural formation exists, though its use is restricted almost entirely to participles, explained later. It is formed by adding *în* for the masculine and *àt* for the feminine. Such a plural is called a sound or unbroken plural. All others are called broken plurals.

(In literary Arabic the sound masculine plural is وْنَ in the nominative case, and يْنَ in the oblique and accusative cases, except when followed by a noun in the genitive, when نَ is dropped. The sound feminine plural is اتٌ in the nominative case, and اتٍ in the oblique and accusative cases; but when the word is definite, the nunation is dropped and the single vowel remains.)

A special form, called the Dual, for only two objects, is regularly used and regularly formed, by adding *ên*; e.g. kitàbên, two books.

(In literary Arabic the dual nominative is انِ, and oblique and accusative ـَيْنِ.)

ELISION AND ASSIMILATION

When the definite article ال *el* is followed by ت *t*, ث *th*, د *d*, ذ *dh*, ر *r*, ز *z*, س *s*, ش *sh*, ص *ṣ*, ض *dh*, ط *ṭ*, ظ *th*, ل *l*, or ن *n*, the ل *l* of the article is assimilated to that letter, which is then doubled, e.g. أَلشَّمْسُ esh shems, the sun. When the article is preceded by a vowel, the *e* of the article should rightly be dropped in transliteration, and the *l* affixed to the preceding word, inasmuch as its corresponding vowel in Arabic disappears in pronunciation; but in this manual the *e* is retained to prevent confusion in the mind of the student, who might regard it as an integral part of the preceding word. Only after certain prepositions is the *l* affixed.

(In literary Arabic, when the consonant preceding the article is quiescent, the alif of the article has kesra with few exceptions, such as كُمْ هُمُ, which give it dhumma, and a few others which give it fet-ḥa.)

WORD LIST

مَرْكَبْ ج مَرَاكِبُ	ship	markab *pl.* maràkib
فُلُوسْ	money	fulûs, flûs
أَعْطِينِي	give me	aʿṭinî
نَهْر ج أَنْهُر . شَطّ ج شُطُوط	river	shaṭṭ, *pl.* shuṭûṭ
بَيْت ج بُيُوت	house	bêt, *pl.* byût, buyût
طَرِيق ج طُرُق	road	darb, *pl.* durûb ṭarîq, *pl.* ṭurq
إِلَى	to	ila
بَلَم ج أَبْلَام	bellum	belam, *pl.* ablàm
حِصَان ج حُصُن . خَيْل	horse	ḥuṣân, *pl.* ḥuṣn, khêl
جِسْر ج جُسُور	bridge	jisr, *pl.* jisûr
مَكْتُوب ج مَكَاتِيب	letter	maktûb, *pl.* makàtîb
اَلْآن	now	hessa, elàn, el ḥîn, tôa
فِي	in	fì, bi
اَلْ	the	el

The names of cities frequently are preceded by *el.*

Exercise 2.

1. Go to Basrah in the bellum. 2. The ship in the river. 3. Give me the money. 4. Bring the horse to the bridge. 5. Take the letters to the house. 6. Go now. 7. Go to the river. 8. Bring a little money. 9. The ships and the horses and the houses.

1. Rûḥ ilal Baṣrah fîl belum. 2. El markab fîsh shaṭṭ. 3. A'tinî el flûs. 4. Jîb el ḥuṣân ilal jisr. 5. Waddi el makàtîb ilal bêt. 6. Rûḥ hessa. 7. Rûḥ ilash shaṭṭ. 8. Jîb shwêya flûs. 9. El maràkib wal khêl wal byût.

١ رُحْ الى البصرة في البلم. ٢ المركب في الشط. ٣ اعطني الفلوس.
٤ اجلب الحصان الى الجسر. ٥ ودِّ المكاتيب الى البيت. ٦ رح الان.
٧ رح الى الشط. ٨ اجلب قليلاً من الفلوس. ٩ المراكب والخيل والبيوت.

WORD LIST: SALUTATIONS

اَلسَّلَامُ عَلَيْكُمْ	Peace on you	Salàm 'alêkum
	(*Reply*)	
وَعَلَيْكُمُ ٱلسَّلَامُ	And on you peace	Wa 'alêkum es salàm
صَبَّحَكُمُ ٱللّٰهُ بِالْخَيْرِ	Good morning	Sabbâḥkum Allâh bil khair
مَسَّاكُمُ ٱللّٰهُ بِالْخَيْرِ	Good evening (any time after noon)	Messàkum Allâh bil khair
تَفَضَّلْ . بِسْمِ ٱللّٰهِ	Come in	Tafadhdhal, Bismillah
اِسْتَرِحْ ج اِسْتَرِيحُوا	Sit down	Istarîḥ, *pl.* istarîḥû
مِنْ فَضْلَكَ	If you please	Min fadhlek
مُتَشَكِّرٌ . مَمْنُونٌ	Thank you	Mimnûn, Muteshekker, Kethther khairek
فِي أَمَانِ ٱللّٰهِ	Good-bye	Fî amàn Illàh

كَيْفَ حَالُكَ	How are you?	Shlôn kêfek, kêf ḥâlek
	(*Reply*)	
اَلْحَمْدُ لِلّٰهِ	Praise God	El ḥamdu lillah
	or	
اَللّٰهُ يُسَلِّمَكَ	God give you peace	Allâh yusellemek
	or	
أَسْأَلُ عَنْ حَالَكَ	I ask after you	Es-el kêfek
جَنَابَكَ ج جَنَابُكُمْ	Your honour	Jinàbek (title of respect)
إِنْ شَاءَ ٱللّٰهُ	If God will	In shâ Allâh
أَهْلاً وَسَهْلاً	Welcome	Ehlen wa sehlen
أَسْتَرْخِصُ	I ask leave to go	Istarkhiṣ

The rider first salaams the walker, the walker the stander, the stander the sitter. It is courteous to salaam one who makes way for you on the road. After the preliminary salutation of *salàm ʿalêkum* said by the visitor at the door, and replied to by the host, good morning or good evening must be said by the host when all are seated, which is also replied to.

ARAB ETIQUETTE

1. The host will assign the place to sit. Even then the visitor, unless he be of undoubted higher social rank, should sit a little lower. Handshaking is quite proper upon entering, and is optional upon leaving. A European is not expected to remove his shoes, but should remove his hat.

2. A sheikh of consequence should always be addressed in the plural.

3. Under no circumstances should one ask after the health of the host's family, if the host be a Moslem. The word for family implies the women folk. A European refers to his own wife as *Jinàb el khâtûn*.

4. The child of the host is referred to by the visitor as *el maḥrûs* or *el makhdûm*.

5. When any one of equal social rank refers to himself as *el faqîr*, or with similar deprecatory terms, the proper ejaculation on the part of the hearer is *jinàbukum*. It is courteous to refer to one's self as *da'ìkum*.

6. If it is necessary to refer to anything regarded as unclean by a Muhammadan, such as shoe or dog, or to mention anything not elegant, such as donkey, garbage, &c., the subject is prefaced by a remark such as *hàshàkum*, *tikram*, *mukerrem man yisma'* or equivalent phrase.

7. Coffee should not be received with the left hand, nor should more than three Arab cups be taken. When giving back the cup and no more is desired, the cup should be slightly shaken. The empty cup should never be placed on the floor nor turned over. Coffee served in Turkish style, in small cup and saucer, is offered only once. A glass of sherbet should not be drained. After drinking water it is customary to say to the drinker *hannîyan*. The proper ejaculation on the part of the drinker is *hannàkum Allâh*. If invited to partake of a meal when a call happens to coincide with it, and the invitation is declined, it should be accompanied by the phrase *'awâfi*.

8. If it is desired to convey the information that a certain one has died, the bald statement, 'He is dead', should not be made; the bad news should be broken or introduced by the use of some such phrase as *râsek ṭayyib*, *ta'ìsh minhu*, or *enta sàlim*.

9. Under no circumstances must the sole of the foot be allowed to point to another.

10. When one is thanked for a favour the reply is *ḥallat el baraka*.

11. The host when wishing to show himself complimented by a visit says, *Sharraftum*. The reply is *sharraf Allâh qadrek*.

'TO HAVE'

The idea of 'having' is expressed in Arabic by the word *'and* (like Hindustani *-pas*), to which are added pronominal suffixes.

عِنْدي	I have	'andi
عِنْدَك	you (*m.*) have	'andek
عِنْدِك	you (*f.*) have	'andech *or* 'andeki
عِنْدُه	he has	'anduh
عِنْدَها	she has	'andeha
عِنْدَنا	we have	'andena, 'adna
عِنْدَكُمْ	you (*pl.*) have	'andekum, 'adkum
عِنْدَهُمْ	they have	'andehum, 'andum

In asking a question the voice is raised without any change in words. (In literary Arabic the question is introduced by هَلْ or أَ.)

An idea like 'The horse has water' is expressed by 'The horse he has water'.

The past 'had' is formed by prefixing كَانَ kàn to the above forms.

Exercise 3.

1. Have you bread? 2. I had a little bread. 3. They have money. 4. Have you some water? 5. We have bread and water. 6. We had bread and water. 7. He has the money. 8. Have you the letter? 9. Has the horse water? 10. We had some money. 11. She had the letter.

1. 'Andek khubz? 2. Kàn 'andi shwêya khubz. 3. 'Andehum flûs. 4. 'Andek shwêya mai? 5. 'Andena khubz wa mai. 6. Kàn 'andena khubz wa mai. 7. 'Anduh el flûs. 8. 'Andek el maktûb? 9. El ḥuṣân 'anduh mai? 10. Kàn 'adna shwêya flûs. 11. El maktûb kàn 'andeha.

١ هل عندك خبز. ٢ كان عندي قليل خبز. ٣ عندهم فلوس. ٤ هل عندك قليل ماء. ٥ عندنا خبز وماء. ٦ كان عندنا خبز وماء. ٧ عنده الفلوس. ٨ هل عندك المكتوب. ٩ هل الحصان عنده ماء. ١٠ كان عندنا قليل من الفلوس. ١١ المكتوب كان عندها.

WORD LIST

كَبِيرٌ ج كِبَارٌ	big	kabîr, *pl.* kibâr chabîr, (*pl.* never *chibâr*)
صَغِيرٌ ج صِغَارٌ	small	ṣaghîr, *pl.* ṣighâr
قَرِيبٌ . قَرِيبَةٌ . أَقْرِبَاءُ	near	qarîb, *pl.* (persons) qarîbîn ,, *pl.* (things) qarîba jarîb
بَعِيدٌ . بَعِيدَةٌ . بُعَدَاءُ	far	ba'îd, *pl.* (persons) ba'îdîn ,, *pl.* (things) ba'îda
حَارٌّ . حَارَّةٌ . حَارُّونَ	hot	ḥârr, *pl.* (persons) ḥârrîn ,, *pl.* (things) ḥârra
بَارِدٌ . بَارِدَةٌ . بَارِدُونَ	cold	bàrid, *pl.* (temperament) bàridîn ,, *pl.* (temperature, things) bàrida bardàn, *pl.* bardànîn (temperature, persons)
كَثِيرٌ . كَثِيرَةٌ . كَثِيرُونَ	many	kathîr, *pl.* (persons) kathîrîn ,, *pl.* (things) kathîra chathîr, &c. wàjid (*vulg.* hwâyi)
كَثِيرٌ او جِدًّا	very	kathîr, kullish wàjid, hwâyi
طَيِّبٌ . طَيِّبَةٌ . طَيِّبُونَ جَيِّدٌ . جَيِّدَةٌ . جِيَادٌ زَيْنٌ . زَيْنَةٌ . زَيْنُونَ	good	ṭayyib, *pl.* (persons) ṭayyibîn ,, *pl.* (things) ṭayyiba khôsh (precedes noun) zên, *pl.* (persons) zênîn ,, *pl.* (things) zêna
رَدِيءٌ . رَدِيئَةٌ . أَرْدِيَاءُ	bad	kharâb, redi, mû zên
مَا . لَيْسَ	not (with *adj.*)	mû, (vulgar) mûsh

The English present 'am, is, &c.' has no equivalent in Arabic; e.g. *The boy is good* becomes *The boy good.*

The adjective follows the noun. When in English the adjective precedes a definite noun, in Arabic the definite article is repeated with the adjective; e.g. *The good boy* becomes *The boy the good.* Otherwise, in general, the order of words in the sentence is as in English. The verb frequently begins the sentence when it contains the main sentiment which is to be expressed.

Exercise 4.

1. The big house. 2. The house is big. 3. The good road. 4. The road is good. 5. The house is very small. 6. The large ship. 7. The ship is large. 8. Is the river large? 9. The house is near. 10. The good water. 11. The water is good. 12. The water is very good. 13. Have you good bread? 14. Cold water. 15. Some hot meat. 16. Hot water. 17. The houses are big. 18. The horses are not small. 19. The water is very bad.

1. El bêt el kabîr. 2. El bêt kabîr. 3. Ed darb eṭ ṭayyib. 4. Ed darb ṭayyib. 5. El bêt kullish ṣaghîr. 6. El markab el kabîr. 7. El markab kabîr. 8. Esh shaṭṭ kabîr? 9. El bêt qarîb. 10. El mai eṭ ṭayyib. 11. El mai ṭayyib. 12. El mai kullish ṭayyib. 13. 'Andek khubz ṭayyib? 14. Mai bàrid. 15. Laḥm ḥârr. 16. Mai ḥârr. 17. El byût kibâr. 18. El khêl mû ṣighâr. 19. El mai kullish mû zên.

١ البيت الكبير. ٢ البيت كبير. ٣ الطريق الطيّب. ٤ الطريق طيّب. ٥ البيت صغير جداً. ٦ المركب الكبير. ٧ المركب كبير. ٨ هل النهر كبير. ٩ البيت قريب. ١٠ الماء الطيّب. ١١ الماء طيّب. ١٢ الماء طيّب جداً. ١٣ هل عندك خبز جيد. ١٤ ماء بارد. ١٥ لحم حارّ. ١٦ ماء حارّ. ١٧ البيوت كبيرة. ١٨ الخيل ما صغيرة. ١٩ الماء ردي جداً ❖

WORD LIST

أَيْنَ	Where ?	Wên, Ên
كَيْفَ	How ?	Kêf, Chêf, Shlôn
مَتَى	When ?	Metta, Yimta
لِمَاذَا	Why ?	Lêsh
كَمْ	How much ? (quantity)	Eshgadr, Shgadr, Shgad
كَمْ	How much ? (price)	Bêsh, Kem, Chem
كَمْ	How many ?	Kem, Chem (with *sing.*)
مَنْ	Who ?	Men
أَيٌّ	Which ?	Ê, Yâ Yâhû (substantive)
هٰذَا	This	Hàdha (not followed by noun)
مَنْ هُوَ	Who is it ?	Menû

Exercise 5.

1. Where is the house ? 2. Where are the horses ? 3. How is the water ? 4. How is the bread ? 5. Why is this ? 6. How much is this ? 7. Where is the road to Basrah ? 8. Which is the road to Basrah ? 9. Where is the big ship ? 10. How many horses have you ? 11. Who is this ? 12. Why is the bridge here ? 13. How much bread have you ? 14. How much money has he ?

1. Wên el bêt ? 2. Wên el khêl ? 3. Shlôn el mai ? 4. Shlôn el khubz ? 5. Lêsh hàdha ? 6. Bêsh hàdha ? 7. Wên ed darb ilal Baṣrah ? 8. Yâhû ed darb ilal Baṣrah ? 9. Wên el markab el kabîr ? 10. Kem ḥuṣân ʿandek ? 11. Menu hàdha ? 12. Lêsh el jisr hina ? 13. Shgad khubz ʿandek ? 14. Shgadr flûs ʿanduh ?

١ اين البيت. ٢ اين الخيل. ٣ كيف الماء. ٤ كيف الخبز. ٥ لماذا هذا. ٦ كم هذا. ٧ اين الطريق الى البصرة. ٨ ايّ هو الطريق الى البصرة.

٩ اين المركب الكبير. ١٠ كم حصانا عندك. ١١ من هذا. ١٢ لماذا الجسر هنا. ١٣ كم عندك من الخبز. ١٤ كم عنده من الفلوس.

WORD LIST

أَنَا	I	ana
أَنْتَ	you (*m.*)	enta, ent
أَنْتِ	you (*f.*)	enti
هُوَ	he, it	hûwa
هِيَ	she	hîya
نَحْنُ	we	naḥnu, naḥen, eḥna
أَنْتُمْ	you (*pl.*)	entu, entum
هُمْ	they	hum, humma

There is no neuter in Arabic. All nouns are either masculine or feminine.

كَانَ	he was	kàn, chàn
كَانَتْ	she was	kànet, chànet
كُنْتَ	you (*m.*) were	kunet, chunet
كُنْتِ	you (*f.*) were	kunti, chunti
كُنْتُ	I was	kunet, chunet
كَانُوا	they were	kànû, chànû
كُنْتُمْ	you (*pl.*) were	kuntum, kuntû, chuntum, chuntû
كُنَّا	we were	kunna, chunna

The present tense of كَانَ kàn is not used in the English sense. Its use will be explained later. The pronoun need not be repeated with كَانَ kàn, but it generally is.

Exercise 6.

1. I was. 2. They were. 3. She was. 4. You (*pl.*) were. 5. You (*f.*) were. 6. We were. 7. It was.

1. Ana kunet. 2. Hûm kànû. 3. Hîya kànet. 4. Entu kuntû. 5. Enti kunti. 6. Eḥna kunna. 7. Hûwa kàn.

١ انا كنتُ. ٢ هم كانوا. ٣ هي كانت. ٤ انتم كنتم. ٥ انتِ كنتِ.
٦ نحن كُنّا. ٧ هو كان.

WORD LIST

فِي	in	fî
مِنْ	from	min
لِ	to	li (in sense of '*and* or after *gal*, he said)
عَلَي	on	'ala
مَعْ . بِ	with	ma', wîya
فَوْق	over	fôq
تَحْتَ	under	taḥt, ḥadr, jôa
دَاخِلْ	inside	dâkhil
خَارِجْ	outside	khârij (barra, *adv.*)
جَوْعَانْ ج جِيَاعْ	hungry	jô'ân, *pl.* jô'ânîn
عَطْشَانْ ج عِطَاشْ	thirsty	'aṭshân, *pl.* 'aṭshânîn
عَسْكَرِيّْ ج عَسْكَرْ . عَسَاكِرْ	soldier	'asker (*sing.* and *pl.*)

The preposition precedes the noun.

Fî with pron. suffixes becomes fîyya, fîk, fîch, fîh, fîha, fîna, fîkum, fîhum.

'Ala " " " 'alêya, 'alêk, 'alêch, 'alêh, 'alêha, 'alêna, 'alêkum, 'alêhum.

Wîya with pron. suffixes becomes wiyày, wiyàk, wiyàch, wiyàh, wiyàha, wiyàna, wiyàkum, wiyàhum.

Li „ „ „ lî, lek, lech, luh, leha, lena, lakum, lahum.

Exercise 7.

1. In the house. 2. On the ship. 3. We were in the house. 4. The soldiers were in the house. 5. He was inside the house. 6. Give me bread with meat. 7. I am very hungry and not thirsty. 8. Go outside. 9. Come inside. 10. Above the house. 11. The soldiers were very thirsty. 12. Are you hungry?

1. Fîl bêt. 2. ʻAlal markab. 3. Eḥna kunna fîl bêt. 4. El ʻasker kànû fîl bêt. 5. Hûwa kàn dâkhil el bêt. 6. Aʻṭinî khubz wîya laḥm. 7. Ana kullish jôʻân wa mû ʻaṭshân. 8. Rûh barra. 9. Taʻâl dâkhil. 10. Fôq el bêt. 11. El ʻasker kànû kullish ʻaṭshânîn. 12. Enta jôʻân?

١ في البيت. ٢ على المركب. ٣ نحن كنا في البيت. ٤ العساكر كانوا في البيت. ٥ هو كان داخل البيت. ٦ اعطني خبزاً مع لحم. ٧ انا جوعان جداً وما عطشان. ٨ رح الى الخارج. ٩ تعال داخل. ١٠ فوق البيت. ١١ العسكر كانوا عطاشاً جداً. ١٢ هل انت جوعان.

WORD LIST

بَيْتٌ	house	bêt
بَيْتِي	my house	bêtî
بَيْتُكَ	your (*m.*) house	bêtek
بَيْتُكِ	your (*f.*) house	bêtech (bêteki)
بَيْتُهُ	his house	bêtuh (bêtuhu)
بَيْتُهَا	her house	bêta (bêteha)

بَيْتُنَا	our house	bêtena
بَيْتُكُمْ	your (*pl.*) house	bêtekum
بَيْتُهُمْ	their house	bêtehum
هٰذَا ٱل	this (with noun) *m.*	hàdhel, hel
هٰذِ ٱل	this (,, ,,) *f.*	hàdhîl, hel (also with *pl.* of impersonal nouns)
ذَاكَ ٱل	that (with noun) *m.*	hadhàk, dhàk
تِلْكَ ٱل	that (,, ,,) *f.*	hadhîk, hadhîch (also with *pl.* of impersonal nouns)
هٰؤُلَاءِ	these	hadhôl
أُولَائِكَ	those	hadhôlàk
رَجُلٌ ج رِجَالٌ	man	rejul, *pl.* rijàl (correct) rijàl, *pl.* rijàjîl (common) riyàl, *pl.* riyàyîl (vulgar)
إِمْرَأَةٌ ج نِسَاءٌ مَرْأَةٌ	woman	ḥarma, mara *pl.* ḥarîm, nisa, niswàn
كِتَابٌ ج كُتُبٌ	book	kitàb, *pl.* kutub
يُوجَدُ	there is, there are	âkû

This house is expressed by *This the house*, Hàdhel bêt. *This is a house* is expressed by *This—house*, Hàdha bêt.

A singular noun ending in *a* generally inserts *t* before the pronominal suffix. E. g. ḥarmatî, *my woman* (wife).

(If the noun ends in ا or ي the sing. 1st pers. suffix is *ya*. E. g. ʻaṣâya, *my stick.*)

A dual noun drops *n* before suffixes. In the 1st pers. sing. it adds *ya*. E. g. yedêya يَدَيَّ my two hands.

Exercise 8.

1. The man was in our house. 2. They were with the women. 3. This book is very good. 4. This woman was inside her house. 5. That woman was in the ship. 6. This bread is bad. 7. Those men are hungry. 8. Those hungry men. 9. These soldiers are not hungry. 10. My meat. 11. Your money. 12. Our ship. 13. Your bread. 14. Give me my money. 15. Is there bread here? 16. There is no water there.

1. Er rijàl kàn fî bêtena. 2. Hum kànû wîya en niswàn. 3. Hel kitàb kullish ṭayyib. 4. Hel ḥarma kànet dâkhil bêta. 5. Hadhîch el ḥarma kànet fîl markab. 6. Hel khubz kharâb. 7. Hadhôlàk er rijàjîl jo'ânîn. 8. Hadhôlàk er rijàjîl el jo'ânîn. 9. Hadhôl el 'asker mû jo'ânîn. 10. Laḥmi. 11. Flûsek. 12. Markabena. 13. Khubzek. 14. A'ṭinî flûsî. 15. Âkû khubz hina? 16. Mâ âkû mai hinàk.

١ الرجل كان في بيتنا. ٢ كانوا مع النساء. ٣ هذا الكتاب جيدٌ جداً.
٤ هذهِ الامرأة كانت داخل بيتها. ٥ تلك الامرأة كانت في المركب.
٦ هذا الخبز ردي. ٧ اولائك الرجال جياع. ٨ اولائك الرجال الجياع.
٩ هولاء العسكر ما جياع. ١٠ لحمي. ١١ فلوسك. ١٢ مركبنا. ١٣ خبزك.
١٤ اعطني فلوسي. ١٥ هل يوجد خبز هنا. ١٦ لا يوجد ماء هناك.

WORD LIST

تَمْرَة ج تَمْر	date	tamra ; *coll.* (dates) tamr
سُكَّر	sugar	sheker
زُبْدَة	butter	zibed
رُزّ	rice	timmen
شَاي	tea	chai
قَهْوَة	coffee	qa-hwa, gâ-hwa

بَلَّامْ ج بَلَّامُونَ مَلَّاحْ ج مَلَّاحُونَ	boatman	bellàm, *pl.* bellàma mellâḥ, *pl.* melàliḥ bellamchi, *pl.* bellamchìa
نَخْلَةٌ ج نَخْلٌ	date-tree	nakhla, *pl.* nakhl
يَوْمٌ ج أَيَّامٌ	day	yôm, *pl.* ayàm
نَهَارٌ ج نُهُرٌ	day (opposite of night)	nahâr
لَيْلَةٌ ج لَيَالٍ	night	lêla, *pl.* layàlì
لَيْلًا او فِي ٱللَّيْلِ	at night	billêl
نَهَارًا او فِي ٱلنَّهَارِ	by day	binnahâr
اَلْيَوْمَ	to-day	elyôm, helyôm
بُكْرَةً او غَدًا	to-morrow	bukra, bàcher, ghada
أَمْسِ او ٱلْبَارِحَةَ	yesterday	ems, embârḥa
كَانَ يُوجَدُ	there was, were	kàn âkû
تَعْبَانٌ ج تَعْبَانُونَ	tired	tâ'bân, *pl.* tâ'bânìn

Exercise 9.

1. I was in the bellum yesterday. 2. Bring dates and bread. 3. Put sugar in the tea. 4. The soldiers were in the ship. 5. The boatmen were tired. 6. To-day we were in the bellum with this man. 7. Those soldiers were very tired at night. 8. Here was a date-tree. 9. Bring the bellum to Basrah to-morrow. 10. There were boatmen yesterday, where are they to-day? 11. I was in the house day and night. 12. This woman was on the bridge. 13. Bring rice and butter with you.

1. Ana kunet fìl belam embârḥa. 2. Jìb tamr wa khubz. 3. Ḥaṭṭ sheker fìl chai. 4. El 'asker kànû fìl markab. 5. El bellàma kànû tâ'bânìn. 6. Helyôm kunna fìl belam ma' her

rejul. 7. Hadhôlàk el ʻasker kànû kullish tâʻbânîn billêl. 8. Hina kànet nakhla. 9. Jîb el belam ilal Baṣrah bàcher. 10. Kàn âkû melàlîh ems, wên hûm helyôm? 11. Ana kunet fîl bêt lêl wa nahâr. 12. Hàdhil ḥarma kànet ʻalal jisr. 13. Jîb timmen wa zibed wiyàk.

١ انا كنت في البلم البارحة. ٢ اجلب تمرًا وخُبزًا ٣ ضع سُكرًا في الشاي. ٤ العسكر كانوا في المركب. ٥ البلّامون كانوا تعبانين. ٦ اليوم كنا في البلم مع هذا الرجل. ٧ اولائك العسكر كانوا تعبانين جداً في الليل. ٨ هنا كان نخلةٌ. ٩ اجلب البلم الى البصرة غداً. ١٠ كان يوجد ملاحون امس اين هم اليوم. ١١ انا كنتُ في البيت ليلاً ونهاراً. ١٢ هذهِ الامرأة كانت على الجسر. ١٣ اجلب رزاً وزبدةً معك.

WORD LIST

نَعَمْ	yes	nâʻam, ênâʻam
بَلَى	certainly	belli
مَعْلُومٌ	of course	maʻlûm
لَا	no	la, lakhair
مَا . لَا	not (with verb)	mâ
قِنِّينَةٌ	bottle	shîsha, *pl.* shîyash
فِنْجَانٌ ج فَنَاجِينُ	cup	finjàn, *pl.* fanàjîn
سَطْلٌ	pail	piyàla, *pl.* piyàlàt (large) baldi, *pl.* baldiyàt
حَبْلٌ ج حِبَالٌ	rope	ḥabl, *pl.* ḥibàl
بُنْدُقِيَّةٌ ج بَنَادِقُ	gun, rifle	tufka, *pl.* tufek
كَلْبٌ ج كِلَابٌ	dog	kelb, *pl.* kilàb chelb, *pl.* chilàb
عَرَبَةٌ ج عَرَبَاتٌ	carriage	ʻarabâna, *pl.* ʻarabâyin

سُوقٌ ج أَسْوَاق	bazaar	sûq, *pl.* aswâq
وَلَدٌ ج أَوْلَادٌ	boy	walad, *pl.* awlàd, wûlid
بِنْتٌ ج بَنَات	girl	bint, *pl.* banàt
بُسْتَانٌ ج بَسَاتِين	garden	bustàn, *pl.* basàtîn
مِفْتَاحٌ ج مَفَاتِيح	key	miftâḥ, *pl.* mafàtîḥ
نَارٌ ج نِيرَانٌ	fire	nâr
بِسُرْعَةٍ	quickly	bil 'âjel, bis sâ'a
لَا بَأْسَ	very well (Fr. bien)	mâ yukhâlif

Exercise 10.

1. Were you in Basrah to-day? Yes. 2. I was not in the bazaar. 3. Come quickly. 4. Bring a pail of water to the house. 5. Put (*pl.*) the rope in the bellums. 6. Have you dogs? 7. The houses are large. 8. I want a carriage. 9. Go to the bazaar with me. 10. The boy and the girl were in the garden. 11. Take this letter to the sahib. 12. Where is the key? 13. Where are the keys? 14. The fire is very hot. 15. Are there dates in the bazaar? 16. Yes, there are a great many. 17. The soldiers had guns. 18. Are you a good boy? Of course. 19. Bring the coffee. Very well.

1. Enta kunet fîl Baṣrah helyôm? Ênâ'am. 2. Ana mâ kunet fîs sûq. 3. Ta'âl bil 'âjel. 4. Jîb baldi mai ilal bêt. 5. Ḥaṭṭu el ḥabl fîl ablàm. 6. 'Andekum chilàb? 7. El byût kibâr. 8. Arîd 'ârabâna. 9. Ta'âl ilas sûq wiyày. 10. El walad wal bint kànû fîl bustàn. 11. Waddi hel maktûb ilas ṣâhib. 12. Wên el miftâḥ? 13. Wên el mafàtiḥ? 14. En nâr kullish ḥârr. 15. Âkû tamr fîs sûq? 16. Belli, âkû kathîr (*or* wàjid, *vulg.* hwâyi). 17. El 'asker kàn 'andehum tufek. 18. Enta khôsh walad? Ma'lûm. 19. Jîb el gahwa. Mâ yukhâlif.

١ هل كنت في البصرة اليوم . نعم. ٢ انا ما كنتُ في السوق. ٣ تعال بسرعة. ٤ اجلب سطل ماء الى البيت. ٥ ضعوا (حطّوا) الحبل في الابلام. ٦ هل عندكم كلاب. ٧ البيوت كبيرة. ٨ اريد عربة. ٩ تَعَال الى السوق معي. ١٠ الولد والبنت كانوا في البستان. ١١ وَدِّ هذا المكتوب الى الصاحب. ١٢ اين المفتاح. ١٣ اين المفاتيح. ١٤ النار حارة جداً. ١٥ هل يوجد تمر في السوق. ١٦ بلى يوجد كثير. ١٧ العساكر كان عندهم بنادق. ١٨ هل انت ولدٌ جيدٌ . معلوم. ١٩ اجلب القهوة . لا بأس .

THE REGULAR VERB

The form of the verb which is found in the dictionary, is the masculine, 3rd person, singular, past tense. E.g. كَتَبَ kéteb, he wrote. Most verbs have a root of three consonants. The different tenses, persons, numbers, and genders are formed by prefixing or suffixing certain letters. The pronoun, as in Latin, is contained in the form, but is frequently repeated for emphasis. In colloquial some forms are indistinguishable from others, except by context.

(Most verbs have as vowels for the consonants of the root *a a a*. Some have *a i a*, and a few have *a u a*. Throughout this manual verb-forms such as duals and fem. plurals, which are not used in colloquial, are omitted in the character.)

The accent ′, placed above a vowel in the transliteration, indicates on which syllable the stress falls.

Active Voice: Past Tense.

كَتَبَ	He wrote	kéteb
كَتَبَتْ	She wrote	kétebet
كَتَبْتَ	You (*m.*) wrote	ketébet
كَتَبْتِ	You (*f.*) wrote	ketébti

كَتَبْتُ	I wrote	ketébet
كَتَبُوا	They wrote	kétebû
كَتَبْتُمْ	You (*pl.*) wrote	ketébtû (ketébtum)
كَتَبْنَا	We wrote	ketébna

Word List.

شَرِبَ	He drank	shéreb
ضَرَبَ	He struck	dhárab
جَلَسَ	He sat	jéles
دَخَلَ	He entered	dákhal

In the above four verbs the first vowel in Arabic is the same, but is modified in pronunciation by the heaviness or lightness of the accompanying consonants.

Exercise 11.

1. They drank. 2. We struck. 3. She entered. 4. You (*m.*) drank. 5. I drank. 6. We sat. 7. You (*pl.*) sat. 8. You (*f.*) struck. 9. He wrote. 10. We drank. 11. They wrote. 12. I entered. 13. I struck.

1. Shérebû. 2. Dharábna. 3. Dákhalat. 4. Sherébet. 5. Sherébet. 6. Jelésna. 7. Jeléstû. 8. Dharábti. 9. Kéteb. 10. Sherébna. 11. Kétebû. 12. Dakhálat. 13. Dharábat.

١ شرِبُوا. ٢ ضربنا. ٣ دخلَت. ٤ شربتَ. ٥ شربتُ. ٦ جلسنا
٧ جلستم. ٨ ضربتِ. ٩ كتب. ١٠ شربنا. ١١ كتبوا. ١٢ دخلتُ.
١٣ ضربتُ.

THE REGULAR VERB (*continued*)

The Present and Future Tenses are identical in form. The first vowel of the present tense varies in the colloquial, but is generally *i* except when followed by a heavy consonant, when the *u* sound predominates, represented by *a*, as in *along* (see above, p. vii). Throughout this manual the present is given with the past.

(In literary Arabic the second vowel is variable, and can be discovered from the dictionary. For decided futurity سَوْفَ precedes the present tense, or the present may take the contraction سَ as a prefix.)

When in English the infinitive would be used after the verb, as e.g. I wish to go, the Arabic has, I wish that I go, in the literary, and I wish I go, You wish you go, &c., in the colloquial.

Active Voice: Present Tense.

يَكْتُبُ	He writes	yíktab
تَكْتُبُ	She writes	tíktab
تَكْتُبُ	You (*m.*) write	tíktab
تَكْتُبِينَ	You (*f.*) write	tiktabī́n
أَكْتُبُ	I write	íktab
يَكْتُبُونَ	They write	yiktabū́n
تَكْتُبُونَ	You (*pl.*) write	tiktabū́n
نَكْتُبُ	We write	níktab

Exercise 12.

1. He drinks. 2. He strikes. 3. He sits. 4. He enters. 5. We enter. 6. They write. 7. You (*m.*) write. 8. You (*f.*) drink. 9. I enter. 10. You strike. 11. You (*pl.*) drink. 12. We drank water yesterday and to-day we drink coffee. 13. The woman entered the house. 14. I drink milk with tea.

15. The boys struck the dogs in the road. 16. They write in their books. 17. She sat inside the house. 18. Bring the key now. 19. I wish to write a letter to Bombay. 20. The horse wishes to drink water. 21. Do you (*pl.*) wish to drink tea? Yes, bring some. 22. The soldiers struck the man.

1. Hûwa yishrab. 2. Hûwa yadhrab. 3. Hûwa yijlas. 4. Hûwa yidkhal. 5. Naḥen nidkhal. 6. Hûm yiktabûn. 7. Enta tiktab. 8. Enti tishrabîn. 9. Ana idkhal. 10. Enta tadhrab. 11. Entu tishrabûn. 12. Sherebna mai ems wa helyôm nishrab gâhwa. 13. El ḥarma dakhalat el bêt. 14. Ana ishrab ḥalîb wîya chai. 15. El awlàd dharabû el kilàb fît ṭarîq. 16. Hûm yiktabûn fî kutubehum. 17. Hîya jeleset dâkhil el bêt. 18. Jîb el miftâḥ hessa. 19. Arîd iktab maktûb ila Bombay. 20. El ḥuṣân yarîd yishrab mai. 21. Tarîdûn tishrabûn chai? Belli jîb shwêya. 22. El 'asker dharabû er rijàl.

١ يشربُ. ٢ يضربُ. ٣ يجلسُ. ٤ يدخلُ. ٥ ندخلُ. ٦ يكتبونَ. ٧ تكتبُ. ٨ تشربينَ. ٩ ادخلُ. ١٠ تضرِبُ. ١١ تشربونَ. ١٢ شربنا ماءً امس واليوم نشربُ قهوة. ١٣ الامراة دخلت البيت. ١٤ اشرب حليباً مع الشاي. ١٥ الاولاد ضربوا الكلاب في الطريق. ١٦ يكتبون في كتبهم. ١٧ جلست داخل البيت. ١٨ اجلب المفتاح الان. ١٩ اريد ان اكتبَ مكتوبًا الى بومبي. ٢٠ لحصان يريد ان يشرب ماء. ٢١ هل تريدون ان تشربوا شاياً . نعم اجلب قليلاً. ٢٢ العساكر ضربوا الرجل.

THE REGULAR VERB (*continued*)

The Imperative is formed by dropping the initial *y* of the 3rd pers. sing. masc. pres. and omitting the *n* in case of feminine and plural.

(In literary Arabic the Imperative is formed by dropping the first syllable from the 2nd pers. masc. sing. pres. and substituting alif wasl with a dhumma if the second syllable have dhumma and otherwise kesra. The final vowel is dropped, except in feminine and plural, where however ن is dropped.)

Imperative.

أُكْتُبْ	write (*m.*)	iktab
أُكْتُبِي	write (*f.*)	iktabî
أُكْتُبُوا	write (*pl.*)	iktabû

The negative imperative is formed by placing لَا là before the 2nd pers. pres. sing. or plur., and in case of fem. and plur. omitting ن *n*.

Exercise 13.

1. Drink (*s. m.*). 2. Strike (*pl.*). 3. Come (*f.*). 4. Enter (*pl.*). 5. Sit (*pl.*) 6. Come (*pl.*) and drink milk. 7. Welcome, Sahib, and drink some coffee. 8. Don't you (*s. m.*) want to sit down and drink some tea? 9. How are you to-day? 10. Don't strike (*pl.*) the dog. 11. Write (*s. m.*) a letter to the man. 12. Come here, boatman, I want your bellum. 13. Don't drink this water. 14. Bring dates in the bellum. 15. Where is the bridge? 16. Don't enter here. 17. Yesterday they shot (struck guns) in the bazaar.

1. Ishrab. 2. Adhrabû. 3. Ta'âli. 4. Idkhalû. 5. Ijlasû. 6. Ta'âlû wa ishrabû ḥalib. 7. Tafadhdhal, Ṣâḥib, wa ishrab shwêya gâhwa. 8. Ma tarîd tijlas wa tishrab shwêya chai? 9. Shlôn kêfek helyôm? 10. Là tadhrabû el kelb. 11. Iktab maktûb ilar rejul. 12. Ta'âl, bellàm, arîd belamek. 13. Là tishrab hel mai. 14. Jib tamr fîl belam. 15. Wên el jisr? 16. Là tidkhal hina. 17. Ems dharabû tufek fîs sûq.

١ اشربْ. ٢ اضربوا. ٣ تعالي. ٤ ادخلوا. ٥ اجلسوا. ٦ تعالوا واشربوا حليباً. ٧ تفضّل صاحب واشرب قليلاً من القهوة. ٨ الا تريد ان تجلس وتشرب قليلاً من الشاي. ٩ كيف حالك اليوم. ١٠ لا تضربوا الكلب. ١١ اكتبْ مكتوباً الى الرجل. ١٢ تعال هنا يا بلام اريد بلمك. ١٣ لا تشرب هذا الماء. ١٤ اجلبْ تمراً في البلم. ١٥ اين الجسر. ١٦ لا تدخل هنا. ١٧ امس اطلقوا بنادق في السوق.

THE REGULAR VERB (*continued*)

The Active Participle is formed by lengthening the first syllable of the root, and vowelling the second syllable with kesra *i*. E.g. كَاتِبْ kàtib. It may denote one or all of three things, *Doing, The doer*, the perfect *Having done*.

E.g. هُوَ كَاتِبْ Hûwa kàtib { He is writing / He is a clerk / He has written

It is regarded as an adjective, and may also take an object.

(In literary Arabic the last syllable takes nunation if indefinite.)

The past tense of intransitive participles is produced by placing كَانَ kàn, inflected for person, number, and gender, before the present participle.

E. g.	Ana kunet jàlis	I was sitting
	Eḥna kunna jàlisîn	We were sitting

The past tense of transitive participles is formed by placing كَانَ kàn, inflected, before the present of the verb.

E. g. Hûwa kàn yiktab He was writing هُوَ كَانَ يِكْتُبْ

From participles, transitive or intransitive, *the pluperfect* results from the above use of kàn, when the participle is used in the perfect tense.

E. g. Ana kunet shàrib el mai I had drunk the water

Usually the pluperfect is produced by placing kàn, uninflected, before the past tense of the verb.

(In literary Arabic قَدْ is generally introduced.)

Exercise 14.

1. He is a clerk in the bazaar. 2. I have drunk water from the river. 3. He is the one who struck the dog. 4. He is the one who entered the house. 5. Are you the writer of this? 6. I was sitting in the house and the man was not there. 7. I have written to Bombay. 8. I had written. 9. They had drunk.

1. Hûwa kàtib fìs sûq. 2. Ana shàrib mai min esh shaṭṭ. 3. Hûwa edh dhârib el kelb. 4. Hûwa ed dâkhil fîl bêt. 5. Enta kàtib hàdha? 6. Ana kunet jàlis fîl bêt war rejul mâ kàn hinàk. 7. Ana kàtib ila Bombay. 8. Ana kunet kàtib. 9. Hûm kàn sherebû.

١ هو كاتبٌ في السوق. ٢ انا شارب ماءً من الشط. ٣ هو الضارب الكلب. ٤ هو الداخل في البيت. ٥ هل انت كاتب هذا. ٦ انا كنتُ جالساً في البيت والرجل ما كان هناك. ٧ قد كتبتُ الى بومبي. ٨ كان قد كتبتُ. ٩ كانوا قد شربوا.

In colloquial an action actually going on is expressed by gâ'id (sometimes shortened to gâ) placed before the present.

Hûwa gâ'id yiktab	He is now writing
Hûm gâ'id yiktabûn	They are now writing

THE REGULAR VERB (*continued*)

The Passive Participle is formed from the root after the model مَكْتُوب maktûb, written, a letter. E.g. هٰذَا ٱلْمَكْتُوبُ hàdhel maktûb, this letter. Hàdha maktûb, This is a letter, or, This is written or has been written. With كَانَ kàn, the pluperfect results.

Exercise 15.

1. The horse has been struck. 2. The water is drunk. 3. The letter had been written.

1. El ḥuṣân madhrûb. 2. El mai mashrûb. 3. El maktûb kàn maktûb.

١ الحصان مضروب. ٢ الماء مشروب. ٣ الخط كان مكتوباً.

THE REGULAR VERB (*continued*)

Nouns of Place or Time are formed by changing the first syllable of the present tense to *ma*.

(In literary Arabic the second vowel agrees with the second vowel of the present tense with few exceptions.)

E. g. مَجْلِس majlis (mejlis), a council-room.

مَسْجِد masjid (mesjid), a mosque, from سَجَد sejed, he worshipped.

مَدْخَل madkhal, an entrance.

مَغْرِب maghrib, sunset, from غَرَب gharab, he (the sun) set.

مَكْتَب maktab (mekteb), a school.

The plurals are regularly formed on the model majàlis.

Nouns of Instrument are formed either

1. On the following model, with the final syllable long; e. g. مِفْتَاح miftâḥ (from feteḥ, he opened), a key. The plural is regularly formed with the last syllable long, mafàtîḥ.

2. On the following model, with the ending ة a. مِكْنَسَة miknesa (from kenes, he swept), a broom. *Pl.* makànis, مَكَانِس.

The Noun of Action is not formed according to uniform model.

E. g. Writing (the art of), kitàba, كِتَابَة.
Drinking (the act or habit of), sherb, شُرْب.
Entering (admission, &c.), dukhûl, دُخُول.

THE IRREGULAR VERB

There are three classes of irregular verbs.

Class I.—Those in which the root contains one or more weak letters. The weak letters are waw, ya, alif.

Class II.—Those in which the second and third consonants are the same.

Class III.—Those which contain a hemza. *Vide* Hemza (Introduction, p. 4).

Class I.

First root-letter weak.			*Second root-letter weak.*			*Third root-letter weak.*		
Past Tense.			*Past Tense.*			*Past Tense.*		
وَقَفَ	He stood	wágaf	قَالَ	He said	gâl	رَمَى	He threw	rama
وَقَفَتْ	She ,,	wágafat	قَالَتْ	She ,,	gâlat	رَمَتْ	She ,,	ramat
وَقَفْتَ	You (*m.*) stood	wagáfat	قُلْتَ	You (*m.*) said	gulat	رَمَيْتَ	You (*m.*) threw	ramêt
وَقَفْتِ	You (*f.*) ,,	wagáfti	قُلْتِ	You (*f.*) ,,	gulti	رَمَيْتِ	You (*f.*) ,,	ramêti
وَقَفْتُ	I ,,	wagáfat	قُلْتُ	I ,,	gulat	رَمَيْتُ	I ,,	ramêt
وَقَفُوا	They ,,	wágafû	قَالُوا	They ,,	gâlû	رَمَوْا	They ,,	ramû
وَقَفْتُمْ	You (*pl.*) ,,	wagáftû	قُلْتُمْ	You (*pl.*) ,,	gultû	رَمَيْتُمْ	You (*pl.*) ,,	ramêtû
وَقَفْنَا	We ,,	wagáfna	قُلْنَا	We ,,	gulna	رَمَيْنَا	We ,,	ramêna

Class I (*continued*).

First root-letter weak.			*Second root-letter weak.*			*Third root-letter weak.*		
Present Tense.			*Present Tense.*			*Present Tense.*		
يَقِفُ	He stands	yógaf	يَقُولُ	He says	yagûl	يَرْمِي	He throws	yarmî
تَقِفُ	She ,,	tógaf	تَقُولُ	She ,,	tagûl	تَرْمِي	She ,,	tarmî
تَقِفُ	You (*m.*) stand	tógaf	تَقُولُ	You (*m.*) say	tagûl	تَرْمِي	You (*m.*) throw	tarmî
تَقِفِينَ	You (*f.*) ,,	togafîn	تَقُولِينَ	You (*f.*) ,,	tagûlin	تَرْمِينَ	You (*f.*) ,,	tarmîn
أَقِفُ	I ,,	ógaf	أَقُولُ	I ,,	agûl	أَرْمِي	I ,,	armî
يَقِفُونَ	They ,,	yogafûn	يَقُولُونَ	They ,,	yagûlûn	يَرْمُونَ	They ,,	yarmûn
تَقِفُونَ	You (*pl.*) ,,	togafûn	تَقُولُونَ	You (*pl.*) ,,	tagûlûn	تَرْمُونَ	You (*pl.*) ,,	tarmûn
نَقِفُ	We ,,	nógaf	نَقُولُ	We ,,	nagûl	نَرْمِي	We ,,	narmî

Imperative.			*Imperative.*			*Imperative.*		
قِفْ	Stand	ógaf	قُلْ	Say	gul	إِرْمِ	Throw	irmi
قِفِي	Stand (*f.*)	ógafî	قُولِي	Say (*f.*)	gûlî	إِرْمِي	Throw (*f.*)	irmî
قِفُوا	Stand (*pl.*)	ogafû	قُولُوا	Say (*pl.*)	gûlû	إِرْمُوا	Throw (*pl.*)	irmû
Active Participle.			*Active Participle.*			*Active Participle.*		
وَاقِفٌ	Standing	wâgif	قَائِلٌ	Saying	gâ-il	رَامٍ	Throwing	râmi
Passive Participle.			*Passive Participle.*			*Passive Participle.*		
مَوْقُوفٌ	Stood	mawgûf	مَقُولٌ	Said	magûl magyûl	مَرْمِيٌّ	Thrown	marmî

Verbs with initial *y* in the root, or final *alif*, are very rare. *In some verbs, as* صَارَ *ṣâr, he became, the* i *vowel predominates instead of* u. *E.g. ṣâr, yaṣîr, ṣiret.*

Notes on Class I, Irregular Verbs.

1. *First root-letter weak.*

It will be noticed that the past is regularly inflected. In literary Arabic, in the present and imperative, the weak letter, when waw, is dropped.

2. *Second root-letter weak.*

In the example above inflected قَالَ gâl, the root originally was قَوَلَ gawala, but the waw of the root has been assimilated and compensated for by lengthening the *a* vowel in the past and the *u* vowel in the present, except when the last consonant was quiescent, in which case the compensation consists in the short *u* vowel. When the original middle consonant was ya, as e.g. صَيَرَ ṣâr, the *i* vowel predominates in the past, and the long *î* vowel in the present; e.g. صَارَ ṣâr, يَصِيرُ yaṣîr, صِرْتَ ṣiret.

3. *Third root-letter weak.*

In the example رَمَى rama, the root originally was رَمَيَ ramaya, but the final ya has been dropped in pronunciation. The ya thus written but not pronounced loses its two dots. The ي reappears in the 2nd and 1st pers. past, because preceded by the heterogeneous vowel fet-ḥa. In the present the final vowel is lost. In the imperative of verbs of this class the ya is entirely lost in the masc. sing.

Word List.

شَافَ يَشُوفُ . رَأَى يَرَى	He saw	shȃf,	*Pres.* yashûf
رَاحَ يَرُوحُ . ذَهَبَ يَذْهَبُ	He went	râḥ	,, yarûḥ
صَارَ يَصِيرُ	He became	ṣâr	,, yaṣîr
بَاعَ يَبِيعُ	He sold	bâʿ	,, yabîʿ
خَافَ يَخَافُ	He feared	khâf (khifet, &c.)	,, yakhâf
مَشَى يَمْشِي	He walked	mesha	,, yimshî

(In colloquial the 2nd and 1st pers. past of shȃf are shifet, shiftû, shifna.)

Exercise 16.

1. Stand here. 2. He stood on the ship. 3. I was standing on the road. 4. What (êsh) did he say? 5. I threw the money into the river. 6. They said he was a good man. 7. The ship stopped (stood). 8. Stop, driver. 9. Why do you stand here? 10. We stood in the water. 11. We said, Yes. 12. What did you say? 13. How do you say this? 14. I said I want to go to Baghdad. 15. Do you want to stand here? 16. Did you see the soldiers? 17. I went and saw the bridge. 18. The man became hungry. 19. Did you become a soldier? 20. Don't be afraid. 21. Do you want to sell this book?

1. Ogaf hina. 2. Hûwa wagaf ʻalal markab. 3. Ana kunet wâgif ʻalad darb. 4. Êsh gâl? 5. Ana ramêt el flûs fîsh shaṭṭ. 6. Gâlû hûwa khôsh rijàl. 7. El markab wagaf. 8. Ogaf, ʻarabachî. 9. Lêsh togaf hina? 10. Wagafna fîl mai. 11. Gulna ê. 12. Êsh gulat? 13. Kêf tagûl hàdha? 14. Gulat arîd arûḥ ila Baghdâd. 15. Tarîd togaf hina? 16. Enta shifet el ʻasker? 17. Ana ruḥat wa shifet el jisr. 18. Er rejul ṣâr jôʻân. 19. Enta ṣiret ʻasker? 20. Là takhâf. 21. Tarîd tabiʻ hel kitâb?

١ قِف هنا. ٢ وقف على المركب. ٣ كنتُ واقفاً على الطريق. ٤ ماذا قال. ٥ رميتُ الفلوس في الشط. ٦ قالوا انه رجل جيد. ٧ المركب وقف. ٨ قِف يا سائِق. ٩ لماذا تقف هنا. ١٠ وقفنا في الماء. ١١ قلنا نعم. ١٢ ماذا قلت. ١٣ كيف تقول هذا. ١٤ قلت اريد ان اذهب الى بغداد. ١٥ هل تريد أن تقف هنا. ١٦ هل شفت العساكر. ١٧ رحتُ وشفتُ الجسر. ١٨ الرجل صار جوعاناً. ١٩ هل صرتَ عسكرياً. ٢٠ لا تخف. ٢١ هل تريد أن تبيع هذا الكتاب.

IRREGULAR VERBS. Class II.

In the verb جَرّ jarr, he pulled, the original form was جَرَر jarar. One can see that if such a verb were inflected regularly an unpleasant repetition of the second consonant would result. In consequence the inflection has been modified in colloquial as indicated below. The imperative has no initial alif.

Past Tense.

جَرّ	He pulled	jarr
جَرَّتْ	She ,,	jarrat
جَرَرْتَ	You (*m.*) pulled	jarrêt
جَرَرْتِ	You (*f.*) ,,	jarrêti
جَرَرْتُ	I ,,	jarrêt
جَرّوا	They ,,	jarrû
جَرَرْتُمْ	You (*pl.*) ,,	jarrêtû
جَرَرْنَا	We ,,	jarrêna

Present Tense.

يَجُرّ	He pulls	yajurr
تَجُرّ	She ,,	tajurr
تَجُرّ	You (*m.*) pull	tajurr
تَجُرِّينَ	You (*f.*) ,,	tajurrîn
أَجُرّ	I ,,	ajurr
يَجُرّونَ	They ,,	yajurrûn
تَجُرّونَ	You (*pl.*) ,,	tajurrûn
نَجُرّ	We ,,	najurr

Imperative.

جُرّ	Pull (*m.*)	jurr
جُرِّي	,, (*f.*)	jurrî
جُرّوا	,, (*pl.*)	jurrû

Active Participle.

جَارّ	Pulling	jârr
جَارَّة	,,	jârra (*f.*) and *impers. pl.*
جَارُّون	,,	jârrîn (*pl.*) persons

Passive Participle.

مَجْرُور	Pulled	majrûr
مَجْرُورَة	,,	majrûra (*f.*) and *impers. pl.*
مَجْرُورُون	,,	majrûrîn (*pl.*) persons

Word List (Irregular Verbs, Class II).

ظَنّ يَظُنّ	He thought (surmised)	dhann, yadhunn
سَدّ يَسُدّ	He closed	sedd, yasidd
حطّ يحطّ . وضعَ يضع	He put	ḥaṭṭ, yaḥuṭṭ
رَدّ يَرُدّ	He returned (*trans.* and *intr.*)	radd, yarudd
عَدّ يَعُدّ	He counted	ʻadd, yaʻudd
حبّ يحبّ	He loved	ḥabb, yaḥibb
خصّ يخصّ	He concerned, was related to It concerned	khaṣṣ, yakhuṣṣ
شدّ يشدّ	He tied	shedd, yashidd
دَخَل يَدْخُل	He entered	deshsh, yadishsh

Exercise 17.

1. Shut the book. 2. He returned from Baghdad. 3. He returned the key to the sahib. 4. I counted the money. 5. Do you like Basrah? 6. He is much beloved. 7. This concerns the man. 8. I tied the horse to the date-tree. 9. Do you think the ship will go to-morrow? 10. It is thought (el madhnûn)

he will not go. 11. The river is closed. 12. He entered the garden. 13. The money is counted and put in the house. 14. I think so. 15. What do you think? 16. I thought he was a good man. 17. Why did you put the book here? 18. Is the horse tied?

1. Sidd el kitàb. 2. Hûwa radd min Baghdad. 3. Hûwa radd el miftâḥ ilaṣ ṣâḥib. 4. Ana ʻaddêt el flûs. 5. Taḥibb el Baṣrah? 6. Hûwa kullish maḥbûb. 7. Hàdha yakhuṣṣ er rejul. 8. Ana shaddêt el ḥuṣân bin nakhla. 9. Tadhunn el markab yarûḥ bàcher? 10. El madhnûn hûwa mâ yarûḥ. 11. Esh shaṭṭ masdûd. 12. Hûwa deshsh fîl bustàn. 13. El flûs maʻdûd wa maḥṭûṭ fîl bêt. 14. Adhunn. 15. Êsh tadhunn? 16. Ana dhannêt hûwa khôsh rejul. 17. Lêsh ḥaṭṭêt el kitàb hina? 18. El ḥuṣân mashdûd?

١ سدّ الكتاب. ٢ هو ردّ من بغداد. ٣ هو ردّ المفتاح الى الصاحب. ٤ عددتُ الفلوس. ٥ هل تحب البصرة. ٦ هو محبوب جدًا. ٧ هذا يخص الرجل. ٨ شددتُ الحصان بالنخلة. ٩ هل تظن المركب يروح غداً. ١٠ المظنون انه لا يروح. ١١ الشط مسدود. ١٢ هو دخل البستان. ١٣ الفلوس معدودة وموضوعة في البيت. ١٤ اظن. ١٥ ماذا تظن. ١٦ ظننت انه رجل جيدٌ. ١٧ لماذا وضعت الكتاب هنا. ١٨ هل الحصان مشدود.

IRREGULAR VERBS. **Class III.**

(*Verbs which have* **hemza** *in the root.*)

In the colloquial the inflection is quite regular, as in keteb, the hemza being regarded as a regular consonant. One exception needs to be noticed. When the final root consonant is hemza, as in قَرَأَ qara, he read, the endings of the past, 2nd and 1st sing. and plur., are as in جَرّ jarr; e.g. qarêt, I read. In the 1st pers. sing. pres. of verbs with initial hemza in the root, the *a* becomes long; e.g. àkul, I eat.

(In literary Arabic one change should be noticed. When the hemza follows a dhumma, or sukun followed by dhumma, the carrier becomes waw; when the hemza follows a kesra or is accompanied by kesra, the carrier becomes ya without dots.)

The hyphen denotes a slight hiatus, as e. g. in *sea-eagle*.

First Consonant Hemza.

أَكَلَ	He ate	akal
يَأْكُلُ	He eats	ya-kul
كُلْ	Eat (*imper. m.*)	ukul
كُلِي	Eat (*imper. f.*)	ukulî
كُلُوا	Eat (*pl.*)	ukulû
آكِلٌ	Eating	àkil
مَأْكُولٌ	Eaten	ma-kûl

Second Consonant Hemza.

سَأَلَ	He asked	se-el
يَسْأَلُ	He asks	yes-el
إِسْأَلْ او سَلْ	Ask (*imper. m.*)	es-el
إِسْأَلِي او سَلِي	Ask (*imper. f.*)	es-elî
إِسْأَلُوا او سَلُوا	Ask (*pl.*)	es-elû
سَائِلٌ	Asking	sà-il
مَسْؤُولٌ	Asked	mas-ûl

Third Consonant Hemza.

قَرَأَ	He read	qara
يَقْرَأُ	He reads	yaqra
إِقْرَأْ	Read (*imper. m.*)	aqra

اِقْرَئِي	Read (*imper. f.*)	aqra-î
اِقْرَأُوا	Read (*pl.*)	aqra-û
قَارِئٌ	Reading	qârî
مَقْرُوءٌ	Read	maqrû

Word List. Class III.

أَمَرَ يَأْمُرُ	He commanded	amar, ya-mur
أَخَذَ يَأْخُذُ	He took	akhadh, ya-khudh

Note.—The imperative of *amar* in colloquial is *âmar*, and of *akhadh* is *ukhudh.*

WORD LIST

قَوِيٌّ ج أَقْوِيَاءُ	Strong	qawi, *pl.* quwai guwi, *pl.* guwai hudâr, *pl.* hudârîn
ضَعِيفٌ ج ضُعَفَاءُ	Weak	dhaʿîf, *pl.* dhuʿâf
رَكِبَ يَرْكَبُ	He rode (mounted)	rekeb, yirkab
" "	He went aboard	" "
طَلَعَ يَطْلَعُ	He went up, out	ṭalaʿ, yiṭlaʿ
صَحْرَاءُ او بَرِّيَّة	Desert	chôl, barr
رَمْلٌ	Sand	raml
دُكَّانٌ ج دَكَاكِين	Shop	dukkàn, *pl.* dukàkîn
رَخِيص ج رَخِيصَة	Cheap	rakhîṣ, *pl.* rakhâṣ
غَالٍ ج غَالِيَةٌ	Dear	ghâli, *pl.* ghâlia
نَزَلَ يَنْزِلُ	He descended	nezel, yinzal
غَسَلَ يَغْسِلُ	He washed	ghasal, yaghsal

Exercise 18.

1. I saw a strong horse. 2. He said, Where is your shop? 3. This is very dear. 4. I was sitting in the shop and the man entered. 5. Descend from your horse. 6. Why don't you (*f.*) wash the cups? 7. She washed the cups with (bi) hot water. 8. I wish to go to the desert. 9. These men are very strong. 10. What did you ask? 11. The cup has been washed in the river. 12. There is much sand in the desert. 13. He mounted his horse and rode to the desert. 14. When will you get aboard? 15. Books are cheap in Bombay, but (làkin) dear here. 16. The ship will leave Bombay to-morrow. 17. When did you leave Bombay? 18. He came out of his house and went to the bazaar. 19. This turned out very dear.

1. Ana shifet ḥuṣân qawi. 2. Hûwa gâl, Wên dukkànek? 3. Hàdha kullish ghâli. 4. Ana kunet jàlis fîd dukkàn wa deshsh er rejul. 5. Inzal min ḥuṣânek. 6. Lêsh mâ taghsalîn el fanàjîn? 7. Hîya ghasalat el fanàjîn bi mai ḥârr. 8. Uríd arûḥ ilal chôl? 9. Her rijàjîl kullish quwai. 10. Êsh se-elet? 11. El finjàn maghsûl fîsh shaṭṭ. 12. Âkû raml hwâyi fîl chôl. 13. Hûwa rekeb ḥuṣânuh wa râḥ ilal chôl. 14. Yimta tirkab? 15. Kutub kullish rakhâṣ fî Bombay làkin ghâlia hina. 16. El markab yiṭla‘ bàcher min Bombay. 17. Yimta ṭalâ‘t min Bombay? 18. Hûwa ṭala‘ min bêtuh wa râḥ ilas sûq. 19. Hàdha ṭala‘ kullish ghâli.

١ شفتُ حصاناً قوياً. ٢ قال اين دكّانك. ٣ هذا غالٍ جداً. ٤ كنتُ جالساً في الدكان ودخل الرجل. ٥ انزل عن حصانك. ٦ لماذا لا تغسلين الفناجين. ٧ هي غسلت الفناجين بماء حارّ. ٨ اريد ان اذهب الى الصحراء. ٩ هؤلاء الرجال اقوياء جداً. ١٠ ماذا سألتَ. ١١ الفنجان مغسول في الشط. ١٢ يوجد رمل كثير في الصحراء. ١٣ هو ركب حصانه وراح الى الصحراء. ١٤ متى تركب. ١٥ الكتب رخيصة جداً في بومبي لكنها غالية هنا. ١٦ المركب سيسافر غداً من بومبي. ١٧ متى خرجت من بومبي. ١٨ هو خرج من بيتهِ وراح الى السوق. ١٩ هذا صار غالياً جداً.

WORD LIST

حُجْرَة ج حُجَر غُرْفَة ج غُرَف	Room	ḥujra, *pl.* ḥujar ghurfa, *pl.* ghuraf gubba, *pl.* gubab ôdha, *pl.* ûwadh
بَلَدٌ ج بِلَادٌ او بُلْدَانٌ	Town	beled, *pl.* buldàn
مَدِينَةٌ ج مُدُنٌ	City	medîna, *pl.* mudn
قَرْيَةٌ ج قُرًى	Village	qarya, *pl.* qura koi, *pl.* koyàt jamâʿa, *pl.* jamâʿàt
غَنِيٌّ ج أَغْنِيَاءُ	Rich	ghani, *pl.* aghnia zengîn, *pl.* zengînîn
فَقِيرٌ ج فُقَرَاءُ	Poor	faqîr, *pl.* fuqarâ
مُنَاخٌ او هَوَاءٌ	Weather, wind	hawa
وَصَلَ يَصَلُ	He arrived	waṣal, yoṣal
سَمِعَ يَسْمَعُ	He heard	semaʿ, yismaʿ
يَلْزَمُ	Must	làzm (with *pres.* tense)
عَمِلَ يَعْمَلُ	He did	sawwa, yusawwî
تَاجِرٌ ج تُجَّارٌ	Merchant	tàjir, *pl.* tujjâr bayyâʿ sherrai, *pl.* tujjâr
قَدَرَ يَقْدُرُ	He could	qadar, yaqdar
لَطِيفٌ لَطِيفَةٌ ج لُطَفَاءُ	Pretty	laṭîf. *pl.* laṭîfîn, laṭîfa ḥulû, *pl.* ḥuluwîn, ḥulwa
حَكَى يَحْكِي	He spoke	ḥaka, yaḥkî ḥacha, yaḥchî
اَلْعَرَبِيَّة . عَرَبِيٌّ	Arabic (lang.) or an Arab	ʿarabî
اَلْعَرَبُ	The Arabs	el ʿarab

ٱلْإِنْكِلِيزِيَّةُ . إِنْكِلِيزِيّ	English (lang.) or an Englishman	anglêzî
ٱلْإِنْكِلِيزُ	The English	el anglêz
ٱلتُّرْكِيَّةُ . تُرْكِيّ	Turkish	turkî
ٱلتُّرْكُ	The Turks	et turk
ٱلْفَارِسِيَّةُ . إِيرَانِيّ	Persian a Persian	fârsî ʿajemî, îrânî
ٱلْإِيرَانِيُّون	The Persians	el ʿajem, el îrâniyîn
ٱلْهِنْدِيَّةُ . هِنْدِيّ	Hindustani or an Indian	hindî
ٱلْهُنُودُ	The Indians	el hinûd
ٱلْفَرَنْسَاوِيَّةُ . فَرَنْسَاوِيّ	French or Frenchman	fransâwî
ٱلْفَرَنْسَاوِيُّون	The French	el fransâwiyîn

Exercise 19.

1. He was in the room. 2. Go and see what they have. 3. We are very poor and have no money. 4. I heard the English went to Baghdad. 5. Do you speak English? 6. Do you speak Persian? 7. I do not speak Arabic. 8. The Arabs went to the desert. 9. The Turks are in Stamboul. 10. The English love the poor and the rich. 11. You must write a letter. 12. I must write a letter. 13. What town is this? 14. The ship arrived last night. 15. What are you doing here? 16. I think he speaks Persian. 17. Can you write Arabic? 18. I cannot go now. 19. I could not go.

1. Hûwa kàn fîl ghurfa. 2. Rûh wa shûf êsh ʿandehum. 3. Naḥen kullish fuqarâ wa mâ ʿadna flûs. 4. Ana semâʿt el anglêz râḥû ila Baghdâd. 5. Taḥkî anglêzî? 6. Taḥchî fârsî? 7. Ana mâ aḥchî ʿarabî. 8. El ʿarab râḥû ilal barr. 9. Et turk fîs Stambûl. 10. El anglêz yaḥibbûn el fuqarâ wal aghnia.

11. Làzm tiktab maktûb. 12. Làzm iktab maktûb. 13. Yâ beled hàdha (hai)? 14. El markab waṣal embârḥa billêl. 15. Êsh tusawwî hina? 16. Adhunn hûwa yaḥkî fârsî. 17. Taqdar tiktab ʿarabi? 18. Ana mâ aqdar arûḥ hessa. 19. Ana mâ qadaret arûḥ.

١ هو كان في الغرفة. ٢ رح وشُف ما عندهم. ٣ نحن فقراء جداً وليس عندنا فلوس. ٤ سمعتُ ان الانكليز ذهبوا لبغداد. ٥ هل تحكي الانكليزيّة. ٦ هل تحكي الفارسية. ٧ لا احكي العربية. ٨ العرب راحوا الى الصحراء. ٩ الترك في استانبول. ١٠ الانكليز يحبون الفقراء والاغنياء. ١١ يلزم ان تكتب مكتوباً. ١٢ يلزم ان اكتبُ مكتوباً. ١٣ ايّ بلد هذا. ١٤ المركب وصل امس ليلاً. ١٥ ماذا تعمل هنا. ١٦ اظن انه يحكي الفارسية. ١٧ هل تقدر ان تكتب في العربية. ١٨ لا اقدر اروح الان. ١٩ ما قدرتُ ان اروح.

WORD LIST

كُلّ	All	kull (with *pl.*)
كُلّ	Every	„ (with *sing.*)
قَتَلَ يَقْتُلُ	He killed	qatal, yaqtal
كَنَسَ يَكْنُسُ	He swept	kenes, yiknas
سَكَنَ يَسْكُنُ	He lived (dwelt)	seken, yiskan
قَعَدَ يَقْعُدُ	He sat	qaʿad, yaqʿad (commonly used instead of jeles)
شَرَدَ يَشْرِدُ . هَرَبَ يَهْرُبُ	He fled	shered, yishrad
مُفِيدٌ	Useful	mufîd
فَانُوس ج فَوَانِيس	Lantern	fânûs, *pl.* fawànîs
جَدِيدٌ ج جُدُدٌ	New	jadîd, *pl.* jided
عَتِيقٌ ج عُتَقَاءُ	Old (not persons)	ʿatîq, *pl.* ʿutuq

مَطَر	Rain	maṭr
تَمْطُر	It rains	tamṭar (lit. she, that is, the heaven, rains)
ثَانِيَةً او أَيْضًا	Again	marra thània, tekrâr
أَيْضًا	Also	aidhan, ham
دُونَ او بِدُونِ	Without	bidûn, mindûn, bighair bila (bilêya)
دُونَ أَنْ	Without (with verb)	bidûn ma, mindûn ma
كَسَرَ يَكْسِرُ	He broke	keser, yiksar
عَرَفَ يَعْرِفُ	He knew	ʿaraf, yaʿraf
عَرَفَ كَيْفَ	He knew how to	,, ,, (followed by verb)

Exercise 20.

1. The soldiers killed the dogs. 2. Bring a lantern with you. 3. You must sweep all the rooms. 4. The house is swept. 5. Where do you live? 6. He sat on the ship. 7. He was sitting in the bazaar. 8. I saw the man sitting in the bazaar. 9. I saw the soldiers walking in the road. 10. This is very useful. 11. These books are very old. 12. It rains very much in Basrah. 13. Do this again. 14. You cannot walk at night without a lantern. 15. You cannot live in Basrah without knowing Arabic. 16. He broke the cup. 17. Do you know how to speak English? 18. I am going to Bombay and my sahib also wishes to go. 19. When the English took Basrah all the Turks fled.

1. El ʿasker qatalû el kilàb. 2. Jîb fânûs wiyàk. 3. Làzm tiknas kull el gubab. 4. El bêt maknûs. 5. Wên tiskan (or Wên sàkin enta)? 6. Hûwa qaʿad ʿalal markab. 7. Hûwa kàn qâʿid fîs sûq. 8. Ana shifet er rejul qâʿid fîs sûq 9. Ana

shifet el ʿasker màshiyîn fìd durb. 10. Hàdha kathîr mufìd. 11. Hel kutub kullish ʿutuq. 12. Tamṭar kathîr fîl Baṣrah. 13. Sawwi hàdha tekrâr. 14. Mâ taqdar timshî billêl bila fânûs. 15. Mâ taqdar tiskan fîl Baṣrah mindûn ma taʿraf ʿarabî. 16. Hûwa keser el finjàn. 17. Taʿraf taḥki anglêzi? 18. Ana râ-iḥ ila Bombay wa ṣâḥibî ham yurìd yarûḥ. 19. Lemma el anglêz akhadhû el Baṣrah kull et turk sheredû.

١ العساكر قتلوا الكلاب. ٢ اجلب فانوساً معك. ٣ يلزم ان تكنس كل الغُرف. ٤ البيت مكنوس. ٥ اين تَسكُن. ٦ هو جلس في المركب. ٧ هو كان جالساً في السوق. ٨ شفتُ الرجل جالساً في السوق. ٩ شفت العساكر ماشية في الطريق. ١٠ هذا مفيد جداً. ١١ هذهِ الكتب عتيقة جداً. ١٢ تمطر كثيرًا في البصرة. ١٣ اعمل هذا ثانيةً. ١٤ ما تقدر ان تمشي ليلاً بدون فانوس. ١٥ ما تقدر ان تسكن في البصرة دون ان تعرف العربية. ١٦ هو كسر الفنجان. ١٧ هل تعرف تحكي الانكليزية. ١٨ انا ذاهبٌ الى بومبي وصاحبي ايضاً يريد ان يروح. ١٩ لمّا الانكليز اخذوا البصرة الترك شردوا كلهم.

POSSESSION

The Arab does not say, 'The house of the man'. He says, 'House the man'. There is an implied vowel change in the Arabic word for 'house' as well as 'man', not possible to represent in English, which indicates the relation between the two words. Since 'house' thus becomes sufficiently defined by being the property of a man, the definite article is discarded in Arabic. 'House' is said to be *in construction* with 'the man'.

(In literary Arabic, in the phrase بَيْتُ ٱلرَّجُلِ, the nunation of بيت has been dropped since بيت has become definite, and only the dhumma remains. The last vowel of الرجل is kesra, indicating the genitive. The last vowel of بيت is dhumma if it is nominative, kesra if oblique, and fet-ḥa if accusative.)

In the strong plural ending in ين ÎN, the ن *n* is dropped in construction.

Examples.

خُبْزُ ٱلْوَلَدِ	The bread of the boy	khubz el walad
تَمْرُ ٱلْبَصْرَةِ	The dates of Basrah	tamr el Baṣrah
دُكَّانُ ٱلتَّاجِرِ	The shop of the merchant	dukkàn et tàjir
فُلُوسُ ٱلتُّجَّارِ	The money of the merchants	flûs et tujjâr
بَلَمُ مُحَمَّدٍ	Muhammad's bellum	belam muḥammad

In colloquial the word مَال *màl* is frequently inserted where English has 'of'. E.g. El khubz màl el walad,
Et tamr màl el Baṣrah.

This *màl* takes the feminine ending ة (generally pronounced *at*), when the antecedent thereof is feminine; e.g. El byût màlat Baghdâd. (*Note.*—All broken plurals of impersonal objects are regarded as feminine singular.)

When adjectives occur, the construction is as follows:

بَيْتُ مُحَمَّدٍ ٱلْقَدِيمُ	Muhammad's old house	bêt Muhammad el ʿatiq
بَيْتُ مُحَمَّدٍ وَٱمْرَأَتُهُ	Muhammad's house and wife	bêt Muhammad wa maratuh

In a sentence like بيت الرجل الطيّب *bet er rejul eṭ ṭayyib*, the meaning may be The good house of the man, or, The house of the good man. In literary Arabic the meaning is known from the final vowels, but in colloquial the meaning is known by the context.

Other expressions used to indicate possession are:

abû belam (lit. Father of the bellum), Bellum owner
râʿi bêt (lit. Shepherd of the house), Landlord
ehl el ablàm (lit. People of bellums), Boatmen
ṣâḥib ed dukkàn (lit. Master of the shop), Shop-owner.

Exercise 21.

1. He went to the house of the man. 2. The water of the river is very cold. 3. The Ashar road is bad. 4. The guns of the soldiers are new. 5. The sand of the desert is hot. 6. He went to his new house. 7. Ahmed's house is not far from here. 8. I do not like Basrah dates. 9. I want the sahib's books and letters. 10. I saw the owner of the bellum and spoke with him. 11. My landlord is very rich. 12. These shops belong to Mustafa.

1. Hûwa râḥ ila bêt er rejul. 2. Mai esh shaṭṭ kullish bàrid. 3. Darb el 'ashâr kullish kharâb. 4. Tufek el 'asker jided. 5. Raml el chôl ḥârr. 6. Hûwa râḥ ila bêtuh el jadîd. 7. Bêt Aḥmed mû ba'îd min hina. 8. Ana mâ aḥibb tamr el Baṣrah. 9. Arîd kutub es ṣâḥib wa makàtîbuh. 10. Ana shifet râ'i el belam wa ḥakêt wiyàh. 11. Ṣâḥib bêtî kullish zengîn. 12. Hel dukàkîn màlat Muṣṭafa.

١ هو راح الى بيت الرجل. ٢ ماء الشط بارد جداً. ٣ طريق العشار رديء. ٤ بنادق العساكر جديدة. ٥ رملُ الصحراء حارٌ. ٦ راح الى بيتهِ الجديد. ٧ بيت احمد ليس بعيداً من هنا. ٨ لا احب تمر البصرة. ٩ اريد كتب الصاحب ومكاتيبهُ. ١٠ شفتُ صاحب البلم وحكيتُ معهُ. ١١ صاحب بيتي غني جداً. ١٢ هذهِ الدكاكين تخصّ مصطفا.

WORD LIST

شَمْسٌ	Sun	shems
قَمَرٌ	Moon	qamr, gamr
رُوبِيَّةٌ ج رُوبِيَّاتٌ	Rupee	rubîa, *pl.* rubiàt
قَرَانٌ ج قَرَانَاتٌ	Kran (4 annas)	qrân, *pl.* qrânàt
ضَوْءٌ	Light (from something)	dhaw

صَيْف او قَيْظ	Summer	ṣêf, gêdh
شِتَاء	Winter	shita
ضَحِكَ يَضْحَكُ	He laughed	dhaḥak, yadhḥak
صَارَ يَصِيرُ	He became	ṣâr, yaṣîr
رَفَعَ يَرْفَعُ	He raised	rafaʿ, yarfaʿ
فَتَحَ يَفْتَحُ	He opened	feteḥ, yiftaḥ fekk, yafukk
رَجَعَ يَرْجِعُ	He returned	rajaʿ, yarjaʿ
مَائِدَة ج مَوَائِدُ	Table	mêz, *pl.* mêzàt, muyûz
سِرَاج ج سُرُج	Lamp	lampa, *pl.* lampàt
فِرَاش ج فُرُش	Bed	firâsh, *pl.* farâshàt, furush
سَرِير ج أَسِرَّة	Bedstead	sarîr (date-stick) charpâya, *pl.* charpâyàt
لٰكِنْ او وَلٰكِنْ	But	làkin, walàkin

Exercise 22.

1. Bring a light. 2. The light of the sun and moon. 3. Why do you laugh? 4. I did not laugh. 5. Don't sit in the sun. 6. At night we see the moon but not by day. 7. He sat on the bed. 8. Put the lamp on the table. 9. Put my bedstead outside. 10. Do you know Arabic? No, I don't know it at all. 11. It has become night. 12. He has become rich. 13. This does not do (is out of the question). 14. When will you return? 15. Raise the book. 16. He removed the table. 17. Open your (*pl.*) books. 18. Give me two rupees and two qrans.

1. Jîb dhaw. 2. Dhaw esh shems wal qamr. 3. Lêsh tadhḥak. 4. Ana mâ dhaḥaket. 5. Là taqʿad fîsh shems. 6. Billêl nashûf el qamr làkin mû binnahâr. 7. Hûwa qaʿad

'alal firâsh. 8. Ḥaṭṭ el lampa 'alal mêz. 9. Ḥaṭṭ charpâyatî barra. 10. Ta'raf 'arabî? Là, kullish mâ a'raf. 11. Sâr el lêl. 12. Hûwa sâr zengîn. 13. Hàdha mâ yasîr. 14. Yimta tarja'? 15. Arfa' el kitàb. 16. Hûwa shâl el mêz. 17. Iftaḥû kutubekum. 18. A'ṭinî rubiatên wa qrânên.

١ اجلب السراج. ٢ ضوء الشمس والقمر. ٣ لماذا تضحك. ٤ ما ضحكتُ.
٥ لا تجلس في الشمس. ٦ في الليل نشوف القمر ولكن ليس في النهار.
٧ جلس على الفراش. ٨ ضع السراج على المائدة. ٩ حط سريري خارجاً.
١٠ هل تعرف العربية. لا. لا اعرفها ابداً. ١١ صار الليل. ١٢ صار غنياً.
١٣ هذا ما يصير. ١٤ متى ترجع. ١٥ ارفع الكتاب. ١٦ هو نقل
المائدة. ١٧ افتحوا كتبكم. ١٨ اعطني روبيتين وقرانين.

THE VERB جَاءَ JÀ—HE CAME

On account of its extensive use and irregular inflection the verb jà, he came, is here inflected in full.

Past Tense.

جَاءَ	He came	jà
جَاءَتْ	She came	jàt
جِئْتَ	You (*m.*) came	jìt
جِئْتِ	You (*f.*) came	jìtî
جِئْتُ	I came	jìt
جَاءُوا	They came	jao (jô)
جِئْتُمْ	You (*pl.*) came	jîtû
جِئْنَا	We came	jîna

Present Tense.

يَجِيءُ	He comes	yîjî
تَجِيءُ	She comes	tîjî
تَجِيءُ	You (*m.*) come	tîjî
تَجِئْنَ	You (*f.*) come	tîjîn
أَجِيءُ	I come	àjî
يَجُوْنَ	They come	yîjûn
تَجُوْنَ	You (*pl.*) come	tîjûn
نَجِيءُ	We come	nîjî

Imperative.

تَعَالَ	Come (*m. sing.*)	ta'âl
تَعَالِي	Come (*f. sing.*)	ta'âlî
تَعَالُوا	Come (*pl.*)	ta'âlû

Participle.

جَاءٍ جَائِيَةْ جَاوُوْنَ	Coming	jai, *pl.* (persons) jâyîn *pl.* (things) jâya

Exercise 23.

1. The ship will come to-morrow. 2. When will the sahib come? 3. We came yesterday. 4. How did the soldiers come? 5. She came but I did not see her. 6. I will not come to your house. 7. Come here. 8. The ship is coming. 9. They came but I did not say anything. 10. Why did you come?

1. El markab yîjî bàcher. 2. Yimta yîjî eṣ ṣâḥib? 3. Jîna embârḥa. 4. Kêf jao el 'asker? 5. Hîya jàt làkin ana mâ shifeta. 6. Ana mâ àjî ila bêtekum. 7. Ta'âl hina. 8. El markab jai. 9. Jao làkin ana mâ gulat shê. 10. Lêsh jît?

١ المركب سيجي غداً. ٢ متى سيجي الصاحب. ٣ نحن جئنا امس. ٤ كيف جاءُوا العساكر. ٥ هي جاءت لكن انا ما شفتها. ٦ انا ما اجيء لبيتكم. ٧ تعال هنا. ٨ المركب جاء. ٩ هم جاءُوا لكن انا ما قلت شيئًا. ١٠ لماذا جئتَ.

GENDERS

Nouns in Arabic are either masculine or feminine. There is no neuter.

Nouns masculine are:

1. Those naturally masculine; e.g. walad (boy), rejul (man).
2. Those not ending in ة *a*, with exceptions as indicated in 3, 4, 5, below.

Nouns feminine are:

1. Those naturally feminine; e.g. أُمّ umm (mother).
2. Those ending in ة *a*. (This ة is silent except before the definite article and in pausâ, when the termination then becomes *at*; see p. 55.)
3. Names of countries, towns, double members of the body e.g. يَدْ yed (hand).
4. Broken plurals of impersonal objects. These take adjective in fem. sing. ة *a*, unless a broken plural of the adjective exists. The verb with broken plurals of impersonal objects is in the fem. sing.; e.g. El maràkib tarûḥ.
5. A few individual nouns;

E.g.	شَمْس	shems (sun)	أَرْض	ardh (earth)
	نَفْس	nefs (soul)	رُوح	rûh (spirit)
	نَار	nâr (fire)	سِكّين	sikkìn (knife)

Nouns ending in ة *a* take a final ت *t* before pronominal suffixes, and in pronunciation before the article. E.g. ḥarmati, my wife; el ḥarmat et ṭayyiba.

Examples.

اَلْبَيْتُ ٱلْقَدِيمُ	The old house	el bêt el 'atîq
اَلْبُيُوتُ ٱلْقَدِيمَةُ	The old houses	el buyût el ʻutuq
اَلْمَائِدَةُ ٱلْعَالِيَةُ	The high table	el mêz el ʻâlî
اَلْاِمْرَأَةُ ٱلْجَيِّدَةُ	The good woman	el ḥarmat et ṭayyiba
اَلسِّرَاجُ ٱلْمَكْسُورُ	The broken lamp	el lampat el maksûra
اَلشَّمْسُ ٱلْحَارَّةُ	The hot sun	esh shems el ḥârra
اَلْأَرْضُ ٱلْكَبِيرَةُ	The large earth	el ardh el kabîra
اَلنَّفْسُ ٱلْعَطْشَانَةُ	The thirsty soul	en nefs el ʻaṭshâna
اَلْيَدُ ٱلصَّغِيرَةُ	The small hand	el yed (*or* îd) eṣ ṣaghîra

NUMERALS

With fem. noun.	*With masc. noun.*		*With masc. noun.*	*With fem. noun.*
وَاحِدَةْ	وَاحِدْ	1	wâḥid	wâḥida
إِثْنَتَانِ	إِثْنَانِ	2	ithnên	thentên
ثَلَاثْ	ثَلَاثَةْ	3	thalàtha	thalàth
أَرْبَعْ	أَرْبَعَةْ	4	arba'a	arba'
خَمْسْ	خَمْسَةْ	5	khamsa	khams
سِتّْ	سِتَّةْ	6	sitta	sitt
سَبْعْ	سَبْعَةْ	7	seb'a	seb'
ثَمَانٍ	ثَمَانِيَةْ	8	thamànya	thamàn
تِسْعْ	تِسْعَةْ	9	tis'a	tis'
عَشْرْ	عَشَرَةْ	10	'ashera	'asher

إِحْدَى عَشْرَةَ	أَحَدَ عَشَرَ	11	idâsh	same
إِثْنَتَى عَشْرَةَ	إِثْنَى عَشَرَ	12	ithnâsh (thnâsh)	,,
ثَلَاثَ عَشْرَةَ	ثَلَاثَةَ عَشَرَ	13	thalathatâsh	,,
أَرْبَعَ عَشْرَةَ	أَرْبَعَةَ عَشَرَ	14	arbatâsh	,,
خَمْسَ عَشْرَةَ	خَمْسَةَ عَشَرَ	15	khamsatâsh (khamstâsh)	,,
سِتَّ عَشْرَةَ	سِتَّةَ عَشَرَ	16	sittâsh	,,
سَبْعَ عَشْرَةَ	سَبْعَةَ عَشَرَ	17	sebatâsh	,,
ثَمَانِيَ عَشْرَةَ	ثَمَانِيَةَ عَشَرَ	18	thamanatâsh (thmantâsh)	,,
تِسْعَ غَشْرَةَ	تِسْعَةَ عَشَرَ	19	tisatâsh	,,
عِشْرُونَ	عِشْرُونَ	20	ʿashrîn	,,
إِحْدَى وَعِشْرُونَ	أَحَدٌ وَعِشْرُونَ	21	wâḥid wa ʿashrîn	wâḥida wa ʿashrîn

NUMERALS (*continued*)

With fem. noun.	*With masc. noun.*		*With masc. noun.*	*With fem. noun.*
ثَلَاثُونَ	ثَلَاثُونَ	30	thalàthîn	same
أَرْبَعُونَ	أَرْبَعُونَ	40	arba'în	,,
خَمْسُونَ	خَمْسُونَ	50	khamsîn	,,
سِتُّونَ	سِتُّونَ	60	sittîn	,,
سَبْعُونَ	سَبْعُونَ	70	seb'în	,,
ثَمَانُونَ	ثَمَانُونَ	80	thamànîn	,,
تِسْعُونَ	تِسْعُونَ	90	tis'în	,,
مِئَةٌ . مِائَةٌ	مِئَةٌ . مِائَةٌ	100	mîa (mîat before vowel)	,,
مِئَةٌ وَوَاحِدَةٌ	مِئَةٌ وَوَاحِدٌ	101	mîa wa wâḥid	mîa wa wâḥida
مِئَتَانِ . مِائَتَانِ	مِئَتَانِ . مِائَتَانِ	200	mîatên	same

ثَلَاثُمِئَةٍ	ثَلَاثُمِئَةٍ	300	thalàth mîa	same
أَلْفٌ	أَلْفٌ	1000	elf	,,
أَلْفَانِ	أُلْفَانِ	2000	elfên	,,
ثَلَاثَةُ آلَافٍ	ثَلَاثَةُ آلَافٍ	3000	thalàthat àlàf	,,
أَحَدَ عَشَرَ أَلْفًا	أَحَدَ عَشَرَ أَلْفًا	11000	idâsh elf	,,
مِائَةُ أَلْفٍ	مِائَةُ أَلْفٍ	100000	mîat elf	,,
مِائَتَا أَلْفٍ	مِائَتَا أَلْفٍ	200000	miatên elf	,,
ثَلَاثُمِئَةِ أَلْفٍ	ثَلَاثُمِئَةِ أَلْفٍ	300000	thalàth mîat elf	,,
مَلْيُونٌ	مَلْيُونٌ	million	milyôn	,,
مَلْيُونَانِ	مَلْيُونَانِ	2 million	milyônên	,,
ثَلَاثَةُ مَلَائِينَ	ثَلَاثَةُ مَلَايِينَ	3 million	thalàth milàyîn	,,

Notes on Numerals.

1. The use of وَاحِدْ *wâḥid* is much the same as that of *one* in English. 'A house' is simply بَيْتْ bêt. *Bêt wâḥid* specifies a single house. The form أَحَدْ *âḥad* (fem. *iḥda*, إِحْدَى) is substantive, though used interchangeably with واحد *wâḥid* in colloquial.

The word فَرْدْ *ferd*, a single one, is often used for the indefinite article; e.g. *ferd walad*, a boy.

2. إِثْنَانِ *ithnên* is used when not accompanied by a noun. Otherwise the dual of the noun is used. E.g. بَيْتَانِ *bêtên*, two houses, but *I saw two* would be *ana shifet ithnên.*

3. With the numerals from 3 to 10 the accompanying noun is in the plural, from 11 on in the singular. E.g.

ثَلَاثُ نِسَاءٍ	thalàth ḥarîm	three women
خَمْسَةُ أَوْلَادٍ	khamsat awlàd	five boys
ثَلَاثَ عَشْرَةَ إِمْرَأَةً	thalathatâsh ḥarma	thirteen women
خَمْسَةَ عَشَرَ وَلَدًا	khamsatâsh walad	fifteen boys

(The gender of the singular noun determines the gender of the plural, with numerals, regardless of the fact that broken plurals of inanimate objects are otherwise regarded as fem. sing.)

4. *One hundred and one pounds* is expressed *hundred and pound.*
One hundred and two pounds is expressed *hundred and pounds* (dual).
One hundred and three pounds is expressed *hundred and three pounds* (pl.).

So with thousands, &c.

5. The order of units, tens, &c., is as follows:

38 eight and thirty
138 hundred and eight and thirty
1138 thousand and hundred and eight and thirty.

Exercise 24.

1. I saw twelve men. 2. Bring two cups of tea. 3. Three rupees. 4. Eighteen women. 5. Six books. 6. 1917. 7. A man. 8. One man. 9. One woman. 10. Two hundred and ninety-nine. 11. Eleven houses. 12. Twelve horses. 13. Two days. 14. Three days. 15. Forty-one boys. 16. Forty-one girls. 17. I saw one of the women. 18. One of the soldiers. 19. Forty-eight rupees.

1. Ana shifet ithnâsh rejul. 2. Jîb finjànên chai. 3. Thalàth rubiàt. 4. Thmantâsh ḥarma. 5. Sitta kutub. 6. Elf wa tis' mîa wa sebatâsh. 7. Rejul. 8. Ferd rejul. 9. Ferd ḥarma. 10. Mîatên wa tis'a wa tis'în. 11. Idâsh bêt. 12. Thnâsh ḥuṣân. 13. Yômên. 14. Thalàthat ayàm. 15. Wâḥid wa arba'în walad. 16. Wâḥida wa arba'în bint. 17. Ana shifet wâḥida min en niswàn. 18. Wâḥid min el 'asker. 19. Thamàn wa arba'în rubîa.

١ شفتُ اثنى عشر رجلًا. ٢ اجلب فنجانين شاي. ٣ ثلاث روبيات.
٤ ثمانِيَ عشرة إمرأةً. ٥ ستة كتب. ٦ الف وتسع مئة وسبعة عشر.
٧ رجلٌ. ٨ رجلٌ واحد. ٩ امرأة واحدة. ١٠ مئتان وتسعة وتسعون.
١١ احد عشر بيتًا. ١٢ اثنى عشر حصانًا. ١٣ يومان. ١٤ ثلاثة ايام.
١٥ واحد واربعون ولدًا. ١٦ احدى واربعون بنتًا. ١٧ رأيتُ احدى
النساء. ١٨ احد العساكر. ١٩ ثمان واربعون روبيةً.

WORD LIST

عَصًا ج عُصِيّ	stick	'aṣa, *pl.* 'uṣî
خَشَبٌ	wood (substance)	khashab
حَطَبٌ	wood (fuel)	ḥaṭab
ضَابِطٌ ج ضُبّاطٌ	officer (military)	dhâbiṭ, *pl.* dhubbâṭ
مَأْمُورٌ ج مَأْمُورُون	officer (civil)	mâ-mûr, *pl.* mâ-mûrîn

عَيْن ج عُيُون	eye	ʿain, *pl.* ʿuyûn
أُذْن ج آذَان	ear	idhn, *pl.* àdhàn
شَعْر	hair	shâʿr (one hair, shâʿra)
رِجْل . سَاق	leg (or foot)	rijl, *pl.* rijûl (riyûl)
أَرْض . قَاع	ground (the earth)	ardh, gâʿ
تُرَاب	ground (soil)	turâb, trâb
عَجَاج . غُبَار	dust	ṭôz, ʿajàj, ghubâr
سَهْل . هَيِّن	easy	sehl, hêyyin
صَعْب	difficult	ṣâʿab, mushkil, zâḥma
حِمَار ج حَمِير	donkey	ḥamâr, *pl.* ḥamîr zamàl, *pl.* zamàyil muṭṭi, *pl.* muṭṭâya
بَعْد	after	bâʿad, ogub
بَعْدَ مَا	after (with verb)	bâʿadma, ogubma

Exercise 25.

1. We struck the dog with the stick. 2. The bellum is of wood. 3. Put wood on the fire. 4. I have two eyes and two ears. 5. We have not three eyes. 6. His eye is large. 7. I am standing on my feet. 8. He is sitting on the ground. 9. We hear with our ears. 10. He threw the money on the floor. 11. There is much dust to-day. 12. The boatman does not see our boat. 13. Arabic is very difficult but Persian is very easy. 14. The donkeys were eating dates. 15. Come after two days. 16. I will come the day after to-morrow. 17. Cut my hair very short. 18. An officer was walking in the road. 19. I went and talked with the officer. 20. We saw three officers sitting in the house.

1. Eḥna dharabna el kelb bil ʿaṣa. 2. El belam min khashab. 3. Ḥaṭṭ ḥaṭab ʿalan nâr. 4. ʿAndi ʿainên wa idhnên. 5. Naḥen mâ ʿadna thalàth ʿuyûn. 6. ʿAinuh kabîra. 7. Ana wâgif ʿala rijlêya (dual). 8. Hûwa gâʿid bil gâʿ. 9. Nismaʿ bi àdhànna. 10. Hûwa rama el flûs ʿalal ardh. 11. Ṭôz wàjid helyôm. 12. El mellâḥ mâ yashûf belamna. 13. ʿArabi kullish sâʿab làkin fârsî kullish sehl. 14. El ḥamîr kànet tà-kul tamr. 15. Taʿâl bâʿad yômên. 16. Ana àjî ogub bàcher. 17. Guṣṣ shâʿri kullish qaṣîr. 18. Ferd mâ-mûr kàn màshi fîd darb. 19. Ana ruḥet wa ḥakêt wìya edh dhâbiṭ. 20. Shifna thalàtha dhubbâṭ gâʿidîn fil bêt.

١ ضربنا الكلب بالعصا. ٢ البلم من خشب. ٣ حط حطباً على النار. ٤ لي عينان واذنان. ٥ ليس لنا ثلاث عيون. ٦ عينهُ كبيرة. ٧ انا واقف على رجليّ. ٨ هو جالس على الارض. ٩ نسمع باذاننا. ١٠ هو رمى الفلوس على الارض. ١١ يوجد عجاج كثير اليوم. ١٢ الملاح ما يشوف بلمنا. ١٣ العربية صعبة جداً لكن الفارسية سهلة جداً. ١٤ الحمير كانت تاكل تمراً. ١٥ تعال بعد يومين. ١٦ اجي بعد الغد. ١٧ قُصّ شعري قصيراً جداً. ١٨ مَأمورٌ كان ماشياً في الطريق. ١٩ رحتُ وحكيتُ مع الضابط. ٢٠ شفنا ثلاثة ضبّاط جالسين في البيت.

ORDINAL NUMBERS

Feminine.	*Masculine.*		*Masculine.*	*Feminine.*
اَلْأُولَى	اَلْأَوَّلُ	1st	el awwal	el ûla, el awwalîa
اَلثَّانِيَةُ	اَلثَّانِي	2nd	eth thànî	eth thània
اَلثَّالِثَةُ	اَلثَّالِثُ	3rd	eth thàlith	eth thàlitha
اَلرَّابِعَةُ	اَلرَّابِعُ	4th	er râbiʻ	er râbiʻa
اَلْخَامِسَةُ	اَلْخَامِسُ	5th	el khâmis	el khâmisa
اَلسَّادِسَةُ	اَلسَّادِسُ	6th	es sàdis, es sàt	es sàdisa, es sàt
اَلسَّابِعَةُ	اَلسَّابِعُ	7th	es sàbiʻ	es sàbiʻa
اَلثَّامِنَةُ	اَلثَّامِنُ	8th	eth thàmin	eth thàmina
اَلتَّاسِعَةُ	اَلتَّاسِعُ	9th	et tàsiʻ	et tàsiʻa
اَلْعَاشِرَةُ	اَلْعَاشِرُ	10th	el ʻâshir	el ʻâshira

أَلْحَادِيَةَ عَشْرَةَ	أَلْحَادِيَ عَشَرَ	11th	el hàdî ʻasher	el hàdia ʻashra
أَلثَّانِيَةَ عَشْرَةَ	أَلثَّانِيَ عَشَرَ	12th	eth thànî ʻasher	eth thània ʻashra
أَلثَّالِثَةَ عَشْرَةَ	أَلثَّالِثَ عَشَرَ	13th	eth thàlith ʻasher	eth thàlitha ʻashra
أَلرَّابِعَةَ عَشْرَةَ	أَلرَّابِعَ عَشَرَ	14th	er râbiʻ ʻasher	er râbiʻa ʻashra
أَلْعِشْرُونَ	أَلْعِشْرُونَ	20th	el ʻashrîn	same
أَلْحَادِيَةُ وَٱلْعِشْرُونَ	أَلْحَادِىْ وَٱلْعِشْرُونَ	21st	el hàdî wa ʻashrîn	el hàdia wa ʻashrîn
أَلْمِئَةُ	أَلْمِئَةُ	100th	el mîa	same
أَلْمِئَةُ وَٱلْحَادِيَةُ	أَلْمِئَةُ وَٱلْحَادِي	101st	el mîa wa wâḥid	el mîa wa wâḥida
أَلْمِئَةُ وَٱلثَّانِيَةُ	أَلْمِئَةُ وَٱلثَّانِي	102nd	el mîa wa thànî	el mîa wa thània
أَلْأَلْف	أَلْأَلْف	1000th	el elf	same

WORD LIST

Arabic	English	Transliteration
إِسْبُوعٌ ج أَسَابِيعٌ	week	isbû', *pl.* asàbi', sabâya'
شَهْرٌ ج أَشْهُرٌ	month	shahr, *pl.* ishhur
سَنَةٌ ج سِنُونَ ، سَنَوَاتٌ	year	sena, *pl.* senîn, senawàt
وَقْتٌ ج أَوْقَاتٌ	time (temps)	waqt, *pl.* awqât
مَرَّةٌ ج مَرَّاتٌ	time (fois)	marra, *pl.* marràt
بَابٌ ج أَبْوَابٌ	door	bàb, *pl.* abwàb, bibàn, bûb
أَوَّلاً	at first	bil awwal, fî awwal el amr

Exercise 26.

1. He came the first day but did not come the second.   2. I am the thirteenth in the house.   3. I came the first of the month and returned the fifteenth.   4. The sixth house on this street.   5. The second door from here.   6. The first time I saw you was in Bombay.   7. He came twice but the second time I did not see him.

1. Hûwa jà el yôm el awwal làkin mâ jà el yôm eth thànî. 2. Ana eth thàlith 'asher fîl bêt.   3. Ana jit el awwal min esh shahr wa raja'at el khâmis 'asher.   4. El bêt es sàdis fî hed darb.   5. El bàb eth thànî minna (min hina).   6. El marrat el ûla (awwal marra) ana shifetek kàn fî Bombay.   7. Hûwa jà marratên làkin el marrat eth thània ana mâ shifetuh.

١ هو جاء في اليوم الأوّل لكن في اليوم الثاني ما جاء. ٢ انا الثالث عشر في البيت. ٣ جئتُ اوّل الشهر ورجعتُ في الخامس عشر. ٤ البيت السادس في هذا الطريق. ٥ الباب الثاني من هنا. ٦ عند ما شفتكَ اوّلاً كنتُ في بومبي. ٧ جاء مرتين لكن المرة الثانية ما شفتُهُ.

WORD LIST

طَبَخَ يَطْبُخُ	He cooked	ṭabakh, yaṭbakh
وَقَعَ يَقَعُ	He fell	waga', yoga'
تَبِعَ يَتْبَعُ	He followed	teba', yitba'
دَرَسَ يَدْرُسُ	He studied	deres, yidras
نَامَ يَنَامُ	He slept	nàm, yanàm (you slept, nimet, &c.)
قَامَ يَقُومُ	He rose	gâm, yagûm
لَمَّا	When (relative)	lemma
قَبْلُ	Before (of time)	gabl
قُدَّامَ	In front of	gadàm, gubàl
قَبْلَ مَا	Before (with verb)	gablama, gabla
بِمَا أَنَّ	Inasmuch as	mà dàm
وَلَوْ . مَعْ أَنَّ	Although	wa law
حَالَمَا	As soon as	awwalma, ḥâlama
قَبْلَ	Ago	gabl (precedes noun)
إِلَى قُدَّامٍ	Straight ahead	gûbal, ila gadàm
يَمِيناً	To the right	ilal yamîn
يَسَاراً	To the left	ilal yisâr
إِلَى ٱلْوَرَاءِ	To the rear (or) backwards	ila wara

Exercise 27.

1. Do you know how to cook? 2. What did you cook? 3. I want cooked meat. 4. The horse fell in the road and

the soldiers came and took the horse away. 5. Don't fall. 6. I wish to become a clerk. 7. The woman followed the child. 8. They studied Turkish in Stamboul. 9. I wish to study Arabic. 10. Why do you laugh when I speak with you? 11. Bring the book before you go to the bazaar. 12. After he went I knew. 13. Although you wish to return you cannot. 14. As soon as you see the ship come here. 15. Inasmuch as you know Turkish why are you afraid? 16. Go straight ahead and after two hours go to the right. 17. The ship goes (walks) astern. 18. He was here three days ago. 19. I came ten months ago.

1. Taʿraf taṭbakh? 2. Êsh ṭabakhat? 3. Arîd laḥm maṭbûkh. 4. El ḥusân wagaʿ fîd darb wal ʿasker jao wa shàlû el ḥuṣân. 5. Là togaʿ. 6. Arîd aṣîr kàtib. 7. El ḥarma tebaʿat el walad. 8. Hûm deresû Turkî fîs Stambûl. 9. Arîd idras ʿarabî. 10. Lêsh tadhḥak lemma aḥkî wiyàk? 11. Jîb el kitàb gabla tarûḥ ilas sûq. 12. Bâʿadma râḥ ʿarafat. 13. Wa law tarîd tarjaʿ mâ taqdar. 14. Awwalma tashûf el markab taʿâl hina. 15. Mâ dàm taʿraf Turkî lêsh takhâf? 16. Rûḥ gûbal wa bâʿad sâʿatên rûḥ ilal yamîn. 17. El markab yimshî ila wara. 18. Hûwa kàn hina gabl thalàthat ayàm. 19. Ana jît gabl ʿasherat ishhur.

١ هل تعرف تطبخ. ٢ ماذا طبختَ. ٣ اريد لحماً مطبوخاً. ٤ الحصان وقع في الطريق وجاءُ العسكر ونقلوهُ. ٥ لا تقع. ٦ اريد ان اصير كاتباً. ٧ الامرأة تبعت الولد. ٨ درسوا التركية في استانبول. ٩ اريد ان ادرس العربية. ١٠ لماذا تضحك لما احكي معك. ١١ اجلب الكتاب قبل ما تروح الى السوق. ١٢ بعد ما راح عرفتُ. ١٣ ولو تريد ان ترجع لكنك ما تقدر. ١٤ حالما تشوف المركب تعال هنا. ١٥ بما انك تعرف التركية لماذا تخاف. ١٦ رح الى قدام وبعد ساعتين رح يميناً. ١٧ المركب يمشي الى الوراء. ١٨ كان هنا قبل ثلاثة ايام. ١٩ انا جئت قبل عشرة اشهرٍ.

PRONOMINAL SUFFIXES OF THE VERB

To denote the object of a transitive verb the following pronominal suffixes are attached to the verbal form required.

نِي	-ni	me	نَا	-na	us
كَ	-ek	you (*m.*)	كُمْ	-kum	you (*pl.*)
كِ	-ech *or* eki	you (*f.*)			
هُ	-uh	him *or* it	هُمْ	-hum	them
هَا	-ha	her			

When the verb form ends in a vowel, the first vowel of the suffix is dropped; e. g. dharabûk, they struck you.

In the present tense, 2nd and 3rd person plural, the ن *n* is dropped; e. g. yadhrabûk, tadhrabûhum.

Examples.

ضَرَبَنِي	He struck me	dharábni
ضَرَبَكَ	He struck you (*m.*)	dharábek
ضَرَبَكِ	He struck you (*f.*)	dharábech
ضَرَبَهُ	He struck him	dharábuh
ضَرَبَهَا	He struck her	dharábha
ضَرَبَنَا	He struck us	dharábna
ضَرَبَكُمْ	He struck you (*pl.*)	dharábkum
ضَرَبَهُمْ	He struck them	dharábhum
يَضْرُبَنِي	He strikes me	yadhrábni
أَضْرُبَكَ	I strike you	adhrábek
ضَرَبْتَنِي	You struck me	dharábetni
ضَرَبْنَاهُ	We struck him	dharabnáh

The stress falls immediately before the suffix except in the 1st and 2nd pers. sing. past, where the stress remains as if without suffix; e.g. dharábetek.

Exercise 28.

1. I saw you in the house. 2. Did you write it? 3. They love me but I do not love them. 4. Why did you follow us? 5. We wrote it but you did not see it. 6. Who said it? 7. Did you say it? 8. No, but they said it.

1. Ana shifetek fîl bêt. 2. Enta ketebetuh? 3. Hûm yaḥibbûni làkin ana mâ aḥibbhum. 4. Lêsh teba'atna? 5. Naḥen ketebnâh làkin entû mâ shiftûh. 6. Men gâluh. 7. Enta gulatuh? 8. Là, làkin hûm gâlûh.

١ شفتكَ في البيت. ٢ هل كتبتهُ. ٣ يحبوني لكن انا لا احبهم.
٤ لماذا تبعتنا. ٥ كتبناهُ لكنك ما شفتهُ. ٦ من قالهُ. ٧ هل قلتهُ.
٨ لا. لكن هم قالوهُ.

WORD LIST

صَدِيقٌ ج أَصْدِقَاءُ	friend	ṣadîq, *pl.* aṣdiqâ, ṣadqân
حَاضِرٌ	ready	ḥâdhir (zàhib)
حَضِّرْ	make ready (*trans.*)	ḥadhdhir, sawwi ḥâdhir
تَحَضَّرْ	get ready (*intr.*)	taḥadhdhar
دَائِماً	always	kull waqt, daiman
كَاغِذٌ . كَاغِدٌ . وَرَقٌ	paper	kàghid
شَيْءٌ ج أَشْيَاءُ	thing	shê, *pl.* eshyà
مُعَلِّم ج مُعَلِّمُون	teacher	mu'allim, *pl.* mu'allimîn
بَيْنَ	between	bên
رُبَّمَا	perhaps	yimkin, rubbama, bilki
سِكِّينٌ ج سَكَاكِينُ	knife	sikkîn, *pl.* sakàkîn

هٰكَذَا	thus	kedha, hàkadha, hîchî
مِثْلَ	like	mithl
مِثْلِي	like me, you, &c.	mithlî, mithlek, &c.
خَلَص	finished	khalaṣ

Exercise 29.

1. I have a friend in India. 2. How many friends have you? 3. I have five friends. 4. Is the bellum ready? 5. Make the bellum ready. 6. The horse is ready, sahib. 7. Why do you always do so? 8. I got (took) paper from the bazaar, but it is bad. 9. I know everything. 10. Do you want these things? 11. The soldiers are between Zobeir and Basrah. 12. Perhaps the ship will come to-morrow. 13. He brought three knives. 14. The teacher came and saw nobody. 15. You talk like an Arab. 16. I am like the teacher. 17. The woman is like you.

1. ʿAndi ṣadîq fil Hind. 2. Kem ṣadîq ʿandek? 3. ʿAndi khamsa ṣadqân. 4. El belam ḥâdhir? 5. Ḥadhdhir el belam. 6. El ḥuṣân ḥâdhir, ṣâḥib. 7. Lêsh kull waqt tusawwî hîchî? 8. Ana akhadhat kàghid min es sûq làkin hûwa kharâb. 9. Ana aʿaraf kull shê. 10. Tarîd hel eshyà? 11. El ʿasker bên ez Zobêr wal Baṣrah. 12. Yimkin el markab yîjî bàcher. 13. Hûwa jàb thalàth sakàkîn. 14. El muʿallim jà wa mâ shàf aḥad. 15. Enta taḥki mithl ʿarabî. 16. Ana mithl el muʿallim. 17. El ḥarma mithlech.

١ لي صديق في الهند. ٢ كم صديقاً لك. ٣ لي خمسة اصدقاء. ٤ هل البلم حاضر. ٥ حَضِّر البلم. ٦ الحصان حاضر يا صاحب. ٧ لماذا تعمل دائماً هكذا. ٨ اخذتُ كاغذاً من السوق لكنه رديء. ٩ اعرف كل شيء. ١٠ هل تريد هذهِ الأشياء. ١١ العساكر بين الزبير والبصرة. ١٢ ربما المركب يجيء غداً. ١٣ هو جلب ثلاث سكاكين. ١٤ المعلم جاء وما شاف احداً. ١٥ تحكي مثل عربي. ١٦ انا مثل المعلم. ١٧ امرأة مثلكِ.

THE RELATIVE PRONOUN

أَلَّذِي	who, which, what (*masc.*)	elledhî, ellî
أَلَّتِي	,, ,, ,, (*fem.*)	elletî (rare)
أَلَّذِينَ	,, (persons) what (*pl.*)	elledhîn
أَللَّاتِي . أَللَّوَاتِي	,, ,, ,, (*pl. fem.*)	(not used)

In colloquial only *elledhî* and *elledhîn* are in common use. *Elledhî* may have as its antecedent a masculine or feminine noun or a broken plural. *Elledhîn* has as its antecedent only plural nouns representing persons.

Examples.

أَلرَّجُلُ ٱلَّذِي جَاءَ	The man who came	er rejul elledhî jà
أَلْأَوْلَادُ ٱلَّذِينَ يَأْكُلُونَ	The boys who eat	el awlàd elledhîn yà-kulûn
أَلْإِمْرَأَةُ ٱلَّتِي تَحْكِي	The woman who speaks	el ḥarma elledhî taḥkî

When in English the relative is a direct object, or is governed by a preposition, in Arabic the relative is introduced immediately after its antecedent, and its corresponding pronominal suffix is repeated after the verb or preposition.

Examples.

أَلرِّجَالُ ٱلَّذِينَ شُفْتُهُمْ

The men whom I saw (The men whom I saw them) — Er rijàl elledhîn shifethum

أَلْوَلَدُ ٱلَّذِي ضَرَبْتُهُ

The boy whom I struck (The boy whom I struck him) — El walad elledhî dharabetuh

أَلْأَوْلَادُ ٱلَّذِينَ جِئْتُ مَعَهُمْ

The boys with whom I came (The boys whom I came with them) — El awlàd elledhîn jît wiyàhum

When there is no antecedent noun expressed, the construction is as follows:

شُفْتُ ٱلّذِينَ جَاءُوا	I saw those who came	Ana shifet elledhîn jao

(In literary Arabic a preposition can be placed directly before the relative; e.g. لِلّذِي.)

Whoever is expressed by	كُلّ مَنْ	kull men
Whatever is expressed by	كُلّ مَا	kullemâ, kullmâ
He to whom can be expressed by	أَلّذِي لَهُ	elledhî lahû *or*
	مَنْ لَهُ	men lahû

Exercise 30.

1. These are not the boys who came yesterday. 2. He who sleeps must rise. 3. This is the house in which we live. 4. Whatever is good is useful. 5. Who has ears to hear. 6. These are the soldiers with whom I came. 7. We saw all those who were soldiers.

1. Hadhôl mû el awlàd elledhîn jao ems. 2. Elledhî yanàm làzm yagûm. 3. Hàdha hûwa el bêt elledhî niskan fih. 4. Kullma ṭayyib mufîd. 5. Men lahû idhnên li yisma‘. 6. Hadhôl hûm el ‘asker elledhîn jît wiyàhum. 7. Shifna kull elledhîn kànû ‘asker.

١ هولاء ليسوا الاولاد الذين جاءُوا امس. ٢ الذي ينام يلزم ان يقوم ٣ هذا هو البيت الذي نسكن فيه. ٤ كل ما جيد هو مفيد. ٥ من له اذنان ليسمع. ٦ هولاء هم العساكر الذين جئتُ معهم. ٧ شفنا كل الذين هم عساكر.

THE MEASURES OF THE VERB

In English some verbs are modified in meaning by internal changes, as e.g. rise—raise, lie—lay, drink—drench, or by prefixes, as e.g. describe, prescribe, &c. In Arabic any verbal root can be changed according to established rules, and the resultant form will give to the root-meaning the modification which the particular form denotes. These derived forms are called by Arab grammarians 'the measures of the verb'. There are fifteen standard measures, of which ten are in common use, though no single root is used in all the measures. The different measures are inflected for person, number, and gender, in the past exactly as in the simple verb, and in the present tense with a change in the vowels as indicated below.

N.B.—It will be noticed that in transliteration sometimes *e* has been used and sometimes *a* for the short vowels; e.g. *teketteb, ta'allam.* The *e* and *a* represent one and the same Arabic vowel sign. When a heavy consonant, such as a guttural, occurs, the Arab pronounces this vowel more like the *a*, but when the consonant is light, as for example a dental, the *e* sound prevails. Likewise when this vowel is lengthened in Arabic, the *á* results when the consonant accompanying it is heavy, and the *à* when the consonant is light. Practice and attention to the impulse of the throat muscles will insure correct pronunciation.

1. Keteb كَتَبَ **Yiktab** يَكْتُبُ

The simple verb. Some verbs are not used in this measure, but appear only as modified in other measures.

2. Ketteb كَتَّبَ **Yukettib** يُكَتِّبُ

The effect of this measure is either

(a) *To intensify the meaning of the original verb*, as e.g.

كَسَرَ keser, he broke كَسَّرَ kesser, he shattered

or

(b) *To make an intransitive verb transitive*, as e.g.

حَسَنَ ḥasan, he was beautiful حَسَّنَ ḥassan, he beautified

or

(c) *To make a verb from a noun*, as e.g.

ذَهَبْ dhahab (dhehb), gold ذَهَّبَ dhahhab (dhehheb), he gilded.

3. Kàteb كَاتَبَ **Yukàtib يُكَاتِبُ**

The effect of this measure is generally one of the following:

(a) *Relation to*, as e.g.

كَاتَبَ kàteb, he wrote to, corresponded with.

(b) *Repetition*, as e.g.

طَالَبَ ṭâlab, he dunned, from ṭalab, he asked.

4. Ekteb أَكْتَبَ **Yuktib يُكْتِبُ**

The force of this measure is

Causative, as e.g.

أَخْرَجَ akhraj, he expelled, from kharaj, he went out.

5. Teketteb تَكَتَّبَ **Yeteketteb يَتَكَتَّبُ**

This measure is *consequential* (generally indicating consequence of Measure 2); e.g.

تَعَلَّمَ ta'allam, he learned, from

عَلَّمَ 'allam, he taught, from

عَلِمَ 'alam, he knew.

6. Tekàteb تَكَاتَبَ **Yetekàteb يَتَكَاتَبُ**

This measure introduces a meaning of *reciprocity*; e.g.

تَضَارَبَ	tadhârab	he fought with some one, from
ضَرَبَ	dharab	he struck.

7. Inketeb إِنْكَتَبَ **Yenketib يَنْكَتِبُ**

This form is the one commonly used in colloquial to indicate the *passive*; e.g.

إِنْكَتَبَ المكتوب	inketeb el maktûb	the letter was written
إِنْكَسَرَ	inkeser	it was broken.

This form is also used to indicate the *impossibility of an action*; e.g. hed darb mâ yenmeshî, this road cannot be walked on.

(A regular passive form exists in literary Arabic, and will be explained later. It is used in writing, but never in ordinary conversation.)

8. Ikteteb إِكْتَتَبَ **Yektetib** يَكْتَتِبُ

This form represents the *state resulting from the action of the original verb*; e. g.

مَزَجَ mezej he mixed إِمْتَزَجَ imtezej it was mixed up with

جَمَعَ jema' he gathered إِجْتَمَعَ ijtema' he foregathered with.

9. Iktebb إِكْتَبَّ **Yektebb** يَكْتَبُّ

This measure is used only to indicate *bodily defects or colours*. (It of course is never used with the root كتب keteb, which is here given only to illustrate the formation). E. g.

إِحْمَرَّ aḥmarr, he blushed, from the *adj.* أَحْمَرُ aḥmar, red

إِصْفَرَّ aṣfarr, he turned pale, from the *adj.* أَصْفَرُ aṣfar, yellow

إِعْرَجَّ a'rajj, he limped, from the *adj.* أَعْرَجُ a'raj, lame.

10. Istekteb إِسْتَكْتَبَ **Yestektib** يَسْتَكْتِبُ

The implication of this measure is generally of *seeking to do*; e. g.

إِسْتَخْبَرَ istakhbar, he inquired, from خَبْرٌ khabr, information

إِسْتَغْفَرَ istaghfar, he asked forgiveness, from غَفَرَ ghafar, he forgave.

THE MEASURES OF THE VERB ILLUSTRATED

It will frequently be difficult to discover how a certain measure of a given root has acquired a certain meaning. The reason will lie somewhere back in the Arab mind, though not explicable according to the foregoing general rules. It is advisable first to discover whether a certain measure of a verb is in use, and what its actual meaning is, before attempting to employ it.

Arabic.	*Colloquial.*	*Meaning of Measure.*	*No.*	*Root.*	*Root Meaning.*
كَذَّبَ	kedhdheb	He gave the lie to	2	kedheb	He lied
كَثَّرَ	kethther	He multiplied	2	kether	To be many
رَاجَعَ	ràja'	He reviewed	3	reja'	He returned
أَنزَلَ	enzel	He caused to descend	4	nezel	He descended
تَقَطَّعَ	taqaṭṭa'	He was cut in pieces	5	qaṭa'	He cut
تَعَارَفَ	ta'âraf	He became acquainted	6	'araf	He knew
إِنْغَلَبَ	inghalab	He was defeated	7	ghalab	He conquered
إِخْتَبَرَ	ikhtabar	He became informed	8	khabar	He tested
إِصْفَرَّ	aṣfaṛr	He turned pale	9	aṣfar (*adj.*)	Yellow
إِسْتَرْخَصَ	istarkhaṣ	He asked permission	10	rakhaṣ	He was cheap
إِسْتَنْظَرَ	istandhar	He expected (*or* waited)	10	nadhar	He looked
إِسْتَعْمَلَ	ista'mal	He used	10	'amal	He did

Word List.

Arabic.	*Meaning of Measure.*	*Past.*	*Present.*	*No.*
إِشْتَغَلَ	He worked	ishtaghal	yashtaghil	8
جَرَّبَ	He tried	jarrab	yujarrib	2
بَدَّلَ	He changed	beddel	yubeddil	2
إِشْتَرَى	He bought	ishtara	yashtarî	8
أَعْطَى	He gave	a'ṭa (anṭa)	yu'ṭî (yanṭi)	4
أَرْسَلَ	He sent	arsal	yursil	4
أَرَادَ	He wished	aràd	yurîd	4
رَادَ	He wished (current)	ràd	yarîd	1

Exercise 31.

1. He worked in the garden two days. 2. He tried to write. 3. He changed the books. 4. He bought a horse. 5. We bought a horse. 6. Do you want to buy a horse? 7. They bought five books. 8. He sent the soldiers to Baghdad. 9. They sent him. 10. He wants to send me. 11. Did you try the gun? 12. I changed my house. 13. Who sent this letter? 14. The English won. 15. The paper was cut in pieces. 16. I became acquainted with this officer in Bombay. 17. Did you ask permission from the sheikh? 18. He said so but I gave him the lie. 19. They multiplied the shops when the soldiers came. 20. We caused the boy to descend from the date-tree. 21. He turned pale when he heard the news. 22. They waited two days and two nights. 23. He returned and reviewed the book. 24. I gave him the money. 25. Please give me this. 26. Whatever you give is good. 27. We gave you all that we have.

1. Hûwa ishtaghal fîl bustàn yômên. 2. Hûwa jarrab yiktab. 3. Hûwa beddel el kutub. 4. Hûwa ishtara ḥuṣân. 5. Ishtarêna ḥuṣân. 6. Tarîd tashtarî ḥuṣân? 7. Ishtarû khamsa kutub. 8. Hûwa arsal el ʻasker ila Baghdâd. 9. Hum arsalûh. 10. Hûwa yarîd yursilnî. 11. Enta jarrabet et tufka? 12. Ana beddelet bêtî. 13. Men arsal hel maktûb? 14. El anglêz ghalabû. 15. El kàghid taqaṭṭaʻ. 16. Ana taʻârafat wîya hedh dhâbiṭ fî Bombay. 17. Istarkhaṣat min esh shêkh? 18. Hûwa gâl kedha làkin ana kedhdhebetuh. 19. Hum keththerû ed dukàkîn lemma jao el ʻasker. 20. Enzelna (nezzelna) el walad min en nakhla. 21. Hûwa aṣfarr lemma semaʻ el khabr. 22. Istandharû yômên wa lêlatên. 23. Hûwa rejaʻ wa ràjaʻ el kitàb. 24. Ana aʻṭêtuh el flûs. 25. Min fadhlek aʻṭinî hàdha. 26. Kullemâ tuʻṭî hûwa ṭayyib. 27. Aʻṭênâk kullemâ ʻandena.

١ اشتغل في البستان يومين. ٢ اجتهد ليكتب. ٣ بدّلَ الكتب. ٤ اشترى حصاناً. ٥ اشترينا حصاناً. ٦ هل تريد ان تشتري حصاناً. ٧ اشتروا خمسة كتب. ٨ ارسل العساكر لبغداد. ٩ ارسلوهُ. ١٠ يريد يرسلني. ١١ هل جرّبت البندقية. ١٢ بدّلتُ بيتي. ١٣ مَن ارسل هذا المكتوب. ١٤ غلب الانكليز. ١٥ تقطّع الكاغذ. ١٦ تعارفتُ مع هذا الضابط في بومبي. ١٧ هل استرخصتَ من الشيخ. ١٨ قال هكذا لكن كذّبتهُ. ١٩ كثّروا الدكاكين لما جاءَ العسكر. ٢٠ انزلنا الولد من النخلة. ٢١ اصفرّ لما سمع الخبر. ٢٢ استنظروا يومين وليلتين. ٢٣ رجع وراجع الكتاب. ٢٤ اعطيتهُ الفلوس. ٢٥ من فضلك اعطني هذا. ٢٦ كلّ ما تعطي هو جيد. ٢٧ اعطيناك كلّ ما عندنا.

SUMMARY OF THE STRONG VERB

No.	*Past.*	*Present.*	*Imperative.*	*Active Part.*	*Pass. Part.*	*Gerund.*
1	كَتَبَ keteb	يَكْتُبُ yiktab	أُكْتُبْ iktab	كَاتِبٌ kàtib	مَكْتُوبٌ maktûb	كِتَابَةٌ kitàba
2	كَتَّبَ ketteb	يُكَتِّبُ yukettib	كَتِّبْ kettib	مُكَتِّبٌ mukettib	مُكَتَّبٌ muketteb	تَكْتِيبٌ tektîb
3	كَاتَبَ kàteb	يُكَاتِبُ yukàtib	كَاتِبْ kàtib	مُكَاتِبٌ mukàtib	مُكَاتَبٌ mukàteb	مُكَاتَبَةٌ mukàtaba
4	أَكْتَبَ ekteb	يُكْتِبُ yuktib	أَكْتِبْ aktib	مُكْتِبٌ muktib	مُكْتَبٌ mukteb	إِكْتَابٌ iktàb
5	تَكَتَّبَ teketteb	يَتَكَتَّبُ yeteketteb	تَكَتَّبْ teketteb	مُتَكَتِّبٌ mutekettib	مُتَكَتَّبٌ muteketteb	تَكَتُّبٌ tekettub
6	تَكَاتَبَ tekàteb	يَتَكَاتَبُ yetekàteb	تَكَاتَبْ tekàteb	مُتَكَاتِبٌ mutekàtib	مُتَكَاتَبٌ mutekàteb	تَكَاتُبٌ tekàtub

7	إنْكَتَبَ inketeb	يَنْكَتِبُ yenketib	إنْكَتِبْ inketib	مُنْكَتِبٌ munketib	مُنْكَتَبٌ munketeb	إنْكِتَابٌ inkitàb
8	إكْتَتَبَ ikteteb	يَكْتَتِبُ yektetib	إكْتَتِبْ iktetib	مُكْتَتِبٌ muktetib	مُكْتَتَبٌ mukteteb	إكْتِتَابٌ iktitàb
9	إكْتَبَّ iktebb	يَكْتَبُّ yektebb	إكْتَبِبْ iktebib	مُكْتَبِبٌ muktebb	مُكْتَبَبٌ muktebb	إكْتِبَابٌ iktibàb
10	إسْتَكْتَبَ istekteb	يَسْتَكْتِبُ yestektib	إسْتَكْتِبْ istektib	مُسْتَكْتِبٌ mustektib	مُسْتَكْتَبٌ mustekteb	إسْتِكْتَابٌ istiktàb

Examples of Gerunds (Verbal Nouns).

4. islàm (Mohammedanism) إسْلَامٌ.
3. muràsala (correspondence) مُرَاسَلَةٌ.
8. iktitàb (enrolment) إكْتِتَابٌ.
2. taḥqîq (corroboration, investigation) تَحْقِيقٌ.
8. ikhtibâr (experience) إخْتِبَارٌ.
6. tebàdul (barter) تَبَادُلٌ.
7. inqilâb (revolution) إنْقِلَابٌ.
9. iḥmirâr (blushing) إحْمِرَارٌ.
10. isti'màl (use) إسْتِعْمَالٌ.

WORD LIST

أَمَرَ يَأْمُرُ	He commanded	amar, ya-mur
بَنَى يَبْنِي	He built	bena, yibnî
بَانَ يَبِينُ . بَيَّنَ يُبَانُ	It appeared	bêyyen, yubêyyin (2)
تَرَكَ يَتْرُكُ	He left, abandoned	terek, yitrak
أَحْرَقَ يُحْرِقُ	He burned (*trans.*)	aḥraq, yuḥriq (4)
إِحْتَرَقَ يَحْتَرِقُ	He burned (*intrans.*)	iḥtaraq, yaḥtariq (8)
حَصَّلَ يُحَصِّلُ	He obtained	ḥaṣṣal, yuḥaṣṣil (2)
حَصَلَ يَحْصُلُ	It was obtainable	ḥaṣal, yaḥṣal (1)
حَفِظَ يَحْفَظُ	He kept	ḥafadh, yaḥfadh
حَمَلَ يَحْمِلُ	He carried	ḥamal, yaḥmal
خَدَمَ يَخْدُمُ	He served	khadam, yakhdam
أَنَّ . أَنِّي . أَنَّكَ . أَنَّكِ . أَنَّهُ . أَنَّهَا . أَنَّنَا . أَنَّكُمْ . أَنَّهُمْ .	That (*conj.*)	ann, anni, annek, annech, annehu, anneha, annena, annekum, annehum

Exercise 32.

1. He commanded me to go to the house. 2. What did you command me to do? 3. It appears the ship will not come to-day. 4. The soldiers abandoned their guns. 5. We burned our books. 6. The paper burned. 7. Butter is not obtainable in the town. 8. I obtained three rupees. 9. They kept their money in the bank. 10. You must take care of (3) your money.

11. I told him to carry the child to his house. 12. What did you give? 13. I served the English three months. 14. He is a servant. 15. Who built this bridge? 16. This bridge is built of wood. 17. You must earn (obtain) your bread. 18. This bread was burned.

1. Hûwa amarni ann arûḥ ilal bêt. 2. Êsh amaratni ann asawwî? 3. Yubêyyin el markab mâ yîjî helyôm. 4. El ʿasker terekû tufekhum. 5. Aḥraqna kutubena. 6. El kàghid iḥtaraq. 7. Zibed mâ yaḥṣal fîl beled. 8. Ana ḥaṣṣalat thalàth rubiyàt. 9. Hum ḥafadhû flûsehum fîl bank. 10. Làzm tuḥâfidh ʿala flûsek. 11. Ana gulat luh ann yaḥmal el walad ila bêtuh. 12. Êsh aʿṭêt? 13. Ana khadamat el anglêz thalàtha ishhur. 14. Hûwa khâdim. 15. Men bena hel jisr? 16. Hel jisr mabnî min khashab. 17. Làzm tuḥaṣṣil khubzek. 18. Hel khubz kàn maḥrûq.

١ أَمرني ان اروح الى البيت. ٢ ماذا امرتني ان اعمل. ٣ يُبان ان المركب ما يجي اليوم. ٤ العسكر تركوا بنادقهم. ٥ احرقنا كتبنا. ٦ الكاغذ احترق. ٧ لا تحصل زبدة في البلد. ٨ حصّلتُ ثلاث روبيات. ٩ حفظوا فلوسهم في البنك. ١٠ يلزم ان تحافظ على فلوسك. ١١ قلتُ لهُ ان يحمل الولد الى بيته. ١٢ ماذا اعطيت. ١٣ خدمتُ الانكليز ثلاثة اشهر. ١٤ هو خادم. ١٥ من بنى هذا الجسر. ١٦ هذا الجسر مبني من خشب. ١٧ يلزم ان تحصّل خبزك. ١٨ احترق هذا الخبز.

SUMMARY OF IRREGULAR VERBS

No.	*Past.*	*Present.*	*Imperative.*	*Active Part.*	*Pass. Part.*	*Gerund.*
	وَقَفَ wagaf	يَقِفُ yogaf	قِفْ ogaf	وَاقِفٌ wâgif	مَوْقُوفٌ mawgûf	وُقُوفٌ wagûf
	قَالَ gâl	يَقُولُ yagûl	قُلْ gul	قَائِلٌ gâ-il	مَقُولٌ magyûl (magûl)	قَوْلٌ gawl
	رَمَى rama	يَرْمِي yarmî	إِرْمِ irmi	رَامٍ râmi	مَرْمِيٌّ marmî	رَمْيٌ ramî
1	جَرَّ jarr	يَجُرُّ yajurr	جُرَّ jurr	جَارٌّ jârr	مَجْرُورٌ majrûr	جَرٌّ jarâra
	أَكَلَ akal	يَأْكُلُ ya-kul	كُلْ ukul	آكِلٌ àkil	مَأْكُولٌ ma-kûl	أَكْلٌ akl
	سَأَلَ se-el	يَسْأَلُ yes-el	إِسْأَلْ . سَلْ es-el	سَائِلٌ sà-il	مَسْؤُولٌ mas-ûl	سُؤَالٌ su-àl
	قَرَأَ qara	يَقْرَأُ yaqra	إِقْرَأْ aqra	قَارِئٌ qârí	مَقْرُوءٌ maqrû	قِرَاءَةٌ qirâ-a

	وَقَّف waggaf	يُوَقِّف yuwaggif	وَقِّف waggif	مُوَقِّف muwaggif	مُوَقَّف muwaggaf	تَوْقِيف tawgîf
	قَوَّل gawwal	يُقَوِّل yugawwil	قَوِّلْ gawwil	مُقَوِّل mugawwil	مُقَوَّل mugawwal	تَقْوِيل tagwîl
	رَمَّى ramma	يُرَمِّي yurammî	رَمِّ rammi	مُرَمِّ murammî	مُرَمَّى muramma	تَرْمِيَة tarmia
2	جَرَّر jarrar	يُجَرِّر yujarrir	جَرِّرْ jarrir	مُجَرِّر mujarrir	مُجَرَّر mujarrar	تَجْرِير tajrîr
	أَكَّل akkal	يُوَكِّل yu-akkil	أَكِّلْ akkil	مُوَكِّل mu-akkil	مُوَكَّل mu-akkal	تَأْكِيل ta-kîl
	سَأَّل se-el	يُسَئِّل yuse-il	سَئِّلْ se-il	مُسَئِّل muse-il	مُسَأَّل muse-el	تَسْئِيل tas-îl
	قَرَّأ qarra	يُقَرِّى yuqarrî	قَرِّ qarri	مُقَرِّى muqarrî	مُقَرَّأ muqarra	تَقْرِئَة taqria

No.	*Past.*	*Present.*	*Imperative.*	*Active Part.*	*Pass. Part.*	*Gerund.*
	وَاقَفَ wâgaf	يُوَاقِف yuwâgif	وَاقِفْ wâgif	مُوَاقِف muwâgif	مُوَاقَف muwâgaf	مُوَاقَفَة muwâgafa
	قَاوَلَ gâwal	يُقَاوِلُ yugâwil	قَاوِلْ gâwil	مُقَاوِل mugâwil	مُقَاوَل mugâwal	مُقَاوَلَة mugâwala
	رَامَى râma	يُرَامِي yurâmi	رَامِ râmi	مُرَامِ murâmi	مُرَامَى murâma	مُرَامَاة murâmàt
3	جَارّ jârar	يُجَارّ yujârir	جَارِرْ jârir	مُجَارِر mujârir	مُجَارَر mujârar	مُجَارَرَة mujârara
	آكَلَ àkal	يُوَاكِلُ yu-àkil	آكِلْ àkil	مُوَاكِل mu-àkil	مُوَاكَل mu-àkal	مُوَاكَلَة mu-àkala
	سَاءَلَ sà-al	يُسَائِلُ yusà-il	سَائِلْ sà-il	مُسَائِل musà-il	مُسَاءَل musà-al	مُسَاءَلَة musà-ala
	قَارَأَ qâra	يُقَارِئُ yuqâri	قَارِئْ qâri	مُقَارِئ muqâri	مُقَارَأ muqâra	مُقَارَأَة muqâra-a

	أَوْقَفَ awgaf	يُوقِفُ yûgif	أَوْقِفْ awgif	مُوقِفٌ mûgif	مُوقَفٌ mûgaf	إِيقَافٌ igâf
	أَقَالَ agâl	يُقِيلُ yugîl	أَقِلْ agil	مُقِيلٌ mugîl	مُقَالٌ mugâl	إِقَالَةٌ igâla
	أَرْمَى arma	يُرْمِي yurmî	أَرْمِ armi	مُرْمٍ murmî	مُرْمًى murma	إِرْمَاءٌ irmâ
4	أَجَرَّ ajarr	يُجِرُّ yujirr	أَجْرِرْ ajirr	مُجِرٌّ mujirr	مُجَرٌّ mujarr	إِجْرَارٌ ijrâr
	آكَلَ àkal	يُؤْكِلُ yû-kil	آكِلْ àkil	مُؤْكِلٌ mû-kil	مُؤْكَلٌ mû-kal	إِيكَالٌ íkàl
	أَسْأَلَ es-el	يُسْئِلُ yus-il	أَسْئِلْ as-il	مُسْئِلٌ mus-il	مُسْأَلٌ mus-al	إِسْآلٌ is-àl
	أَقْرَأَ aqra	يُقْرِئُ yuqri	أَقْرِئْ aqri	مُقْرِئٌ muqri	مُقْرَأٌ muqra	إِقْرَاءٌ iqrâ

No.	*Past.*	*Present.*	*Imperative.*	*Active Part.*	*Pass. Part.*	*Gerund.*
	تَوَقَّفَ tawaggaf	يَتَوَقَّفُ yatawaggaf	تَوَقَّفْ tawaggaf	مُتَوَقِّفْ mutawaggif	مُتَوَقَّفْ mutawaggaf	تَوَقُّفْ tawagguf
	تَقَوَّلَ tagawwal	يَتَقَوَّلُ yatagawwal	تَقَوَّلْ tagawwal	مُتَقَوِّلْ mutagawwil	مُتَقَوَّلْ mutagawwal	تَقَوُّلْ tagawwul
	تَرَمَّى taramma	يَتَرَمَّى yataramma	تَرَمَّ taramma	مُتَرَمٍّ mutarammí	مُتَرَمًّى mutaramma	تَرَمٍّ tarammî
5	تَجَرَّرَ tajarrar	يَتَجَرَّرُ yatajarrar	تَجَرَّرْ tajarrar	مُتَجَرِّرْ mutajarrir	مُتَجَرَّرْ mutajarrar	تَجَرُّرْ tajarrur
	تَأَكَّلَ ta-akkal	يَتَأَكَّلُ yata-akkal	تَأَكَّلْ ta-akkal	مُتَأَكِّلْ muta-akkil	مُتَأَكَّلْ muta-akkal	تَأَكُّلْ ta-akkul
	تَسَآَّلَ tese-el	يَتَسَآَّلُ yetese-el	تَسَآَّلْ tese-el	مُتَسَيِّلْ mutese-il	مُتَسَآَّلْ mutese-el	تَسَآُّلْ tese-ul
	تَقَرَّأَ taqarra	يَتَقَرَّأُ yataqarra	تَقَرَّأْ taqarra	مُتَقَرِّئ mutaqarri	مُتَقَرَّأْ mutaqarra	تَقَرُّوْ taqarru

	تَوَاقَفَ tawâgaf	يَتَوَاقَفُ yatawâgaf	تَوَاقَفْ tawâgaf	مُتَوَاقِفٌ mutawâgif	مُتَوَاقَفٌ mutawâgaf	تَوَاقُفٌ tawâguf
	تَقَاوَلَ tagâwal	يَتَقَاوَلُ yatagâwal	تَقَاوَلْ tagâwal	مُتَقَاوِلٌ mutagâwil	مُتَقَاوَلٌ mutagâwal	تَقَاوُلٌ tagâwul
	تَرَامَى tarâma	يَتَرَامَى yatarâma	تَرَامَ tarâma	مُتَرَامٍ mutarâmî	مُتَرَامًى mutarâma	تَرَامٍ tarâmî
6	تَجَارَّ tajârar	يَتَجَارُّ yatajârar	تَجَارَرْ tajârar	مُتَجَارِرٌ mutajârir	مُتَجَارَرٌ mutajârar	تَجَارٌّ tajârur
	تَآكَلَ ta-àkal	يَتَآكَلُ yata-àkal	تَآكَلْ ta-àkal	مُتَآكِلٌ muta-àkil	مُتَآكَلٌ muta-àkal	تَآكُلٌ ta-àkul
	تَسَاءَلَ tasà-al	يَتَسَاءَلُ yatasà-al	تَسَاءَلْ tasà-al	مُتَسَائِلٌ mutasà-il	مُتَسَاءَلٌ mutasà-al	تَسَاؤُلٌ tasà-ul
	تَقَارَأَ taqâra	يَتَقَارَأُ yataqâra	تَقَارَأْ taqâra	مُتَقَارِئٌ mutaqâri	مُتَقَارَأٌ mutaqâra	تَقَارُؤٌ taqâri

No.	*Past.*	*Present.*	*Imperative.*	*Active Part.*	*Pass. Part.*	*Gerund.*
	إِنْوَقَف inwagaf	يَنْوَقِف yanwagif	إِنْوَقِف inwagif	مُنْوَقِف munwagif	مُنْوَقَف munwagaf	إِنْوِقَاف inwigâf
	إِنْقَال ingâl	يَنْقَال yangâl	إِنْقَل ingal	مُنْقَال mungâl	مُنْقَال mungâl	اِنْقِيَال ingiyâl
	إِنْرَمَى inrama	يَنْرَمِي yanramî	إِنْرَمِ inrami	مُنْرَمٍ munramî	مُنْرَمًى munrama	إِنْرِمَاء inrimâ
7	إِنْجَرّ injarr	يَنْجَرّ yanjarr	إِنْجَرِر injarir	مُنْجَرّ munjarr	مُنْجَرّ munjarr	إِنْجِرَار injirâr
	إِنْأَكَل in-akal	يَنْأَكِل yan-akil	إِنْأَكِل in-akil	مُنْأَكِل mun-akil	مُنْأَكَل mun-akal	إِنْئِكَال in-ikâl
	إِنْسَأَل inse-el	يَنْسَئِل yense-il	إِنْسَئِل inse-il	مُنْسَئِل munse-il	مُنْسَأَل munse-el	إِنْسِئَال insi-àl
	إِنْقَرَأ inqara	يَنْقَرِى yanqari	إِنْقَرِى inqari	مُنْقَرِى munqari	مُنْقَرَأ munqara	إِنْقِرَاء inqirâ

اِتَّقَفَ ittagaf	يَتَّقِفُ yattagif	اِتَّقِفْ ittagif	مُتَّقِفٌ muttagif	مُتَّقَفٌ muttagaf	اِتِّقَافٌ ittigâf
اِقْتَالَ iqtâl	يَقْتَالُ yaqtâl	اِقْتَلْ iqtal	مُقْتَالٌ muqtâl	مُقْتَالٌ muqtâl	اِقْتِيَالٌ iqtiyâl
اِرْتَمَى irtama	يَرْتَمِي yartamî	اِرْتَمِ irtami	مُرْتَمٍ murtamî	مُرْتَمًى murtama	اِرْتِمَاءٌ irtimâ
اِجْتَرَّ ijtarr	يَجْتَرُّ yajtarr	اِجْتَرِرْ ijtarir	مُجْتَرٌّ mujtarir	مُجْتَرٌّ mujtarr	اِجْتِرَارٌ ijtirâr
اِيتَكَلَ ittàkal	يَأْتَكِلُ yattàkil	اِيتَكِلْ ittàkil	مُوتَكِلٌ muttàkil	مُوتَكَلٌ muttàkal	اِيتِكَالٌ ittikàl
اِسْتَأَلَ iste-al	يَسْتَئِلُ yeste-il	اِسْتَئِلْ iste-il	مُسْتَئِلٌ muste-il	مُسْتَأَلٌ muste-el	اِسْتِئَالٌ isti-àl
اِقْتَرَأَ iqtara	يَقْتَرِئُ yaqtari	اِقْتَرِئْ iqtari	مُقْتَرِئٌ muqtari	مُقْتَرَأٌ muqtara	اِقْتِرَاءٌ iqtirâ

No.	*Past.*	*Present.*	*Imperative.*	*Active Part.*	*Pass. Part.*	*Gerund.*
	إستوقف istawgaf	يَستوقِف yastawgif	إستوقِف istawgif	مُستوقِف mustawgif	مُستوقَف mustawgaf	إستيقاف istîgâf
	إستقال istagâl	يَستقِيل yastagîl	إستقِل istagil	مُستقِيل mustagîl	مُستقال mustagâl	إستقالة istigâla
	إسترمى istarma	يَسترمِي yastarmî	إسترِم istarmi	مُسترم mustarmî	مُسترمى mustarma	إسترماء istirmâ
10	إستجرّ istajarr	يَستجِرّ yastajirr	إستجرِر istajrir	مُستجِرّ mustajirr	مُستجَرّ mustajarr	إستجرار istijrâr
	إستأكَل istà-kal	يَستأكِل yastà-kil	استأكِل istà-kil	مُستأكِل mustà-kil	مُستأكَل mustà-kal	إستيكال isti-kàla
	إستسأل istes-al	يَستسئِل yestes-il	إستسئِل istes-il	مُستسئِل mustes-il	مُستسأَل mustes-el	إستسآل istis-àl
	إستقرأ istaqra	يَستقرى yastaqri	إستقرِي istaqri	مُستقرِي mustaqri	مُستقرأ mustaqra	إستقراء istiqrâ

Note.—Attention need be called only to the 8th measure. In verbs with initial *waw* و, the *waw* is assimilated into the characteristic *t* of the measure, which is doubled to compensate. Likewise the initial hemza in أَكَلَ *akal*, in colloquial.

Exercise 33.

1. We made them eat (2) the bread. 2. I saw him standing behind the house. 3. He taught (2) the boy reading. 4. I do not like the food in the bazaar. 5. You are responsible (pass. part. 1, se-el). 6. Have you read this book? 7. Sṭand up and read. 8. I contracted with him (6, gâl). 9. I have a contract with him (gerund, 3, gâl). 10. They shot at each other (6, rama). 11. Pull the punkah. 12. Ask whatever you wish. 13. The bread has been eaten. 14. The bread cannot be eaten (7). 15. They made them stand in the bazaar (4 or 2). 16. Why do you ask this question? 17. I learned reading and writing. 18. Standing on the feet (foot) is difficult. 19. The book was taken from the table. 20. The horse is tied. 21. The house is closed. 22. I saw the money put on the table. 23. The water spread (8, medd) to the desert. 24. The men conferred with (3, reja‘) the soldiers. 25. He goes back and forth (5, radd). 26. He was lying down (act. part., 5, medd). 27. He made me afraid (2). 28. We took a walk (5, mesha).

1. Akkalnâhum el khubz. 2. Ana shifetuh wâgif wara el bêt. 3. Hûwa ‘allam el walad qirâya (qirâ-a). 4. Ana mâ aḥibb el akl fîs sûq. 5. Enta mas-ûl. 6. Enta qârî hel kitàb? 7. Ogaf wa aqra. 8. Ana tagâwalat wiyàh. 9. ‘Andi mugâwala wiyàh. 10. Tarâmû. 11. Jurr el punkah. 12. Es-el kullmâ tarîd. 13. El khubz ma-kûl. 14. El khubz mâ yan-akil. 15. Awgafûhum (waggafûhum) fîs sûq. 16. Lêsh tes-el hes suwàl (su-àl)? 17. Ana ta‘allamat qirâya wa kitàba. 18. El wagûf ‘alar rijl zaḥma. 19. El kitàb in-akhadh min el mêz. 20. El ḥuṣân mashdûd. 21. El bêt masdûd. 22. Ana shifet el flûs maḥṭûṭ ‘alal mêz. 23. El mai emtedd ilal chôl. 24. Er rijàl râja‘û el ‘asker. 25. Hûwa yataraddad. 26. Hûwa kàn mutamaddid. 27. Hûwa khawwafni. 28. Temeshshênâ.

١ أكّلناهم الخبز. ٢ شفتهُ واقفاً وراء البيت. ٣ علّمَ الولد القراءة. ٤ لا احبّ الأكل في السوق. ٥ انت مسؤول. ٦ هل قرأت هذا الكتاب. ٧ قِف وٱقرأْ. ٨ تقاولتُ معهُ. ٩ لي مقاولة معهُ. ١٠ تَرَامُوا. ١١ جرّ البانكة. ١٢ سَلْ كل ما تُريد. ١٣ قد إناأكل الخبز. ١٤ لا ينأكل الخبز. ١٥ اوقفوهم في السوق. ١٦ لماذا تسأل هذا السؤال. ١٧ تعلمتُ القراءة والكتابة. ١٨ الوقوف على الرجل صعب. ١٩ إناأخذ الكتاب عن المائدة. ٢٠ الحصان مشدود. ٢١ البيت مسدود. ٢٢ شفتُ الفلوس موضوعة على المائدة. ٢٣ امتدّ الماء الى الصحراء. ٢٤ راجعوا الرجال مع العسكر. ٢٥ يتردّد. ٢٦ كان متمدِّداً. ٢٧ خوّفَني. ٢٨ تمشّيْنا.

WORD LIST: ADJECTIVES FOR COLOURS, ETC.

Plur.	*Fem.*	*Masc.*		*Masc.*	*Fem.*	*Plur.*
حُمْر	حَمْرَاءُ	أَحْمَرُ	Red	aḥmar	ḥamra	ḥumr
سُودٌ	سَوْدَاءُ	أَسْوَدُ	Black	aswad	sôda	sûd
زُرْق	زَرْقَاءُ	أَزْرَقُ	Blue	azraq	zirqa	zirq
بِيضٌ	بَيْضَاءُ	أَبْيَضُ	White	abyadh	bêdha	bîdh
خُضْر	خَضْرَاءُ	أَخْضَرُ	Green	akhdhar	khadhra	khudhr
صُفْر	صَفْرَاءُ	أَصْفَرُ	Yellow	aṣfar	ṣafra	ṣufr
شُهْبٌ	شَهْبَاءُ	أَشْهَبُ (أَمْلَحُ)	Grey	ramâdî	ramadîa	
			„ (of hair)	abyadh, &c.		
مُنَقَّطُونَ	مُنَقَّطَةٌ	مُنَقَّطٌ	Speckled	munaqqaṭ	munaqqaṭa	

WORD LIST (*continued*)

Plur.	*Fem.*	*Masc.*		*Masc.*	*Fem.*	*Plur.*
بُقْعٌ	بَقْعَاءُ	أَبْقَعُ	Spotted *or* piebald	abqaʿ	baqʿa	buqʿ
مُخَطَّطُونَ	مُخَطَّطَةٌ	مُخَطَّطٌ	Striped	mukhaṭṭaṭ	mukhaṭṭaṭa	
عُمْيٌ او عُمْيَانٌ	عَمْيَاءُ	أَعْمَى	Blind	aʿma	ʿamya	ʿamyàn ʿamyànîn
طُرْشٌ	طَرْشَاءُ	أَطْرَشُ	Deaf	aṭrash	ṭarsha	ṭursh
خُرْسٌ	خَرْسَاءُ	أَخْرَسُ	Dumb	akhras	kharsa	khurs khursîn
عُرْجٌ	عَرْجَاءُ	أَعْرَجُ	Lame	aʿraj	ʿarja	ʿurj
بُرْصٌ	بَرْصَاءُ	أَبْرَصُ	Leprous	abraṣ	barṣa	burṣ burṣîn
		أَىّ جِنْسٍ . أَىّ شِكْلٍ	What kind of ?	ê jins ? ê shikl ? yâ shikl ?		

Note.—Adjectives for bodily defects and colours are all formed after the above model. Broken plurals take a broken plur. adj. when such exists.

Exercise 34.

1. The blacks live in the Sudan. 2. The woman is black and the man is white. 3. We have three white horses. 4. The paper is yellow. 5. My eyes are blue. 6. The date-tree is green. 7. My dog is spotted white and black. 8. Their hands are red. 9. The girl is white. 10. We are white but you are black. 11. The house is grey. 12. What kind of book have you? 13. All the blind and lame came. 14. There are many lepers in Basrah. 15. Are you deaf?

1. Es sûd yiskanûn fîs sudàn. 2. El ḥarma sôda war rejul abyadh. 3. 'Andena thalàtha ḥuṣn bîdh. 4. El kàghid aṣfar. 5. 'Ayûnî zirq. 6. En nakhla khadhra. 7. Kelbî abqa' abyadh wa aswad. 8. Idêhum ḥumr. 9. El bint bêdha. 10. Eḥna bîdh làkin entû sûd. 11. El bêt ramâdî. 12. Ê shikl kitàb 'andek? 13. Kull el 'amyàn wal 'urj jao. 14. Burṣ (burṣîn) wàjid fîl Baṣrah. 15. Enta aṭrash?

١ السود يسكنون السودان. ٢ الامرأة سوداء والرجل ابيض. ٣ عندنا ثلاثة حُصُن بيضاء. ٤ الكاغذ اصفر. ٥ عيناي زرقاوَانِ. ٦ النخلة خضراء. ٧ كلبي ابقع ابيض واسود. ٨ ايديهم حمراء. ٩ البنت بيضاء. ١٠ نحن بيض وانتم سود. ١١ البيت املح. ١٢ اي شكل كتاب عندك. ١٣ جاءَ كل العمي والعرج. ١٤ يوجد بُرص كثيرون في البصرة. ١٥ هل انت اطرش.

WORD LIST

عِوَضاً عَنْ	Instead of	'iwadh
عِوَضاً عَنْ أَنْ	Instead of (with verb)	'iwadhma
عَوَّضَ يُعَوِّضُ	He substituted	'awwadh, yu'awwidh
إِمَّا — أَوْ	Either—or	amma—aw, yô—yô
لَا — وَلَا	Neither—nor	la—wa la

إِسْمٌ ج أَسْمَاءٌ	Name	ism, asàmî, ismà
مَا ٱسْمُ	What is the name of	shism
إِبْنٌ ج بَنُونَ . أَبْنَاءٌ	Son	ibn, *pl.* benîn, ibnà *pl.* (before *gen.*) benî
بِنْتٌ ج بَنَاتٌ	Daughter	bint, *pl.* banàt
بِقَدْرِ مَا	In proportion as	bigadrma, bigadma
وَدَعَ يَدَعُ . سَمَحَ يَسْمَحُ	He let	khalla, yukhallî
إِجْتَهَدَ يَجْتَهِدُ	He endeavoured	ijtehed, yejtehid

Exercise 35.

1. I want this instead of that. 2. Instead of going to Basrah why don't you go to Baghdad? 3. It is either white or black. 4. It is neither here nor there. 5. You must either buy or sell. 6. Whose son is this? 7. He is my son. 8. How many sons have you? 9. I have four sons and two daughters. 10. What is your name? 11. What is their name? 12. What is the name of this town? 13. In proportion as you try you learn. 14. Let us go to the bazaar. 15. He will not let me go. 16. I let him go but he did not wish to. 17. They substituted horses for men. 18. How many children (walad) have you? 19. Leave me alone. 20. The children of Israel.

1. Arîd hàdha ʿiwadh dhàk. 2. ʿIwadhma tarûḥ ilal Baṣrah lêsh mâ tarûḥ ila Baghdâd? 3. Hûwa yô abyadh yô aswad. 4. Hûwa la hina wa la hinàk. 5. Làzm amma tashtarî aw tabîʿ. 6. Ibn men hàdha? 7. Hûwa ibnî. 8. Kem ibn ʿandek? 9. ʿAndi arbaʿa benîn wa bintên. 10. Shismek? 11. Shismehum? 12. Shism hel beled? 13. Bigadma tejtehid tataʿallam. 14. Khallina narûḥ ilas sûq. 15. Hûwa mâ yukhallîni arûḥ. 16. Ana khallêtuh yarûḥ làkin hûwa mâ ràd yarûḥ. 17. ʿAwwadhû rijàl bi khêl. 18. Kem walad ʿandek? 19. Khallini. 20. Benî Israîl.

١ اريد هذا عوضاً عن ذاك. ٢ عوضاً عن ان تروح الى البصرة لماذا لا تروح الى بغداد. ٣ هو إما ابيض او اسود. ٤ هو لا هنا ولا هناك. ٥ يلزم إما ان تشتري او تبيع. ٦ ابنُ مَن هذا. ٧ هو ابني. ٨ كم ابناً عندك. ٩ عندي اربعة بنين وبنتان. ١٠ ما ٱسمُك. ١١ ما ٱسمهم. ١٢ ما اسم هذا البلد. ١٣ بقدر ما تجتهد تتعلم. ١٤ دعنا نروح الى السوق. ١٥ هو لا يدعني ان اروح. ١٦ انا سمحتُ لهُ ان يروح لكنه ما اراد. ١٧ عوّضوا الرجال بخيل. ١٨ كم ولداً عندك. ١٩ اتركني. ٢٠ بنو اسرائيل.

FRACTIONS AND ARITHMETIC

نُصْف	Half	nuṣf, nuṣṣ
ثُلْث ج أَثْلَاث	Third	thulth, *pl.* athlàth
ثُلْثَانِ	Two thirds	thulthên
رُبْع ج أَرْبَاع	Quarter	rub', *pl.* arbâ' (chàrik, *pl.* chawàrîk, Turk.)
ثَلَاثَةُ أَرْبَاعٍ	Three quarters	thalàthat arbâ'
خُمْس ج أَخْمَاس	Fifth	khums, *pl.* akhmâs
سُدْس ج أَسْدَاس	Sixth	suds, *pl.* asdàs
سُبْع ج أَسْبَاع	Seventh	sub', *pl.* asbâ'
ثُمْن ج أَثْمَان	Eighth	thumn, *pl.* athmàn
تُسْع ج أَتْسَاع	Ninth	tus', *pl.* atsà'
عُشْر ج أَعْشَار	Tenth	'ushr, *pl.* a'shâr
جُزْء ج أَجْزَاء	Part, portion	juz, *pl.* ajzà
جُزْءٌ مِنْ أَحَدَ عَشَر	Eleventh	juz min idâsh
جُزْآنِ مِنْ أَحَدَ عَشَر	Two elevenths	juz-ên min idâsh

ثَلَاثَةُ اَجْزَاءٍ مِنْ أَحَدَ عَشَرَ	Three elevenths	thalàthat ajzà min idâsh &c., &c., &c.
وَاحِدٌ وَنُصْفٌ	$1\frac{1}{2}$	wâḥid wa nuṣf
وَاحِدٌ وَرُبْعٌ	$1\frac{1}{4}$	wâḥid wa rubʿ
إِلَّا	Except, less	illa
ثَلَاثَةٌ إِلَّا رُبْعٍ	$2\frac{3}{4}$	thalàtha illa rubʿ
ثَلَاثَةٌ وَثَلَاثَةُ أَثْمَانٍ	$3\frac{3}{8}$	thalàtha wa rubʿ wa thumn
ثَلَاثَةٌ وَخَمْسَةُ أَثْمَانٍ	$3\frac{5}{8}$	thalàtha wa nuṣf wa thumn
فِي ٱلْمِئَةِ	Per cent.	bil mîa
وَ	Plus	wa
إِلَّا	Minus, less	illa
فِي	Times	fî (followed by number)
عَلَى	Divided by	ʿala
ضَرَبَ يَضْرِبُ	He multiplied	dharab, yadhrab
طَرَحَ يَطْرَحُ	He subtracted	ṭaraḥ, yaṭraḥ
جَمَعَ يَجْمَعُ	He added	jamaʿ, yijmaʿ
قَسَمَ يَقْسِمُ	He divided	qasam, yaqsam
	Total, result	
ٱلْمَجْمُوعُ	of addition	
ٱلْبَاقِي	,, subtraction	el yakûn
ٱلْحَاصِلُ	,, multiplication	
ٱلْخَارِجُ	,, division	

TIME OF DAY

أَلسَّاعَةُ	o'clock	es sâʿa
كَم آلسَّاعَةُ	What time is it ?	es sâʿa kem ? bêsh es sâʿa ?
دَقِيقَةٌ ج دَقَائِقُ	Minute	daqîqa, *pl.* daqâyiq
أَلسَّاعَةُ خَمْسٌ	Five o'clock	es sâʿa bi khamsa
أَلسَّاعَةُ وَاحِدَةٌ	One o'clock	es sâʿa bi wâḥida
أَلسَّاعَةُ وَاحِدَةٌ وَخَمْسُ دَقَائِقَ	1.05	wâḥida wa khamsa
„ „ وَعَشْرُ دَقَائِقَ	1.10	wâḥida wa ʿashera
„ „ وَرُبْعٌ	1.15	wâḥida wa rubʿ (chàrik)
„ „ وَثُلْثٌ	1.20	wâḥida wa thulth
„ „ وَنِصْفٌ إِلَّا خَمْسِ دَقَائِقَ	1.25	wâḥida wa nuṣf illa khamsa
„ „ وَنِصْفٌ	1.30	wâḥida wa nuṣf
„ „ وَنِصْفٌ وَخَمْسُ دَقَائِقَ	1.35	wâḥida wa nuṣf wa khamsa
أَلسَّاعَةُ إِثْنَتَانِ إِلَّا ثُلْثٍ	1.40	thentên illa thulth
„ „ „ رُبْعٍ	1.45	thentên illa rubʿ

TIME OF DAY (*continued*)

الساعة إثنتان إلا عشر دقائق	1.50	thentên illa ʿashera
,, ,, ,, خمس دقائق	1.55	thentên illa khamsa
الساعة إثنتان	2 o'clock	es sâʿa bi thentên
,, واحدة وثماني عشرة دقيقة	1.18, &c.	wâḥida wa thmantâsh daqîqa
,, إثنتان إلا آثنتى عشرة دقيقة	1.48, &c.	thentên illa thnash daqîqa
ساعة	Watch	sâʿa, *pl.* sâʿàt
ساعة حائط	Clock	sâʿa màlat ḥâyiṭ
ساعاتي	Watchmaker	sâʿachî, *pl.* sâʿachîya
عقرب ج عقارب	Watch-hand	ʿaqrab (lit. scorpion)
الساعة تمشي	The watch goes	es sâʿa timshî
الساعة وقفت	The watch has stopped	es sâʿa wâgifa
نصب ينصب	He wound	naṣab, yanṣab
زنبرك	Spring	zambrak
جامة	Glass, crystal	jàma, balûra

WORD LIST

أَبٌ ج آبَاءٌ	Father	àb, *pl.* àbà, àbahàt
أُمٌّ ج أُمَّهَاتٌ	Mother	umm, *pl.* ummahàt
أَخٌ ج إِخْوَةٌ	Brother	âkh, *pl.* ikhwa, ikhwàn
أُخْتٌ ج أَخَوَاتٌ	Sister	ûkht, *pl.* khawàt
جَدٌّ ج أَجْدَادٌ او جُدُودٌ	Grandfather	jidd, *pl.* ajdàd
جَدَّةٌ ج جَدَّاتٌ	Grandmother	jidda, *pl.* jiddàt
عَمٌّ ج أَعْمَامٌ	Paternal uncle	ʿamm, *pl.* aʿmàm
عَمَّةٌ ج عَمَّاتٌ	Paternal aunt	ʿamma, *pl.* ʿammàt
خَالٌ ج أَخْوَالٌ	Maternal uncle	khâl, *pl.* akhwâl, khawâl
خَالَةٌ ج خَالَاتٌ	Maternal aunt	khâla, *pl.* khâlàt
إِبْنُ ٱلْعَمِّ . بِنْتُ ٱلْخَالِ . الخ	Cousin	ibn ʿamm, bint khâl, &c. (according to parentage)
قَرِيبٌ ج أَقْرِبَاءُ	Relation	qarîb, *pl.* qarâyib
يَخُصُّ	He is related to	hûwa yakhuṣṣ
عَائِلَةٌ ج عَائِلَاتٌ او عِيَالٌ	Family	ʿayela, *pl.* ʿayelàt, ʿayàl
عَشِيرَةٌ ج عَشَائِرُ	Tribe	ʿashîra, *pl.* ʿashâyir

The inflection of أَبٌ àb, and أَخٌ âkh is somewhat irregular.

أَبُو	abû	in construction with following noun. E.g. àbû Yûsuf
أَبِي	abûi	my father

أَبُوكَ	abûk	your father
أَبُوكِ	abûch (abûki)	your (*f.*) father
أَبُوهُ	abûh	his father
أَبُوهَا	abûha	her father
أَبُونَا	abûna	our father
أَبُوكُمْ	abûkum	your (*pl.*) father
أَبُوهُمْ	abûhum	their father

(In literary Arabic the inflection is as follows:

	أَبُو	abû	Nominative in construction and with suffixes
	أَبِي	abî	Genitive and Dative in constr. and with suffixes
	أَبَا	abâ	Accusative in constr. and with suffixes
E.g.	جَاءَ أَبُوكَ	jâ'a abûka	Your father came
	كُنْتُ مَعْ أَبِيكَ	kuntu maʿ abîka	I was with your father
	هُوَ ضَرَبَ أَبَاكَ	huwa dharaba abâka	He struck your father.)

WORD LIST

بَعْضُ	Some	bâʿdh, shê
بَعْضُ مِنْ	Some of	el bâʿdh min
بَعْضُنَا بَعْضاً	Each other (we)	bâʿdhena bâʿdh
بَعْضُكُمْ بَعْضاً	Each other (you)	bâʿdhekum bâʿdh
بَعْضُهُمْ بَعْضاً	Each other	bâʿdhehum bâʿdh
أَحَدٌ	Any (with negative)	aḥad

Illustrations.

جَاءَ بَعْضُ ٱلْعَسَاكِرِ	Some of the soldiers came	bâ'dh el 'asker jao *or* el bâ'dh min el 'asker jao
شُفْنَا بَعْضُنَا بَعْضاً	We saw each other	shifna bâ'dhena bâ'dh
شُفْتُمْ بَعْضُكُمْ بَعْضاً	You saw each other	shiftû bâ'dhekum bâ'dh
شَافُوا بَعْضُهُمْ بَعْضاً	They saw each other	shàfû bâ'dhehum bâ'dh
كَتَبُوا لِبَعْضِهِمْ بَعْضٍ	They wrote to each other	ketebû bâ'dhehum ilal bâ'dh *or* tekàtebû
أَخَذُوا فُلُوساً مِنْ بَعْضِهِمْ بَعْضٍ	They took the money from each other	akhadhû el flûs min bâ'dhehum *or* bâ'dhehum min el bâ'dh
ضَرَبُوا بَعْضُهُمْ بَعْضاً	They struck each other	dharabû bâ'dhehum bâ'dh *or* tadhârabû
مَا رَأَيْتُ (شُفْتُ) أَحَداً	I did not see anybody	ana mâ shifet aḥad
مَا جَاءَ أَحَدٌ	Nobody has come	mâ aḥad jà

CONDITIONAL SENTENCES

Simple: *Idha* or *in kàn* with present—present.

If I go, I shall see the ship
Idha arûḥ ashûf el markab (*In kàn arûḥ ashûf el markab*).

Probable: *Idha* or *law* with past—*kàn* (inflected) with present.

If I should go, I should see the ship
Idha ruḥat kunet ashûf el markab (*Law ruḥat*, &c.).

Contrary to fact: *Law kàn* with past—*kàn* (uninflected) with past.

If I had gone, I should have seen the ship
Law kàn ruḥat kàn shifet el markab.

The apodosis in contrary to fact conditions is frequently preceded by فَ fa. E.g. I should have seen the ship, *fa kàn shifet el markab.*

The phrase 'If it had not been for' is expressed by *law la.*

E.g. If it had not been for the soldiers, we would not be here.
Law la el ʿasker fa naḥen mu hina.

If it had not been for his writing, we would not have known he had come.
Law la kitàbatuh fa mâ ʿarafna hûwa jai.

(The Semitic theory of tenses being so entirely at variance with Occidental ideas, it is impracticable here to give in detail the literary usage of conditional sentences. The above are sufficient for all ordinary composition.)

COMPARISON OF ADJECTIVES

The Comparative is formed on the model كَبِيرْ أَكْبَرُ kabir, akbar.

The English 'than' is expressed by مِنْ min (lit. from).

E.g. The boy is bigger than the girl
El walad akbar min el bint
أَلْوَلَدُ أَكْبَرُ مِنَ ٱلْبِنْتِ

Comparatives and superlatives have no plural form.

When the second and third consonants of the positive are alike, they are brought together in the comparative.

E.g. قَلِيلٌ qalîl, أَقَلّ aqall.

When a participle beginning in *m* is to be compared, the participle itself is not altered, but the comparative is indicated by introducing أَكْثَرُ akthar, 'more'.

E.g. akthar mukhtebir more informed.

Likewise frequently for the sake of euphony.

E.g. akthar ʿaṭshân more thirsty.

The Superlative is formed by prefixing the article اَلْ el to the comparative.

E.g. الأَكْبَرُ el akbar the biggest.

When the superlative is in construction with a following noun, the article is of course dropped.

E.g. He is the largest of all the boys

هُوَ أَكْبَرُ كُلِّ ٱلأَوْلَادِ Hûwa akbar kull el awlàd

or

هُوَ الأَكْبَرُ مِنْ كُلِّ ٱلأَوْلَادِ Hûwa el akbar min kull el awlàd.

(In literary Arabic there is a special form for the fem. superl.; e.g. *kabîrun*, fem. superl. *el kubra* كَبِيرٌ ٱلْكُبْرَى.)

Illustrations.

الأَقْوَى	أَقْوَى	قَوِيٌّ	strong	qawi, aqwa, el aqwa
الأَضْعَفُ	أَضْعَفُ	ضَعِيفٌ	weak	dhaʿîf, adhʿaf, el adhʿaf
الأَجْهَلُ	أَجْهَلُ	جَاهِلٌ	ignorant	jàhil, ajhal, el ajhal
الأَحْكَمُ	أَحْكَمُ	حَكِيمٌ	wise	ḥakîm, aḥkam, el aḥkam
الأَغْنَى	أَغْنَى	غَنِيٌّ	rich	ghani, aghna, el aghna
الأَبْرَدُ	أَبْرَدُ	بَارِدٌ	cold	bàrid, abrad, el abrad

الأَحَرّ	أَحَرّ	حَارّ	hot	ḥârr, aḥarr, el aḥarr
الأَوْضَح	أَوْضَح	وَاضِح	evident	wâdhiḥ, awdhaḥ, el awdhaḥ
الأَحْسَن	أَحْسَن	حَسَن	beautiful	ḥasan, aḥsan, el aḥsan

IDIOMATIC EXPRESSIONS

The English 'too' with an adjective or adverb has no Arabic equivalent. 'Too much' is rendered by كَثِير kathîr, 'much', sometimes by زَائِد zàyid. E.g. This is too long

Hàdha kathîr ṭawîl (This is very long)

or

Hàdha ṭûluh zàyid (This its length is excessive).

The English 'enough' with an adjective or adverb also has no Arabic equivalent. Sometimes the idea is conveyed by كَافِي kàfi, 'enough'.

E. g. This is long enough

Hàdha ṭûluh kàfi

(This its length is enough).

The above, however, is not purely Semitic. An Arab would not use it, though he would understand it.

The English 'on the point of' is frequently expressed in colloquial by رَاح râḥ.

E. g. He is on the point of falling

Hûwa râḥ yogaʿ

Or by *ràd* for the past, *yarîd* for the present.

E. g. He is on the point of falling

Hûwa yarîd yogaʿ.

He was on the point of falling

Hûwa ràd yogaʿ.

'He began to' can be rendered by the usual إِبْتَدَأ *ibteda*, 'he began', but frequently and idiomatically by

صَار *ṣâr*, e.g. He began to walk, *Hûwa ṣâr yimshî*

or by قَام *gâm*, e.g. *hûwa gâm yimshî*,

or by أَخَذ *akhadh*, e.g. *hûwa akhadh yimshî.*

'Ought to have' is expressed by *kàn làzm*, with present verb following, or by *kàn*, with past verb following.

E.g. You ought to have written
Kàn làzm tiktab or
Kàn ketebet.

'The same' has no exact Arabic equivalent. The following are used to convey the idea.

He and I saw the same ship
Ana wa hûwa shifna nefs el markab.

He and I came in the same ship
Ana wa hûwa jîna fî markab wâḥid.

These two houses are the same
Hel bêtên wâḥid or *Hel bêtên mithl bâʿdheha.*

This is the same as that
Hàdha mithl dhàk.

WORD LIST

كَيْفَمَا كَانَ	However	kêf mâ kàn
كَلِمَةٌ ج كَلِمَاتٌ	Word	kalima, *pl.* kalimàt
اَلْحِينَ او فِي ٱلْوَقْتِ ٱلْحَاضِرِ	At present	el ḥîn, fîl ḥâdhir
أَرْسَلَ عَلَى او بَعَثَ عَلَى	He sent for	baʿath ʿala (yibʿath)
شَوَّفَ يُشَوِّفُ	He showed	rawwa, yurawwî (2 from ra-a)
فِي ٱلْبَيْتِ	At home	fîl bêt
فَهِمَ يَفْهَمُ	He understood	fehem, yifham, *or* iftehem, yeftehim (8)
لِذٰلِكَ او لِهٰذَا ٱلسَّبَبِ	Therefore	lidhàlik, *or* min hes sebeb
سَابِقًا	Formerly	gabl, sàbiqan

مِنْ بَعْدُ	Afterwards	fîma bâ'ad
مُنْذُ مُدَّة	For a long time (past)	min zamàn
إِلَى مُدَّةٍ	For a long time (future)	ila mudda
اَلْمَرَّةُ الْأَخِيرَةُ	The last time	el marrat el akhîra ed def'at el akhîra en nôbat el akhîra
كُلِّيًّا	Entirely	bil kullîa

Exercise 36.

1. Some English words are like Arabic words. 2. There are no ships in the river at present. 3. He sent for me but I did not want to come. 4. He showed me the road. 5. Please show me the road. 6. Do you want me to show you? 7. Is the sahib at home? 8. Do you understand when I talk Arabic? 9. I am poor, therefore I cannot buy this. 10. Formerly when the Turks were here, we could not do so. 11. He arrived afterwards. 12. I haven't seen you for a long time. 13. He will work for a long time. 14. The last time we saw them was in Bombay.

1. Bâ'dh el kalimàt el anglêzîa mithl kalimàt 'arabîa. 2. Mâ âkû maràkib fîsh shaṭṭ fîl ḥâdhir. 3. Hûwa ba'ath 'alêya làkin ana mâ ridet àjî. 4. Hûwa rawwâni ed durb. 5. Min fadhlek rawwini ed durb. 6. Tarîd urawwîk? 7. Es ṣâḥib fîl bêt? 8. Tifham lemma aḥkî 'arabî? 9. Ana faqîr lidhàlik (min hes sebeb) mâ aqdar ashtarî hàdha. 10. Gabl lemma kànû et turk hina mâ qadarna nusawwî hîchî. 11. Hûwa waṣal fîma bâ'ad. 12. Ana min zamàn mâ shifetek. 13. Hûwa yashtaghil illa mudda. 14. El marrat el akhîra shifnâhum kàn fî Bombay.

١ بعض الكلمات الانكليزية مثل الكلمات العربية. ٢ لا يوجد مراكب في الشط للحين. ٣ هو بعث عليّ لكني ما اردتُ ان اجئُ. ٤ هو

شوّفني الطريق. ٥ من فضلك شوفني الطريق. ٦ هل تريد ان اشوّفك. ٧ هل الصاحب في البيت. ٨ هل تفهم لما احكي العربية. ٩ انا فقير لذلك لا اقدر اشتري هذا. ١٠ سابقاً لما كان الترك هنا ما قدرنا نعمل كذا. ١١ هو وصل من بعد. ١٢ منذ مدة ما شفتُك. ١٣ هو يشتغل الى مدة. ١٤ عندما شفناهم المرة الاخيرة كان في بومبي.

WORD LIST

حُمّى	Fever	sakhûna
مَحْمُوم	Fevered	musakhkhan
سَاعَدَ يُسَاعِدُ	He helped	sâ'ad, yusâ'id (3)
أَيّ كَانَ	Any one at all	kàyin men kàn
مَهْمَا كَانَ	Whatever it be	kullmâ kàn, êshmâ kàn
تَقَيّدْ او إعْتَنِ	Be careful	taqayyid, dir bàlek
إبْتَدَأَ يَبْتَدِئُ	He began	ibteda, yebtedi (8)
غَالِطٌ	Mistaken	ghalṭân
نَسِيَ يَنْسَى	He forgot	nesi, yensa
كَنِيسَةٌ ج كَنَائِسُ	Church	kanîsa, *pl.* kanàyis
مُكْتَفٍ	Satisfied	muktefi, râdhi
شَبْعَانٌ	Satisfied (with food)	sheb'ân
إحْتَاجَ يَحْتَاجُ	He needed	iḥtàj, yaḥtàj (8)
مُحْتَاجٌ	Needy	muḥtàj
مَرّ يَمُرُّ. عَبَرَ يَعْبُرُ	He passed	fàt, yafût

Exercise 37.

1. There is much fever in Basrah. 2. I have fever. 3. They helped us very much. 4. Do you want me to help you? 5. Help me with this. 6. Any one can learn Arabic. 7. Bring all that you see, whatever it be. 8. Be careful when you go aboard. 9. You are mistaken. 10. I forgot my money. 11. Don't forget. 12. I have forgotten. 13. I am afraid you will forget. 14. How many churches are there in Basrah? 15. As many as there are mosques. 16. Are you satisfied with what you earn? 17. We need a clerk who knows English and Arabic. 18. The man passed my house yesterday. 19. Get out of the way. 20. I saw him pass. 21. The time is up.

1. Âkû sakhûna wàjid fîl Baṣrah. 2 Ana musakhkhan. 3. Hûm sâʻadûna kathîr. 4. Tarîd usâʻidek? 5. Sâʻidni bi hàdha. 6. Kàyin men kàn yaqdar yataʻallam ʻarabî. 7. Jîb kullmâ tashûf, êshmâ kàn. 8. Taqayyid lemma tirkab. 9. Enta ghalṭân. 10. Ana nesît flûsî. 11. Là tinsa. 12. Ana nàsi. 13. Akhâf tinsa. 14. Kem kanîsa âkû fîl Baṣrah? 15. Bigadma âkû masàjid (jawàmiʻ). 16. Enta râdhi bi-mâ tuḥaṣṣil? 17. Naḥtàj kàtib elledhî yaʻraf anglêzî wa ʻarabî. 18. Er rejul ems fàt min bêtî. 19. Fût. 20. Ana shifetuh fàyit. 21. El waqt fàyit.

١ يوجد حمّى كثيرة في البصرة. ٢ انا محموم. ٣ ساعدونا جداً. ٤ هل تريد ان اساعدك. ٥ ساعدني بهذا. ٦ ايّ كان يقدر يتعلم العربية. ٧ اجلب مهما تشوف كل ما كان. ٨ تقيّد لما تركب. ٩ انت غالط. ١٠ نسيتُ فلوسي. ١١ لا تنسى. ١٢ انا نسيتُ. ١٣ اخاف لِئلا تنسى. ١٤ كم كنيسة يوجد في البصرة. ١٥ بقدر ما يوجد جوامع. ١٦ هل انت مكتفٍ بما تُحصّل. ١٧ نحتاج الى كاتب الذي يعرف الانكليزية والعربية. ١٨ الرجل مرّ على بيتي البارح. ١٩ اخرج عن الطريق. ٢٠ شفتهُ ماراً. ٢١ صار الوقت.

DAYS AND MONTHS

يَوْمُ ٱلْأَحَدِ	Sunday	yôm el aḥad, *or* el aḥad
,, ٱلْإِثْنَيْنِ	Monday	,, el ithnên
,, ٱلثَّلَاثَاءِ	Tuesday	,, eth thalàthà
,, ٱلْأَرْبَعَاءِ	Wednesday	,, el arba'â
,, ٱلْخَمِيسِ	Thursday	,, el khamîs
,, ٱلْجُمْعَةِ	Friday	,, el jum'a
,, ٱلسَّبْتِ	Saturday	,, es sebt
كَانُونُ ٱلثَّانِي	January	kànûn thànî
شُبَاطُ	February	shabâṭ
أَذَارُ	March	âdhâr
نِيسَانُ	April	nîsàn
أَيَّارُ	May	âyâr
حَزِيرَانُ	June	ḥazîràn
تَمُّوزُ	July	tamûz
آبُ	August	àb
اَيْلُولُ	September	êlûl
تِشْرِينُ ٱلْأَوَّلُ	October	tishrîn awwal
تِشْرِينُ ٱلثَّانِي	November	tishrîn thànî
كَانُونُ ٱلْأَوَّلُ	December	kànûn awwal

The day is generally reckoned by Arabs as beginning at sunset. E.g. *lêlat el aḥad* is Saturday night, though *mesa el aḥad* is Sunday evening. *Mesa*, evening, is counted from noon till late evening.

صُبْحْ	Morning	ṣubḥ, ṣabâḥ
ضَحَاءْ	Mid-morning	dhaḥa
ظُهْرْ	Noon	dhuhr (*pron.* dhu-hr)
عَصْرْ	Mid-afternoon	'aṣr
مَغْرِبْ	Sunset	maghrib
مَسَاءْ	Evening	mesa
نِصْفُ ٱللَّيْلِ	Midnight	nuṣf el lêl
فَجْرْ	Dawn	fijr, ghubsha (daybreak)

Examples.

Sunday morning	ṣabâḥ el aḥad, el aḥad es ṣubḥ
Next Sunday	el aḥad el jai, el aḥad el àtî
Last Sunday	el aḥad el mâdhî, el aḥad el fàyit
A week from Sunday	el aḥad bâ'ad thamànyat ayàm
A week ago Sunday	el aḥad gabl thamànyat ayàm
Two weeks from to-day	bâ'ad khamstâsh yôm
Three weeks ago yesterday	embârḥa gabl 'ashrîn yôm
Day after to-morrow	bâ'ad bàcher, ogub bàcher
Day before yesterday	awwal embârḥa (ems)
Last year	el 'âm
Year before last	awwal el 'âm

WORD LIST

تَقْرِيباً . نَحْوَ	About, almost	taqrîban, naḥw
حَسَبَ	According to	ḥasab
عَبْرَ	Across	'abar, 'abr
ضِدَّ . على	Against	dhudd, 'ala
بَيْنَ . فِيمَا بَيْنَ	Among	bên, fîma bên

حَوْلَ	Around	ḥawl, dàyir madàyir
مَا عَدَا	Besides (except)	mâ ʿada
بِجَانِب	By the side of	bijànib, yem
بَعِيدًا عَنْ	Beyond	ghâdî
مِنْ جِهَةِ . فِي خُصُوصِ . عَنْ	Concerning	min jehet, fî khuṣûṣ
مِنْ سَبَبِ	On account of	min sebeb
لِخَاطِرِ . مِنْ أَجْلِ . لِأَجْلِ	For the sake of	khâṭir, min ejel, li ejel
مِنْ سَبَبِ . مِنْ حَيْثُ . لِأَنْ	Because	min sebeb, min ḥêth, li-an
فِي أَثْنَاء . اثناء	During	fî ithnà
أَبَدًا	Never	ebeden (with negative)

Exercise 38.

1. I almost fell. 2. He has about one thousand rupees. 3. You must do according to the order. 4. It is three o'clock by my watch. 5. Can you see across the river? 6. I want to go across the river. 7. The ship goes against the water. 8. Why do you speak against me? 9. If you wish to learn Arabic you must live among the Arabs. 10. There are soldiers all around the town. 11. I have two houses here, and besides these I have four in Baghdad. 12. He was sitting beside me. 13. Who is that beside you? 14. The bridge is beyond the city. 15. I don't know anything about the war. 16. Ships cannot come here on account of the war. 17. I will do this for your sake. 18. During the night I heard the soldiers passing. 19. I will never learn Arabic. 20. Never do this again. 21. They came because there is work here. 22. Will you do this for my sake?

1. Ana taqrîban wagaʿat. 2. ʿAnduh taqrîban elf rubîa. 3. Làzm tusawwî ḥasab el amr. 4. Hûwa es sâʿa bi thalàtha ḥasab sâʿati. 5. Taqdar tashûf ʿabar esh shaṭṭ. 6. Arîd arûḥ ʿabar esh shaṭṭ. 7. El markab yimshî dhudd el mai. 8. Lêsh

taḥkî ʻalêya ? 9. Idha tarîd tataʻallam ʻarabi làzm tiskan bên el ʻarab. 10. Âkû ʻasker dàyir madàyir el beled. 11. ʻAndi bêtên hina wa mâ ʻada hàdhi ʻandi arbaʻa fî Baghdâd. 12. Hûwa kàn gâʻid yemmî. 13. Men hàdha yemek ? 14. El jisr ghâdi el wilàya. 15. Ana mâ aʻraf shê min jehet el ḥarb. 16. El maràkib mâ taqdar tîjî hina min sebeb el ḥarb. 17. Ana usawwî hàdha min ejelek. 18. Fî ithnà el lêl semaʻat el ʻasker fàyitîn. 19. Ana ebeden mâ ataʻallam ʻarabî. 20. Ebeden là tusawwî hàdha bâʻad. 21. Jao min ḥêth âkû shughl hina. 22. Tusawwî hàdha khâṭirî ?

١ تقريباً وقعتُ. ٢ عنده نحو الف روبيه. ٣ يلزم ان تعمل حسب الامر. ٤ الساعة الثالثة حسب ساعتي. ٥ هل تقدر تشوف عبر الشط. ٦ اريد ان اذهب عبر الشط. ٧ المركب يمشي ضد الماء. ٨ لماذا تحكي عليّ. ٩ اذا تريد ان تتعلم العربية يلزم ان تسكن بين العرب. ١٠ يوجد عسكر حول البلد. ١١ عندي بيتان هنا وما عداها عندي اربعة في بغداد. ١٢ كان جالساً بجانبي. ١٣ من هذا بجانبك. ١٤ الجسر بعيد عن المدينة. ١٥ لا اعرف شيئاً عن الحرب. ١٦ المراكب لا تقدر ان تجي هنا من سبب الحرب. ١٧ انا اعمل هذا لخاطرك. ١٨ اثناء الليل سمعتُ العسكر عابراً. ١٩ ما اتعلم العربية ابداً. ٢٠ لا تعمل هذا مرة ثانية. ٢١ جاءُوا من سبب يوجد شغل هنا. ٢٢ هل تعمل هذا لخاطري.

WORD LIST

أَقَلًّا	At least	aqallan, aqall mâ yakûn
عَلَى كُلِّ حَالِ	In any case	ʻala kulli ḥâl
بَعْدُ . لَا زَالَ	Still, yet	bâʻad
مِثْلَمَا . كَمَا	Like as	mithlma, kema
مِنْ أَيْنَ	Whence ?	min ên ?
إِلَى أَيْنَ	Whither ?	ila wên ? liwên ? wên ?

مَرَّةً	Once upon a time	ferd marra, ferd yôm
فَقَطْ	Only	faqaṭ, bess
حَتَّى	Until	ḥatta, lîmâ (with verb)
حَتَّى . لِكَيْ	In order that	ḥatta
حَتَّى	Even	ḥatta
غَيْر	Un-	ghair
بَاكِرًا	Early	min waqt
مُتَأَخِّرًا	Late	muta-akhkhir, fàyit waqt
مَجَّانًا	Gratis	bilàsh, majjànan

Exercise 39.

1. He has at least a hundred rupees. 2. You can at least try 3. He has not come yet. 4. He is still here. 5. Why don't you speak as you write? 6. Where have you come from? 7. Where do you want to go? 8. I speak only English. 9. Don't come until you have washed yourself. 10. He sat until evening. 11. Even the women work. 12. I told you this in order that you might learn. 13. Bring the tea early. 14. They give books gratis to all.

1. 'Anduh aqallan mîat rubîa. 2. Taqdar tujarrib aqall mâ yakûn. 3. Hûwa bâ'ad mâ jà. 4. Hûwa bâ'ad hina. 5. Lêsh mâ taḥkî mithlma tiktab. 6. Enta min ên jai? 7. Wên (liwên) tarid tarûḥ? 8. Ana aḥkî faqaṭ anglêzî. 9. Là tîjî ḥatta taghsal nefsek. 10. Hûwa gâ'ad ḥatta el mesa. 11. Ḥatta en niswàn yashtaghilûn. 12. Ana gulat lek hàdha ḥatta tata-'allam. 13. Jîb el chai min waqt. 14. Yu'ṭûn kutub bilàsh ilal kull.

١ اقلاً عندهُ مئة روبية. ٢ اقلاً تقدر ان تجرب. ٣ ما اتى بعدُ. ٤ هو هنا بعد. ٥ لماذا لا تحكي كما تكتب. ٦ من اين جئت. ٧ الى اين تريد ان تروح. ٨ احكي الانكليزية فقط. ٩ لا تجئُ حتى تغسل

نفسك. ١٠ جلس حتى المساء. ١١ حتى النساء يشتغلن. ١٢ قلتُ لك هذا حتى تتعلم. ١٣ اجلب الشاي باكرًا. ١٤ يعطون كتب مجّانًا للكل.

THE DIMINUTIVE

Mesopotamian Arabs, and especially those along the rivers, are very fond of using the diminutive. It is regularly formed on the model:

كَلْبٌ	كُلَيْبٌ	كِتَابٌ	كُتَيْبٌ
kelb, a dog;	kulêb, a little dog;	kitàb, book;	kutêb, a little book;
وَلَدٌ	وُلَيْدٌ		
walad, a boy;	wulêd, a little boy.		

Lês.

The word لَيْسَ lês, *not*, is a quasi-verb and is inflected as follows:

لَيْسَ	lês
لَيْسَتْ	lêsat
لَسْتَ	lesta
لَسْتِ	lesti
لَسْتُ	lestu
لَيْسُوا	lêsû
لَسْتُمْ	lestum
لَسْنَا	lesna

It is not inflected except in literary Arabic; in rather higher colloquial lês is the only form used.

E.g. A friend is not a brother, eṣ ṣadîq lês el âkh.

THE LITERARY PASSIVE

The Seventh Measure, e.g. إِنْكَتَبَ inketeb, conveys the idea of the passive in which the agent is totally disregarded. The regular literary passive, inflected below, is used when the agent is mentioned or the agent's presence is implied. It does not occur in colloquial, save in rare instances, as يُسْتَعْمَل yusta'mal, *it is used*, قِيل qîl, *it was said*. The vowel changes in the derived measures can be easily mastered by a student of the literary language.

قُتِلَ He was killed	قُتِلَتْ She was killed	قُتِلْتَ You (*m.*) were killed
	قُتِلْتِ You (*f.*) were killed	
قُتِلْتُ I was killed	قُتِلُوا They were killed	قُتِلْتُمْ You (*pl.*) were killed
	قُتِلْنَا We were killed	
يُقْتَلُ He is killed	تُقْتَلُ She is killed	تُقْتَلُ You (*m.*) are killed
	تُقْتَلِين You (*f.*) are killed	
أُقْتَلُ I am killed	يُقْتَلُونَ They are killed	تُقْتَلُونَ You are killed
	نُقْتَلُ We are killed	

Yakûn.

The present form of كَان kàn is inflected as below. It does not, however, convey the meaning of 'am, is, are', but is used to indicate only the future.

E.g. You will be responsible *Takûn mas-ûl*

Yakûn may also mean *It is probable.*

The imperative is used as in English.

E.g. Be polite *Kun adîb*

يَكُونُ	He will be	yakûn
تَكُونُ	She will be	takûn
تَكُونُ	You will be	takûn
تَكُونِينَ	You (*f.*) will be	takûnîn
أَكُونُ	I shall be	akûn
يَكُونُونَ	They will be	yakûnûn
تَكُونُونَ	You (*pl.*) will be	takûnûn
نَكُونُ	We shall be	nakûn

Imperative.

كُنْ	Be (*m.*)	kun
كُونِي	Be (*f.*)	kûnî
كُونُوا	Be (*pl.*)	kûnû

BIBLIOGRAPHY

Palmer, *A Grammar of the Arabic Language*, **1874. (Old, but complete, with treatise on prosody.)**

Socin, *Arabic Grammar*, **3rd ed., 1885; 7th ed. (no Engl. trans.), 1913. (Very compact and terse.)**

Thatcher, *Arabic Grammar of the Written Language*, **1911. (Practical and complete, with numerous exercises.)**

Wright, *A Grammar of the Arabic Language*, **3rd ed., 2 vols., 1896–8. (An exhaustive treatise, especially useful for reference.)**

Thornton, *Elementary Arabic.* **(An abridgement of Wright's Arabic Grammar; see above.)**

Sterling, *A Grammar of the Arabic Language*, **1904. (Complete, with excellent hand-book of idioms.)**

Van Ess, *An Aid to Practical Written Arabic*, **1920. (Affords practice in the language of newspapers, contracts, letters, etc., and in handwriting.)**

PART II

VOCABULARY

The English infinitive is rendered by the Arabic 3rd pers. masc. sing. of the past tense. In the Vocabulary, when an Arabic verb is followed by a preposition or a noun, this is given after the past only, and is to be understood after the present. Some English adjectives and adverbs are rendered by a preposition and a noun, or by a participle; English adjectives beginning with 'in' and ending in 'able' or 'ible' are generally rendered by the negative and a participle or by the negative and the 3rd pers. masc. sing. of the present tense. P. = Persian ; T. = Turkish.

A

abandon : terek, yitrak.
abdomen : baṭn.
ability : iqtidâr; (mental) idrâk.
able : muqtedir. See also **can.**
ablution : *n.* wadhu ; *v.* to perform an ablution, tawadhdha, yatawadhdha.
abolish : baṭṭal, yubaṭṭil; algha, yulghî.
abominable : makrûh.
abominate : kereh, yikrah.
about : (concerning) min jehet, fî khuṣûṣ; (around) ḥawl; dàyir madàyir; (nearly) taqrîban, naḥw.
above : fôq.
above-mentioned : madhkûr.
abscess : demla, *pl.* demlàt.
absence : ghiyàb.
absent : ghâyib.
absolute : see **monarchy.**
absolutely : muṭlaqan.
abstain : tejenneb ʿan, yetejenneb; imtenaʿ ʿan, yemteniʿ; jàz, yajûz.
absurd : muḥâll; ghair maʿqûl.
abundant : mabdhûl, wâfir.
abuse : *v.* ḥaqqar, yuḥaqqir; rezzel, yurezzil; *n.* sû istiʿmàl.
accept : qabal, yaqbal.
acceptable : maqbûl.
accident : muṣîba, muṣâyib.
accidentally : bi taṣâduf.
accompany : râfaq, yurâfiq.
accomplish : temmem, yutemmim.
according to : ḥasab; bi mûjib.
accordingly : bi hel mûjib.
account : *n.* ḥisàb, *pl.* ḥisàbàt; account book, defter, *pl.* defàtir; on account of, min sebeb.
accountant : muḥâsib (muḥâsibchi, T.).
accumulate : *v. trans.* jamaʿ, yijmaʿ; *v. intrans.* tarâkam, yatarâkam.
accuracy : tadqîq.
accurate : mudaqqaq.
accursed : malʿûn.
accusation : shikàya, *pl.* shikàyàt.
accuse : ishteka ʿala, yeshteki.
accustom to : ʿâwwad ʿala, yuʿâwwid.

accustomed to: muta'âwwad 'ala.
ache: *n.* waja'; *v.* awja', yûja'.
acid: ḥâmidh, àsîd.
acknowledge: qarr, yaqurr.
acquainted: *v.* become a., ta'âraf, yata'âraf; *part.* a. with (things), mukhtebir.
acquire: ḥaṣṣal, yuḥaṣṣil.
acquit: abra, yubri.
acquitted: *v.* to be acquitted, teberra, yeteberra.
across: 'abar, 'abr; (crosswise) 'ardh.
act: *n.* 'aml, *pl.* â'màl; *v.* taṣarraf, yataṣarraf.
action: (at law) dâ'wa, *pl.* da'âwi; (in war) 'arka, *pl.* 'arkàt.
active: nashîṭ, *pl.* nashîṭîn.
actual: ḥaqîqî.
actually: bil ḥaqîqa.
acute: (pain) shadîd; (mind) dhekî.
adapt: ṭabbaq, yuṭabbiq; rehhem, yurehhim.
adapted to: *v.* to be adapted to, rehem 'ala, yerhem.
add: jama', yijma'.
addition: jum'; in add. to, 'alâwatan 'ala.
address: (by speaking) *v.* khâṭab, yukhâṭib; *n.* khaṭba; (in writing); *v.* kàteb, yukàtib; *n.* 'anwàn.
adequate: kàfi.
adieu: fì amàn Illàh.
adieu: *v.* to bid adieu to, tawâda' ma', yatawâda'.
adjacent: mujâwir.
adjective: ṣifa, *pl.* ṣifât.
administer: dâr, yadîr.
administration: (direction) idâra; (government) ḥukm.
admire: 'ajjab, yu'ajjib (with object admired as subject).
admission: (entrance) dukhûl; (confession) qarâr.
admit: (allow to enter) dakhkhal, yudakhkhil; (confess) qarr, yaqurr.
admonish: nebbeh, yunebbih.
adorn: zêyyen, yuzeyyin.
adult: bàligh es sin.
adulterer: zàni.
adulteress: zània.
adultery: zina.
advance: *v. intrans.* taqaddam, yataqaddam; *n.* taqaddam; (money) 'arabûn.
advantage: fàyida, *pl.* fawàyid.
advantageous: mufîd.
advertise: a'lan, yu'lin.
advertisement: i'làn.
advice: naṣîha, *pl.* naṣâyih; (information) khabr.
advise: naṣah, yinṣah.
advocate: *n.* wakîl dâ'wa; awkâṭ; muḥâmî.
aeroplane: ṭayyâra, *pl.* ṭayyâràt.
affable: bashûsh.
affair: amr, *pl.* umûr; not my affair, mâ yakhuṣṣni.
affectionate: muḥibb.
affirmative: îjàb, îjàbî.
afraid: khâif, khâyif.
after: bâ'ad (bâ'd), ogub; (with verb) bâ'adma, ogubma.
afternoon: bâ'ad edh dhuhr; mid-afternoon, 'aṣr.
afterwards: fîma bâ'ad.
again: tekrâr; marra thània; aidhan.
against: dhudd, 'ala.
age: (of persons, &c.) 'amr.
aged: (man) shâyib, *pl.* shiyàb; (woman) 'ajûz, *pl.* 'ajâyiz.
agent: wakîl, *pl.* wukalâ.
ago: gabl (precedes noun).
agree: wâfaq, yuwâfiq.

agreeable: (pleasant) mustaḥibb; (suitable) muwâfiq.
ague: bàrida.
aid: *v.* sâ'ad, yusâ'id; 'âwan, yu'âwin; *n.* musâ'ada.
aim: *v.* (gun) akhadh nîshàn; (purpose) qaṣad, yaqṣad; *n.* (gun) nîshàn; (purpose) qaṣd.
air: hawa.
alas: (interjection expressing sorrow, disgust, &c.) âkh.
alcohol: spirito.
alien: ajnabi, *pl.* ajànib.
alight: *v.* nezel, yinzal; ḥawwal, yuḥawwil.
alike: mithl bâ'dheha (bâ'dhehum, &c.).
alive: ḥai, *pl.* aḥyà; ṭayyib.
all: kull (with *pl.*).
allege: iddâ'a, yaddâ'î.
allegiance: ṭâ'a.
alliance: mu'âhada.
allow: rakhkhaṣ, yurakhkhiṣ; semaḥ, yismaḥ.
allowable: jàyiz.
ally: ḥalîf, *pl.* ḥulafâ; muttaḥid, *pl.* muttaḥidîn.
almighty: qâdir 'ala kull shê; qâdir.
almost: taqrîban, naḥw.
alms: ṣadaqàt.
alone: waḥdi (I), waḥdek (you), &c.
along: (with) mâ', wîya; (beside) bi jànib.
aloud: bi ṣawt 'âli.
alphabet: àlif bà.
already: (no equivalent in colloquial Arabic).
also: aidhan, ham.
alter: ghayyar, yughayyir; beddel, yubeddil.
alteration: taghyîr, tabdîl.
alternately: bi dôr.
although: wa law; mâ' ann.
altogether (ensemble): sûwa
always: daiman; kull waqt.
amass: jama', yijma'; lamm, yalimm.
ambassador: safîr, *pl.* sufarâ.
ambush: kamîn.
among: bên; fîma bên.
amount: *n.* miblagh, *pl.* mabàligh.
amount to: *v.* sawwa, yusawwî.
amputate: gaṣṣ, yaguṣṣ.
amuse: wennes, yuwennis; farraj, yufarrij.
amused: *v.* to be amused, tewennes, yetewennes; tafarraj, yatafarraj.
ancestor: jidd, *pl.* ajdàd.
anchor: *v.* debb angar, yadibb; *n.* angar.
anchored: dabb angar; ṭâriḥ.
ancient: qadîm, *pl.* (persons) qudamâ.
and: wa.
anecdote: qaṣṣa, *pl.* qaṣṣaṣ; ḥikàya, *pl.* ḥikàyàt; sàlifa, *pl.* sawàlif.
angel: malàk, *pl.* malàyika.
anger: zâ'l.
angle: zâwiya, *pl.* zawàya.
angry: za'lân, ghadhbân, mughtâdh.
animal: ḥaiwân, *pl.* ḥaiwânàt, haiwawîn.
annihilate: demmer, yudemmir.
announce: khabbar, yukhabbir; a'lan, yu'lin.
annoy: kedder, yukeddir; az'aj, yuz'ij.
annual: senawî.
annul: baṭṭal, yubaṭṭil.
another: ghair, âkhar.
answer: *v.* jàwab, yujàwib, *n.* jawàb, *pl.* ajwiba, jawàbàt.
ant: nimla, *pl.* niml.

antique: *adj.* qadîm; *n.* antîqa.
anxious: (disturbed) bil fikr; (eager) mushtâq.
any: any body, aḥad; anything, shê; any one at all, kàyin men kàn; anything at all, êsh mâ kàn.
apart: 'an bâ'dheha ('an bâ'dhehum, &c.).
apologize: ṭalab 'âfu, yaṭlab.
apostle: rasûl, *pl.* rusul.
apparent: wâdhiḥ, bêyyen.
appear: bêyyen, yubêyyin.
appearance: bayàn, dhuhûr.
appendix: tadhyîl.
appetite: ishtihà.
apple: tuffâḥa, *coll.* tuffâḥ.
appoint: 'ayyan, yu'ayyin.
appointed: mu'ayyan.
appointment: tâ'yîn.
apprentice: ṣâni', *pl.* ṣannâ'; khalfa, *pl.* khalfàt.
approach: taqarrab, yataqarrab; tedenna, yetedenna.
appropriate: *adj.* muwâfiq, làyiq, munàsib.
approve: istaḥsan, yastaḥsin; istensab, yestensib.
apricot: mishmish.
April: nîsàn.
apron: ṣadrîa.
Arab: 'arabî, *pl.* 'arab.
Arabia: bilàd el 'arab; jazîrat el 'arab.
Arabic: 'arabî.
argue: taḥàjaj, yataḥàjaj.
arise: gâm, yagûm.
arithmetic: ḥisàb.
arm: *n.* kitf, *pl.* aktàf; dhrâ', *pl.* udhru'.
arms: (weapons) islâḥ, asliḥa.
army: jêsh, *pl.* juyûsh.
around: ḥawl; dàyir madàyir.
arrange: debber, yudebbir; retteb, yurettib.
arrangement: tadbîr, *pl.* tadàbîr; tartîb, *pl.* taràtîb.
arrival: wuṣûl.
arrive: waṣal, yoṣal.
arsenal: tereskhâna.
artery: damâr, *pl.* damâràt.
article: (thing) shê, *pl.* ashyà; (item)bend, màdda, *pl.* mawàd.
artificial: iṣṭinâ'î, 'amalî.
artillery: ṭôbchîa.
as: mithl; as soon as you come, ḥâlama tîjî; as good as, ṭayyib mithl.
ascend: ṣa'ad, yiṣ'ad.
ascent: ṣa'da.
ascertain: ḥaqqaq, yuḥaqqiq.
ashamed: mustaḥî, khajlàn.
ashes: ramâd.
aside: 'ala ṣafḥa.
ask: (inquire) se-el, yes-el; (demand) ṭalab, yaṭlab.
asleep: nàyim.
ass: ḥamâr, *pl.* ḥamîr; zamàl, *pl.* zamàyil.
assault: *v.* hejem, yihjam; *n.* hujûm.
assemble: *v. trans.* jamma', yujammi'; *v. intrans.* tajamma', yatajamma'.
assembly: jamâ'a.
assent: radhi, yardha; *n.* ridhâ.
assist: sâ'ad, yusâ'id; 'âwan, yu'âwin.
associate: *v. intrans.* tarâfaq, yatarâfaq; *n.* rafîq, *pl.* rufaqâ; sharîk, *pl.* shurakâ.
astonish: *v. trans.* 'ajjab, yu'ajjib.
astonished: *v.* to be astonished, ta'ajjab, yata'ajjab.
astronomy: 'ilm er nujûm.
at: (near) 'and; at home, fîl bêt; at first, fî awwal el amr;

at last, akhîran ; at once, ḥâlan, bis sâ'a ; at least, aqallan ; aqall ma yakûn.
athletics: jimnastîk, pehlawàn.
attack: *v.* hejem 'ala, yihjam ; *n.* hujûm.
attempt: *v.* ijtehed, yejtehid ; jarrab, yujarrib ; *n.* tajriba.
attend: ḥadhar, yaḥdhar.
attendance: ḥudhûr.
attention: intibàh; pay attention, entebeh, yentebih ; dâr bàl, yadîr bàl.
attentive: muntebih.
attract: jedheb, yijdhab.
attribute: *v.* neseb ila, yinsab.
auction: màzàd.
August: àb.
aunt: (paternal) 'amma, *pl.* 'ammàt ; (maternal) khâla, *pl.* khâlàt.
author: mu-ellif.
authority: (dignity) saṭwa ; (government) ḥakûma ; (power) ḥukm.
avarice: ṭam'.
avaricious: ṭammâ'.
average: *n.* mu'addal.
aviator: ṭayyâr, *pl.* ṭayyârîn.
awake: *v.* ga''ad, yugâ''id ; *adj.* gâ'id, ḥâsis, yaqdhân.
aware: muntebih, mukhtebir.
away: (absent) ghâyib ; far away, ba'îd ; go away (*imper.*), rûḥ.
axe: fàs.

B

baby: ṭafl, *pl.* aṭfâl.
bachelor: sagurtî.
back: *n.* dhahr, *pl.* dhuhûr ; gafa ; (back of book, back of boat, &c.) akhîr, âkhar ; *v.* come back, raja', yarja' ; give back, rajja, yurajji' ; back up, radd ila wara, yarudd.
backwards: ila wara.
bacon: laḥm khanzîr.
bad: kharâb, redi, mû zên (gone bad) kharbân.
bag: kîs, *pl.* akyàs ; (sack) gonîa, *pl.* gawânî.
baggage: aghrâdh.
bake: (bread, &c.) khabaz, yakhbaz ; (brick) aḥraq, yuḥriq.
baker: khabbàz, *pl.* khabbàzîn.
balance: (scales) mîzàn ; (account) mîzànîa ; (remainder) bâqî.
bald: aqra', *f.* qar'â, *pl.* qur'.
bale: farda, *pl.* fardàt, afrâd.
ball: ṭôpa, *pl.* ṭôpàt.
bamboo: khaizaràn.
band: (music) muzîqa, jôq ; (company) jamâ'a, *pl.* jamâ'àt ; (that binds) rabâṭ.
bandage: laffàfa, rabâṭ, shedda.
banish: ṭarad, yaṭrad ; anfa, yunfî.
bank: (for money) bank, *pl.* bunuk ; (of river) jurf, *pl.* jurûf.
banker: abu bank ; ṣaḥib bank.
bank-note: nôt, *pl.* anwât.
bankrupt: maksûr, muflis.
banner: bêraq, *pl.* bayâriq ; ṣanjaq, *pl.* ṣanàjiq.
baptism: 'amàd.
baptize: 'ammad, yu'ammid.
baptized: *v.* to be baptized, ta'ammad, yata'ammad.
bar: (hindrance) màni', *pl.* mawàni' ; (sand) shelha, *pl.* shelhàt.
barbarian: waḥshî, *pl.* wuḥûsh.
barber: muzêyyin.
barefoot: ḥâfi, *pl.* ḥafai.

bargain: *v.* 'âmal, yu'âmil; *n.* mu'âmala.
bark: *v.* nebaḥ, yinbaḥ; *n.* gishr.
barley: sha'îr.
barracks: qishla.
barrel: pîp, *pl.* apyàp; barmîl, *pl.* baràmîl.
barter: tebàdul.
base: *n.* asàs; *adj.* denî, *pl.* edniyà.
base: *v.* esses, yu-essis.
bashful: musteḥî.
bashfulness: mustaḥa.
basin: (for washing) legen; (reservoir) ḥôdh.
basis: asàs.
basket: sella, *pl.* salàl; zembîl, *pl.* zanàbîl.
bat: (animal) khashàf el lêl.
bath: ḥamàm; bath-tub, ḥôdh; bath-room, ḥamàm.
bathe: taḥammam, yataḥammam.
battle: muḥâraba, *pl.* muḥârabàt.
bay: *n.* (sea) khalîj; *adj.* (colour) aḥmar.
bayonet: sengi.
bazaar: sûq, *pl.* aswâq.
be: kàn, yakûn.
beach: sâḥil.
beads: nimnim; (rosary) sibḥa.
beak: minqâr.
beam: (wood) khashab, jisr; (of the sun) shu'â', *pl.* shu'â'at.
bear: *v.* (carry) ḥamal, yaḥmal; (endure) taḥammal, yataḥammal; (bring forth) walad, yolad; *n.* (animal) dibb.
beard: leḥya, *pl.* liḥa.
bearer: ḥammàl, *pl.* ḥamàmîl.
beast: ḥaiwân, *pl.* ḥaiwâwîn.
beat: dharab, yadhrab; daqq, yaduqq; (overcome) ghalab, yaghlab.
beautiful: ḥasan, *pl.* ḥasana; laṭîf, *pl.* laṭâf; ḥulu, *pl.* ḥuluwîn.
beautify: ḥassan, yuḥassin; zêyyen, yuzêyyin.
because: min sebeb; min ḥêth; li-an; min kawn.
beckon: awma, yûmî.
become: ṣâr, yaṣîr.
becoming: (proper) làyiq.
bed: firâsh, *pl.* firâshàt, furush; bedstead, charpâya, *pl.* charpâyàt; bedstead (date-stick), sarîr.
bedding: firâsh.
bedroom: gubbat en nôm; manàm.
bee: zambûr, *pl.* zanàbîr.
beef: laḥm hôsh; laḥm baqr.
beetroot: shwandar.
before: *prep.* (in front of) gadàm, jadàm, gubàl; *adv.* gabl; *conj.* gablama, gabla.
beg: gedda, yugeddî; ista'ṭa, yasta'ṭî.
beggar: mugeddi, *pl.* mugàdî.
begin: *v. trans.* abda, yubdi; *v. intrans.* ibteda, yebtedi; begin to do, &c., gâm, yagûm (*or* sâr *or* akhadh), followed by the present tense (see p. 108).
beginning: bidàya, ibtidà.
behalf: on b. of, khâṭir, li ejel.
behave: taṣarraf, yataṣarraf.
behaviour: taṣarruf, sîra.
behead: gaṭa' râs, yagṭa'.
behind: wara, khalf.
belief: i'tiqâd.
believe: i'taqad, ya'taqid; àman, yû-min; (credit) ṣaddaq, yuṣaddiq.
believer: mu-min.

bell: jurs, *pl.* jurûs.
bellows: manfâkh.
belly: baṭn.
belong to: khaṣṣ, yakhuṣṣ.
beloved: maḥbûb.
below: *adv.* and *prep.* taḥt, ḥadr, jôa.
bench: takhat, *pl.* tukhût.
bend: *v. trans.* 'awwaj, yu'awwij; *v. intrans.* in'awaj, yan'awij; tagawwas, yatagawwas; *n.* (small) 'oja, *pl.* 'ojàt; (of a river) dôra, *pl.* dôràt.
beneath: see **below.**
beneficial: mufîd, nàfi'.
benefit: fàyida, *pl.* fawàyid.
bent: *part.* mu'awwaj; *n.* (inclination) mêl.
beseech: iltemes, yeltemis; terejja, yeterejja.
beside: yem, bijànib.
besides: *prep.* mâ 'ada; *adv.* fadhla, 'alâwa.
besiege: ḥâṣar, yuḥâṣir.
best: el aḥsan; el akhair.
bet: *v.* tashâraṭ, yatashâraṭ.
betray: khân, yakhûn.
betroth: nêshan, yunêshin.
better: aḥsan, khair.
between: bên; mâ bên.
beware of: taqayyad min, yataqayyid.
beyond: *adv.* and *prep.* ghâdî.
bible: el kitàb el muqaddas.
big: kabîr, chabîr, *pl.* kibâr (never chibâr).
bigness: kubr.
bigoted: muta'aṣṣib.
bile: ṣafra.
bill: (account) hisàb; (of a bird) minqâr.
bind: rabaṭ, yarbaṭ; shedd, yashidd.
bird: ṭêr, *pl.* ṭuyûr.
birth: wilàda.
birthday: wilàda; yôm wilàda.
bit: (bridle) lijàm; (portion) shwêya.
bite: 'adhdh, ya'adhdh.
bitter: murr.
bitterness: marâra, marûra.
bitumen: gîr, jîr.
black: aswad, *f.* sôda, *pl.* sûd.
blacksmith: ḥaddàd, *pl.* ḥaddàdîn.
blame: *v.* làm, yalûm; *n.* lôm.
blanket: planket, *pl.* planketàt.
blaspheme: kefer, yikfar.
blasphemy: kufr.
bleed: ṭala' dem, yiṭla'.
bless: bârak, yubârik.
blessed: mubârak.
blessing: baraka.
blind: a'ma, *f.* 'amya, *pl.* 'amyàn, 'amyànîn.
block: *v.* 'akkas, yu'akkis; *n.* khashba.
blockade: ḥiṣâr.
blood: dem, *pl.* dimà.
bloodmoney: faṣl.
bloodshed: sefk dimà.
blossom: *v.* zahar, yizhar; *n.* zahra, *pl.* zuhûr.
blot: lekka, *pl.* lekkàt, lekkek.
blotting-paper: kàghid nashshàf.
blow: *v.* habb, yahibb; *n.* (hit) ṣawâb, dharba.
blue: azraq, *f.* zirqa, *pl.* zirq.
blunt: (of a knife) a'ma (lit. blind).
board: *v.* (a ship) rekeb, yirkab; *n.* (plank) lôḥa, *pl.* lôḥ, alwâḥ.
boast: *v.* tafâkhar, yatafâkhar.
boat: (without power) safîna, *pl.* sufn, safàyin. See also **gun-boat, launch, motor, steam-boat.**

body: jised, *pl.* ajsàd; beden, *pl.* abdàn; (body of people) jamâ'a, khalq.
boil: *v. trans.* **fawwar**, yufawwir; *v. intrans.* **fâr**, yafûr; ghala, yaghlî.
bold: jàsûr, *pl.* jàsûrîn; (forward) mutajàsir.
bolt: *v.* (door) qaffal, yuqaffil; *n.* (of iron) burghi, *pl.* barâghî; (of cloth) ṭol, ṭul, ṭâqa.
bomb: qanbala, *pl.* qanâbil.
bombard: aṭlaq madàfi', yuṭliq; dharab ṭôp, yadhrab.
bond: *v.* ta'ahhad, yata'ahhad; *n.* sened, *pl.* senedàt; (tie) irtibâṭ.
bone: 'adhm, *pl.* a'dhâm.
book: kitàb, *pl.* kutub. See also **pocket-book**.
bookbinder: mujellid kutub.
book-keeper: màsik defàtir.
book-keeping: mesk defàtir.
bookseller: beyyâ' kutub.
boot: qandara, *pl.* qanâdir, qandaràt; (top boot) juzma.
bootmaker: qanderachi.
booty: nahîba, kesb, chesb, ghanîma.
border: *v.* (adjoin) ittaṣal wîya, yattaṣil; *n.* (boundary) ḥadd, *pl.* ḥudûd; (edge) ḥâfa, ḥâshia.
born: mawlûd.
borrow: istaqradh, yastaqridh; tadàyan, yatadàyan.
both: (they both) ithnênehum; (you both) ithnênekum; (we both) ithnênena.
bottle: shîsha, *pl.* shîyash, ashyàsh.
bottom: esfel.
bound: *v.* (leap) ṭafar, yaṭfar; naṭṭ, yanuṭṭ; *v.* (limit) ḥaddad, yuḥaddid.
bounds: ḥudûd.
bow: *n.* (of boat) ṣadr.
bowels: maṣârîn.
bowl: ṭâsa, *pl.* ṭasàt; mâ'un, *pl.* mawâ'în.
box: ṣandûq, *pl.* ṣanâdîq.
boy: walad, *pl.* awlàd, wulid; ṣabai, *pl.* ṣabyàn.
brain: mukh, dimâgh.
bran: nakhâla.
branch: *n.* ghaṣn, *pl.* ghaṣûna, aghṣân; (date) ṣa'f.
brass: prinj.
brave: shajjâ', *pl.* shajjâ'a jàsûr, *pl.* jàsûrîn.
brazier: manqala, *pl.* manâqil.
bread: khubz.
breadth: 'ardh.
break: *v. trans.* keser, yiksar; *v. intrans.* inkeser, yenkesir; *n.* kesra.
breakfast: rayûq, fuṭûr.
breast: ṣadr, *pl.* ṣudûr.
breath: nefs, nefes.
breathe: teneffes, yeteneffes.
breeches: pantalûn.
bribe: *v. trans.* barṭal, yubarṭil; give a bribe, a'ṭa reshwa, yu'ṭî; take a bribe, irtesha, yerteshî; *n.* barṭîl, reshwa.
brick: (burned) ṭâbûqa, *pl.* ṭâbûq; (mud) liben.
bride: 'arûs.
bridegroom: 'arîs.
bridge: jisr, *pl.* jisûr.
bridle: *n.* lijàm.
brigand: luṣṣ, *pl.* luṣuṣ; ḥarâmî, *pl.* ḥarâmîa.
bright: (shining) làmi'.
bring: jàb, yajîb.
broad: 'arîdh, *pl.* 'arâdh.
broker: dallàl, *pl.* dallàlîn.
broom: miknesa, *pl.* mikànis.
broth: mai laḥm, shorba.

brother: âkh, *pl.* ikhwa, ikhwàn.
brother-in-law: nasîb.
brown: esmer, *f.* samra, *pl.* sumr.
bruise: *v.* ʻawwar, yuʻawwir; *n.* ʻawâr.
brush: *v.* farrach, yufarrich; *n.* furcha, *pl.* furach.
brutal: waḥshî.
brute: *n.* waḥsh, *pl.* wuḥûsh.
bucket: bàldi, *pl.* bàldiyàt; saṭl.
buckle: *n.* ebzîm.
bugle: bûrî, *pl.* bûriyàt; burazân.
build: bena, yibnî; ʻammar, yuʻammir.
builder: benna, *pl.* bennai.
building: *n.* bunyàn; (art of) bina, taʻmîr.
bull: thôr, *pl.* thîrân.
bullet: raṣâṣa, *pl.* raṣâṣ; fishga, *pl.* fisheg.
bullock: see **bull.**
bundle: (of clothing) bukcha, *pl.* bukech; (of wood) ḥuzma, *pl.* ḥuzam.
burden: ḥiml, *pl.* aḥmàl.
bureau: (furniture) qantôr; (office) idâra.
burial: defn.
buried: madfûn.
burn: *v. trans.* aḥraq, yuḥriq; *v. intrans.* iḥtaraq, yaḥtariq.
burst: *v. trans.* shaqq, yashuqq; *v. intrans.* inshaqq, yanshaqq.
bury: defen, yidfan.
bush: ʻulêq, ʻagûl.
business: (affair) shughl, shoghl, *pl.* ashghâl; (trade) tajâra.
busy: mashghûl.
but: làkin, walàkin.
butcher: gaṣṣâb, *pl.* gaṣâṣîb.
butt: (of rifle), qandâgh, kaʻb, chaʻb.
butter: zibed.
button: dugma, *pl.* dugam.
buy: ishtara, yashtarî; shara, yishrî.
buyer: mushtarî.
by: (near) qarîb, ʻand; (according to) ḥasab; by means of, bi wâsiṭat; by day, binnahâr.

C

cabbage: lahâna.
cabin: qamâra, *pl.* qamâyir.
cage: qafs.
cake: kêk; pan ispanya.
calamity: balîa, *pl.* balàyà.
calculate: ḥasab, yaḥsab.
calculation: ḥisàb.
calendar: taqwîm, ruznàma.
calf: ʻijl, *pl.* ʻujûl.
call: *v. trans.* and *intrans.* ṣâḥ, yaṣîḥ; *v. trans.* (call on, visit) zâr, yazûr; *n.* (hail) ṣiyâḥ; (visit) ziyâra.
calm: *v. trans.* sekken, yusekkin; *adj.* hàdi, sàkin, sàkit; *n.* (no wind) sawàli.
camel: jemel, *pl.* jimàl, ajmàl; baʻîr, *pl.* abâʻir, baʻârîn.
camel-driver: jammàl, *pl.* jammàlîn.
camp: *v.* khayyam, yukhayyim; *n.* muʻaskar.
camphor: kàfûr.
can: *v.* (be able) qadar, yaqdar.
canal: (small) nahr, *pl.* anhur, nahrân; (great, e.g. Suez) turʻa, bughâz.
candle: shemaʻ, pl. shamâʻ.
cane: (material) khaizaràn; (walking-stick), ʻaṣa, bâston.
cannon: medfaʻ, *pl.* madàfiʻ; ṭôp, *pl.* aṭwâp.
cannon-ball: gulla, *pl.* gulel.
canopy: dhalàl.
canvas: (cloth) chitrî.

cap: (European) kàp; (skull-cap) 'araqchîn; percussion cap, kapsûn.
capable: muqtedir.
capacious: wâsi', râhî.
capacity: (size) wus'; (official) ṣifa.
cape: (headland) râs.
capital: *n.* (city) 'âṣima, pai-takht; capital letter, ḥarf kabîr; *adj.* (good) 'âl.
captain: (naval) qapṭân, *pl.* qapâṭîn; (military) yôzbâshî, *pl.* yôzbâshîa.
captive: asîr, *pl.* usarâ.
capture: (seize) mesek, yimsak; (take captive) esser, yu-essir; *n.* akhdh.
caravan: karwân, *pl.* karâwîn; qâfila, *pl.* qawâfil.
carcass: jiththa, *pl.* jitheth; leshsha.
card: kârt; pack of cards, desta.
care: *v.* care for, ihtemm bi, yehtemm; i'tenî, ya'tenî; *v.* take care, taqayyad, yataqayyad; dâr bàl, yadîr.
careful: mutaqayyid.
careless: ghâfil.
carelessness: ghafla.
cargo: ḥiml.
carpenter: najjâr, *pl.* najâjîr.
carpet: zûlîa, *pl.* zawàlî.
carriage: 'arabâna, *pl.* 'arabâyin; 'araba, *pl.* 'arabàt.
carrier ḥammàl, *pl.* ḥamàmîl.
carrion: faṭîs, *pl.* faṭâyis.
carrot: juzr.
carry: ḥamal, yaḥmal; shàl, yashîl.
cartridge: fishga, *pl.* fisheg.
case: (box) ṣandûq, *pl.* ṣanâdîq; (for knife, instrument, &c.) bêt; (legal affair) qadhîa; in case, idha, in kàn; in any case, 'ala kulli ḥâl.
cash: *n.* nuqûd; *adv.* naqdan.
cast: *v. trans* debb, yadibb; ṭaraḥ, yaṭraḥ.
castle: qaṣr, *pl.* quṣûr; jil a, *pl.* jilâ'.
castor-oil: see oil.
cat: bazzûna, *pl.* bazàzîn.
catalogue: qaima, *pl.* qawâyim.
catch: *v.* mesek, yimsak; lezem, yilzam.
catholic: kàtulîk.
cattle: mawàshî.
cauliflower: qarnabîṭ.
cause: *v. trans.* sebbeb, yusebbib; ja'al, yaj'al; *n.* sebeb, *pl.* asbàb.
caution: *v.* nebbeh, yunebbih; *n.* (care) intibàh, taqyàd.
cavalry: sawârîa.
cease: *v. trans.* and *intrans.* baṭṭal, yubaṭṭil.
ceiling: sagf.
celebrate: (feast) 'ayyad, yu'ayyid.
celebrated: mashhûr, shahîr.
celery: krafas.
cellar: sardâb, *pl.* saràdîb.
cement: chemento.
cemetery: maqbara.
censure: *v.* wabbakh; yuwabbikh; *n.* tawbîkh.
census: 'adad nufûs.
centre: *n.* (of circle, of government) markaz, *pl.* maràkiz; (middle) wasṭ.
century: mîat sena; qarn, *pl.* qurûn.
ceremony: iḥtifàl.
certain: (sure) akîd; (a certain one) aḥad; (so and so) fulàn.
certainly: ma'lûm, belli.
certificate: shahàda.

chaff: *n.* tiben, gishr.
chain: zanjîl, *pl.* zanàjîl; silsala, *pl.* salàsil.
chair: kursî, *pl.* karàsî; skumli, *pl.* skumliyàt.
chalk: ṭabâshîr.
change: *v. trans.* beddel, yubeddil; ghayyar, yughayyir; *v. trans.* (money) ṣarraf, yuṣarrif; *v. intrans.* taghayyar, yataghayyar; tebeddel, yetebeddel; *n.* tabdîl, taghyîr; (money) khurda, qusûr; see also **money**.
channel: mejra.
chapter: faṣl, fuṣûl; bàb, abwàb; (of bible) aṣḥaḥ, *pl.* aṣḥaḥàt.
character: (nature) ṭabî'a, akhlàq; (letter) ḥarf, *pl.* ḥurûf, aḥruf.
charcoal: faḥm Karâchî; faḥm ḥaṭab.
charge: *v.* waṣṣa, yuwaṣṣi; *v.* (attack) hejem 'ala, yihjam.
charm: (amulet) ḥirs.
cheap: rakhîṣ, *pl.* rakhâṣ.
cheapness: rukhṣ.
cheat: *v.* ghishsh, yaghishsh; *n.* ghashshàsh.
cheek: khadd, *pl.* khudûd.
cheese: jiben.
cheque: ḥawàla, *pl.* hawàyil; chek.
chess: saṭranj.
chest: (breast) ṣadr, fuwàd. See also **box**.
chew: 'alas, ya'las.
chicken: dajàja, *pl.* dajàj.
chief: *n.* raìs, *pl.* ruasâ; *adj.* raisî.
chiefly: khâṣatan, aghlab.
child: walad, *pl.* awlàd.
childbirth: wilàda.
childhood: ṣughr.
chimney: medkhana, *pl.* medâkhin.
chin: dhuqn.
china: (crockery) forfûri.
China: Ṣîn, Chîn.
chisel: minqâr.
choke: *v. trans.* khanaq, yakhnaq; *v. intrans.* ikhtanaq, yakhtaniq.
cholera: ez zû'; kolêra.
choose: ikhtâr, yakhtâr; khayyar, yukhayyir.
Christ: el Masîḥ; 'Îsa el Masîḥ.
Christian: masîḥî, *pl.* masîḥiyîn; naṣrânî, *pl.* naṣâra.
Christianity: el masîḥîa; ed diyànat el masîḥîa.
Christmas: 'îd el mîlàd.
church: kanîsa, *pl.* kanàyis; bî'a, *pl.* bî'àt.
cigar: charût.
cigarette: jigâra, *pl.* jigâyir.
circle: dàyira, *pl.* dàyiràt.
circular: mudawwar, mustadîr.
circulate: *v. intrans.* jara, yijrî.
circumcise: ṭahhar, yuṭahhir; khatan, yakhtan.
circumcision: ṭuhûr, khitàn.
circumstance: ḥâl, *pl.* aḥwâl.
cistern: ḥôdh.
city: wilàya, *pl.* wilàyàt; medîna, mudn.
civil: (polite) adîb, *pl.* adîbîn, udabà; (not military) ehelî; see also **procedure**.
civilization: temeddun.
civilized: mutemedden.
claim: *v.* idda'a, yadda'î; *n.* da'wa, *pl.* da'âwî.
claimant: mudda'î.
clap: *v.* ṣaffaq, yuṣaffiq.
class: *n.* (in school) ṣaff, *pl.* ṣufûf; *v.* see **rank, rate**.
claw: *n.* dhafîr, *pl.* adhâfîr.

clean: *adj.* nadhîf, *pl.* nadhâf; *v.* nadhdhaf, yunadhdhif.
clear: (bright) ṣâfî; (evident) wâdhiḥ, dhâhir; *v. trans.* (clarify) ṣaffa, yuṣaffî.
clearly: wâdhiḥan.
clergyman: qass, *pl.* qassàn, qusûs.
clerk: kàtib, *pl.* kuttàb.
clever: shâṭir, *pl.* shaṭṭâr.
climate: hawa, manâkh.
climb: *v.* ṣa'ad, yiṣ'ad.
cloak: 'aba, *pl.* 'ubi.
clock: sâ'a màlat ḥâyiṭ.
close: *v.* sedd, yasidd.
close: *adj.* dhayyiq.
closet: (water-closet) edeb, edeb-khâna, khala.
cloth: khâm; (print) chît.
clothe: lebbes, yulebbis; kesa, yiksî; chesa, yichsî.
clothed in: làbis.
clothes: hudûm, thiyàb, kiswa, chiswa.
cloud: ghêma, *pl.* ghêm, ghuyûm.
cloudy: mugheyyem.
club: (of wood) khashba; (society) jam'ia, klub.
coal: faḥm.
coarse: khushn.
coarseness: khashûna.
coast: sâḥil, *pl.* sawâḥil.
coat: sitra, kôt; (overcoat) paltô.
cobbler: raggâ'.
cock: dîk, *pl.* duyûk; dîch, *pl.* duyûch.
cocoa: kuku.
coco-nut: jôz nargîl.
coffee: gâhwa.
coffee-shop: gâ-hwa.
coffin: tàbût, ṣandûq.
coin: *n.* sikka, *pl.* sikek.
cold: (temperature, of things) bàrid; (do., of persons), bardàn, *pl.* bardànîn; (temperament of persons) bàrid, *pl.* bàridîn; *n.* (temperature) bard; have a cold, *part.* manshûl.
collar: yâkha, *pl.* yâkhàt.
collect: *v. trans.* jama', yijmà'; *v. intrans.* ijtama', yajtamai'.
college: kullîya.
colonel: mîr alai; (lt.-col.) qaimaqâm.
colour: lôn, *pl.* alwân; rang.
coloured: mulawwan.
colt: muhr.
column: (pillar) 'âmûd, *pl.* 'awâmîd; (of figures) 'âmûd.
comb: *n.* mishṭ; *v.* mashshaṭ, yumashshiṭ.
come: jà, yîjî; ata, yà-ti; *imper.* ta'âl.
comfort: *v.* 'azza, yu'azzi; sella, yusellî; *n.* ta'zia, taslia.
comfortable: (of thing) murîh; (of person) mustarîh.
command: *v.* amar, ya-mur; *n.* amr, *pl.* awâmir; ḥukm.
commander-in-chief: qâid 'âm; kommandân.
commence: see **begin**.
commerce: tajâra; bi' wa shara.
commercial: tajârî.
commit: *v. trans.* sellem, yusellim; (a fault) ghalaṭ, yaghlaṭ.
common: *adj.* (ordinary) âdî; (universal) 'umûmî.
commonly: 'âdatan.
communion: (holy) ishtirâk muqaddas.
companion: rafîq, *pl.* rufaqâ; rafîj; rub' (*pl.* only).
company: jamâ'a; (mil.) buluk.
comparison: in comparison with, bi nisba ila.
comparison: muqâbala.

compare: qâbal wîya, yuqâbil.
compass: (mariners') qiblanàma; (dividers) pargâl.
compel: ajbar, yujbir.
compelled: majbûr.
compensate: 'awwadh, yu'awwidh.
compensation: ta'wîdh.
complaint: (accusation) shikàya, *pl.* shikàyàt.
complain: ishtaka, yashtekî.
complete: *v.* temmem, yutemmim; khallaṣ, yukhalliṣ; qadha, yaqdhi; *adj.* kàmil, tàmm.
completed: to be completed, khalaṣ, yikhlaṣ; inqadha, yanqadhi.
completely: bil kullîa.
completion: ikmàl.
compliments: taḥyiyàt.
composed of: muḥtawî 'ala.
composition: (substance) tarkîb.
comprehend: derek, yidrak.
comprehension: idrâk.
compulsion: ijbâr; by compulsion, bil jabr.
comrade: see **companion**.
conceal: akhba, yukhbî; akhfa, yukhfî.
concealed: mukhtebî, mukhtefî, mukhfî.
conceive: (imagine) taṣawwar, yataṣawar; (become pregnant) ḥabalat, taḥbal.
concerned: (anxious) bil fikr.
concerning: min jehet; fî khuṣûṣ; min ṭarf.
conclude: (deduce) istantaj, yastantij; (finish) khatam, yakhtam.
condemn: ḥakam, yaḥkam.
condemned: maḥkûm.
condition: (state) ḥâl, *pl.* aḥwâl; (contingency) sharṭ, *pl.* shurûṭ; on condition that, bi sharṭ an.
conditional: taḥt sharṭ.
conduct: *v. trans.* dell, yadill; *v.* conduct oneself, taṣarraf, yataṣarraf.
conduct: *n.* taṣarruf, sîra, silûk.
confess: qarr, yaqurr; i'taraf, ya'tarif.
confession: iqrâr, i'tirâf.
confidence: thiqqa.
confident: muthiqq.
confirm: ḥaqqaq, yuḥaqqiq.
confiscate: dhabaṭ, yadhbaṭ.
confiscation: dhabṭ.
confusion: qalabalagh.
congratulate: bârak li, yubârik; henna, yuhennî.
congratulations: tahnia, tabrîk.
congregation: jamâ'a.
conjecturally: takhmînam.
conjecture: dhann, yadhunn.
conjugate: ṣarraf, yuṣarrif.
conjugation: taṣrîf.
conjunction: (gram.) ḥarf 'aṭf.
connect: *v. trans.* waṣṣal ila, yuwaṣṣil; *v. intrans.* ittaṣal, yattaṣil.
connected with: muttaṣal wîya; (of persons) mansûb ila.
connexion: in this connexion, min hel qabîl.
conquer: intaṣar, yantaṣir; ghalab, yaghlab; (conquer a city) fetaḥ, yiftaḥ.
conqueror: muntaṣir, ghâlib.
conscience: dhamîr.
consecutive: mutatàbi'.
consecutively: bi tatàbu'.
consent: *v.* radhi, yardha; *n.* ridhâ.
consequence: natîja, *pl.* natàyij.

consider: ifteker, yeftekir; tefekker bi, yetefekker.
consist of: iḥtawa, yaḥtawî.
construct: see **build**.
consul: qunṣal, *pl.* qunâṣil; balyôz.
consulate: qunṣal khâna.
consult: shâwar, yushâwir.
consultation: mashâwara.
contagious: sàrî.
contain: (hold) wasa', yasa'; (have inside) aḥwa, yaḥwî.
contempt: ikrâh, taḥqîr.
contented: râdhi.
context: qarîna.
continual: dàyimî.
continually: daiman; kull waqt.
contraband: mamnû'.
contract: *v.* taqâwal, yataqâwal; *n.* muqâwala, kontrât.
contradict: 'âradh, yu'âridh.
contradiction: munâqadha.
contrary: *adj.* 'aksî; *prep.* dhudd; on the contrary, bil'aks.
conversation: ḥaki, ḥachi, tekellum.
converse: ḥaka, yaḥkî; tekellem, yetekellem.
convert: *n.* muhtedî.
convict: *v. trans.* ḥakam 'ala, yahkam.
cook: *v. trans.* ṭabakh, yaṭbakh; *v. intrans.* inṭabakh, yanṭabikh; *n.* ṭabbâkh, *pl.* ṭabbâkhîn; àschî; àschîa (*f.*).
copper: naḥâs.
copy: *v. trans.* nesekh, yinsakh; *n.* niskha, *pl.* nisakh; kôpya.
corkscrew: burghî.
corner: zâwia, *pl.* zawâya.
corpse: jinàza, *pl.* janàyiz.
correct: *v.* ṣallaḥ, yuṣalliḥ; *adj.* tamàm.
correspondence: muràsala.
correspond with: (write) kàteb, yukàtib; (agree) wâfaq, yuwâfiq.
corrupt: *v.* afsad, yufsid; *adj.* fàsid, *pl.* fàsidîn.
corruption: fasàd.
cost: *v.* kellef, yukellif; *n.* qîma, *pl.* aqyàm.
cotton: gutan.
cough: gaḥḥ, yaguḥḥ; *n.* gaḥḥa.
council: majlis, mejlis.
counsellor: mustashâr.
count: 'add, ya'udd.
counterfeit: *adj.* sakhta, taqlîd.
countless: la tu'add; bila'adad.
country: (patrie) waṭn, *pl.* awtân; (geo.) memleka, *pl.* mamàlik; bilàd, *pl.* buldàn, bilàdîn; in the country (outside town), fîl khârij.
couple: zôj, *pl.* azwàj.
courage: shajâ'a.
court: (of law) maḥkama, *pl.* maḥâkim; (court-yard) ḥôsh; court martial, dîwàn ḥarb; dîwàn 'urfi.
cousin: ibn 'amm, bint 'amm, ibn (or bint) 'amma, khâl, khâla, &c. (according to parentage).
cover: *v.* ghaṭṭa, yughaṭṭi; *n.* ghaṭa.
covered: mughaṭṭa.
covet: ṭama' bi, yiṭma'.
cow: hàsha, *pl.* hôsh; baqara, *pl.* baqr.
coward: khawwâf, jabbàn.
cradle: qârôq, mahd.
crawl: zaḥaf, yizḥaf.
cream: gêmer.
create: khalaq, yakhlaq.
creation: (act of) khalq; (universe) khalîqa.

creator: khâliq.
creature: (created thing) makhlûq.
credit: *v.* ṣaddaq, yuṣaddiq; on credit, bi dên.
creditor: ṭâlib.
creed: i'tiqâd.
creep: see **crawl.**
crescent: hilàl.
crier: dallàl.
crime: janàya.
criminal: mujrim; see also **procedure.**
cripple: *adj.* saqaṭ.
crooked: a'waj, *fem.* 'ôja.
crop: *n.* (of field) ḥâṣil.
cross: *v. intrans.* 'abar, ya'bar; *v. trans.* 'abbar, yu'abbir; *n.* ṣalîb.
crow: *n.* (bird) ghurâb, *pl.* ghirbân; *v.* ṣaḥ, yasîh.
crowd: *v.* izdaḥam, yazdaḥim; *n.* jamâ'a, khalq.
crown: tàj; pl. tîjân.
crucify: ṣallab, yuṣallib.
cruel: qâsî.
cruelty: qasâwa.
crush: saḥaq, yisḥaq.
cry: (weep) beka, yibkî; (aloud) ṣaḥ, yaṣîḥ; ṣarakh, yaṣrakh; *n.* siyâḥ, ṣurâkh.
cucumber: khiyâr.
cultivate: 'ammar, yu'ammir; felaḥ, yiflaḥ.
cultivation: falâḥa, ta'mîr.
cultivator: see **peasant.**
cup: (small) finjàn, *pl.* fanàjîn; (large) piyàla, *pl.* piyàlàt.
cupboard: dûlàb, *pl.* dawàlîb.
cure: ashfa, yushfî; shàfa, yushàfî; *n.* shifà.
currants: qishmish.
current: *adj.* jàrî; (of money) râ-ij; *n.* jaryàn.
curse: *v.* la'an, yil'an; *n.* la'na.
cursed: mal'ûn.
curtain: parda, *pl.* pardàt.
cushion: makhadda, *pl.* makhâdît.
custom: 'âda, *pl.* 'awâyid.
custom-house: gumruk.
customs: (dues) resm, *pl.* rusûmàt.
cut: *v.* gaṣṣ, yaguṣṣ; qaṭa', yaqṭa'.

D

dagger: khanjar, *pl.* khanàjir.
daily: *adj.* yômî; *adv.* yômîan.
damage: *v.* dharr, yadhurr; *n.* dharar, madharra.
damp: nedi, murṭib.
dance: *v.* raqaṣ, yarqaṣ; *n.* raqṣ.
danger: khaṭar, *pl.* akhṭâr; derekîya.
dangerous: mukhṭir.
dare: tajàsar, yatajàsar.
dark: mudhlim; (in colour) 'amîq, tôkh.
darkness: dhulma.
date: (time) târîkh; (fruit) *sing.* tamra, *coll.* tamr.
dated: mu-arrakh.
daughter: bint, *pl.* banàt.
dawn: fijr.
day: yôm, *pl.* ayàm; (opposite night) nahâr.
daybreak: ghubsha.
dead: mêyyit.
deadly: muqtil.
deaf: aṭrash, *f.* ṭarsha, *pl.* ṭursh.
dealer: (seller) bayyâ'.
dear: (in price) ghâli; (beloved) 'azîz, *pl.* a'izzà; maḥbûb, *pl.* maḥbûbîn.
dearness: ghala.
death: mawt.
debt: dên, *pl.* duyûn.

decay: fesed, yifsad; kharab, yakhrab.
deceit: ghish.
deceitful: ghashshàsh, ḥayyàl.
deceive: ghashsh, yaghishsh.
December: kànûn awwal.
decide: (determine) 'azam, ya'zam; (distinguish) mêyyez, yumêyyiz.
declare: a'lan, yu'lin.
decoration: (official) nîshàn.
decree: *v.* a'lan, yu'lin; amar, ya-mur; *n.* amr, i'làn, fetwa.
deduct: ṭaraḥ, yaṭraḥ; naqqaṣ, yunaqqiṣ.
deed: (of title) sened tâpô; ḥijja.
deem: ḥasab, yaḥsab.
deep: 'amîq; ghamîq, ghamîj.
depth: 'umq.
defeat: *v. trans.* ghalab 'ala, yaghlab.
defence: mudàfa'a.
defend: dàfa' 'an, yudàfi'; ḥâma 'an, yuḥâmi.
defendant: (at law) mudda'a 'alêh.
defender: mudàfi'.
defile: *v.* nejjes, yunejjis.
defiled: to be, tenejjes, yetenejjes.
degree: daraja, *pl.* darajàt.
delay: *v. trans.* 'aṭṭal, yu'aṭṭil; akhkhar, yuakhkhir; *v. intrans.* ta'aṭṭal, yata'aṭṭal; taakhkhar, yata-akhkhar; *n.* ta'tîl, ta-khîr.
delicious: ladhîdh.
deliver: sellem, yusellim.
delivery: teslîm.
demand: ṭalab, yaṭlab; *n.* ṭalba, *pl.* ṭalabàt; ṭalâba.
denial: inkâr, tankîr.
dentist: murekkib asnàn; murekkib sunûn; asnànchî.
deny: neker, yinkar.
depart: râḥ, yarûḥ; (on journey) sàfar, yusàfir.
departed: (dead) marḥûm.
departure: rawâḥ.
depose: 'azzal, yu'azzil; khala', yikhla'.
deposed: to be, in'azal, yan'azil.
deposit: *v.* (place) ḥaṭṭ, yaḥutt; *n.* (in bank) dapuzît; see also **pledge**.
deprive: aḥram, yuḥrim.
deputy: nàyib, *pl.* nawwâb; wakîl, *pl.* wukalâ.
deride: qashmar, yuqashmir.
derision: qashmara.
descend: nezel, yinzal.
descendant: min dhurrîat.
descent: (incline) nezla.
describe: waṣaf, yoṣaf.
description: tawṣîf.
desert: *v.* terek, yitrak.
desert: *n.* chôl, barr, bàdia.
deserve: istaḥaqq, yastaḥiqq; istehel, yestehil.
deserving: mustaḥiqq, mustehil.
desire: *v.* ràd, yarîd; ishteha, yashtehi; *n.* iràda, raghba, ishtihà.
desist: baṭṭal, yubaṭṭil.
despair: yàs; in despair, mayûs.
despise: kereh, yikrah; akrah, yukrih.
despotic: mustabidd.
destroy: kharrab, yukharrib; demmer, yudemmir.
destroyer: (naval) mudemmira, *pl.* mudemmiràt.
destruction: halàk, tadmîr, itlàf.
detail: (of a narrative) tafṣîl, *pl.* tafâṣîl.
detain: 'aṭṭal, yu'aṭṭil.

devil: shêtân, *pl.* shêyâtîn; iblîs, *pl.* abàlîs.
devout: taqi, *pl.* atqiyà; khâ-if Allâh.
dew: nida.
diameter: 'ardh.
diamond: elmàss.
diarrhoea: ishàl (*pron.* is-hàl).
dictionary: qâmûs, *pl.* qawâmîs.
die: màt, yamût; (of persons only) tawaffa, yatawaffa.
differ: ikhtalaf, yakhtalif.
difference: farq.
different: mukhtelif; (another) ghair (before noun); (various) mutanawwa'.
difficult: ṣâ'ab, mushkil, zâḥma.
difficulty: ṣa'ûba, *pl.* ṣa'ûbàt.
dig: ḥafar, yaḥfar.
digest: hadham, yahdam; ṣarraf, yuṣarrif.
digest: *n.* mulakhkhas, zibda.
digestion: hadhm ṭa'âm.
dignity: saṭwa, hêba.
diligence: himma.
diligent: muhtemm.
diminish: *v. trans.* naqqaṣ, yunaqqiṣ; *v. intrans.* naqaṣ, yanqaṣ; qall, yaqill.
dine: (at noon) taghadda, yataghadda; (in evening) ta'ashsha, yata'ashsha.
dining-room: ṣufra khâna.
dinner: (noon) ghada; (evening) 'asha.
diploma: shahàda.
direct: *v.* (regulate) dâr, yadîr; direct to, dell ila, yadill; *adj.* râsan.
direction: (toward) ṭarf; (instruction) kêfîat isti'màl; (regulation) idâra.
directly: (at once) ḥâlan, hessa.
director: mudîr, *pl.* mudarâ.
dirt: wasakh.
dirty: wasikh, *pl.* wasikhîn.
disagree: mâ ittafaq, yattafiq.
disagreement: 'adm ittifâq.
disappear: ghâb, yaghîb.
disappearance: ghiyàb.
disappoint: khayyab, yukhayyib.
disappointed: khâyib.
discharge: (cargo) nafadh, yanfadh; farragh, yufarrigh; (duty) adda, yu-addi; (dismiss) baṭṭal, yubaṭṭil.
discipline: *v.* eddeb, yu-eddib; *n.* nidhâm.
discover: keshef, yikshaf.
discovery: keshf.
disease: mardh, *pl.* amrâdh; waj', *pl.* aw'jâ'.
disgrace: *n.* 'aib.
dish: *n.* mâ'ûn, *pl.* mawâ'în; ṣaḥn, *pl.* ṣuḥûn.
dismiss: see **discharge**.
dismount: ḥawwal, yuḥawwil.
disobedience: 'adm iṭâ'a.
disobedient: 'âṣi, *pl.* 'âṣiyîn.
disperse: *v. trans.* ṭashshar, yuṭashshir; shettet, yushettit; *v. intrans.* taṭashshar, yataṭashshar; teshettet, yeteshettet.
displeased: mû râdhî; ghair râdhî.
dispute: see **quarrel**.
distance: masàfa.
distant: ba'îd.
distinct: wâdhiḥ.
distinguish: mêyyez, yumêyyiz.
distinguished: mumtàz.
distress: 'ankara.
distribute: wazza', yuwazzi'.

distributed: to be, tawazza', yatawazza'.
distribution: tawzî'.
district: nâḥiya, *pl.* nawâḥî.
disturb: ṣadda', yuṣaddi'.
disturbance: tashwîsh.
ditch: khandaq, *pl.* khanâdiq.
dive: ghâṣ, yaghûṣ; ghaṭṭas, yughaṭṭis.
diver: ghawwâṣ, *pl.* ghawâwîṣ.
divide: *v. trans.* qasam, yaqsam; qassam, yuqassim.
divine: *adj.* ilàhî.
divinity: làhût.
divorce: *v.* ṭallaq, yuṭalliq; *n.* ṭallâq.
divorced: *v.* to be divorced, taṭallaq, yataṭallaq.
do: sawwa, yusawwî.
doctor: ḥakîm, *pl.* ḥukamâ; ṭabîb, *pl.* aṭibbâ; dokhtor, *pl.* dakhâtir.
doctrine: ta'lîm, *pl.* ta'âlîm.
dog: kelb, *pl.* kilàb; chelb, *pl.* chilàb.
dome: gubba.
donkey: ḥamâr, *pl.* ḥamîr; zamàl, *pl.* zamàyil; muṭṭi, *pl.* muṭṭâya.
door: bàb, *pl.* abwàb, bîbàn, bûb.
double: mudhâ'af, qâṭên.
doubt: *v.* shekk, yashikk; *n.* shekk.
dough: 'ajîn.
down: *adv.* ḥadr, taḥt; downstairs, ḥadr, taḥt, jôwa.
dragoman: tarjumàn, *pl.* tarjumànîa.
draper: bazzàz, *pl.* bazzàzîn.
draughts: dàma.
draw: jarr, yajurr; jedheb, yijdhab; (picture) resem, yirsam.
drawer: (of table or chest) majarr, *pl.* majarràt.
drawers: (garment) libàs, sharwâl.
drawing: (art of) taṣwîr, tarsîm.
drawing-room: diwànîa.
dream: *n.* ḥulm, *pl.* aḥlàm; *v.* ḥalam, yaḥlam.
dress: *v. trans.* lebbes, yulebbis; *v. intrans.* (clothe one's self) lebes, hudûm yilbas, *n.* libs
drill: *v.* 'allam, yu'allim; *n.* ta'lûm.
drink: *v.* shereb, yishrab; *n.* sherba.
drive: *v.* sâq, yasûq.
driver: (of carriage) 'arabachî; *pl.* 'arabachîa.
drown: gharaq, yaghraq.
drug: *n.* dawa, *pl.* adwia.
drum: *n.* ṭabl, *pl.* ṭubûl.
drunk: sakrân, *pl.* sakâra.
drunkard: sakrân, *pl.* sakâra; sakîr.
drunkenness: sikr.
dry: *v. trans.* yebbes, yuyebbis; neshshef, yuneshshif; *v. intrans.* yebes, yêbes (têbes, &c.); *adj.* yàbis, nàshif.
duck: besh, *pl.* bushûsh.
dull: (wearying) mu'ajjiz.
dumb: akhras, *f.* kharsa, *pl.* khurs, khursîn.
dung: zibl, zibàla.
dung-heap: mezbela.
during: fî ithnà.
dust: *n.* ṭôz, 'ajàj, ghubâr.
duty: (obligation) wàjib, *pl.* wàjibàt; (customs) resm, *pl.* rusûmàt.
dwell: seken, yiskan.
dye: *v.* ṣabagh, yaṣbagh; *n.* ṣubgh.
dynamite: dinamît.
dysentery: ishal dem; dizánterî.

E

each: kull; each one, kull wâḥid; each other, (3rd pers.) bâ'dhehum bâ'dh; (2nd pers.) bâ'dhekum bâ'dh; (1st pers.) bâ'dhena bâ'dh.
ear: idhn, *pl.* àdhàn.
early: *adv.* min waqt.
earth: ardh; (soil) trâb.
ease: *n.* râḥa; with ease, bi râḥa; bi suhûla.
east: sharq; *adj.* sharqî; eastward, sharqan.
Easter: el 'îd el kabîr; 'îd el qiyàma.
eastern: sharqî; *pl.* (orientals), sharqiyîn.
easy: sehl, hêyyin.
eat: akal, ya-kul.
edge: ḥadd, *pl.* ḥudud; ṭarf, *pl.* aṭrâf.
editor: mu-ellif.
educate: rabba, yurabbî.
education: tarbiya.
effect: *v.* (bring about) sebbeb, yusebbib; *n.* (result) natîja, *pl.* natàyij.
egg: bêdha, *pl.* bêdh, bêdhàt; dahrûja, *pl.* dahârîj.
eight: (*with masc.*) thamànya; (*with fem.*) thamàn.
eighteen: thmantâsh, thamanatâsh.
eighteenth: thàmin 'asher.
eighth: *n.* thumn, *pl.* athmàn; *adj.* thàmin.
eightieth: eth thamànîn.
eighty: thamànîn.
either: (either — or) amma — aw; yô — yô.
elbow: 'aks.
elect: *v.* ikhtar, yakhtar; intakhab, yantakhib.
election: intikhab.
electricity: kahraba-ìa, lektrik.
electric: lektrîkî.
elementary: ibtida-î.
elephant: fîl, *pl.* afyàl.
elevate: see **raise**.
elevation: irtifâ'.
eleven: idâsh.
eleventh: *adj.* hàdî 'asher (*masc.*); hàdia 'ashra (*fem.*); *n.* juz min idâsh.
eloquent: faṣih, balîgh.
embark: rekeb, yirkab.
embassy: sifàra.
emperor: imperator, sulṭân.
empire: memleka, *pl.* memàlik.
employ: istakhdam, yastakhdim.
employment: khidma, istikhdàm.
empress: sulṭâna.
empty: *adj.* khâlî, fârigh; *v.* farregh, yufarrigh.
encamp: khayyam, yukhayyim.
enclose: see **inclose**.
encyclopaedia: dàirat el mu'ârif.
end: *v. trans.* enha, yunhî; *v. intrans.* inteha, yentehi; *n.* nihàya.
endeavour: *v.* ijtehed, yejtehid; *n.* ijtihàd.
endless: bila nihàya.
endure: taḥammal, yataḥammal.
enemy: 'adû, *pl.* 'adwàn, a'dâ.
enmity: 'adâwa.
engine: makîna, *pl.* makàyin.
engineer: (mechanical) osta, *pl.* ostawàt; (civil) muhendis, *pl.* muhendisîn.
England: anglaterra.
English: (language or person) anglêzî; the English el anglêz.
engrave: naqash, yanqash.
enjoy: kêyyef bi, yukêyyif.

enjoyment: kêf.
enlarge: wassa', yuwassi'.
enlargement: tawsî', takbîr.
enlist: keteb fîl 'askarîya.
enough: kàfi, bes.
enquire: se-el, yes-el; **istakh**bar, yastakhbir.
enrolment: iktitàb.
enter: dakhal, yidkhal; deshsh, yadishsh; khashsh, yakhishsh.
entire: kull.
entirely: bil kullîa; kullish.
entrance: *n.* madkhal.
entreat: iltemes, yeltemis; terejja, yeterejja.
envelope: *v.* ḥawwaṭ, yuḥawwiṭ; *n.* ghalf, *pl.* ghalfat; dharf, dhurûf.
envious: ḥasûd.
environs: nawâhî.
envy: ḥasad.
equal: *adj.* sawa, sûwa, musâwa; *v.* sâwa, yusâwî.
equipment: 'adawàt, muhimmàt.
err: ghalaṭ, yaghlaṭ.
error: ghalaṭ, *pl.* aghlâṭ.
escape: *v.* inhezem, yenhezim; shered, yishrad; *n.* hazîma.
especially: khaṣûṣan, makhṣûṣ.
establish: thebbet, yuthebbit; (put, &c.) ḥaṭṭ, yaḥuṭṭ.
esteem: *v.* (respect) i'tabar, ya'tabir; *v.* (deem) ḥasab, yaḥsab; *n.* i'tibâr, iḥtirâm.
estimate: *v.* khamman, yukhammin.
et cetera: ila âkhirihi; wa enta râyiḥ.
eternal: ebedî.
eternally: ilal ebed.
etiquette: àdàb.
etymology: aṣl el kalima; ishtiqâq.
eunuch: khaṣî, *pl.* khiṣyân; mukhṣî, *pl.* makhâṣî.
Europe: urôpa.
European: uropâwî, *pl.* uropâwiyîn; franjî, frangî, *pl.* franj.
Europeanized: *v.* to become E., tafarnaj, yatafarnaj.
even: *adj.* sawa, *pl.* sûwa; (straight) 'âdil; *adv.* ḥatta.
evening: mesa.
event: ḥâditha, *pl.* ḥawâdith.
ever: (always) daiman; kull waqt; e. g. have you *ever* seen? (not used).
every: kull (with *sing.*).
everywhere: fî kull makàn.
evidence: shahàda; (proof) barhân, *pl.* barâhîn.
evident: wâdhiḥ, bêyyen.
evil: *adj.* sharîr, *pl.* ashrâr; *n.* sharr.
ewer: ibrîq, *pl.* abârîq.
exaggerate: bàlagh, yubàligh.
exaggeration: mubàlagha.
examination: imtiḥân, faḥs.
examine: imtaḥan, yamtaḥin; faḥaṣ, yifḥaṣ.
example: methel, *pl.* amthàl; for example, methelen.
exceedingly: kullish.
excellent: 'âl, fâkhir.
except: *v.* istethna, yestethnî; *prep.* illa.
exception: istithnà.
exchange: *v.* beddel, yubeddil; 'awwadh, yu'awwidh; *n.* tabdîl; (of money) ṣarâfa.
excite: hêyyej, yuhêyyij.
excited: muhêyyej.
excitement: hêyejàn.
excuse: *v.* 'adhdhar, yu'adhdhir; *n.* 'udhr, *pl.* 'udhûr.
excused: mâ'dhûr; (allowed to go) markhûṣ.

exercise: *n.* (physical) riyâdha; (written) tamrîn, *pl.* tamârîn; *v.* take exercise, akhadh riyâdha.
exist: wajad, yojad; in existence, *part.* mawjûd.
existence: wujûd.
exile: *n.* (state) nefî; (person) manfî.
expect: intadhar, yantadhir; istandhar, yastandhir.
expel: ṭarad, yaṭrad.
expense: maṣraf, *pl.* maṣârif.
expensive: ghâli.
experience: ikhtibâr, ikhtibârîa.
experienced: mukhtabir.
explain: fesser, yufessir; wadhdhaḥ, yuwadhdhiḥ.
explanation: tafsîr, tawdhîḥ, sharḥ.
export: *v.* ba'ath, yib'ath.
express: *v.* 'abbar, yu'abbir.
expressly: khuṣûṣan, makhṣûṣ.
expulsion: ṭard.
extend: *v. trans.* madd, yamudd; *v. intrans.* emtedd, yemtedd.
exterior: khârij, burrât.
exterminate: maḥa, yamḥî.
extinguish: ṭaffa, yuṭaffî.
extraordinary: khârij; fôq el 'âda.
extremely: ghâyatan.
eye: 'ain, *pl.* 'uyûn.
eyebrow: ḥàjib, *pl.* ḥawàjib.
eyelid: jifn, *pl.* jifûn.

F

fable: qaṣṣa, *pl.* qaṣaṣ.
face: wajh, *pl.* wujûh.
facing: qubàl, muqâbil.
fact: ḥaqîqa, *pl.* ḥaqâyiq; in fact, bil ḥaqîqa.
factory: karkhâna, fabrîka.
fade: keshef, yikshaf.
faint: *v.* ghâbat er rûḥ, taghib; ughma 'ala, yughma.
faith: îmàn; (belief) i'tiqâd, medhheb.
faithful: amîn, *pl.* amînîn.
fall: waga', yoga'; ṭaḥ, yaṭîḥ; (of city) saqaṭ, yasqaṭ; *n.* suqûṭ.
false: kidhb, kàdhib.
falsehood: kidhb.
fame: shuhra.
family: (household) 'ayela, *pl.* 'ayelàt, 'ayàl (among Moslems refers to women).
famine: jû'; qaḥṭ.
famous: mashhûr, *pl.* mashhûrîn.
fan: maheffa, *pl.* mahàfîf.
fanatical: muta'aṣṣib.
fanaticism: ta'aṣṣub.
far: ba'îd.
farewell: *v.* to bid farewell, tawâda', yatawâda'; *n.* see **good-bye**.
fast: *adj.* (quick) sarî'; (firm) thàbit; *v.* ṣâm, yaṣûm; *n.* ṣôm.
fat: samîn, *pl.* samàn.
fatal: muqtil, mumit.
fate: ejl, qadr.
father: àb (before *gen.*, àbû), *pl.* àbà, àbahat; wàlid.
fault: 'aib, *pl.* 'uyûb; (blame) taqṣîr, quṣûr, sûch.
favour: *v.* fadhdhal, yufadhdhil; *n.* fadhla; in favour of, muwâfiq ila.
fear: *v.* khâf min, yakhâf; *n.* khôf.
feast: *n.* dhiyàfa; 'azîma, *pl.* 'azâyim; (festival) 'îd, *pl.* ayàd.
feather: rîsha, *pl.* rîsh.
February: shabâṭ.
feebl: dha'îf, *pl.* dhu'âf.

feed: *v. trans.* ṭa''m, yuṭa''im; *v. intrans.* taṭa''m, yataṭa''m.
feel: ḥass, yaḥiss; (touch) lemes, yilmas; (be affected by) te-ethther min, yete-ethther.
feeling: ḥiss.
feelings: ḥâsiyàt.
female: *n.* (of animal) nithya, *pl.* nithàya; *adj.* unàthî. See also **woman**.
feminine: mu-ennath.
ferry: mu'êber.
fertile: mukhṣib.
fertility: khuṣb.
festival: 'îd, *pl.* a'yàd.
fever: *n.* sakhûna; *v.* to have fever, sakhkhan, yusakhkhin; fevered *part.* musakhkhan.
few: qalîl; *pl.* qalîlîn.
field: mazra'a, *pl.* mazâri'; battle-field, mêdàn el ḥarb.
fifteen: khamsatâsh, khamstâsh.
fifteenth: khâmis 'asher.
fiftieth: el khamsîn.
fifth: *n.* khums, *pl.* akhmâs; *adj.* khâmis.
fifty: khamsîn.
fig: tîna, *pl.* tîn.
fight: *v.* ta'ârak, yata'ârak; *v.* (battle) taḥârab, yataḥârab; *n.* 'arka, *pl.* 'arkàt.
figure: raqam, *pl.* arqâm.
file: (instrument) mabrad; (of soldiers) ṣaff, *pl.* ṣufûf.
fill: teres, yitras; emla, yimlî.
filled: matrûs.
filth: wasakh, najàsa.
filthy: wasikh.
finally: akhîran.
find: wajad, yojad; lega, yilgî.
fine: *v.* akhadh jiza, ya-khudh; *n.* jiza; *adj.* (not coarse) nâ'im; (excellent) 'âl.
finger: uṣbu', *pl.* aṣâbi', ṣub' ṣabâya'.
finish: *v. trans.* khallaṣ, yukhalliṣ; kemmel, yukemmil.
finished: khalaṣ.
fire: nâr.
fireplace: bukhârî.
firm: *adj.* (strong) thàbit, qawî; (resolute) muṣirr; *n.* (company) shirka, sherika.
first: awwal, *f.* awwalîa, ûla.
firstborn: bikr.
fish: *coll.* semek, semech; *sing.* semka, semcha: *v.* ṣâd semek, yaṣîd
fisherman: semmàk, *pl.* semmàka; ṣayyâd semek, *pl.* sayyâdîn.
fit: *n.* sar', inṣirà'; *adj.* muwâfiq, munàsib.
five: (*with masc.*) khamsa; (*with fem.*) khams.
fix: *v.* (make firm) thebbet, yuthebbit; (appoint) 'ayyan, yu'ayyin.
fixed: mu'ayyan.
flag: bêraq, *pl.* bayâriq; ṣanjaq, *pl.* ṣanàjiq; bandêra, *pl.* bandêràt.
flat: 'âdil, musaṭṭaḥ.
flavour: ṭa'âm.
flay: ṣallakh, yuṣallikh.
flea: bargûth, *pl.* barâghîth.
flee: see **escape**.
flesh: laḥm.
fling: dabb, yadibb; rama, yarmî; shammar, yushammir.
flock: qaṭî'.
flog: baṣṣaṭ, yubaṣṣiṭ; degg, yadigg.
flood: zôd.
flour: ṭaḥîn.
flow: jara, yijrî.
flower: warad, *pl.* wurûd.

flute: mâṣûla.
fly: *v.* ṭar, yaṭîr: *n.* dhabàna, *pl.* dhabbàn.
foal: filu.
fodder: (of cows and sheep) 'alaf; (of horses) 'alîj.
fog: dhabâb.
fold: ṭawa, yaṭwî.
folded: maṭwî.
follow: teba', yitba'.
follower: tàbi', *pl.* tàbi'în.
food: ṭa'âm, ekl.
fool: jàhil, *pl.* juhàl; aḥmaq.
foolish: see **fool**.
foot: (part of body) rijl, *pl.* rijûl, riyûl; (measure) qadam, *pl.* aqdàm.
for: li ejel; khâṭir.
forbid: mena', yimna'.
forbidden: mamnu', yaṣaq.
force: *v.* ajbar, yujbir; *n.* jabr, qûwa.
forehead: gaṣṣa, jabin.
foreign: gharîb, *pl.* ghurabâ; ejnabî, *pl.* ajànib.
foreigner: ejnabî, *pl.* ajànib.
foreleg: rijl qadmanîa; îd.
forenoon: ṣubḥ; gabl edh dhuhr.
forgery: sakhtakâr loghîa.
forget: nesi, yinsa.
forgive: ghafar, yaghfar.
forgiveness: ghafrân; (from men) 'afu.
fork: chingâl, shôka.
form: *v.* shekkel, yushekkil; *n.* shikl, *pl.* ashkàl; ṣûra, *pl.* ṣûar.
former: sàbiq.
formerly: gabl, sàbiqan.
forsake: terek, yitrak.
fort: qal'a, jil'a, *pl.* aqlâ', ajlâ'.
fortieth: el arba'în.
fortify: istaḥkam, yastaḥkim.
fortified: muḥkam, mustaḥkam.
fortification: istiḥkàm.
fortune: ḥadhdh.
fortunate: ḥadhdh zên; ḥadhîdh.
forty: arba'în.
foul: see **filthy**.
found: esses, yu-essis.
foundation: asàs.
fountain: 'ain, *pl.* 'uyûn.
four: (*with masc.*) arba'a; (*with fem.*) arba'.
fourteen: arbatâsh.
fourteenth: râbi' 'asher (*masc.*); râbi'a 'ashra (*fem.*).
fourth: *adj.* râbi'; *n.*, see **quarter**.
fowl: ṭêr, *pl.* ṭuyûr; dujàja, *pl.* dujàj.
fragment: waṣla, *pl.* waṣl.
frame: *n.* (of picture) châhar chûba.
fraternal: akhawî.
free: *adj.* ḥurr, *pl.* aḥrâr; serbest; (gratis) bilàsh, majjànan; *v.* aṭlaq, yuṭliq; fakk, yafukk.
freedom: ḥurrîya.
freely: bi ḥurrîya.
freemason: farmasônî, *pl.* farmasôn.
freeze: jemed, yijmad.
freight: (cargo) ḥiml; (charges) nôl.
French: fransâwî, *pl.* fransâwiyîn.
frequent: *adj.* mukerrer; kathîr yaḥdath.
frequently: kathîr; kathîr marràt.
fresh: (not stale) jadîd, tàzi', ṭari; (of paint) akhdhar.
freshly: jadîd.
friction: tafrîk; (fig.) munàza'a.
Friday: yôm el jum'a.
friend: ṣadîq, *pl.* ṣadqân, aṣdiqâ.

friendly: muḥibb.
friendship: ṣadâqa.
fright: khôf.
frighten: khawwaf, yukhawwif.
frightful: mukhawwif.
fringe: sharshûb, *pl.* sharàshîb.
frivolous: khafîf.
fro: to and fro, e.g. he goes to and fro, yarûḥ wa yîjî.
frog: ʻaqrôq.
from: min, ʻan.
front: *n.* wajh; (of boat) ṣadr; (of book) râs; in front of, qadàm.
frontier: ḥadd, *pl.* ḥudûd.
fronting: muqâbil; mutawajjih ila.
frown: *v.* ʻabas, yaʻbas.
frowning: ʻabûs, muʻabbas.
frozen: jàmid.
frugal: muqtaṣid.
fruit: thamra, *pl.* athmâr; fàkiha, *pl.* fawàkih; (figurative) natîja, ḥâṣil.
fruitful: muthmir, khaṣîb, mukhṣib.
fruitfulness: khuṣb.
fruitless: (lit. and fig.) bila thamra; bila fàyida.
frustrate: baṭṭal, yubaṭṭil.
fry: gala, yaglî; fried, muglî.
frying-pan: ṭâwa.
fuel: (wood) ḥaṭab.
fugitive: farrâr, *pl.* farrârîya.
fulfil: kemmel, yukemmil.
fulfilment: ikmàl.
full: matrûs, malyàn; (of ship) shâḥin, muḥammal; full of, matrûs min; in full, tamàman.
full-dress: hudûm resmîya.
fully: tamàman.
fume: *n.* bukhâr.
fumigate: bakhkhar, yubakhkhir.
fumigation: tabkhîr.
fun: wunsa, kêf; in fun, bi shaqqa; *v.* make fun of, qashmar, yuqashmir.
function: wadhîfa, *pl.* wadhâyif.
fund: (capital) râs màl, ṣarmâya; (place of deposit) ṣandûq.
fundamental: asàsî.
fundamentals: mabàdî.
fundamentally: asàsan.
funds: màlîya.
funeral: jinàza, defn.
funnel: (of ship) medkhena; (instrument) raḥâtî.
funny: (strange) gharîb; (ridiculous) mudhḥik.
fur: shaʻr, faru.
furious: (angry) zaʻlân, mughtâdh; (intense, of fire) shadîd.
furlough: rukhṣa.
furnace: kûra.
furnish: (a house) farash, yafrash; (supply) qaddam, yuqaddim.
furniture: mafrûshàt; agrâdh bêtîya.
furrow: *n.* khaṭṭ, *pl.* khuṭûṭ; ḥafra, *pl.* hafràt.
further: (more distant) abʻad; (in addition) baʻad, ghair hàdha; (additional) ghair; *v.* sâʻad, yusâʻid.
fuse: *v.* laḥam, yilḥam; *n.* fatîla, *pl.* fatàyil.
fuss: tashwîsh.
futile: bila fàyida; ʻabath.
futility: ʻadm fàyida.
future: mustaqbil; in future, fil mustaqbil; future tense, mustaqbil; future life, el âkhira.

G

gain: *v.* ḥaṣṣal, yuḥaṣṣil; rabaḥ, yarbaḥ; keseb, yiksab; gain ground, taqaddam, yataqaddam; *n.* ribḥ, maḥṣûl, kesb.

gait: meshî.
gaiter: leffàfa.
gale: dharba.
gall: *v.* (figurative) kedder, yukeddir; *n.* ṣafra, marrâra.
gallop: *v.* gafa', yagfa'.
gallows: meshneqa, ṣallâba.
gamble: la'ab qumâr, yil'ab.
gambler: qumârchî.
gambling: qumâr.
game: *n.* (play) la'ab; (birds, &c.) ṣêd.
gang: jamâ'a.
gangrene: khazn.
gangway: derj.
gaol: ḥabs.
gap: shaqq.
gape: bâwa', yubâwi'; daḥḥaq, yudaḥḥiq.
garbage: zabàla.
garden: bustàn, *pl.* basàtîn; (small garden) baghcha.
gardener: bustànchî.
gargle: *v.* gharghar, yugharghir; *n.* gharghara.
garlic: thûm.
garment: (under garment) thôb, *pl.* thiyàb. See also **cloak, coat.**
garrison: muḥâfadha.
gas: ghâz.
gasp: *v.* sheheg, yishheg; *n.* shehga.
gate: bàb, *pl.* abwàb.
gather: *v. trans.* jema', yijma'; lemm, yalimm; *v. intrans.* ijtema', yajtamî'.
gauge: *v.* (estimate) khamman, yukhammin; *n.* miqyàs, qiyàs.
gaunt: dha'îf, naḥîf.
gay: farḥân, mustenis.
gaze: *v.* daḥḥak, yudaḥḥik.
gazelle: ghazàl, *pl.* ghazlàn.
gazette: jarîda, *pl.* jaràyid; ghazetta.
gelding: ḥuṣân mukhṣî.
gem: jôhar, *pl.* jawâhir.
gendarme: dhabṭî, *pl.* dhabṭîya.
gendarmerie: zhandarma.
gender: jins, *pl.* ajnàs.
genealogy: silsala.
general: *adj.* 'umûmî; in general, 'umûman; *n.* general commanding, qâid 'âm, mushîr; lieutenant-general, farîq awwal; major-general, amîr liwa; farîq; quarter-master-general, mâmûr el i'âsha.
generally: akthar el awqât.
generation: jîl, *pl.* ajyàl.
generosity: sakhâwa; kerm.
generous: karîm, sakhî.
Genesis: (book of) takwîn.
genitive: ḥâl el idhâfa.
genius: jinnî, *pl.* jinn.
gentle: (meek) mutawâdhi', laṭîf, maskîn.
gently: yawâsh yawâsh.
genuine: ṣaḥîḥ, ḥaqîqî.
genuineness: ṣaḥḥa, ḥaqîqa.
geographical: jôghrâfî.
geography: jôgrâfia.
geology: 'ilm ṭabaqàt el ardh.
geometry: hendesa.
George: jarjis.
germ: jarthûma, *pl.* jaràthîm.
German: allamânî, *pl.* allamân; jarmanî, *pl.* jarman.
Germany: allamânia; bilàd el jarman.
gesture: ḥaraka, *pl.* ḥarakàt.
get: ḥaṣṣal, yuḥaṣṣil; (become) ṣâr, yaṣîr; get to (reach), waṣal, yoṣal.
ghee: dihn.
ghost: khiyàl.
Ghost, Holy: er rûḥ el qudus.
Gibraltar: jebel ṭâriq.
giddiness: dôkha.

giddy: dàyikh.
gift: (present) hadîya, *pl.* hadàya; (mental) môhaba, *pl.* mawàhib.
gild: dhehheb, yudhehhib.
gilded: mudhehheb.
gimlet: mithqab.
gin: (spirit) ʽaraq.
ginger: zanjafîl, zanjabîl.
gipsy: kawli, *pl.* kawâwala.
gird: *v. trans.* ḥazzam, yuḥazzim; *v.* be girt, taḥazzam, yataḥazzam.
girder: jiṣr, *pl.* jisûr.
girdle: *n.* ḥizâm, *pl.* aḥzima, ḥizàmàt.
girl: bint, *pl.* banàt; bunêya, *pl.* bunêyàt.
girt: see **gird**.
girth: (of saddle) baṭân.
gist: khulâṣa, zibda.
give: aʽṭa, yuʽṭî (vulg. anṭa, yanṭî).
given: muʽṭa.
giver: muʽṭî.
giving: ʽaṭa.
glad: farḥân, *pl.* farḥânîn.
gladden: farraḥ, yufarriḥ.
gladly: bi farḥ.
gladness: farḥ.
glance: *v.* iltefet, yeltefit; *n.* lefta.
glare: *n.* lemaʽân.
glaring: (dazzling) làmiʽ.
glass: jàm; (of watch) jàma, balûra; (for drinking) glâs, *pl.* glâsàt; (telescope) darbîn; (magnifying) mukebbira; *adj.* min jàm.
glasses: (spectacles) mandhara, *pl.* mandharàt, manâdhir.
glazed: maṣqûl, madhûn, emles.
glib: (of tongue) talq; khafîf el lisàn.
glimpse: *n.* nadhra.
glitter: *v.* lemaʽ, yilmaʽ.
globe: kurra.
gloom: (fig.) gham, kedr.
gloomy: ḥazîn, *pl.* ḥazînîn (pers.).
glorify: mejjed, yumejjid.
glorious: majîd, jalîl.
glory: mejd; (honour) shuhra.
glossy: maṣqûl, yilmaʽ.
glove: keff, *pl.* kufûf.
glow: *v.* aḥmarr, yaḥmarr.
glue: *n.* ṣamagh, ghira, katîra.
go: râḥ, yarûḥ; dheheb, yidhhab; (of ship, machine, &c.) mesha, yimshî; ishtaghal, yashtaghil.
goal: (purpose) nîya, qaṣd; (in game) ḥadd, *pl.* ḥudûd.
goat: (he-goat) tês, *pl.* tuyûs; (she-goat) ʽanza, *pl.* ʽanzàt.
go-between: wasîṭ.
God: Allâh; (heathen god) ilàh, *pl.* àliha; God willing, in shâ allâh; would to God, ʽalawâh.
going: *n.* rawâḥ, dhahàb.
gold: *n.* dhehb; *adj.* (golden) dhehebî.
goldsmith: ṣâyigh, *pl.* ṣayyâgh.
gone: gone away, râyiḥ; (finished) khalaṣ.
gong: nâqûs, *pl.* nawâqîs.
good: ṭayyib, *pl.* ṭayyibîn; zên, *pl.* zênîn; (useful) mufîd; no good, mâ yinfaʽ; good for, yaṣlaḥ ila; make good (amends for), ʽawwadh, yuʽawwidh.
good-bye: fi amàn Illàh; awdaʽnâkum; sellem ʽalêkum; khâṭirikum.
good-mannered: adîb, *pl.* adîbîn, udaba; mu-eddeb, *pl.* mu-eddebîn.
good-natured: laṭîf, *pl.* laṭâf, laṭîfîn.

goods: agrâdh, amwàl.
goose: baṭṭa, *pl.* buṭûṭ.
gorgeous: fâkhir.
gospel: injîl, *pl.* anàjîl.
gossip: *v.* nemmem, yunemmim; *n.* namîma.
gout: mardh el mulûk.
govern: ḥakam 'ala, yaḥkam.
government: ḥakûma. See also **power**.
governmental: 'âyid ila el ḥakûma.
governor: ḥâkim, *pl.* ḥukkàm.
grab: *v.* qamash, yaqmash; qadhdh, yaqudhdh.
grace: ni'ma.
gracious: laṭîf.
gradation: tadrîj.
grade: daraja, *pl.* darajàt.
gradual: tadrîjî.
gradually: tadrîjan.
graduate: *v.* (from school) ṭala', yiṭla'; akhadh shahàda, yakhudh.
graft: *v.* (arb.) rekkeb, yurekkib.
grain: (in bulk) ṭa'âm, ḥabûbàt; (single seed) ḥabba, *pl* ḥubûb; ḥabbâya, *pl.* ḥabbâyàt.
grammar: naḥu wa ṣarf.
grammatical: naḥwî.
grammatically: naḥwî, naḥwîyan.
gramme: ghrâm, *pl.* ghrâmàt.
granary: makhzan.
grand: 'adhîm.
grandchild: ḥafîd, *pl.* ḥafada.
grandeur: 'adhama.
grandfather: jidd, *pl.* ajdàd.
grandmother: jidda, *pl.* jiddàt.
grant: *v.* a'ṭa, yu'ṭî; *n.* i'âna.
granted: *v.* take for granted, faradh, yafradh.
grapes: 'anab.
grape-vine: tislàga, aṣmâya.
grasp: *v.* lezem, yilzam; qamash, yaqmash; (mentally) derek, yidrak.
grasping: (covetous) ṭammâ', *pl.* ṭammâ'în.
grass: ḥashîsh.
grate: *v.* ḥakk, yaḥukk; *n.* (fireplace) bukhârî.
grateful: mimnûn, *pl.* mimnûnîn; muteshekkir, *pl.* muteshekkirîn.
gratify: serr, yusirr.
grating: (lattice-work) mushebbek.
gratis: bilàsh, majjànan.
gratitude: mimnûnîa.
gratuitous: majàni.
grave: *n.* qabr, qubûr; *adj.* (important) muhimm; (of illness) mukhṭir.
gravel: ḥaṣu.
graveyard: maqbara, *pl.* maqâbir.
gravitate: injedheb, yenjedhib.
gravitation: qûwa jàdhibîya.
gravy: marq.
graze: ra'a, yar'a.
grease: *v.* dehhen, yudehhin: *n.* dihn.
greasiness: dihûna.
greasy: dahîn.
great: 'adhîm, *pl.* 'udhamâ. See also **large**.
greatly: kullish.
greatness: 'adhama.
Greece: bilàd el yônàn.
greedy: (covetous) ṭammâ', *pl.* ṭammâ'în; *v.* be greedy, see **overeat**.
Greek: yônàni, *pl.* yônàn.
green: akhdhar, f. khadhra, *pl.* khudhr; (fresh) ṭarî.
greengrocer: baqqâl, *pl.* baqâqîl.

greenhorn: ghashîm, *pl.* ghushama.
greenness: khudhra, khadhâr.
greens: khadhra, mukhadhdharat, sebzawàt.
greet: sellem 'ala, yusellim; tarahhab bi, yatarahhab.
greetings: tahyiyàt.
grenade: qanbala, *pl.* qanàbil.
grey: ramâdî, eshheb; (of horse, of eyes) azraq, *pl.* zirq; (of hair) abyadh.
greyhound: salûgi, *pl.* salugiyàt; silga, *pl.* sileg.
grief: huzn.
grievance: shekwa, *pl.* shekwàt.
grieve: *v. intrans.* tekedder, yetekedder; inhadham, yanhadhim.
grill: *v.* shawa, yashwî.
grilled: (of meat) mashwî.
grime: wasakh.
grind: (sharpen) senn, yasinn; haddad, yuhaddid; (meal) tahan, yathan.
grindstone: charkh.
grit: (sand) raml.
groan: *v.* wann, yawunn.
grocer: baqqâl, *pl.* baqâqîl.
groceries: baqâla.
groom: sais, *pl.* sayyàs; (bridegroom) 'arîs; *v.* hass, yahiss.
groove: hafra, hazz.
gross: *adj.* (the whole) kull; *n.* (twelve dozen) thnâsh darzen.
ground: *v.* (run aground) sheleh, yishlah; *n.* (land) ardh, *pl.* arâdhî; gâ', *pl.* gî'ân; (basis) asàs; (reason) sebeb, *pl.* asbàb; (place of action) mêdàn.
groundless: bila asàs.
group: *n.* jamâ'a; *v.* jama', yijma'.
grouse: *v.* ishteka, yeshteki.
grow: *v.* nema, yanmu; (increase) zàd, yazîd; (become) şâr, yaşîr; (raise) zara', yizra'.
growl: hammar, yuhammir.
growth: namu.
gruff: 'abûs.
grumble: tadhammar, yatadhammar.
guarantee: *v.* emmen, yu-emmin; keffel, yukeffil; *n.* tàmîn. See also **pledge**.
guard: *v.* hâfadh, yuhâfidh; hâras, yuhâris; naţar, yanţar; *n.* (sentinel) nôbachî, *pl.* nôbachîa; nâţûr, *pl.* nawâţîr; *v.* be on one's **guard**, taqayyad, yataqayyad.
guardian: weli, *pl.* awlia.
guess: *v.* hazar, yahzar.
guest: dhêf, *pl.* dhuyûf.
guest-room: madhîf.
guidance: irshàd.
guide: *v.* dell, yadill; hada, yahdî; sêyyer, yusêyyir; *n.* dalîl, *pl.* adilla; musêyyir, *pl.* musêyyirîn.
guilt: dhenb.
guilty: mudhnib.
guise: ţarz.
gulf: khalîj, *pl.* khuljàn.
gulp: *v.* saraţ, yasraţ.
gum: (for sticking) şamagh; (of the teeth) liththa, *pl.* liththàt.
gun: (rifle) tufka, *pl.* tufek; (cannon) ţôp, *pl.* aţwâp; medfa', *pl.* madàfi'; (machine-gun) rashshàsh, mitralyôz.
gun-barrel: lûla.
gun-boat: manwar, *pl.* manâwir; markab harbî.
gunner: ţôpchî, *pl.* ţôpchîa.
gunpowder: bârûd.
gunsmith: chekmakchî.
gurgle: *v.* baqbaq, yubaqbiq.

gut: maṣrân, *pl.* masârîn.
gutter: sâqia, *pl.* sawâqî.
guttural: ḥalqî.
gymnasium: zôrkhâna.
gymnastics: jimnastîk, pehlawàn.
gypsum: juṣṣ.

H

habit: (custom) 'âda, *pl.* 'awâyid.
habitable: to be habitable, inseken, yensekin.
habitation: mesken, *p.* masàkin.
habitual: 'âdi; (repeated) mukerrer.
habitually: daiman, 'âdatan.
habituate: 'awwad, yu'awwid.
habituated: muta'awwid.
hack: *v.* (cut in pieces) qaṭṭa', yuqaṭṭi'; *n.* (horse) kadîsh, *pl.* kiddesh.
had: (possessed) kàn 'and (see p. 13); *pluperfect*, kàn with past of verb (see p. 30 f.).
haft: maqbadh.
haggard: hazîl.
haggle: ta'âmal, yat'âmal.
haggling: *n.* mu'âmala.
hail: *v.* (call) ṣâḥ, yaṣîh; *n.* (call) ṣiyâḥ; (hailstones) ḥâlûb.
hair: shâ'ra, *pl.* shâ'r; (camel's) wabr.
hair-brush: furcha lish sha'r.
hairdresser: muzêyyin.
hairy: musha'ar; (made of) min sha'r.
half: nuṣf, nuṣṣ.
half-boiled: 'ala nuṣṣ.
half-brother: ibn àb *or* ibn umm.
half-caste: mujennes.
half-dead: nuṣṣ mêyyit.
half-moon: rub 'esh shahr.
half-pay: nuṣṣ ma'âsh.
half-way: nuṣṣ ed darb.
half-yearly: kull sitt ishhur.
hall: (passage) majàz; (large room) ṣâlon, marsaḥ.
halo: dàyira.
halt: *v. trans.* waggaf, yuwaggif; *v. intrans.* wagaf, yogaf; *imp.* (command) ogaf, *pl.* ogafû.
halter: reshma.
ham: fakhdh khanzîr; zhambon.
hammer: *v.* daqq, yaduqq; ṭarraq, yuṭarriq; *n.* châkûch, maṭraqa.
hamper: *n.* sella, *pl.* aslàl; guffa, *pl.* gufaf; *v.* 'aṭṭal, yu'aṭṭil.
hand: yed, *pl.* êdî; îd, *pl.* êdî; my (two) hands, yedêya; (of watch) 'aqrab; *adj.* second-hand, musta'mal; on the one hand, min jeha wâḥida; on hand, ḥâdhir; *v.* (pass) nawwash, yunawwish; have a hand in, ishterek, yeshterik.
hand-breadth: qabdha, qadhba.
hand-cuff: kelebcha.
handed: right, yimnâwî; left, yisrâwî.
handful: ḥafna, *pl.* ḥafnàt.
handkerchief: kefîya, *pl.* kafàfî; mendîl, *pl.* manàdîl.
handle: *v.* (manage) dâr, yadîr; *n.* yed, îd.
hand-mill: raḥa.
handsome: ḥulu, ḥasan, laṭîf, ḥasîn.
handwriting: khaṭṭ.
handy: sehl; (dexterous) musta'idd.
hang: *v. trans.* 'allaq, yu'alliq; (execute) shanaq, yashnaq;

ṣalab, yaṣlab; *v. intrans.* ta'allaq, yata'allaq.
hank: rabṭa, *pl.* rabṭàt.
hanker: ishteha, yeshtehî.
haphazard: shlôn ma kàn.
happen: (come to pass) ṣâr, yaṣîr; jara, yijrî; ittafaq, yattafiq; happen on (encounter) ṣâdaf, yuṣâdif.
happening: *n.* ḥâditha, *pl.* ḥawâdith.
happily: min ḥusn el ḥadhdh.
happy: farḥân, *pl.* farḥânîn; masrûr, *pl.* masrûrîn; sa'îd, *pl.* su'adâ.
harass: az'aj, yuz'ij; shawwash, yushawwish.
harbour: *n.* bandar, *pl.* banàdir; mîna, *pl.* mîyan.
harbour-master: mir baḥr; mudîr el mîna.
hard: (not soft) qawi; (difficult) ṣa'ab, zaḥma, mushkil; *adv.* kathîr, kullish.
harden: *v. trans.* jemmed, yujemmid; qawwa, yuqawwî; *v. intrans.* jemed, yijmad; qawa, yaqwa.
hard-hearted: qâsî el qalb.
hardly: (scarcely) bil kàd; bi ṣa'ûba.
hardness: (opposite of softness) qûwa; (difficulty) ṣa'ûba.
hardship: mashaqqa, shaqqa, 'anqara.
hardy: qawi, *pl.* qawai.
harem: (place of women) ḥarm; (the women) ḥarîm.
harlot: fâḥisha, *pl.* fawâḥish; gaḥba, *pl.* gaḥâb.
harm: *v.* dharr, yadhurr; *n.* dharar, madharra.
harmful: mudharr.
harmless: mâ yu-edhdhi.
harmonium: muzîqa.
harmoniously: bi ittifâq; (without quarrelling) bi maḥabba.
harmonize: *v. trans.* ṭâbaq, yuṭâbiq; *v. intrans.* wâfaq, yuwâfiq.
harness: *v.* dharab takhm, yadhrab; *n.* takhm.
harsh: (rough) khashn; (severe) sert, ṣârim.
harvest: *v.* ḥaṣad, yaḥṣad; *v.* (fruit) jena, yijnî; *n.* ḥaṣâd.
hash: *v.* faram, yafram; *n.* laḥm mafrûm.
haste: 'ajala, 'ajl; in haste, musta'jil.
hasten: *v. trans.* 'ajjal, yu'ajjil; *v. intrans.* ista'jal, yasta'jil.
hastily: bil 'ajl.
hasty: (quick) 'ajûl; (of temper) ḥadd.
hat: shefqa, *pl.* shefqàt; qâpûs.
hatch: *v. intrans.* faqas, yafqas.
hatchet: fàs, qadûm.
hate: *v.* baghadh, yabghadh; kereh, yikrah; *n.* bughdh.
haughty: mutekebbir.
haul: *v.* (a load) jarr, yajurr.
haunch: qaṭ'a.
haunted: maskûn.
have: (possess) 'and, followed by noun or pronominal suffix (see p. 13); perfect, active participle (see p. 30); have on (wearing), làbis; have one do (*v. trans.*), khalla, yukhallî; kellef, yukellif.
hawk: *v.* (peddle) dawwar, yudawwir; *n.* (bird) ṣagr.
hay: qishsh.
haze: dhabâb.
hazy: mudhabbab.
he: hûwa.
head: (part of body) râs, *pl.*

ru-ûs; (top) râs, *pl.* ru-ûs; (chief) ra-îs, *pl.* ru-asâ.
headache: waja' râs.
headed toward: mutawwajih ila.
heading: (of letter, &c.) 'anwàn.
headland: râs, *pl.* ru-ûs.
headman: ra-îs, *pl.* ru-asâ.
head-quarters: markaz, *pl.* maràkiz.
headship: riyàsa.
headstrong: 'anîd.
head wind: hawa 'aks.
heal: *v. trans.* shàfa, yushàfî; *v. intrans.* shefa, yishfa.
healing: *n.* shifa.
health: ṣaḥḥa, 'âfia.
healthful: mufîd liṣ ṣaḥḥa.
healthy: ṣâḥî; muta'âfî; fi ṣaḥa jêyyida.
heap: *v.* kawwam, yukawwim; *n.* kôma, pl. komàt.
hear: sema', yisma'.
hearer: sàmi', *pl.* sami'în.
hearing: (sense of) sem'; (legal) muḥâkama.
hearsay: rawâya.
heart: qalb, *pl.* qulûb; (inner part) baṭn.
heartily: (with appetite) bi ishtihà; (with all the heart) qalbîyan.
heat: *n.* (of summer) ḥarr; (of fire) ḥarâra; (of temper) ḥidda; *v. trans.* aḥma, yuḥmî; *v. intrans.* taḥamma, yataḥamma.
heathen: wathanî, *pl.* wathaniyîn; 'âbid aṣnâm; 'abadat aṣnâm.
heathenish: wathanî; (rude) waḥshî, mutawaḥḥish.
heave anchor: jarr angar, yajurr.
heaven: sema, *pl.* semàwàt.
heavenly: semàwî.
heaves: *n.* (efforts to vomit) sqaw, maqaw.
heavily: bi thuql; thaqîl.
heavy: thaqîl, *pl.* thaqâl.
Hebrew: 'abrânî.
hedge: siyàj.
hedgehog: qanfadh.
heed: bàla, yubàlî; dâr bàl, yadîr.
heedless: ghâfil.
heel: ka'ab.
Hegira: hijra; Mohammedan year, sena hijrîa.
heifer: 'ijl, *pl.* 'ujûl.
height: 'ilu, irtifâ'; (high place) makàn 'âli.
heighten: (raise) 'alla, yu'alli; (increase) zàd, yazîd.
heir: wàrith, *pl.* waratha.
heir apparent: weli 'ahd.
hell: jahennam.
helm: sakkàn.
helmet: (sun) shefqa, *pl.* shefqât.
helmsman: sakkànî; sakkànchî, *pl.* sakkànchîa.
help: *v. trans.* sâ'ad, yusâ'id; 'âwan, yu'âwin; it cannot be helped, mâ luh chàra; it does not help, mâ yufîd; *n.* musâ'ada.
haemorrhage: nezf.
haemorrhoids: bâsûr, *pl.* bawâsîr.
hen: dujàja, *pl.* dujàj.
hence: (from here) min hina, minna; (therefore) li dhàlik.
henceforth: min hessa wa ba'ad; min elàn fa ṣâ'idan.
her: *pron. suffix*, ha or eha (see pp. 13, 18 f., 69).
herb: 'ushb; baql, *pl.* buqûl.
herbage: 'ushb.
herd: *n.* qaṭî'.

herdsman: râ'î, *pl.* ru'ât.
here: hina.
hereafter: *adv.* min hessa wa ba'ad; min elàn fa ṣâ'idan; *n.* el âkhira.
hereby: bi hàdha; bi hel wâsiṭa.
hereditary: irthî, waràthî.
herein: fî hàdha.
hereof: min hàdha; (concerning) 'an hàdha.
heresy: dhalâl.
heretic: khârijî, *pl.* khawârij.
hereto: (thus far) ila hina; ḥatta hina.
heretofore: gabl, sàbiqan.
hereupon: 'ala hàdha.
herewith: ma' hàdha.
heritage: waràtha, irth.
hernia: fataq.
hero: jabbâr, jàsûr.
heroism: shujâ'a.
hers: màleha, màla.
herself: nefsa, nefsuha; by herself, bi waḥda; bi waḥdiha; bi nefsa; bi nefsiha.
hesitate: taraddad, yataraddad.
hesitation: taraddud, tawagguf.
hew: *v.* (with axe) qaṭṭa', yuqaṭṭi'; qaṣṣ, yaquṣṣ; (with chisel) ḥafar, yaḥfar.
hibernate: shetta, yushettî.
hiccough: *v.* tafâwaq, yatafâwaq; *n.* bufâg, bilfâg.
hidden: makhfî, mukhfa, khafî.
hide: akhfa, yukhfî; khabba, yukhabbi; (keep secret) ketem, yiktam.
hideous: bish', qabîḥ.
hiding-place: makhba.
high: 'âli, murtefa'; (wind) 'âli; (expensive) ghâli; high tide, medda 'âlia; *v.* become high, 'ala, ya'lû.
high-born: sharîf el aṣl.
higher: a'la.
highest: el a'la.
high-flown: (of language) faṣîḥ.
highway: darb; darb sulṭânî.
hill: jebel, *pl.* jibàl; (mound) tell, *pl.* tulûl.
hilt: gabdha.
him: *pron. suffix*, uh, h, or hu (see pp. 13, 18 f., 69).
himself: nefsuh, nefsuhu; by himself, bi nefsuh; bi nefsihi; waḥduh; wahduhu; bi dhàtuh; bi dhàtihi.
hind: (part) khalfânî, akhîr.
hinder: 'aṭṭal, yu'aṭṭil; 'âradh, yu'âridh; (prevent), mena', yimna'.
hind-leg: rijl warânîa; *dual* rijlên warânîa.
hindrance: màni', *pl.* mawàni'.
Hindu: hindî, *pl.* hinûd; banyàni, *pl.* banyàn.
Hindustani: hindî.
hinge: *n.* narmada, *pl.* narmadàt.
hint: *v.* ashâr, yushîr; *n.* ishâra, *pl.* ishâràt.
hip: warq, warj.
hire: *v. trans.* kera, yikrî; (labourers, house) istà-jar, yastà-jir; *n.* karwa, îjâr.
hireling: ajîr, *pl.* ujarâ.
hirer: mustà-jir, kàrî.
his: *pron. suffix*, uh, hu (see p. 19); it is his, màluh, màluhu.
historical: târîkhî.
history: târîkh, *pl.* tawârîkh.
hit: *v. trans.* dharab, yadhrab; ṣâb, yaṣîb; daqq, yaduqq; *n.* ṣawâb.
hitch: *v. trans.* (horse) rabaṭ-yarbaṭ; shedd, yashidd; *n.* (hindrance) màni', *pl.* ma, wàni'.

hither: ila hina; hither and thither, râyiḥ jai; ila gadàm wa ila wara.
hitherto: ila hessa; ilal elàn.
hoarse: mabḥûḥ.
hoe: *n.* sakhîn.
hog: khanzîr, *pl.* khanâzîr.
hoist: rafa', yarfa'; 'alla, yu'allî.
hold: (grasp) mesek, yimsak; lezem, yilzam; (detain) waggaf, yuwaggif; (contain) wasa', yasa'; ḥawa, yaḥwî; (defend) dhabaṭ, yadhbaṭ; (keep) dhabaṭ, yadhbaṭ; ḥafadh, yaḥfadh; (office) tawadhdhaf, yatawadhdhaf; (consider) i'taqad, ya'taqid; hold back from, imtena', yamteni'; hold out (last) dâm, yadûm; hold good, jara, yijrî; *n.* (of ship) 'ambâr, *pl.* 'anâbîr; *n.* (grasp) qabdha, meska.
holder: (of property) ṣâḥib, *pl.* aṣḥâb.
holding: *n.* iltizàm, *pl.* iltizàmàt.
hole: nugra, *pl.* nugar; thuqb, *pl.* thuqûb; (in ground) nugra, *pl.* nugar; ḥafra, *pl.* hafràt.
holiday: (vacation) rukhṣa; (school-vacation) ta'ṭîl; (festival) 'îd, *pl.* a'yàd.
holiness: qadàsa.
Holland: hulanda.
Hollander: hulandî.
hollow: fârigh, khâlî; *n.* nugra, *pl.* nugar; *v.* jawwaf, yujawwif.
holy: muqaddas; (of God) quddûs.
holy war: jihàd.
homage: iḥtirâm.
home: (house) bêt, *pl.* buyût; (country) waṭan, *pl.* awṭân; at home, fîl bêt; gâ'id.
home-sick: mutawaḥḥish.
home-sickness: dà waṭn.
homogeneous: mutajànis.
hone: *v.* senn, yasinn; *n.* masinn.
honest: ṣâdiq, *pl.* sâdiqîn; amîn, *pl.* amînîn.
honesty: amàna, ṣadq, emnîa.
honey: 'asal.
honorary: fakhrî.
honour: *v.* (respect) iḥtarem, yaḥtarim; ekrem, yukrim; (accept and pay) i'taber, ya'tabir; *n.* (respect) iḥtirâm, ikrâm; (good name) sharf, nàmûs; (title) laqab, nîshàn; in honour of, ikrâman ila; on my honour, bi sharfî.
honourable: (man) mu'tabar; (action) sharîf.
hoof: ḥâfir, *pl.* ḥawâfir.
hook: *v.* chengel, yuchengil; *n.* chingâl, *pl.* chanàgîl; (fish-hook) shuṣṣ.
hop: qamaz, yaqmaz.
hope: *v.* raja, yarjû; te-emmel, yete-emmel; *n.* rija, eml; it is hoped that, el eml an; el mà-mûl an.
hopeless: (despairing) mà-yûs; (without hope) maqṭû' er rija; gâṭi' er rija.
horizon: 'ufq.
horizontal: 'âdil.
horn: (of animal) qarn, *pl.* qurûn; (musical) bûrî, *pl.* bûriyàt.
horrible: mukhîf.
horrify: khawwaf, yukhawwif; ar'ab, yur'ib.
horse: ḥuṣân, *pl.* ḥuṣn, khêl.
horseback: ràkib, *pl.* rakibîn; khayyàl, *pl.* khayyàla.
horse-dealer: ḥuṣṣân, *pl.* ḥuṣṣâna.
horse-dung: rôdh, serjîl.

horseman: khayyàl, *pl.* khayyàla.
horsemanship: rukb el khêl.
horse-power: qûwat ḥuṣân.
horse-race: sharṭ, musàbaqa, muṭârada.
horse-shoe: na'al.
horse-shoer: na'al bend.
hose: (leather tube) anbûb; (stockings) jawàrîb.
hospitable: muḥibb lidh dhêf.
hospital: khastakhâna, *pl.* khastakhânàt; musteshfa, *pl.* musteshfiyàt.
hospitality: dhiyàfa; give hospitality, adhâf, yudhîf; take hospitality, dhâf, yadhîf.
host: ṣâḥib el maḥall; (great number) khalq, jamhûr; (sacramental) qarbân.
hostile: mudhâdd, dhudd.
hostility: 'adâwa, dhaddîya.
hot: ḥârr, *pl.* ḥârrîn.
hotel: loqanda, ôtel.
hotly: (with temper) bi ḥidda; (violently) shadîd.
hound: *n.* salûgî, *pl.* salûgiyàt; silga, *pl.* sileg.
hour: sâ'a, *pl.* sâ'àt.
hourly: kull sâ'a.
house: bêt, *pl.* byût, buyût; ḥôsh, *pl.* ḥawâsh; House of Commons, bêt en nawâb; House of Lords, bêt el umarâ; mejlis ashrâf.
house-keeping: tadbîr el bêt.
how: kêf, chêf, shlôn; how many, kem, chem (with *sing.*); how much, shqadr, shqad, ê miqdâr; how far, shqad ba'îd; how long, shqad.
however: kêf mâ kàn, shlôn mâ kàn; however big, mahma kàn kabîr.
howl: *v.* ṣâḥ, yaṣîḥ; ṣêyyeḥ, yuṣêyyiḥ; *n.* ṣiyâḥ.
hug: *v.* (embrace) 'ânaq, yu'âniq; (keep close to) lezem, yilzam.
huge: 'adhîm, jasîm.
hull: *v.* (husk rice) hebbesh, yuhebbish; *n.* (of rice) gishr; (of ship) jised.
hum: *v.* denden, yudendin.
human: *adj.* besherî; the human race, el jins el besherî.
humble: mutawâdhi'; nefsuh ṣaghîra.
humble: *v.* dhellel, yudhellil.
humbly: bi tawâdhu'.
humdrum: *adj.* mumill.
humid: nedi, murṭib.
humidity: raṭûba.
humility: tawâdhu'.
humorous: mudhḥik.
humour: *v.* radhdha, yuradhdhî; ṭayyab khâṭir, yuṭayyib; *n.* (temper) khulq, ṭab'; good humour, bashàsha.
hump: (deformity) ḥadba; (of camel) sanàm; (of bullock) tibba.
hump-backed: aḥdab.
hundred: mîa (mîat before vowel).
hundredth: el mîa.
Hungarian: majârî.
Hungary: majâristàn.
hunger: jû'.
hungry: jô'ân, *pl.* jô'ânîn, jowâ'a.
hunt: *v.* ṣâd, yaṣîd; (search for) dawwar, yudawwir; fettesh 'ala, yufettish.
hunter: ṣayyâd, *pl.* ṣayyâdîn.
hunting: *n.* ṣêd.
hurl: rama, yarmî; shammar, yushammir.
hurricane: dharba.
hurriedly: bi 'ajala.

hurry: *n.* isti'jàl; in a hurry, musta'jil; *v.*, see **hasten.**
hurt: *v. trans.* 'awwar, yu-'awwir; *v. intrans.* waja', yoja'; *n.* waj'.
hurtful: mudharr.
husband: zôj, *pl.* azwàj; rejul, *pl.* rijàl; *vulg.* rijàl (riyàl), *pl.* rijàjîl (riyàyîl).
hush: *v. trans.* sekket, yusek-kit; *v. intrans.* seket, yiskat; *n.* sukût; *interjection,* iskat, huss.
husk: gishr, *pl.* gushûr; *v.* (husk rice) hebbesh, yuhebbish.
husky: (of voice) mabḥûḥ.
hussar: khayyàl, *pl.* khayyàla.
hut: (mat) ṣarîfa, *pl.* ṣarâyif; (mud) bêt ṭîn, *pl.* byût ṭîn.
hybrid: mujennes.
hydrophobia: keleb.
hygiene: ḥifdh es ṣaḥḥa.
hygienic: ṣaḥḥi.
hymn: tarnîma, *pl.* tarnîmàt.
hyphen: shakhṭa.
hypnotism: tanwîm.
hypochondria: sôda.
hypocrisy: nifâq, marâyàt.
hypodermic: taḥt el jild; needle, ibra.
hypothesis: fardh.
hypothetical: iftirâdhî.

I

I: (pers. pron.) ana.
ice: thelej.
iceberg: jebel thelej.
icecream: dandarma.
idea: fikr, *pl.* afkâr; rai, *pl.* ârâ.
ideal: *adj.* kema làzm; *n.* (person) muqteda; (thing) ghardh.
identical: (alike) mithl ba'dh; the identical one, nefs el.
identify: 'araf, ya'raf.
identity: dhàtîya.
i. e.: ya'ni.
idiom: iṣṭilâḥ, *pl.* iṣṭilâḥàt.
idiomatic: iṣṭilâḥi.
idiomatically: iṣṭilâḥîan.
idiot: mukhabbal.
idle: (not employed) baṭṭâl, *pl.* baṭṭâlîn; (lazy) keslàn, *pl.* kesàla, keslànîn; tembil, *pl.* tenàbil; (unprofitable) bâṭil.
idleness: (laziness) kesl.
idol: ṣanam, *pl.* aṣnâm.
idolator: 'âbid aṣnâm, *pl.* 'abadat aṣnâm.
idolatry: 'abàdat aṣnâm.
if: idha, in kàn, law (see p. 106); (introducing condition contrary to fact) law kàn (see p. 106); if it had not been for, law la (see p. 106).
ignite: *v. trans.* sha'al, yish'al; *v. intrans.* ishta'al, yashta'il.
ignition: ishti'âl.
ignoramus: jàhil, *pl.* juhàl.
ignorance: jahàla.
ignorant: *adj.* jàhil; (uninformed) ghashîm, *pl.* ghu-shamâ; *v.* to be ignorant of, jehel, yijhal.
ignore: mâ dâr bàl, yadîr.
ill: *adj.* (sick) marîdh, *pl.* mar-dha; waj'ân, *pl.* waj'ânîn; kêfsiz; khasta; (bad) redi; mt zên; *n.* (evil) sû; *v.* to be ill, tamarradh, yatamarradh.
ill-bred: min dûn tarbiya; tarbiyatsiz.
ill-defined: ghair wâdhiḥ.
illegal: ghair jàyiz; khilàf el qânûn.
illegally: mukhâlif el qânûn.
illegible: mâ yanqari.
ill-fated: mashûm, ogharsiz.

illiterate: ummî; mâ ya'raf yaqra wa yiktab.
ill-luck: naḥs; sû ḥadhdh.
illness: mardh, *pl.* amrâdh; waj', *pl.* awjâ'.
ill-omened: mashûm.
ill-timed: mû fî waqtuh.
ill-treat: ahàn, yuhîn.
ill-treatment: sû mu'âmala.
illumination: tanwîr.
illusion: takhayyul.
illustrate: (make clear) wadhdhaḥ, yuwadhdhiḥ; (with pictures) ṣawwar, yuṣawwir.
illustrated: (made clear) muwadhdhaḥ; (with pictures) muṣawwar.
illustration: (example) methl, *pl.* amthàl; (picture) taṣwîr.
illustrious: mashhûr, shahîr.
image: (likeness) ṣûra, *pl.* ṣûwar; (idol) ṣanam, *pl.* aṣnâm; (statue) timthàl, *pl.* tamàthîl.
imagination: (faculty) takhayyul; (false idea) wahm.
imagine: taṣawwar, yataṣawwar; takhayyal, yatakhayyal.
imbecile: see **idiot.**
imbed: nezzel, yunezzil.
imbibe: resekh fîl fikr, yarsakh.
imitate: qallad, yuqallid.
imitation: taqlîd.
immaterial: (unimportant) ghair muhimm.
immature: (person) ghair bàligh; (thing) nâqiṣ.
immeasurable: la yuqâs; la yuḥadd.
immediate: (present) ḥâlî; (without anything intervening) min dûn wâsiṭa.
immediately: bis sâ'a; hessa; ḥâlan.
immense: 'adhîm.
immensely: kullish, kathîr.
immerse: ghaṭṭas, yughaṭṭis.
immigrant: muhàjir, *pl.* muhàjirîn.
immigration: muhàjara.
immobile: la yataḥarrak.
immoderate: khârij; fôq el ḥadd.
immodest: safîh, *pl.* sufaha.
immodesty: qillat el ḥaya.
immoral: fàsid, *pl.* fàsidîn.
immorality: fasàd, fujûr.
immortal: la yamût; khâlid.
immortality: khulûd.
immovable: la yataḥarrak.
immunity: mu'âf.
impair: dharr, yadhurr.
impart: a'ṭa, yu'ṭî.
impartial: min dûn maḥâbàt.
impassable: mâ aḥad yafût bi.
impassionate: ḥârr.
impatience: 'adm ṣabr.
impatient: bila ṣabr.
impede: 'aṭṭal, yu'aṭṭil.
impediment: màni', *pl.* mawàni'.
impel: sâq, yasûq; ḥethth, yaḥithth.
impend: qarab, yaqrab.
impending: qarîb.
impenetrable: (substance) mâ yanthaqib.
impenitent: mâ muteneddim.
imperative: (mood) amr; (necessary) dhurûrî, làzim.
imperceptible: mâ yuḥass bi.
imperfect: *adj.* nâqiṣ; *n.* (tense, as in Greek) mâdhî.
imperfection: naqṣ, nuqṣân, naqîṣa, 'aib.
imperial: sulṭânî.
imperil: ḥaṭṭ fîl khaṭr, yaḥuṭṭ.
impertinent: waqîḥ, *pl.* wuqâḥ, wuqqaḥ.

impetuous : ḥâdd el mizàj.
impetus : qûwa dàfi'a.
implant : (figuratively) gharas, yaghras.
implement : àla, *pl.* àlàt.
implicate : tehem, yit-ham.
implication : istintàj.
implicit : (e. g. of confidence) tàmm.
implicitly : bi tamàm.
implore : iltemes, yeltemis.
imply : (signify) tadhamman, yatadhamman.
impolite : mû adîb; ghair adîb; khashan.
impolitic : ghair siyàsî.
import : *v. trans.* jeleb, yijlab; *n.* jelb; *n.* imports, dâkhilàt, wâridàt.
importance : ahemmiya; *v.* attach importance, istahamm, yastahimm.
important : muhimm.
importer : jàlib.
importune : laḥḥ, yaluḥḥ; lejj, yalijj.
importunity : ilḥaḥ.
impose : ḥaṭṭ, yaḥuṭṭ; wadha', yodha'; impose condition, ashraṭ, yushriṭ; impose upon (deceive) ghashsh, yaghishsh.
imposing : mu-eththir.
imposition : (placing) wadh'; (deceit) ghishsh.
impossibility : 'adm imkàn.
impossible : mâ mumkin; muḥâll.
impost : resm, *pl.* rusûm.
impostor : ghashshàsh, kadhdhàb.
impotent : 'âjiz.
impoverish : faqqar, yufaqqir.
impracticable : mâ yimkin.
imprecation : masebba, tashtûm.
impregnable : mâ yan-akhadh.
impress : *v.* (force) sakhkhar, yusakhkhir; (fix on mind) rassakh fìdh dhihn, yurassikh.
impression : (influence) tathîr; (idea) fikr, *pl.* afkâr.
impressive : mu-eththir.
imprison : ḥabas, yaḥbas.
imprisonment : ḥabs.
improbable : mâ muḥtemel.
improper : ghair làyiq; mâ munàsib.
improperly : khilàf el làzm.
improve : *v. trans.* ḥassan, yuḥassin; aṣlaḥ, yuṣliḥ; *v. intrans.* ḥasan, yaḥsan; (recover from illness) ṭâb, yaṭîb.
improvement : (advance) taqaddum; e.g. a great improvement, iṣlâḥ; taqaddum.
improvident : mitlàf, mubedhdhir.
imprudent : mihdhâr.
impudent : lisàn ṭawîl; waqîḥ
impugn : kedhdheb, yukedhdhib.
impulse : sebeb muḥarrik.
impulsive : sarî' et te-eththur.
impunity : min dûn qaṣâṣ.
impure : (dirty) wasikh; (ceremonially) nejis; (morally) fàsid.
impurity : najàsa.
imputation : madhemma; (charge) tuhma.
impute : neseb ila, yinsab.
in : fî, bi; in order to, ḥatta, likê; in case, idha, in kàn (see also **if**).
inability : 'ajz; 'adm iqtidâr.
inaccessible : mâ yoṣal ila.
inaccurate : mâ madhbûṭ; mâ mudaqqaq.
inaction : baṭâla.
inactive : wâgif.

inadequate: ghair kàfi; mâ yikfî.
inadmissible: mâ maqbûl.
inane: fàhî, fârigh.
inanimate: mâ mutaḥarrik; jàmid.
inapplicable: mâ muṭabbaq.
inappropriate: ghair làyiq.
inasmuch: mà dàm; bima ann.
inattentive: ghâfil.
inaudible: mâ yansami'.
inaugurate: (begin) ibteda fî, yebtedi; (into office) naṣab, yanṣab.
inborn: gharîzî, ṭabî'î.
incalculable: la yuḥsab wa la yu'add.
incapable: mâ muqtedir.
incarnate: *adj.* mujessem, mujessed.
incautious: ghâfil.
incense: 'ûd, bakhûr.
incentive: tashwîq; sebeb muḥarrik.
incessant: mustamirr.
incessantly: bila inqiṭâ'.
inch: inch, *pl.* inchàt.
incident: *n.* ḥâditha, *pl.* ḥawâdith; wâqi'a, *pl.* waqâyi'.
incidentally: ṣadfatan.
incinerator: dôgha, *pl.* duwagh.
incite: heyyej, yuheyyij.
incitement: sebeb.
incivility: qillat edeb.
inclination: mêl.
incline: *v. trans.* amàl, yumîl; *v. intrans.* màl, yamîl; *n.* (up) ṣa'da; (down) nezla.
inclined: màyil.
inclose: *v. trans.* ḥawwaṭ, yuḥawwiṭ; (as in letter) leff, yaliff.
inclosure: (place) ḥoṭa; in letter, marsûl ṭêhi.
include: ḥawa, yaḥwî; shemel, yishmal.
included: dâkhil; (reckoned) maḥsûb.
incoherent: mukharbaṭ.
incombustible: mâ yashta'il.
income: wàridàt.
incomparable: la lahu nadhîr.
incomparably: bila qiyàs.
incompatible: mudhâdd.
incompetent: mâ muqtedir.
incomplete: nâqiṣ.
incomprehensible: mâ yenfehem.
inconceivable: la yutaṣawwar.
inconsiderate: ghair mubàlî.
inconsistent: mughâyir.
inconstant: mutaqallib.
inconvenient: mâ muwâfiq.
incorporate: *v.* (include) dhamm, yadhumm.
incorrect: ghalaṭ, yaghnish, ghalṭân.
increase: *v. trans.* and *intrans.* zàd, yazîd; *n.* izdiyàd, ziyàda.
increasingly: bi izdiyad.
incredible: muḥâll; la yuṣaddaq.
incriminate: tehhem, yutehhim.
incrimination: tuhma.
inculcate: gharaz, yaghraz.
incumbent: mutawadhdhaf.
incur: expense, kellef nefsuh, yukellif; danger, jarr khaṭr, yajurr.
incurable: la luh shifa.
indebted: madyûn ila.
indebtedness: dên.
indecent: mukhâlif el àdàb.
indeed: (really) bil ḥaqîqa; (exclamation) yâ bâ.
indefinite: (uncertain) mâ ma'lûm; (unlimited) mâ maḥdûd.

indefinitely: (endlessly) ilal ebed; bila ḥadd.
indemnify: 'awwadh, yu'awwidh.
indent: ṭalab, yaṭlab.
independence: istiqlàl.
independent: mustaqill; ḥurr, *pl.* aḥrâr.
independently: (alone) kull men bi waḥduh; (independently of one) min dûn mushâwara.
indescribable: la yûṣaf.
indeterminate: ghair mafayyan.
index: (pointer) dalîl; (table of contents) fihrist.
India: el hind; hindustàn.
Indian: hindî, *pl.* hinûd.
indicate: dell, yadill; bêyyen, yubêyyin.
indication: 'alàma, *pl.* 'alàmàt.
indict: ethem, yut-him.
indifference: ihmàl.
indifferent: (careless) la yubàlî; (ordinary) dûnî; (all the same) kulluh wâḥid.
indigestion: jàli.
indignant: za'lân, mughtâdh.
indiscriminately: min dûn tamyîz.
indispensable: làzm, làzim, dharûrî.
indisposed: (ill) munḥarif el mizàj; (disinclined to) mutanàfir min.
indistinct: (confused) mushawwash; (hardly discernible) mâ yanshàf.
indistinguishable: la yumêyyez.
individual: *adj.* shakhṣî; *n.* nefer, *pl.* anfâr; shakhṣ, *pl.* ashkhâṣ.
individually: wâḥid wâḥid; ferd ferd.
indorse: (on paper) dhahhar, yudhahhir; jêyyer, yujêyyir; (support) sened, yisnad.
indorsement: jîrû; (sanction) ridhâ, taṣdîq.
induce: raghghab, yuraghghib; qanna', yuqanni'; (produce) sebbeb, yusebbib.
inducement: targhîb, tashwîq, sebeb.
indulge: (gratify) semaḥ, yismaḥ.
indulge in: (e. g. pleasure) inhamaq, yanhamiq.
indulgent: muyessir.
industrial: ṣanâ'i.
industrious: mujtehid.
industry: (diligence) ijtihàd; (trade) ṣan'a, *pl.* ṣanâyi'.
ineffective: min dûn tà-thîr.
inefficient: 'âjiz; mâ muqtedir.
ineligible: munàsib.
inequality: ikhtilàf.
inestimable: la yuthemmen.
inevitable: la khalâṣ minhu.
inexcusable: min dûn 'udhr.
inexhaustible: la lahu nihàya.
inexpedient: mâ munàsib; mâ muwâfiq.
inexperienced: mâ mukhtebir; ghashîm.
inexplicable: la yufesser
inexpressible: la yu'abbar.
infallible: ma'ṣum min el khaṭa.
infancy: ṣughr.
infantry: piyàda.
infection: iṣâba.
infectious: sàri, mu'dî.
infer: istentej, yestentij.
inference: istintàj.
inferior: dûn, edna; (unimportant) dûnî.
infest: (road) lezem, yilzam.

infidel: kàfir, *pl.* kuffâr.
infidelity: kufr.
infinite: bila ḥadd; ghair maḥdûd.
infinitive: maṣdar.
inflame: heyyej, yuheyyij.
inflamed: (of wound) multehib.
inflammable: yushta'al, yaḥtariq.
inflammation: (of wound) iltihàb.
inflate: nafakh, yanfakh.
inflect: (*gram.*) ṣarraf, yuṣarrif.
inflexion: (*gram.*) taṣrîf.
inflict: (punishment) qâṣaṣ, yuqâṣiṣ.
influence: *v. trans.* qanna', yuqanni'; *n.* (power) nufûdh, saṭwa; *n.* (effect) ta-thir.
influential: muteneffidh; ṣâḥib saṭwa.
inform: akhbar, yukhbir.
informal: ghair resmî.
informally: ghair resmîyan.
information: khabr; (knowledge) ma'rifa.
informed: mukhtebir.
infraction: kesr, mukhâlafa.
infrequent: nàdir.
infringe: ta'adda, yata'adda.
ingenious: ḥâdhiq, *pl.* ḥâdhiqîn.
ingenuity: ḥadhâqa, dhekà.
ingratitude: 'adm mimnûnîa; nekràn ni'ma.
ingredient: juz, *pl.* ajzà.
inhabit: seken, yiskan.
inhabitable: yensekin.
inhabitant: sàkin, *pl.* sakkàn.
inhabited: maskûn.
inhale: teneffes, yeteneffes.
inherent: gharîzî.
inherently: ṭab'an.
inherit: warath, yorath.
inheritance: irth, waràtha, mîràth.
inhospitable: mâ muḥibb lidh dhêf.
inhuman: waḥshî; min dûn insànîa.
inimical: mudhâdd ila.
inimitable: la luh nadhîr.
iniquitous: khabîth, sharîr.
iniquity: sharr, ithm.
initial: *n.* ijàz; *v.* keteb ijàz, yiktab; *adj.* awwal, awwalî.
initiation: ta'lîm el uṣûl.
initiative: mubàdàt; take the initiative, kàn el awwal, yakûn.
inject: ṭa''m, yuṭa''im.
injection: (subcutaneous) dharab ibra; (anal.) dharab ḥaqna.
injudicious: min dûn baṣîra.
injunction: amr, *pl.* awâmir.
injure: dharr, yadhurr; àdha, yu-edhdhî; (hurt) 'awwar, yu'awwir.
injurious: mudharr.
injury: dharar, madharra.
injustice: dhulm.
ink: ḥibr.
inkstand: dawâya.
inkling: ishâra.
inland: dâkhil.
inlay: *v.* nezzel fî, yunezzil.
inmost: bâṭinî.
inn: khân, *pl.* khânàt.
innate: gharîzî.
innately: gharîzîyan, ṭab'an.
inner: dâkhilî.
innings: (turn) nôba.
innkeeper: khânchî, *pl.* khânchîa.
innocence: barà-a.
innocent: beri; (simple) basîṭ, meskîn.
innocently: bila ma'rifa.
innumerable: la yu'add.
inoculate: laqqaḥ, yulaqqiḥ.
inoculation: talqîḥ.
inoffensive: mâ yadhurr.

inopportune: mû fî waqtuh.
inorganic: jàmid.
inquire: se-el, yes-el; istakhbar, yastakhbir; inquire into, fettesh ʻala, yufettish.
inquiry: suwàl, istikhbâr.
insane: majnûn, *pl.* majànîn; mukhabbal, *pl.* makhâbîl; mukhtell esh shuʻûr.
insanity: junûn, khabâl.
insatiable: la yishbaʻ.
inscribe: see **write, engrave.**
inscription: kitàba, kitba.
insect: baqq; ḥashara, *pl.* ḥasharàt.
insecure: mû ma-mûn.
insensible: bila ḥass.
insert: dakhkhal, yudakhkhil.
inside: dâkhil, jôwa.
insight: iṭṭilâʻ.
insignia: niyàshîn.
insignificant: min dûn ahemmîya.
insincere: munàfiq.
insipid: fàhî.
insist: aṣarr, yuṣirr.
insistence: iṣrâr.
insolence: waqâḥa.
insolent: waqîḥ, *pl.* waqqaḥ.
insoluble: la yanḥall.
insolvency: iflàs.
insolvent: muflis, maksûr.
inspect: fettesh, yufettish.
inspection: teftîsh.
inspector: mufettish, *pl.* mufettishîn.
inspiration: waḥî, ilhàm; (impetus) taḥrîdh.
inspire: (give impetus to) ḥarradh, yuḥarridh.
inspiring: muḥarridh.
instability: ʻadm thabàt.
instalment: qasṭ, *pl.* aqsâṭ.
instance: (example) methel; (occurrence) ḥâditha; for instance, methelen; in the first instance, fî awwal el amr.
instant: *n.* (moment) daqîqa; this instant (immediately) ḥâlan.
instantaneous: fî waqtuh; fî sâʻatuh.
instantly: hessa.
in statu quo: kema kàn.
instead of: ʻiwadh; ʻiwadhan ʻan; (with verb) ʻiwadhma.
instigate: ḥethth, yaḥithth; waswas, yuwaswis.
instigation: taḥrîk.
instigator: muḥarrik.
instinct: fiṭra.
instinctively: fiṭratan.
institute: *v.* (establish) esses, yu-essis; (appoint) ʻayyan, yuʻayyin.
institution: (act of establishing) tà-sîs; (society) jamʻîa.
instruct: (teach) ʻallam, yuʻallim; (command) amar, ya-mur.
instruction: (teaching) taʻlîm; (order) amr, *pl.* awâmir.
instructive: mufîd.
instructor: muʻallim.
instrument: àla, *pl.* àlàt; (means) wâsiṭa, *pl.* wasâyiṭ; (document) warqa, *pl.* awrâq.
instrumental: (aiding in) wâsiṭa.
insubordination: ʻadm ṭâʻa; ʻaṣyàn.
insufferable: la yataḥammal.
insufficient: mû kàfi; ghair kàfi; qâṣir.
insulate: lebbes, yulebbis.
insulation: telbîs.
insulator: marfaʻ.
insult: *v.* ahàn, yuhîn; ḥaqqar, yuḥaqqir; *n.* ihàna, taḥqîr.

insulting: muhîn, muḥaqqir.
insuperable: la yughlab.
insurance: tà-mîn, sagurto, dhamân.
insure: sôgar, yasôgar.
insurrection: thôra, ikhtilàl.
intact: 'ala ḥâluh.
integrity: (uprightness) istiqâma; (wholeness) ibqâ.
intellect: 'aql, *pl.* 'uqûl; dhihn, *pl.* adhhàn.
intellectual: 'aqlî; (well informed) fahîm.
intellectually: 'aqlan, 'aqlîyan.
intelligence: (understanding) 'aql, fehem; (news) akhbâr.
Intelligence Department: dàyirat el mukhâbaràt.
intelligent: 'âqil, *pl.* 'uqqâl; fahîm, *pl.* fahîmîn.
intelligently: bi 'aql.
intelligible: mafhûm, yenfehim.
intemperance: (drunkenness) sukr.
intemperate: (addicted to drink) see **drunkard**; intemperate language, kalàm khârij.
intend: qaṣad, yaqṣad; 'azam, ya'zam; nawa, yanwî.
intended: maqṣûd.
intense: qawî; shadîd.
intensely: kullish; bi shidda.
intensify: shedded, yusheddid.
intensity: shidda.
intention: maqṣad, *pl.* maqâṣid; qaṣd; niyya.
intentional: bi qaṣd.
intentionally: qaṣdan, 'amdan.
intercede: tawassaṭ, yatawassaṭ; shefa', yishfa'.
intercession: tawassuṭ, shafâ'a.
intercessor: wasîṭ, shafî'.
interchange: *v.* tabàdal, yatabàdal; *n.* tabàdul, mubàdala.
interchangeably: bi tabàdul.
intercourse: mukhâlaṭa, mu'âshara.
interest: *v.* (concern) khaṣṣ, yakhuṣṣ; *n.* (advantage) menfa'a; (concern) maṣlaḥa; (connexion) 'alâqa; (on money) faidh; *v.* take interest in, ihtemm, yehtemm.
interesting: (cannot be adequately expressed in Arabic).
interfere: taḥarrash, yataḥarrash; ta'âradh, yata'âradh.
interference: taḥarrush, ta'arrudh, mu'âradha.
interim: ithnà.
interior: *n.* dâkhil; department of the interior (i. e. Home Office), dâkhilîya; *adj.* dâkhilî.
interline: keteb bên es suṭûr, yiktab.
intermarriage: tazàwuj.
intermarry: tazàwaj, yatazàwaj.
intermediate: mutawassiṭ.
intermittent: mutaqaṭṭa'.
internal: dâkhilî.
international: duwalî.
interpose: *v. intrans.* tawassaṭ, yatawassaṭ.
interposition: tawassuṭ.
interpret: (translate) tarjam, yutarjim; (explain) fesser, yufessir.
interpretation: (explanation) tefsîr.
interpreter: tarjamàn, *pl.* tarjamànîya.
interrogation: istifhàm.
interrogative: istifhàmî.
interrupt: (in work) 'aṭṭal, yu-

'aṭṭil; (in speech) qaṭa' kalàm, yaqṭa'.

(If necessary to interrupt another's speech, the proper ejaculation is: kalàmek fî khâṭirik.)

interruption: (hindrance) 'âyiq, 'awâyiq; màni', *pl.* mawàni'.

intersect: qaṭa', yaqṭa'.

interval: mudda; in the interval, fî ithnà dhàlik; at intervals, min waqt ila waqt.

intervene: tawassaṭ, yatawassaṭ; tadâkhal, yatadâkhal.

intervention: tawassuṭ, tadâkhul.

interview: *v.* wàjah, yuwàjih; *n.* muwàjaha.

intestines: maṣârîn.

intimacy: ṣuḥba, ṣadâqa.

intimate: *v.* ashâr ila, yushîr; *adj.* muḥibb, mukhlis.

intimidate: khawwaf, yukhawwif.

intimidation: takhwîf.

into: fî.

intolerable: mâ yataḥammal.

intolerance: ta'aṣṣub.

intolerant: muta'aṣṣib.

intoxicate: sekker, yusekkir.

intoxicated: sakrân, *pl.* sakâra.

intoxication: sikr.

intransitive: làzim.

intrench: taḥaṣṣan, yataḥaṣṣan

intrenchments: *n. pl.* khanâdiq, istiḥkàmât.

intricate: ghawîs.

intrigue: *n.* dasîsa, *pl.* dasàyis; *v.* desses, yudessis; eften yuftin.

intriguer: mudessis, muftin.

intrinsic: haqîqî.

introduce: (bring in) dakhkhal, yudakhkhil; (make known) 'arraf, yu'arrif.

introduction: (bringing in) idkhâl; (making known) ta'rîf; (preface) muqaddama; letter of introduction, tawṣiya.

intrude: ta'adda, yata'adda.

intrust: emmen, yu-emmin.

inundate: gharraq, yugharriq.

inundation: feyadhân.

invade: dakhal, yidkhal.

invalid: (null) bâṭil; (ill) 'alil.

invalidate: baṭṭal, yubaṭṭil; fesekh, yifsakh.

invaluable: la yuthemmen.

invariable: la yataghayyar.

invariably: daiman.

invasion: dukhûl.

invent: ikhtara', yakhtari'.

invention: ikhtirâ', *pl.* ikhtirâ'àt.

inventory: qaima.

invert: qalab, yaqlab.

inverted: maqlûb.

invest: with authority, wadhdhaf, yuwadhdhif; money, shaghghal flûs, yushaghghil; ḥaṭṭ flûs, yaḥuṭṭ.

investigate: fettesh, yufettish; faḥaṣ, yifḥaṣ.

investigation: teftîsh, taḥqîq.

investment: tajâra.

inveterate: muzmin.

invigorate: qawwa, yuqawwî.

invincible: mâ yanghalib.

inviolable: la yumess.

inviolate: sàlim.

invisible: mâ yanshàf; ghair mandhûr.

invitation: da'wa.

invite: da'â, yad'û; (to a meal) 'azzam, yu'azzim.

invited: mad'u, ma'zûm.

invocation: du'â.

invoice: qaima.
involuntary: ghair ikhtiyârî.
involuntarily: min dun ikhtiyâr.
involve: (imply) ḥawa, yaḥwî; (implicate) eshrek, yushrik.
involved: mushtebik.
inward: ila dâkhil.
ipso facto: bi dhàt el 'aml.
Ireland: irlanda.
Irish: irlandî.
iron: *n.* ḥadîd; (sheet) ṣâch; flat iron, ûti; *v.* dharab ûti, yadhrab; *adj.* min ḥadîd.
ironmonger: bàyi' ḥadàyid.
irons: pringa.
irrational: mukhâlif lil 'aql.
irreconcilable: mâ yataṣâlaḥ.
irregular: khilàf el qânûn; min dûn tertîb.
irregularity: 'adm tertîb.
irrelevant: mâ yakhuṣṣ el mesela.
irresistible: la yuqâwam.
irresolute: ḥâyir.
irrespective of: min dûn nadhr ila.
irrigate: saqa, yasqî.
irrigation: rê, saqî.
irritable: ḥâdd el mizàj.
irritate: (physically) ḥakk, yaḥukk; (mentally) kedder, yukeddir.
is: (not ordinarily expressed); there is, âkû, mawjûd.
Islam: islàm.
island: jazîra, *pl.* jazàyir.
isolate: qaṭa', yaqṭa'.
isolated: munqaṭa'.
isolation: infirâd, inqitâ'.
Israel: isra-îl.
issue: *v. intrans.* (happen) ṣadar, yaṣdar; *v. trans.* (distribute, allot) wazza', yuwazzi'; (give currency to, publish) edrej, yudrij; *n.* (result) natîja, *pl.* natàyij; (matter under consideration) mesela.
isthmus: barzakh.
it: hûwa.
Italian: îṭâliyànî.
Italy: îṭâliya.
itch: *v.* ḥakk, yaḥukk; *n.* ḥakka.
item: màdda, *pl.* mawàd.
itinerary: raḥla.
itinerate: (lead a wandering life) sâḥ, yasîḥ.
itself: nefsuh, nefsuhu.
ivory: 'âj.

J

jackal: wâwî, *pl.* wâwîya.
jacket: sitra, chàket.
Jacob: ya'qûb.
jagged: masnûn.
jail: *v.* ḥabas, yaḥbas: *n.* ḥabs.
jailor: urdiyàn, sejjàn.
jam: marabba.
janitor: bawwàb.
January: kànûn thànî.
Japan: yâbân.
Japanese: yâbânî.
jar: *n.* (of stone) jarra, *pl.* ajrar; (of metal) maskhana, *pl.* masâkhin.
jaundice: àbû ṣafâr.
jaunt: *n.* siyâḥa.
jaw: fekk, fech.
jealous: ḥasûd, *pl.* ḥasûdîn; be jealous of, ḥasad, yaḥsad.
jealously: bi ghîra.
jealousy: ḥasad.
jerk: *v.* hezz, yahizz; *n.* hizza.
Jerusalem: el quds.
jest: *v.* tashâqa, yatashâqa; *n.* shaqqa, mazâḥ.
jetty: eskela.
Jew: yahûdî, *pl.* yahûd.
jewel: jôhar, *pl.* jawâhir.

jewelled: muraṣṣa'.
jeweller: jôharchî, *pl.* jôharchîya.
Jewess: yahûdîya.
jingle: *v.* rann, yarunn.
job: shughl, *pl.* ashghâl.
jockey: *n.* musàbiq.
John: yuḥanna, ḥanna.
join: *v. trans.* waḥḥad, yuwaḥḥid; jama', yijma'; *v. intrans.* (associate with) ishterek, yeshterik; (as road) tawaḥḥad, yatawaḥḥad.
joiner: najjâr, *pl.* najjàjîr.
joint: *n.* (of bones) 'uqda, *pl.* 'uqad, 'uqûd; mafṣal, *pl.* mafâṣil; (mechanical) shelemma; out of joint, maflûsh; *adj.* mushterik.
jointed: shelemma.
jointly: suwîyatan, ma'an.
joist: jisr, Zanzibar; chandal.
joke: see **jest**.
jolly-boat: jalbût, *pl.* jawàlbît.
Joseph: yûsuf.
jostle: da'am, yid'am.
journal: (day-book) defter yômî; (newspaper) jarîda, *pl.* jaràyid.
journey: *v.* sàfar, yusàfir; *n.* sefer, *pl.* seferàt.
joy: farḥ.
joyful: masrûr; making joyful, gladdening, musirr, mufarriḥ.
judge: *v.* ḥakam, yaḥkam; (regard as) ḥasab, yaḥsab; *n.* (religious) qâdhî; (civil) ra-îs maḥkama.
judgement: (sentence) ḥukm; (opinion) rai; (discernment) tamyîz; last judgement, dênûna; yôm ed dîn.
judicatory: maḥkama.
judicial: 'adli.
judicious: 'âqil.
jug: jak, ibriq.
juice: mai, 'asîr.
juicy: reyyàn.
July: tamûz.
jump: *v.* ṭafar, yaṭfar; *n.* ṭafra.
junction: mejma'.
June: ḥazîràn.
jungle: ghâba, *pl.* ghâbàt.
junior: aṣghar, edna.
Jupiter: (planet) el mushterî.
jurisdiction: ḥukm.
jurisprudence: fiqh.
jury: mejlis maḥkama.
just: *adj.* (equitable) 'adil; *adv.* (exactly) tamàm; just now, hessa, ṭôwa.
justice: (equity) 'adàla, 'adl; department of justice, el 'adlîya; *v.* administer justice, ḥakam, yaḥkam; see also **procedure**.
justifiable: jàyiz.
justifiably: bil ḥaqq.
justification: (sufficient reason) sebeb kàfi.
justify: berrer, yuberrir.
justly: bil 'adl.
jut: ṭala', yiṭla'.
jute: jinfâṣ.

K

keel: ka'ab.
keen: (sharp) ḥâdd; (clever) shâṭir, ḥâdhiq; (eager) munhemiq fî.
keep: *v. trans.* (retain) dhamm, yadhumm; khalla 'and, yukhallî; ḥafadh, yaḥfadh; (delay) 'aṭṭal, yu'aṭṭil; (protect) ḥâfadh 'ala, yuḥâfidh; (observe, solemnize) lezem, yilzam; keep from (prevent), mena', yimna'; keep at, dàwam 'ala, yudàwim; keep on, dhall, yadhull; dàwam, yudàwim; istamarr, yastamirr; *v. in-*

trans. (last), dhall, yadhull; keep from (refrain from), imtena' 'an, yemtena'; keep up, dàwam, yudàwim; keep up with, laḥaq, yilḥaq.
keeper: ḥâris, *pl.* ḥurrâs.
keepsake: tidhkâr; yadigâr.
keg: pîp, *pl.* apyàp.
kernel: (of fruit) nawâya, *pl.* nawâyàt; libb, *pl.* lubûb; (of grain) ḥabb, *pl.* ḥubûb.
kettle: (tea) kêtli; (large) jidr, *pl.* jidûr.
key: miftâḥ, *pl.* mafàtîḥ.
kick: refes, yirfas.
kid: jedî, *pl.* jidà; sakhla, *pl.* sukhûl.
kidney: kilwa, *pl.* kilàwî.
kill: qatal, yaqtal; dhebeḥ, yidhbaḥ.
kiln: kûra, *pl.* kûwar; dôgha, *pl.* dûwagh.
kilometre: kilomêtro, *pl.* kilomêtrowàt.
kilt: tanûra.
kind: *adj.* laṭîf, *pl.* laṭîfîn, laṭâf; *n.* (genus) jins, *pl.* ajnàs; no', *pl.* anwâ'; shikl, *pl.* ashkàl.
kindle: *v. trans.* sha'al, yish'al; *v. intrans.* ishta'al, yashta'il.
kindly: bi luṭf.
kindness: luṭf, iḥsàn.
kindred: *n. pl.* qaràyib.
king: melek, *pl.* mulûk.
kingdom: memleka, *pl.* mamàlik.
kinsman: qarîb, *pl.* qarâyib.
kiss: bàs, yabûs; qabbal, yuqabbil: *n.* bôsa, qubla.
kit: (soldier's) aghrâdh; (mechanic's) 'idda.
kitchen: maṭbakh, *pl.* maṭâbikh.
kite: (for flying) ṭayyâra, *pl.* ṭayyâràt.
kitten: farkh bazzûn, *pl.* furûkh.
knack: (dexterity) mahâra.
knapsack: ṭorba.
knead: 'ajan, ya'jan.
knee: rukba, *pl.* rukûb.
kneel: raka', yarka'; (of camel) berek, yibrak.
kneeling: (prostrate) rukû'.
knife: sikkîn, *pl.* sakàkîn. See also **pen-knife, pocket-knife.**
knit: (with thread) nesej, yinsaj; (cause to join, of broken bone) jeber, yijbar.
knob: 'uqda.
knock: (hit) dharab, yadhrab; (at door) daqq, yaduqq; *n.* dharba, ṣawâb.
knot: *v.* 'aqqad, yu'aqqid; *n.* 'uqda.
know: 'araf, ya'raf; dere, yidrî; indell, yendell.
knowledge: ma'rifa, 'ilm; (information) khabr.
known: ma'rûf; *v.* make known, 'arraf, yu'arrif.
knuckle: 'uqda, *pl.* 'uqûd.
Koran: qur-ân.

L

label: 'anwàn.
laboratory: ma'mal.
laborious: mut'ib.
laboriously: bi ta'ab.
labour: *v.* ishtaghal, yashtaghil; *n.* shughl; labour corps, 'ammàla.
lace: *n.* ôya; (of boot) sharîṭ; *v.* shedd, yashidd.
lack: *v.* 'âz, ya'ûz; *n.* naqṣ.
lacking: (missing) nâqiṣ.
lad: ṣabî (ṣabai), *pl.* ṣabyàn.

ladder: sullam, derej.
lading: bill of, setemî, *pl.* setemiyàt.
lady: khâtûn, *pl.* khawâtîn.
lag: ta-akhkhar, yata-akhkhar.
laid: (put) maḥṭûṭ.
lake: buḥéra, *pl.* buḥêràt.
lamb: ṭalî, *pl.* ṭalyàn.
lame: a'raj, *f.* 'arja, *pl.* 'urj; saqaṭ.
lamented: marḥûm.
lamp: lampa, *pl.* lampàt.
lance: ramḥ, *pl.* armâḥ; lance-corporal, wakîl ôn bâshî.
lancer: rammâḥ, *pl.* rammâḥa.
lancet: neshter.
land: *v. trans.* nezzel, yunezzil; *v. intrans.* nezel, yinzal; *n.* ardh, *pl.* arâdhî; gâ', *pl.* gi'ân; mulk, *pl.* amlàk; native land, waṭan, *pl.* awṭân; crown land, arâdhî sanîya.
landing-place: eskela, menzel.
landlord: (of land) mallàk, *pl.* mallàka; (of house) ṣâḥib bêt; râ'î bêt.
landmark: nîshàn, *pl.* nayàshîn.
land-tax: (fixed) resm jarîb; (proportional) khums, 'ushr.
language: logha, *pl.* loghàt; lisàn, *pl.* elsina.
languid: mutarâkhî.
languor: tarâkhî.
lantern: fânûs, *pl.* fawànîs; magic lantern, fânûs siḥrî.
lap: *v.* (in drinking) laqq, yaluqq; *n.* (knees) ḥadhn.
lapse: *v.* fesekh, yifsakh; *n.* lapse of time, murûr ez zamàn.
larceny: sirqa.
lard: *n.* dihn khanzîr.
large: kabîr, *pl.* kibâr.
largely: (mostly) ekther.
largeness: kubr.
larvae: dûd.
lash: *v.* (whip) jeled, yijlad; (tie) shedd, yashidd; *n.* (whip) qâmchî.
lass: bunêya.
lassitude: tarâkhî.
last: *v.* dàm, yadûm; dàwam, yudàwim; *n.* (of shoe) qâlib, *pl.* qawâlib; *adj.* âkhir, akhîr, *pl.* âkhirîn; last night, el lêlet el mâdhia; *adv.* at last, akhîran. See also **year.**
lasting: bâqî, dâyim, thàbit.
latch: chekelek.
late: (tardy) muta-akhkhir, mubṭi; (deceased) marḥûm; late news, akhbâr akhîra; it is late, fàyit waqt; it is too late, fàt el waqt.
lately: akhîran.
latent: mukhfa.
later: bâ'ad; (afterwards) fîma bâ'ad.
laterally: 'ala jànib; 'ala ṣafḥa.
lathe: charkh.
Latin: làtînî.
latitude: (geographical) 'ardh.
latter: akhîr.
latterly: akhîran.
lattice: mushebbek.
laudable: mustaḥiqq el medḥ.
laugh: *v.* dhaḥak, yadhḥak; *n.* dhaḥka.
laughable: mudhḥik.
laughing: *n.* dhaḥk.
launch: *v.* ṭeyyeḥ, yuṭeyyiḥ; *n.* markab ṣaghîr; lânch.
laundress: ghassàla.
laundry: (place) maghsal; (linen) hudûm el ghasîl.
lavender: lawanta.
lavish: *v.* bedhdher, yubedhdhir; *adj.* musrif.
law: (rule) qânûn, *pl.* qawânîn; religious law, shar'; criminal law, qânûn jinà-î; martial

law, ḥukm 'askarî; go to law, aqâm da'wa; taḥâkam, yataḥâkam.
lawful: jàyiz, mubâḥ.
lawfully: qânûnîyan.
lawfulness: jawàz.
lawless: mukhâlif el qânûn.
lawlessness: 'adm en nidhâm.
lawsuit: da'wa, *pl.* da'âwî.
lawyer: wakîl da'wa; awkât, *pl.* awkâtîya.
lax: rakhu.
laxative: mushil (*pron.* mushil).
laxity: rakhâwa.
lay: *v.* (put) ḥaṭṭ, yaḥuṭṭ; khalla, yukhallî; lay out (plan), retteb, yurettib; lay up (save), dhamm, yadhumm; lay eggs, bâdh, yabîdh.
layer: ṭabaqa, *pl.* ṭabaqât.
lazily: bi kesl.
laziness: kesl.
lazy: keslàn, *pl.* kesàla, keslàîn; tembil, *pl.* tenàbil.
lead: *v.* (guide) qâd, yaqûd; lead to (direction), râḥ, yarûḥ; wadda, yuwaddî; lead life, 'âsh, ya'îsh; take lead, taqaddam, yataqaddam.
lead: *n.* (metal) raṣâṣ.
leader: qâ-id.
leadership: qiyàda, riyàsa.
leading: *adj.* (principal) ra-îsî.
leaf: (of paper or plant) warqa, *pl.* awrâq.
league: *n.* (alliance) mu'âqada, muḥâlafa; (three miles) farsakh, *pl.* farâsikh; in league with, muttefiq ma'.
leak: *v.* kharr, yakhurr; *n.* khararân.
lean: *adj.* dha'îf, naḥîf; *v.* màl, yamîl; lean on, sened 'ala, yisnad; itteka, yetteki.
leap: *v.* ṭafar, yaṭfar.
leap-year: kabîsa.
learn: ta'allam, yata'allam.
learned: 'âlim, *pl.* 'ulemâ.
learner: telmîdh, *pl.* telàmîdh.
learning: *n.* 'ilm, *pl.* 'ulûm.
lease: *v.* ejjer, yu-ejjir; *n.* (period) muddat îjâr; (document) warqat îjâr; (rental) îjâr.
least: (of number) aqall; (of quality) edna; at least, aqallan; aqall mâ yakûn.
leather: jiled; of leather, min jiled.
leave: *v. intrans.* (depart) râḥ, yarûḥ; sàfar, yusàfir; *v. trans.* (abandon) terek, yitrak; (allow) khalla, yukhallî; (bequeathe) khallaf, yukhallif; leave off, baṭṭal, yubaṭṭil.
leave: *n.* (permission) rukhṣa; on leave, bi rukhṣa; by your leave, bi rukhṣatek; *v.* take leave, tawâda', yatawâda'.
leaven: *v.* khammar, yukhammir; *n.* khamîr, khamra.
leavened: mukhtamar.
leavings: fadhalàt.
lecture: *n.* khiṭâb; *v. intrans.* khaṭab, yakhṭab; *v. trans.* (instruct) derres, yuderris.
led: *v.* to be led, inqàd, yanqàd.
ledger: defter istàdh.
left: yisâr, shamàl; to the left, ilal yisâr; left handed, yisrâwî.
leg: rijl, *pl.* rijûl, riyûl.
legacy: wiràtha, irth.
legal: qânûnî; (permitted by law) jàyiz.
legality: qânûnîya.
legalize: ṣaddaq, yuṣaddiq.
legally: qânûnîyan.
legatee: wàrith, *pl.* waratha.
legation: sifâra.

legend: khurâfa; qaṣṣa, *pl.* qaṣaṣ.
legible: yanqarî.
legislate: ḥakam, yaḥkam.
legislation: ḥukm.
legitimate: jàyiz, qânûnî.
leisure: farâgha; at leisure, fârigh.
leisurely: ʿala kêf (with *pron. suff.*).
lemon: lîmûn.
lemonade: lîmunâta, *vulg.* namlêt.
lend: aqradh, yuqridh.
lender: dàyin, muqridh.
length: ṭûl; length of time, mudda; at length, akhîran.
lengthen: ṭawwal, yuṭawwil.
lengthways: ʿala ṭûl.
leniency: shefeqa.
lenient: lêyyin.
lens: jàma.
Lent: (season) eṣ ṣôm el kabîr.
lentils: ʿades.
leopard: fehed.
leper: abraṣ, *fem.* barṣa, *pl.* burṣ, burṣîn.
leprosy: barṣ.
leprous: see **leper.**
less: *adj.* aqall; (minus) nâqiṣ; less than, aqall min; *prep.* illa.
lessee: mustà-jir.
lessen: qallal, yuqallil; naqqaṣ, yunaqqiṣ.
lesson: ders, *pl.* durûs.
lest: khôfan la; li-ella.
let: (permit) khalla, yukhallî (*imp.* khalli); let alone, khalla, yukhallî; let down, nezzel, yunezzil; let go, fekk, yafukk.
letter: maktûb, *pl.* makàtîb; khaṭṭ, *pl.* khuṭûṭ; (character) ḥarf, *pl.* ḥurûf; capital letter, ḥarf kabîr.
letter-carrier: muwazziʿ makàtîb.
lettuce: khess.
Levant: esh sharq el aqrab.
level: *v.* ʿaddal, yuʿaddil; *n.* (instrument for surveying) irtifâʿ; *adj.* ʿâdil, mutasâwî.
lever: makhal.
levity: khiffa.
levy: *v.* (levy money) kellef, yukellif; (levy troops) ḥashad, yaḥshad; *n.* (troops) iḥtishàd.
lewd: fàsiq.
lewdness: fujûr.
liability: (debt) dên, *pl.* duyûn.
liable: qâbil; (responsible) mas-ûl.
liar: kedhdhàb, *pl.* kedhdhàbîn.
liberal: karîm, sakhî, musrif; (free) ḥurr, *pl.* aḥrâr.
liberality: kerm, sakhâwa.
liberally: bi kuthra.
liberate: fekk, yafukk; aṭlaq, yuṭliq.
liberty: ḥurrîya; at liberty (leisure), fârigh; take the liberty, tajàsar, yatajàsar.
library: mekteba.
license: *v.* rakhkhaṣ, yurakhkhiṣ; *n.* (permission) rukhṣa.
licensed: murakhkhaṣ.
licentious: fàsid, fàsiq.
licentiousness: fujûr.
lick: laḥas, yilḥas.
licorice: sûs.
lid: ghaṭa, qapagh.
lie: *v.* (tell falsehood) kedheb, yikdhab; (rest horizontally, of person), nàm, yanàm; (rest horizontally, of thing), maḥṭûṭ; *n.* (falsehood) kidhb.
lien: ṭalab.
lieu: in lieu of, ʿiwadh.

lieutenant: (military) mulàzim, *pl.* mulàzimìn; first lieutenant, m. awwal; second lieutenant, m. thànì; lieutenant-general, farìq awwal; (agent) nàyib.
life: (vitality) ḥayàt; (lifetime) ʻamr; (mode of life) ʻìsha; life to come, el âkhira.
life-insurance: dhamân el ḥayàt.
lifeless: mêyyit.
lift: *v.* rafaʻ, yarfaʻ; shàl, yashìl; *n.* (elevator) jarr athqâl.
ligament: ʻiṣâba.
ligature: rabṭa.
light: *v. trans.* (kindle) shaʻal, yishʻal; *v. intrans.* (be kindled) ishtaʻal, yashtaʻil; light on (happen on) ṣâdaf, yuṣâdif; come to light, dhahar, yadhhar; give light, dhawwa, yudhawwì; make light of, istakhaff, yastakhiff; *n.* (of lamp) dhaw; (of sun) nûr; *adj.* (not heavy) khafìf, *pl.* khafâf; (nimble) khafìf, nashìṭ; (easy) sehl, hêyyin; (bright) mudhwì; (of colour) kàshif, âchiq; (slight) juz-ì, khafìf.
lighten: *v. intrans.* (flash) lemaʻ, yilmaʻ; *v. trans.* (make light) khaffaf, yukhaffif.
lighter: *adj.* akhaff, akhfaf; *n.* (boat) châya, *pl.* châyàt; *v.* become lighter (fade in colour) nafadh, yanfadh.
lighterage: resm ech châya.
lighterman: mellâḥ, *pl.* melàlìḥ.
light-headed: khafìf, *pl.* khafâf.
light-hearted: bashûsh.
lighthouse: manâra, *pl.* manâyir.
lightly: khafìf; bi khiffa.
lightness: khiffa.
lightning: barq.
like: *v.* ḥabb, yaḥibb; *n.* mithl, nadhìr; (similar) mithl, yishbah; like this, hìchì, hàkadha; like as, mithlma, kema.
likely: (probable) muhtemil, qâbil.
liken: shebbeh, yushebbih.
likeness: (picture) ṣûra.
likewise: kadhàlik, aidhan.
liking: (inclination) mêl; (pleasure) kêf.
limb: (of body) ʻadhu, *pl.* aʻdhâ; (of tree) ghaṣn, *pl.* ghaṣûna, aghṣân.
limber: (supple) lêyyin.
lime: (material) juṣṣ; (fruit) lûmì; limejuice, mai lumì; Rose's Limejuice, laimjûsh.
limekiln: kûra, *pl.* kûwar.
limestone: kels.
limit: *n.* ḥadd, *pl.* ḥudûd; *v.* ḥaddad, yuḥaddid.
limited: (bounded) maḥdûd; (narrow) dhayyiq; (restrained) maḥṣûr.
limitless: bila ḥadd.
limp: *v.* aʻrajj, yaʻrajj.
limpness: rakhâwa.
line: *v. trans.* (cover inside) baṭṭan, yubaṭṭin; (arrange in line) ṣaffat, yuṣaffit; (draw line) saṭṭar, yusaṭṭir; *v. intrans.* line up, iṣṭaff, yaṣṭaff; *n.* (string) khaiṭ, *pl.* khuyûṭ; (rope) ḥabl, *pl.* ḥibàl; (mark) khaṭṭ, *pl.* khuṭûṭ; (of print) saṭr, *pl.* asṭur; (row) ṣaff, *pl.* ṣufûf; (shipping company) sherika.
linen: kattàn; (garments) hudûm.
linger: baṭa, yabṭi.
lingering: *adj.* (e.g. of disease) mubṭi, muzmin.

linguist: loghawî.
linguistic: loghawî.
liniment: dihn, merham.
lining: baṭâna.
link: *n.* (of chain) ḥalaqa, *pl.* ḥalaqàṭ; *v.* rabaṭ, yarbaṭ.
linseed: bizr kattàn.
lion: seb', *pl.* sibâ'; esed, *pl.* usûd.
lip: shifa, *pl.* shifaf.
liquefy: dhawwab, yudhawwib.
liquid: mithl mai; sàyil.
liquidate: ṣaffa ḥisàb, yuṣaffî.
liquidation: taṣfia ḥisàb.
liquor: (strong drink) muskir, *pl.* muskiràt.
lisp: lagath, yilgath.
list: *n.* (register, catalogue) qâima, *pl.* qâimàt; (canting over of ship) mêl.
listen: istema', yestemi'; iṣṭanaṭ, yaṣṭaniṭ.
listless: fàtir.
literally: ḥarfîyan.
literary: edebî.
literature: edebiyàt, àdàb; (books) kutub.
lithograph: *v.* ṭaba' fî ḥajr, yaṭba'.
litigant: mukhâṣim, mudda'î.
litigation: muḥâkama.
little: *adj.* ṣaghîr, *pl.* ṣighâr; *n.* shwêya, qalîl; *adv.* qalîl, shwêya; little by little, shwêya shwêya.
littleness: ṣughr, qilla.
liturgy: ṭaqs.
live: *v.* (dwell) seken, yiskan; qa'ad, yaq'ad; (exist) 'âsh, ya'îsh; *adj.* (alive), see **living**.
livelihood: ma'îsha.
lively: *adj.* (active) nashîṭ, *pl.* nashâṭ; *adv.* bi himma.
liver: (anat.) kebed.
live-stock: mawâshî, dawàb.
living: *adj.* ḥai, *pl.* aḥyà; ṭayyib; fî qaid el ḥayàt; *n.* (subsistence) ma'îsha.
lizard: àbû brêṣ.
load: *v. trans.* ḥammal, yuḥammil; (load gun) teres, yitras; *n.* ḥiml, thuql.
loaded: (burdened) muḥammal; (of gun) matrûs.
loaf: of bread, ṣâmûna, *pl.* ṣâmûnàt; of sugar, râs qand.
loan: *n.* qardha, istiqrâdh.
loathe: kereh, yikrah.
loathesome: karîh.
lobster: saraṭân.
local: maḥallî.
locality: mawqa'.
localize: ḥaṣar, yaḥṣar.
locate: *v. trans.* leqa, yilki.
located: wâqi', ṣâyir.
location: mawqa'.
lock: *v. trans.* qaffal, yuqaffil; *v. intrans.* inqafal, yanqafil; *n.* qufl, *pl.* qufûl; (of gun) zinàd; (of dam) bàb, *pl.* abwàb.
locomotive: jarrâra.
locust: (insect) jarâd; (tree) kharnûb, barhâm.
lodge: *v. trans.* bêyyet, yubêyyit; bàt, yabàt; *v. intrans.* (alight) nezel, yinzal.
lodger: nazîl, *pl.* nezel.
lodging: (place) menzil, mesken.
loftiness: 'ulu.
lofty: 'âli.
log: jidh', *pl.* jidhû'.
logic: manṭiq.
logical: ma'qûl.
logician: manṭiqî.
loin: khâṣira.
loiter: ta-akhkhar, yata-akhkhar; baṭa, yabṭi.
loneliness: waḥsha, waḥda.
lonely: mutawaḥḥish, munferid.

long: ṭawîl, *pl.* ṭawâl; as long as, ṭûlma; mà dàm; ṭâlama; before long, 'an qarîb; how long (time), shqad; ila yimta. See also **time.**
long for: *v.* ishtâq, yashtâq.
longer: aṭwal; (any more) bâ'ad.
longest: el aṭwal.
longevity: ṭûl 'amr.
longing: *n.* ishtiyâq, shôq; *adj.* mushtâq.
longitude: ṭûl.
long-suffering: *adj.* ṭawîl er rûḥ.
long-winded: kathîr el kalàm.
look: *v.* shâf, yashûf (*imper.* shuf); bâwa', yubâwi'; isṭaba, yasṭabi; look at, bâwa' bi, yubâwi'; look after, dâr bàl 'ala, yadîr; look into, fettesh, yufettish; look out, dâr bàl, yadîr; look for, dawwar, yudawwir; fettesh 'ala, yufettish; *n.* nadhra.
looker-on: muteferrij, *pl.* muteferrijîn.
looking-glass: marâya, 'aina.
look-out: *n.* (watching) ḥirâsa; (watchman) nôbachî.
loom: *n.* jûma.
loop-hole: nôcha, *pl.* nôchàt.
loose: *adj.* (unbound) maḥlûl, mafkûk; (not tight) rakhu; *v.* get loose, iftekk, yeftekk; let loose, fekk, yafukk.
loosen: (untie) ḥall, yaḥull; fekk, yafukk; (make less tight) rakhkha, yurakhkhî.
looseness: (laxity) rakhâwa; (flux) ishàl (*pron.* is-hàl).
lord: *v.* tasallaṭ, yatasallaṭ; *n.* (God) 'er rabb; (master) sêyyid; (nobleman) sharîf, *pl.* ashrâf; House of Lords, see **house.**
lordship: siyàda.
lose: *v.* (e.g. wealth) khasar, yakhsar; (e.g. way, money) dhêyya', yudhêyyi'.
loser: khâsir.
loss: (pecuniary) khasâra; (e.g. of an article) faqd; *v.* be at loss, taḥayyar, yataḥayyar.
losses: (in battle) telefiyàt.
lost: (not to be found) dhâyi', mafqûd; (e.g. of a ship) gharqân, râyiḥ; (financially) makhsûr.
lot: (state) ḥâl; (share) qasm, *pl.* aqsàm; ḥaṣṣa, *pl.* ḥaṣaṣ; (fate) naṣîb; (chance) qar'a; lot of people, jumla.
lottery: ya naṣîb.
loud: bi ṣawt 'âli.
louse: qamla, *pl.* qaml.
lovable: yanḥabb.
love: *v.* ḥabb, yaḥibb; *n.* maḥabba.
lovely: ḥulu, laṭîf, ḥasan.
low: *adj.* nâṣî; (of price) rakhîṣ; (mean) denî, *pl.* edniyà.
lower: *v. trans.* nezzel, yunezzil; (morally) denna, yudennî; *adj.* anṣa.
lowest: el anṣa; (morally) el edna.
lowness: of ground, naṣu; of character, denàwa.
low-water: jezer.
loyal: amîn, *pl.* amînîn.
loyalty: amàna, emnîya.
lubricate: dehen, yidhan.
lubrication: tadhîn.
lucerne: jett.
lucid: (clear) wâdhiḥ; (transparent) ṣâfî.
lucidity: ṣafâwa.
luck: ḥadhdh, naṣîb; good luck, ḥadhdh zên; bad luck, naḥs; good luck to you, Allâh wiyàk.

luckily: min ḥusn et tôfîq.
lucky: ṣâḥib ḥadhdh.
lucrative: muksib.
ludicrous: mudhḥik.
luggage: aghrâdh.
lukewarm: fàtir.
lull: sekta.
lumbago: waj' dhahr.
lumber: lôḥ, khashab.
luminous: mudhwî.
lump: (piece) waṣla, *pl.* waṣl; qaṭ'a; (mass) qaṭ'a; in a lump, bil jumla; *v.* kawwam, yukawwim.
lumpy: mu'aqqad.
lunar: hilàlî, qamrî; lunar month, shahr qamrî; lunar year, sena hijrîya.
lunatic: majnûn, *pl.* majànîn.
lunch: (noon meal) ghada; *v.* taghadda, yataghadda.
lung: (*colloq.*) ma'lâq; (*literary*) riya, *dual,* riyatên.
lurch: *v.* indefa' ila ṣafḥa, yendefi'.
lurk: ikhtaba, yakhtabi.
luscious: ladhîdh.
lust: shehwa.
lustre: leme'ân; (renown) shuhra.
luxuriant: athîth.
luxurious: mutana''im.
luxury: tana''am.

M

macaroni: makarônî, makârana.
machine: makîna, *pl.* makàyin.
machine-gun: rashshàsh, mitralyôz.
machinery: makîna, àlàt.
machinist: osta, *pl.* ostawàt.
mad: (insane) majnûn, *pl.* majànîn.
madden: khabbal, yukhabbil.
made: ma'mûl.
mad-house: mâristàn.
madness: junûn, khabâl.
magazine: (store-house) makhzan, *pl.* makhâzin; (paper) jarîda, *pl.* jaràyid.
maggot: dûda, *pl.* dûd.
magic: *n.* siḥr; *adj.* siḥri; magic lantern, fânûs siḥrî.
magician: sâḥir, *pl.* saḥara.
magistrate: ḥâkim, *pl.* ḥukkàm.
magnanimous: sharîf en nefs.
magnet: maghnaṭîs.
magnetic: maghnaṭîsî.
magnificence: (grandeur) jilàl; (pomp) fakhfakha.
magnificent: fâkhir, 'adhîm.
magnify: (enlarge) kebber, yukebbir; (enhance) 'adhdham, yu'adhdhim.
magnitude: kubr, 'adhama; (importance) ahemmiya.
maiden: bint, *pl.* banàt.
mail: (letters) posṭa; *v.* ba'ath yib'ath.
maim: saqqaṭ, yusaqqiṭ.
maimed: saqaṭ.
mainly: bil ekther; el aghlab.
maintain: (keep) ḥafadh, yaḥfadh; (support with food) 'ayyash, yu'ayyish; (affirm) idda'a, yadda'i; (continue) istamarr 'ala, yastamirr.
maintenance: (sustenance) ma'âsh; (preservation) muḥâfadha.
maize: idhrat esh shàm.
majesty: His Majesty, jalàlat el melek.
major: *n.* (officer) bînbâshî; major-general, amîr liwa; farîq; sergeant-major, bâsh

châwûsh; *adj.* (of age) bàligh; (the greater) el ekther.
majority: (greater number) el ektherîya; (full age) sinn el bulûgh; rank of major, ritba bînbâshî.
make: (do) sawwa, yusawwî; (compel) ejber, yujbir; ghaṣab, yaghṣab; (amount to) sàwa, yusàwî; make money, ḥaṣṣal, yuḥaṣṣil; make up deficiency, kemmel, yukemmil; make up (reconcile) taṣâlaḥ, yataṣâlaḥ; make up (compose) rekkeb, yurekkib; make up mind, nawa, yinwî; *n.* (manufacture) shughl, shoghl.
malady: dà, waj', mardh.
malaria: sakhûna.
male: (human) dhikr, *pl.* dhukûr; (beast) faḥl, *pl.* fuḥûl.
malefactor: mudhnib, *pl.* mudhnibîn.
malice: khubth.
malign: khabîth.
mallet: daqmâq.
maltreat: àdha, yu-àdhi.
maltreatment: adhîya.
man: *n.* (opposite of woman) rejul, *pl.* rijàl; rijàl, *pl.* rijàjîl; riyàl, *pl.* riyàyîl; (opposite of beast) insàn, *pl.* unàs, nàs; (person) àdamî, *pl.* awàdim; (individual) nefer, *pl.* neferàt, anfâr; *v.* jehhez, yujehhiz.
manacle: *v.* kettef, yukettif; *n.* pringa.
manage: debber, yudebbir; dâr, yadîr.
management: idâra, tadbîr.
manager: mudîr, *pl.* mudarâ.
mane: ma'ârif.
manfully: bi jasâra.
manner: (mode) ṭarîqa; (kind) nô', *pl.* anwâ'; jins, *pl.* ajnàs; (custom) 'âda, *pl.* 'awâyid; in this manner, hîchî, kedha, hàkadha; good manners, àdàb; bad manners, sû àdàb.
mannerly: adîb, *pl.* adîbîn.
manœuvre: *v.* taḥarrak, yataḥarrak; *n.* ḥaraka; military manœuvre, manâwara.
manslaughter: qatl min dûn ta'ammud.
mantle: 'aba, *pl.* 'ubi.
manual: *adj.* shughl yed.
manufactory: kirkhâna, fabrîka.
manufacture: *v.* ṣana', yaṣna'.
manufacturer: ṣâḥib fabrîka.
manure: *n.* samàd; *v.* semmed, yusemmid.
manuscript: *n.* warqa, *pl.* awrâq; *adj.* kitàbat yed; kitbet îd.
many: kathîr, chathîr, wàjid, hwâyi; how many, shqad, shqadr, kem (with singular noun).
map: *n.* kharîṭa, *pl.* kharâyiṭ; khârṭa, *pl.* khârṭât.
mar: (hurt) dharr, yadhurr.
maraud: ghaza, yaghzu.
marauder: beleshtî, *pl.* beleshtîya.
marble: marmar; (little ball) bîl, *pl.* abyàl.
march: *v. trans.* meshsha, yumeshshî; *v. intrans.* mesha, yimshî; *n.* (movement of troops) masîr.
March: (month) âdhâr.
mare: fars, *pl.* afràs.
margin: (edge) ḥâfa; (of book) ḥâshia, *pl.* ḥawâshî.
marine: baḥrî.
mariner: baḥrî, *pl.* baḥrîya; nôkhadha, *pl.* nawâkhadha.

maritime: baḥrî.
mark: *v*. (make mark) nêshen, yunêshin; (observe) lâḥadh, yulâḥidh; *n*. (token) 'alàma, *pl*. 'alàmàt; marka, *pl*. markàt; (indication) ishâra, *pl*. ishâràt; (trace) ether; (target) nîshàn, *pl*. niyàshîn.
marked: munêshen; (evident) mubêyyen, bêyyen.
market: *v*. *intrans*. tasawwaq, yatasawwaq; *n*. sûq, *pl*. aswâq.
marketing: miswâq, tasawwuq.
market-price: si'r es sûq.
marksman: nêshenchî, *pl*. nêshenchîya.
marmalade: marabba portugâl.
marriage: (act) zawàj; (rite) nikâḥ, barrâkh; (wedding) 'urs.
marriageable: qâbil ez zawàj.
married: mutazzawaj, muteehhel.
marrow: (substance in bone) mukhkh.
marry: *v*. *trans*. zawwaj, yuzawwij; kellel, yukellil; barrakh, yubarrikh; *v*. *intrans*. tazawwaj, yatazawwaj.
Mars: (planet) marîkh.
marsh: hôr, *pl*. ahwâr; mustenqa'a.
marshal: *v*. *trans*. ṣaff, yaṣuff; *n*. mushîr.
marshalled: muṣṭaffîn.
marshy: hôr.
martial: ḥarbî; martial law, ḥukm 'askarî; court martial, dîwàn ḥarb; dîwàn 'urfi.
martyr: shahîd, *pl*. shuhadà.
martyrdom: istishhàd.
marvel: *v*. ta'ajjab, yata'ajjab; *n*. 'ajîba, *pl*. 'ajâyib.
marvellous: 'ajîb.
Mary: miryam.
masculine: mudhekker.
mash: *v*. *trans*. khabaṭ, yakhbaṭ; *n*. ma'jûn.
mask: *v*. (hide) akhfa, yukhfî.
mason: benna, *pl*. bennai; freemason, farmasônî.
mass: *v*. *trans*. jamma', yujammi'; *n*. (lump) keff; (quantity) jumla; (sacrament) qaddàs.
massacre: *v*. dhebeḥ, yidhbaḥ; *n*. medhbaḥa.
massage: *v*. ferek, yifrak; *n*. ferk.
massive: jasîm.
mast: dugal, *pl*. dugalàt.
master: *v*. ghalab 'ala, yaghlab; istawla, yastawlî; *n*. (teacher) mu'âllim, *pl*. mu'allimîn; (proprietor) ṣâḥib, *pl*. aṣḥâb; (chief) ra-îs, *pl*. ru-asâ; master of ship, qapṭân, *pl*. qapâṭîn; master of arts, istàdh el funûn.
mastery: siyàda, riyàsa.
masticate: 'alas, ya'las.
mat: (rough) bària, *pl*. bawârî; (fine) haṣîr, *pl*. haṣrân; (cloth) basâṭ.
match: *v*. (equal) wâfaq, yuwâfiq; (suit) ṭâbaq, yuṭâbiq; *n*. (contest) musàbaqa; (equivalent) akhu, muṭâbiq; (lucifer) kibrît; shakhâṭa, *pl*. shakhâṭ.
mate: *n*. (companion) rafîq, *pl*. rufaqâ; (of bird) rafîq; (of ship) mu'allim.
material: (equipment) lawàzim, mawàd; *adj*. màddî; (important) muhimm.
mathematician: istàdh fîr riyâdhiyàt.
mathematics: riyâdhiyàt.

matriculate: *v. trans.* qayyad, yuqayyid; *v. intrans.* taqayyad, yataqayyad.
matriculation: qaid.
matrimony: zawàj.
matter: *n.* (substance) màdda; (affair) mes-ela, *pl.* mesàyil; qadhîya, *pl.* qadhâyâ; (pus) mudd; what is the matter? êsh âkû; what is the matter with you? êsh bîk; what does it matter to you? êsh yakhuṣṣek; it doesn't matter, mâ yukhâlif; la bàs.
matting: *n.* (coco-nut) qambâr; (straw) haṣîr, *pl.* haṣrân.
mattress: dôshek, *pl.* dawâshik.
mature: *v. intrans.* (fruit) istawa, yastawî; (person) belegh, yiblagh; (bill) istaḥaqq, yastaḥiqq; *adj.* (fruit) mustawî; (person) bàligh; (bill) mustaḥaqq.
maturity: (person) bulûgh; (bill) istiḥqâq.
maund: menn, *pl.* emnan (weight for dates, 154 to 168 lb.).
mauve: mâwî.
maxim: (rule) qâ'ida, *pl.* qawâ'id; (gun) rashshàsh.
maximum: nahàya; a'la daraja; *adj.* kull.
may: *v. aux.* (perhaps) yimkin; may I go? yaṣîr arûḥ; âkû rukhṣa; may it be so, 'alawâh.
May: (month) âyâr.
mayor: ra-îs beledîya.
me: *pron. suffix*, ni, after verb (see p. 69); i, after preposition ending in cons. (see p. 13); aya, êyya, ya, î, after preposition ending in vowel (see p. 18 f.).
meagre: qalîl.
meal: (ground grain) ṭaḥîn; (repast) ekl.
mean: *adj.* (low) denî, *pl.* edniyà; (intermediate) mutawassiṭ, mu'tedil; *v.* (intend) qaṣad, yaqṣad; (signify) 'ana, ya'nî.
meaning: ma'na, *pl.* ma'ânî.
meanness: denàwa.
means: wâsiṭa, *pl.* wasâyiṭ; by means of, bi wâsiṭat; by all means, 'ala kull ḥâl; by no means, ebeden.
meantime: in the meantime, fî dhâk el ithnà.
measles: ḥaṣba.
measure: *v.* (by size) qâs, yaqîs; qaddar, yuqaddir; (by capacity) kàl, yakîl; (by weight) wazan, yozan; *n.* (standard) qiyàs; (of capacity) kêl; (of weight) wazn; (of size) qadr; beyond measure, fôq el ḥadd; in some measure, no'an mâ; *v.* take measures, debber, yudebbir.
measurement: qiyàs; (of land) masâḥa.
mechanic: osta, *pl.* ostawàt.
mechanical: makànîkî.
mechanically: bi wâsiṭat àlàt.
mechanics: makànikiyàt.
mechanism: terkîb.
medal: nîshàn, *pl.* niyàshîn.
meddle: *v.* (interfere) tafâdhal, yatafâdhal; (play) la'ab, yil'ab.
meddler: fadhûlî.
meddlesome: fadhûlî.
meddling: *n.* tafâdhul.
mediaeval: min el qurûn el wusṭa.
medial: mutawassiṭ.
mediate: tawassaṭ, yatawassaṭ.
mediation: tawassuṭ.

mediator: wasîṭ, *pl.* wusaṭâ; (religious) shafî', *pl.* shufa'â.
medical: ṭubbî.
medically: ṭubban.
medicine: dawa, *pl.* edwiya; (science of) eṭ ṭubb.
mediocre: mutawassiṭ.
meditate: te-emmel, yete-emmel; tefekker, yetefekker; (purpose) qaṣad, yaqṣad.
meditation: te-emmul, tefekkur.
Mediterranean: el baḥr el mutawassiṭ.
medium: (means) wâsiṭa, *pl.* wasâyiṭ; wasîla; *adj.* mutawassiṭ.
meek: miskîn, *pl.* masàkîn; mutawâdhi'; faqîr.
meekness: wadâ'a, tawâdhu'.
meet: *v. trans.* (encounter) lâqa, yulâqî; *v. intrans.* (encounter) talâqa, mâ' yatalâqa; (assemble) ijtema, yajtemi'; (become acquainted with) ta'âraf mâ', yata'âraf; meet face to face, wàjah, yuwàjih; *adj.* làyiq, munàsib.
meeting: ijtimâ'; (interview) muwàjaha; (athletic) manâdhara.
melancholic: sodâwî.
mêlée: ma'raka.
mellow: (ripe) nàdhij; (of sound) rakhîm.
melody: (tune) naghma.
melon: (water) reggî; (musk) baṭîkh.
melt: *v. trans.* dhawwab, yudhawwib; *v. intrans.* dhàb, yadhûb; mâ', yamû'.
member: (of body or society) 'adhu, *pl.* a'dhâ.
membership: 'adhawîya.
membrane: ghasha.
memento: tidhkâr; yâdigâr (T.).
memorable: mashhûr.
memorandum: mufekkira.
memorial: (monument) tidhkâr.
memorize: ḥafadh 'ala el qalb, yaḥfadh.
memory: (faculty) edh dhàkira; in memory (recollection), fî bàl; from memory, ghaiban.
menace: *v.* (threaten) hedded, yuheddid; *n.* (danger) khaṭr, mukhâṭara, derekîya.
menacing: muheddid.
mend: *v. trans.* ṣallaḥ, yuṣalliḥ; *v. intrans.* taṣallaḥ, yataṣallaḥ.
menial: denî, *pl.* edniyà.
mensuration: masâḥa.
mental: 'aqli.
mentally: 'aqlan.
mention: *v.* dheker, yidhkar; *n.* dhikr.
mentioned: madhkûr.
mercantile: tujârî.
mercenary: (greedy) ṭammâ', *pl.* ṭammâ'în.
merchandise: amwàl tujârîya.
merchant: tàjir, *pl.* tujjâr.
merciful: raḥûm, *pl.* raḥûmîn; raḥîm, *pl.* ruḥamâ.
mercifully: bi raḥma.
merciless: bila raḥma.
mercury: (quicksilver) zîbaq.
Mercury: (planet) 'aṭârid.
mercy: *n.* raḥma; *v.* have mercy on, raḥam, yarḥam.
mere: *adj.* ṣirf.
merely: faqaṭ.
merge: *v. trans.* waḥḥad, yuwaḥḥid; *v. intrans.* tawaḥḥad, yatawaḥḥad.
meridian: khaṭṭ el hàjira.

merit: *v.* istaḥaqq, yastaḥiqq; istehel, yestehil; *n.* istiḥqâq.
merited: mustaḥaqq.
meritorious: mustehil.
merry: masrûr, farḥân.
mesh: fetḥa.
mess: *v. intrans.* (eat) akal, ya-kul; *n.* (officers') ṣufrat edh dhubbâṭ; (confusion) khabṣa; make a mess of, khabbaṣ, yukhabbiṣ.
message: (notice sent) risàla, khabr.
messenger: rasûl, ṭârish, sâ'î.
Messiah: el messîḥ.
Messrs.: el khawàjàt.
metal: *n.* ma'dan, *pl.* ma'âdin: *adj.* min ma'dan.
metaphor: mushàbaha.
meteorology: 'ilm el jô.
method: (way of doing) ṭarîqa, uslûb; (order) nidhâm, tertîb.
methodical: muntadhim.
methylated spirits: spirito.
metre: (French measure) metro, *pl.* metrowàt; (poetic) wazn.
metropolis: akbar medîna; (capital) 'âṣima, *pl.* 'awâṣim.
mettle: ḥammîya, ḥidda.
mew: *v.* mawwa, yumawwî.
miasma: wakhm.
microbe: mikrôb.
microscope: mikroskôp, mukebbir, mijhar.
mid: nuṣṣ, nuṣf.
middle: *n.* wasṭ, nuṣf, nuṣṣ; *adj.* wasṭânî.
middle-aged: kehel.
midnight: nuṣf el lêl; nuṣṣ el lêl.
midshipman: mulàzim.
midst: wasṭ, nuṣf, nuṣṣ.
midsummer: nuṣṣ el gêdh, nuṣṣ eṣ ṣêf.
midway: nuṣṣ ed darb; nuṣṣ eṭ ṭarîq.
midwinter: nuṣṣ esh shita.
might: *v. aux.* yimkin; kàn yimkin; *n.* qûwa.
mighty: (powerful) qawî; (great) 'adhîm; (of God) qâdir, qadîr.
migrate: hàjar, yuhàjir.
migration: muhàjara.
mild: (gentle) laṭîf; (e.g. of tobacco) bàrid.
mildew: 'afûna.
mildness: luṭf.
mile: mîl, *pl.* amyàl.
militant: muḥârib.
military: *adj.* 'askarî; *n.* el 'askarîya.
militate against: dhâdad, yudhâdid.
milk: ḥalîb.
milky: mithl ḥalîb.
mill: (for grinding, large) maṭḥana; (for grinding, by hand) raḥa, *pl.* ruḥi; (factory) kirkhâna.
miller: ṭaḥḥân.
millet: dakhn.
million: milyôn, *pl.* malàyin.
millstone: raḥa.
mimic: *v.* qallad, yuqallid; *n.* muqallid.
mimosa: shammûṭ baḥr.
minaret: manâra, *pl.* manâyir.
mince: *v.* ferem, yafram.
mind: *v. trans.* (heed) bàla, yubàlî; (take care of) dàra, yudàrî; *n.* (intelligence) 'aql; (purpose) nîyya; (opinion) rai; *v.* bear in mind, tedhekker, yetedhekker; change mind, ghayyar fikr, yughayyir; make up mind, 'azam, ya'zam; never mind, là bàs; là tubàli.
mindful of: muhtemm bi.

mine: (of minerals) ma'dan, *pl.* ma'âdin; (in war) lughm, *pl.* alghâm; *v.* (dig) ḥafar, yaḥfar; *v.* place mines, lagham, yalgham; *pron.* màlî.
mineral: ma'dan, *pl.* ma'âdin.
mingle: *v. trans.* mezej, yimzaj; *v. intrans.* imtezej, yemtezij.
mingled: mumtezij.
miniature: *n.* taṣghîr; *adj.* ṣaghîr.
minim: (drop) qaṭra, *pl.* qaṭràt.
minimum: aqall; el aqall.
minister: *n.* (diplomatic) safîr, *pl.* sufarâ; (clergyman) qass, qasîs, *pl.* qassàn; prime minister, ṣadr; cabinet minister, nâdhir, wazîr; *v. trans.* minister to, khadam, yakhdam.
ministration: khidma.
ministry: (ecclesiastical) qasûnîya; (place or office in cabinet) nadhâra.
minor: (less) aqall; (smaller) aṣghar; *n.* (under age) qaṣîr, *pl.* quṣṣar.
minority: (lesser number) aqallîya; (under age) qaṣr.
mint: (place of coinage) sikkakhâna; (plant) na'nâ'.
minus: *adj.* nâqis; *prep.* illa.
minute: *n.* (60 seconds) daqîqa, *pl.* daqâyiq; (record) khulâṣa; 'amra; *adj.* (small) daqîq.
minute-hand: 'aqrab ed daqàyiq.
minutely: bi tadqîq.
miracle: mu'jiza, *pl.* mu'jizàt; 'ajûba, *pl.* 'ajâyib.
miraculous: 'ajîb.
mirage: sarâb.
mire: waḥl, ṭîn.
mirror: mirâya, 'aina.
mirth: farḥ.
miry: mutawaḥḥil.
misadventure: balîya.
misapprehension: sû istifhàm.
misappropriate: ikhteles, yakhtelis.
misbehave: sâ et taṣarruf, yasî, tawakkaḥ, yatawakkaḥ.
misbehaviour: sû taṣarruf.
miscalculate: ghalaṭ, yaghlaṭ.
miscarry: (of plans) habaṭ, yahbaṭ.
miscellaneous: mutanawwa'.
mischance: qadha.
mischief: (evil) sharr; (damage) dharar.
mischievous: (of persons) mufsid; (of children) waqîḥ, *pl.* wuqqâḥ.
misconception: sû fehm.
misconduct: see **misbehaviour**.
misdemeanour: qabâḥa.
miser: bakhîl, *pl.* bukhala.
miserable: (of health) munḥaṭṭ; (of living conditions) ta'îs; kasîf; (of quality) denî.
misery: (physical) ta'âsa; (mental) shaqâwa, shaqqa.
misfortune: (mishap) muṣîba, *pl.* maṣâyib; (ill-luck) sû ḥadḥ.
misgiving: shekk.
misgovernment: sû idâra.
mishap: see **misfortune**.
misinformed: mâ mukhtebir es ṣaḥîḥ.
mislay: dhayya', yudhayyi'.
mislead: ghashsh, yaghishsh.
mismanage: khabbaṣ, yukhabbiṣ.
mismanagement: sû tedbîr.
misplaced: mû fî makànuh.
mispronounce: ghalaṭ fît talaffudh, yaghlaṭ.

misrepresent: mâ bêyyen el ḥaqîqa, yubêyyin.
misrule: *n.* teshwîsh.
miss: *n.* (opposite of hit) khaṭa; (young lady) khâtûn; *v.* (opposite of hit) khaṭa, yakhṭî; (not attain) mâ laḥaq, yilḥaq; (feel absence of) makànuh bêyyen, yubêyyin.
missent: marsûl bil wehm.
missing: mafqûd, dhâyi'.
mission: (commission) mamurîya; (society) irsàlîya; mishen.
missionary: *n.* mursal, *pl.* mursalîn.
misspelling: *n.* ghalaṭ fît tehjia.
mist: dhabâb.
mistake: *v.* make a mistake, ghalaṭ, yaghlaṭ; *n.* ghalaṭ, *pl.* aghlâṭ.
mistaken: ghalṭân.
mister: ṣâḥib, mister.
mistranslate: ghalaṭ fît tarjuma (cp. **mistake**).
mistress: (proprietress) ṣâḥiba.
mistrust: *v.* shekk fî, yashikk; *n.* shekk.
misunderstand: mâ iftehem tamàm, yeftehim.
misunderstanding: sû istifhàm.
misuse: *v.* behdel, yubehdil; *n.* sû isti'màl.
mitigate: khaffaf, yukhaffif.
mitigation: takhfîf.
mitten: keff, *pl.* kufûf.
mix: *v. trans.* khalaṭ, yakhlaṭ; mezej, yimzaj; *v. intrans.* ikhtalaṭ, yakhtaliṭ; imtezej, yemtezij.
mixed: (compounded) makhluṭ, mamzûj; (confused) mushawwash.
mixture: (compound) khalîṭ, mazîj.
moan: *v.* wenn, yawunn; *n.* anîa.
mob: *v.* thâr 'ala, yathûr; *n.* thàyirin.
mobile: khafîf el ḥaraka.
mobility: khiffa fîl ḥaraka.
mobilize: *v. trans.* jamma', yujammi'; ḥashad, yaḥshad; *v. intrans.* tajamma', yatajamma'.
mock: *v.* (imitate) qallad, yuqallid; (ridicule) qashmar, yuqashmir; istehza bi, yestehzi.
mockery: qashmara, istihzà.
mode: (method) ṭarîqa, kêfîya; (fashion) môda; (custom) 'âda, *pl.* 'awâyid.
model: (pattern) namûna; *v. trans.* ṣawwar, yuṣawwir.
moderate: *adj.* (not extreme) mu'tedil, mutawassiṭ; *v. trans.* khaffaf, yukhaffif; qallal, yuqallil; *v. intrans.* khaff, yakhuff.
moderation: i'tidàl.
moderately: mu'tedil; bi i'tidàl.
modern: jadîd, *pl.* jided; ḥadîth.
modest: muḥteshim, musteḥî.
modesty: (opposite of conceit) tawâdhu', ḥaya; (chastity) 'iffa.
modification: taghyîr.
modify: (change) ghayyar, yughayyir; (lighten) khaffaf, yukhaffif.
modus operandi: kêfîyat el 'aml.
Mohammed: muḥammad.
Mohammedan: muslim, *pl.* muslimîn.

Mohammedanism: islàm.
moist: nedî.
moisten: nagga, yunaggi'.
moisture: raṭûba.
molar: *n.* (tooth) dhirṣ, *pl.* dhurûṣ.
molasses: dibes.
molest: *v.* qârash, yuqârish; ḥârash, yuḥârish.
mollify: lêyyen, yulêyyin.
molten: madhyûb.
moment: (of time) daqîqa, *pl.* daqâyiq.
momentarily: kull sâ'a.
momentary: waqtî.
momentous: muhimm.
momentum: qûwa dàfi'a.
monarch: sulṭân, *pl.* salâṭîn.
monarchical: mulûki, sulṭânî.
monarchy: salṭana; absolute monarchy, salṭana mustabidda; limited monarchy, salṭana maḥdûda.
monastery: dêr, *pl.* adyâr.
monastic: rahbânî.
monasticism: rahbânîya.
Monday: yôm el ithnên; el ithnên.
money: flûs, fulûs; make money, see **make**.
money-changer: ṣarrâf, *pl.* ṣarârîf.
moneyed: mutamawwal.
monk: râhib, *pl.* rahbân.
monkey: shàdî, *pl.* shawàdî.
monogamy: akhdh ḥarma wâḥida.
monopolize: iḥteker, yaḥtekir.
monopoly: iḥtikàr.
monosyllable: maqṭa' wâḥid.
monotheism: et tawḥîd.
monotheist: muwaḥḥid.
monotonous: mu'ajjiz.
monsoon: baraṣât.
Montenegro: jebel aswad; qaradâgh (T.).
month: shahr, *pl.* ishhur.
monthly: *adj.* shahrî; *adv.* shahrîyan; monthly pay, shahrîya.
monument: tidhkâr.
mood: (temper) khulq; (of verb) ṣîgha.
moody: 'abûs.
moon: qamr, gamr; new moon, hilàl; full moon, bedr.
moonlight: qamrîya.
moor: *v. trans.* (tie ship) rabaṭ, yarbaṭ; *v. intrans.* (anchor ship) dabb angar, yadibb.
Moor: maghrabî, *pl.* maghâraba.
moorage: marsa.
moorings: marsa.
moral: *adj.* edebî; (virtuous) adîb.
morality: àdàb.
morally: edebîyan.
morals: àdàb, akhlâq.
more: akthar, ekther, ezyed; any more (again), bâ'ad; more and more, ekther fa ekther; more or less, taqrîban, bên ez zàyid wa en nâqis; the more—the more, bi qadrma.
moreover: 'alâwatan 'ala hàdha.
morning: ṣubḥ, ṣabâḥ; mid-morning, dhaḥa; good morning, ṣabbâḥkum Allâh bil khair.
Morocco: marâkish.
morphine: rûḥ efyûn; murfîn.
morsel: luqma.
mortal: *adj.* (subject to death) fànî; (deadly) qâtil, mumît; (human) besherî; *n.* besher.
mortality: (rate of death) wafiyyàt.

mortally: (unto death) lil môt.
mortar: (for bricks) juṣṣ.
mortgage: *v.* rahan, yarhan; *n.* ruhn, rahanîya.
mortified: maqhûr.
mortify: qahhar, yuqahhir.
mortmain: waqf; amlàk mawqûfa.
Mosaic: (pertaining to Moses) mûsawî.
Moses: mûsa.
Moslem: muslim, *pl.* muslimîn.
mosque: jàmi', *pl.* jawàmi'; masjid, *pl.* masàjid.
mosquito: *sing. and pl.* baqq; mosquito-curtain, kulla, *pl.* kulel.
most: *adj.* el ekther; el ezyed; el aghlab; at the most, ekther ma yakûn; make more of, debber, yudebbir.
mostly: el ekther; el aghlab.
moth: (cloth-eating) 'ith.
mother: umm, *pl.* ummahàt; wàlida; mother country, el waṭn el aṣalî.
mother-in-law: ḥamàt.
motion: *n.* (movement, gesture) ḥaraka, *pl.* harakàt; to make motion (parliamentary), awrad rai, yûrid; to second motion (parliamentary), thenna rai, yuthennî; motion was (is) carried (parliamentary), fàz er rai, yafûz.
motionless: sàkin; bila ḥaraka.
motive: (actuating principle) sebeb; muḥarriq.
motley: mukhtelif.
motor: motor cycle, motor saikel; motor car, tanbîl, *pl.* tanàbîl; trâm; motor boat, markab gàz, motor bôt.
motto: 'anwàn.
mould: *v. trans.* shekkel, yushekkil; *v. intrans.* (mildew) ta'affan, yat'affan; *n.* (form, model) qâlib, *pl.* qawâlib; *n.* (mildew) 'afûna.
moulding: parwàz, ḥâshia.
mouldy: mu'affan.
moult: *v.* beddel, yubeddil.
mound: tell, *pl.* tulûl.
mount: *v. trans.* mount horse, rekeb, yirkab; mount picture, rekkeb, yurekkib; mount guard, ḥaṭṭ nôbachi, yaḥuṭṭ; *v. intrans.* ṣa'ad, yaṣ'ad; ṭala', yiṭla'; *n.* (animal) dàbba, *pl.* dawàb.
mountain: jebel, *pl.* jibàl, ajbàl.
mountainous: jebelî.
mounted: (on horseback) ràkib, *pl.* ràkibîn.
mourn: ḥazan, yaḥzan.
mourner: fâqid, *pl.* fâqidîn.
mournful: ḥazîn, *pl.* ḥazàna.
mourning: ḥuzn; in mourning, ḥazîn.
mouse: fâr, *pl.* fîrân.
moustache: shawârib.
mouth: (of person) *colloquial*, ḥalq, *pl.* ḥulûq; *literary*, fàh, *pl.* afwàh; (of river) ṣadr, maṣabb; (of cave) ḥalq, medkhal.
mouthful: luqma.
movable: mutaḥarrik.
move: *v. trans.* (put in motion) ḥarrak, yuḥarrik; (transfer) naqal, yanqal; *v. intrans.* (be in motion) taḥarrak, yataḥarrak; (be transferred) intaqal, yantaqil.
movement: ḥaraka, *pl.* ḥarakàt.
mow: ḥashsh, yaḥishsh.
mown: maḥshûsh.
much: *adj. and adv.* kathîr; how much? (price and quan-

tity), shqadr, shqad; as much as, biqadrma; so much, helqad.
mucilage: ṣamagh.
muck: siyàn.
mud: ṭîn, waḥl.
muddle: *v.* (confuse) shawwash, yushawwish; (make a mess of) khabbaṣ, yukhabbiṣ.
muddy: mutawaḥḥil.
muffle: *v.* (cover) ghaṭṭa, yughaṭṭî; lethem, yiltham; (lessen sound of) waṭṭa, yuwaṭṭî.
mug: mashrab.
mulberry: tukkî.
mule: baghl, *pl.* baghâl.
muleteer: baghghâl, *pl.* baghghâla; makàri, *pl.* makàrîya.
multiplication: (arithmetical) dharb; (increase) takthîr.
multiplicity: kuthra.
multiply: (in arithmetic) dharab, yadhrab; (increase) *v. intrans.* kether, yikthar, *v. trans.* kethther, yukeththir.
multitude: (of people) jamâ'a; (great number) kuthra.
municipal: beledî.
municipality: beledîya.
munitions: jubakhâna.
murder: *v.* qatal, yaqtal; *n.* qatl.
murderer: qâtil, *pl.* qâtilîn.
murky: mudhabbab.
murmur: (protest) *v.* qamqam, yuqamqim.
muscle: habra, *pl.* habr.
muscular: muhabbar.
museum: muzakhâna, mat-haf.
mush: ḥarîsa.
mushroom: fuṭar.
music: muzîqa.
musical: muzîqî.
musician: muzîqachî, *pl.* muzîqachîya.
Muslim: see **Moslem**.
muslin: kham raqîq.
must: làzm; e.g. I must go, làzm arûḥ, &c.
mustard: khardal.
muster: *v.* jama', yijma'.
musty: mu'fina.
mute: *adj. and n.* akhras, *f.* kharsa, *pl.* khurs, khursîn.
mutilate: shawwah, yushawwih.
mutinous: 'âṣî, *pl.* 'âsiyîn.
mutiny: *n.* thôra, 'aṣyân; *v.* 'aṣa, ya'ṣî.
mutton: laḥm ghanam.
mutual: mutabàdil.
muzzle: *v.* leththem, yuleththim.
my: *pron. suffix*, î (see p. 19); màlî (after noun).
myrtle: yàs.
myself: nefsî.
mysterious: ghâmidh.
mystery: (secret) sirr, *pl.* asrâr; (something not understood) mesela ghâmidha.
mysticism: taṣawwuf.
myth: khurâfa, *pl.* khurâfàt.
mythical: khurâfî.

N

nail: *v.* besmer, yubesmir; *n.* (of iron) bismâr, *pl.* basàmîr; mismâr, *pl.* masàmîr; (finger nail) dhafr, *pl.* adhâfir.
naked: muṣallakh, 'aryân, (of truth) mujerred.
nakedness: (nudity) 'arya.
name: *v.* semma, yusemmî; (appoint) 'ayyan, yu'ayyin; *n.* ism, *pl.* asàmî, ismà; proper name, ism khâṣṣ; what is the name of...? shism.
named: musemma.

namely: ya'nî.
nap: *v.* taqayyal, yataqayyal; *n.* qêlûla.
nape: (of neck) 'ilba.
naphtha: nafadh.
napkin: peshqîr, *pl.* pashàqîr.
narcotic: mukhaddir.
narrate: ḥaka, yaḥkî; qaṣṣ, yaquṣṣ.
narrative: *n.* rawàya.
narrow: dhayyiq; narrow-minded, muta'aṣṣib.
narrowly: (with difficulty) bil kàd.
narrowness: dhîq.
nasty: (filthy) wasikh.
nation: umma, *pl.* umam.
national: ummî.
nationality: jinsîya.
native: *adj.* waṭanî, *pl.* waṭanîyîn; *n.* ibn el bilàd, *pl.* ehl el bilàd.
natural: ṭabî'î.
naturalize: tejennes, yetejennes.
naturalized: mujennes.
naturalization: tejnîs.
naturally: ṭabî'î, ṭab'an.
nature: ṭabî'a; (kind) jins, *pl.* ajnàs; (created things) 'âlim eṭ ṭabî'a.
naught: *v.* come to naught, baṭal, yabṭal; set at naught, istakhaff, yastakhiff.
naughty: waqîḥ, *pl.* wuqqâḥ.
nausea: la'b en nefs.
nauseate: la''b en nefs, yula''ib.
nautical: baḥrî.
naval: baḥrî.
navigable: yenmeshî bi safîna.
navigate: meshsha markab, yumeshshî.
navigation: (art of) malâḥa; (act of) meshi maràkib.
navigator: rabbân.
navy: baḥrîya.
near: qarîb, jarîb; *v.* come near, tedenna, yetedenna.
nearly: taqrîban; he nearly fell, ràd yoga' (cp. p. 108).
nearness: qurb.
neat: (clean) nadhîf, *pl.* nadhâf; (orderly) muretteb.
neatly: (orderly) bi nidhâm.
necessaries: lawàzim.
necessarily: bidh dharûra.
necessary: làzm, lâzim, dharûrî.
necessitate: elzem, yulzim; awjab, yûjib.
necessity: luzûm, dharûra.
neck: (human) ruqba; (of land) lisàn; (of bottle) ḥalq.
necklace: ṭôq, qilâda.
necktie: boyunbâgh.
need: *v.* iḥtàj, yaḥtàj; lezem, yilzam; 'âz, ya'ûz (used in 3rd pers. with pron. suffix of person needing).
need: ḥàja, *pl.* ḥàjàt; iḥtiyàj, *pl.* iḥtiyàjàt; in case of need, 'and el luzûm; in need of, muḥtàj ila.
needle: ibra, *pl.* ibar.
needless: mâ làzm.
needlessly: 'abath, ṣadan.
needle-work: shughl khiyâṭa.
needy: muḥtàj.
negation: inkâr.
negative: *adj.* selbî.
negatively: selban.
neglect: *v.* ghafal 'an, yaghfal; ehmel 'an, yuhmil; *n.* ihmàl.
neglected: matrûk.
negligence: ihmàl, taghâful.
negligent: ghaflân.
negotiable: yatadâwal.
negotiate: (treat with) tadhàkar, yatadhàkar; (negotiate a bill) bâ', yabî'.

negotiation: mukhâbara, mudhàkara.
negro: 'abd, *pl.* 'abîd.
neigh: *v.* ṣahal, yaṣhal; *n.* ṣahîl.
neighbour: jâr, *pl.* jîrân; *v.* jâwar, yujâwir.
neighbourhood: maḥalla.
neighbouring: mujâwir.
neither: neither — nor, la — wa la.
nephew: ibn âkh *or* ibn ûkht.
nerve: (anatomical) 'aṣab, *pl.* a'ṣâb; (courage) jasâra.
nervous: (with affected nerves) aṣabî; (agitated) maqlûq.
nervousness: (affection of nerves) 'aṣabîya.
nest: 'ish.
net: (for fish) shebeka, shebcha; (against mosquitoes) kulla, *pl.* kulel; *adj.* (resultant) ṣâfî.
netting: *n.* mushebbek.
nettle: *v.* (irritate) kedder, yukeddir.
neuralgia: nawàzîl.
neuter: (gender) jàmid.
neutral: mutaḥâyid.
neutrality: ḥiyàda.
neutralize: baṭṭal, yubaṭṭil.
never: ebeden (with negative).
nevertheless: mâ' dhàlik.
new: jadîd, *pl.* jided; make new, jedded, yujeddid.
newly: min jadîd; (recently) fî hel qurb.
news: khabr, *pl.* akhbâr; ḥawâdith.
newspaper: jarîda, *pl.* jaràyid.
next: thànî; the next day, el yôm eth thànî; next month, esh shahr el àtî; esh shahr el jai; esh shahr el muqbil; *adv.* thumma; bâ'ad hàdha.
nice: (good) ṭayyib, 'âl; (exact) madhbûṭ.
nicely: (well) ṭayyib.
nick: nick of time, fî daqîqatuh.
nickel: nîkel.
nickname: laqab, *pl.* alqâb.
niece: bint el âkh or bint el ûkht.
niggardly: bakhîl, mumsik.
night: lêla, *pl.* layàlî; to-night, hel lêla; by night, bil lêl; day and night, lêl wa nahâr.
night-clothes: gêjalik; hudûm el lêl.
nile: en nîl.
nimble: khafîf.
nimbleness: khuffa.
nine: (*with masc.*) tis'a; (*with fem.*) tis'.
ninefold: tis' marràt.
nineteen: tisatâsh (tis'atâsh).
nineteenth: tàsi' 'âsher.
ninetieth: et tis'în.
ninety: tis'în.
ninth: *n.* tus', *pl.* atsà'; *adj.* tàsi'.
nippers: minqâsh.
nipple: memma.
nitre: shûra.
nitrogen: nitrôjîn.
no: la, lakhair; no one, maḥad; (not) mâ.
nobility: (dignity, rank) sharf; the nobility, el ashrâf.
noble: *adj.* sharîf, najîb; *n.* sharîf.
nobleness: najàba.
nobody: maḥad; la aḥad.
nod: *v.* nekkes er râs, yunekkis; *n.* neksa.
noise: (sound) ḥiss; (clamour) ṣiyâḥ; (uproar) qalabâligh.
noiseless: bila ḥiss; bi sukût.
noisy: see **noise**.
nomad: bedwî, *pl.* bedu.
nominal: bil ism.

nominally: isman.
nominate: 'aradh, ya'radh.
nomination: taqdîm ism.
nominative: marfû'.
none: (person) aḥad (with negative); (thing) shê (with negative).
non-observance of: ihmàl 'an.
nonsense: *n.* laghwa.
noon: dhuhr (*pron.* dhu-hr).
nor: la, wa la.
normal: 'âdî; normal school, dâr el mu'allimîn.
north: shamàl.
north-east: shamàl sharq.
northern: shamàlî.
northward: shamàlan.
north-west: shamàl gharb.
Norway: nàrûj.
Norwegian: nàrûjî.
nose: khashm.
nose-ring: khazàma.
nostril: mankhara, *pl.* manâkhir.
not: (with verb) mâ; (with noun or adj.) mû, (vulgar) mûsh; (negative imperative) la; is not, are not, lês.
notable: (man, personage) sharîf, *pl.* ashrâf, a'yàn.
notably: (especially) khaṣûṣan.
notary: musejjil.
note: *v.* (set down in writing) qayyad, yuqayyid; (observe) lâḥadh, yulâḥidh; *n.* (short letter) teskera, *pl.* tasàkir; (comment in book) ḥâshia, *pl.* ḥawâshî; sharḥ; (bank-note) nôt, *pl.* anwât; (promissory) kampiyàla, *pl.* kampiyàlàt.
note-book: defter, *pl.* dafàtir.
noted: (famous) mashhûr; (observed) mulâhadh, mâ'lûm.
nothing: hîch; là shê; for nothing (gratis) bilàsh, majjànan; good for nothing, mâ yinfa'; he has nothing, mâ 'anduh shê.
notice: *v.* dâr bàl 'ala, yadîr; lâḥadh, yulâḥidh; *n.* (intimation) khabr; (advertisement) i'làn; (consideration, regard) i'tibâr.
noticeable: yan'arif.
notify: bellegh, yubelligh.
notoriety: shuhra.
notorious: mashhûr bi sharr.
notwithstanding: *conj.* mâ' hàdha; *prep.* ghaṣban 'an.
noun: ism, *pl.* asàmî, ismà; proper noun, ism khâṣṣ.
nourish: *v.* (feed) ṭa''am, yuṭa''im.
nourishing: muqawwî.
nourishment: ekl.
novel: *adj.* jadîd, gharîb; *n.* rawâya, *pl.* rawâyàt.
November: tishrîn thànî.
novice: ghashîm, *pl.* ghushamâ.
now: hessa, elàn, el ḥîn, tôa; now and then, aḥyànan.
nowadays: fî hel ayàm.
nowhere: mâ . . . fî ai makân.
noxious: karîh.
nucleus: aṣl, libb.
nuisance: dôkha.
null and void: bâṭil.
nullify: baṭṭal, yubaṭṭil.
numb: mukhaddar.
number: *v.* 'add, ya'idd; ḥasab, yaḥsab; *n.* 'adad; (quantity) miqdâr; singular number, mufrid; plural number, jam'.
numberless: la yu'add.
numbers: a'dàd, arqâm.
numerically: bil 'adad.
numerous: 'adîd, kathîr.
nurse: *v.* dàra, yudàrî; *n.* mudària, *pl.* mudàriyàt.

nut: (walnut) jôza, *pl.* jôz; pistachio, fistiq; (monkey nut) fistiq 'abîd; (for bolt), ṣamûna, *pl.* ṣamûnàt.
nutmeg: jôzbû'.

O

oak: balûṭ.
oar: mijdhàf, *pl.* majàdhîf.
oasis: wâḥa, *pl.* wâḥàt.
oath: yamîn; take oath, ḥalaf yamîn, yaḥlaf.
oatmeal: wetmîl.
obdurate: 'anîd, *pl.* 'anîdîn.
obedience: ṭâ'a.
obedient: ṭâyi', muṭî'.
obey: ṭâ', yaṭî'.
object: *v.* i'taradh, ya'taridh; *n.* (thing) shê, *pl.* ashyà; (purpose) qaṣd, ghardh; (grammatical) maf'ûl bihi.
objection: i'tirâdh, *pl.* i'tirâdhàt.
objectionable: mâ maqbûl.
obligation: (duty) wàjib, wajûb; (coercion) ijbâr.
obligatory: làzm, làzim.
oblige: (constrain) ejber, yujbir; (do favour) 'amal ma'rûf, ya'mal.
obliged: (required) majbûr; malzûm; (grateful) mimnûn.
obliging: ṣâḥib ma'rûf.
oblique: màyil.
oblong: mustaṭîl.
obscene: fâḥish.
obscure: (figurative) ghâmidh.
observance: (performance) ijrâ; (custom) 'âda, *pl.* 'awâyid.
observant: mulâḥidh.
observation: (remark) mulâḥadha; (seeing) nadhr, temyîz; (notice) murâqaba.
observe: (notice) lâḥadh, yulâḥidh; observe holiday, lezem, yilzam.
obsolete: matrûk, mulgha.
obstacle: mànî', *pl.* mawànî'.
obstinacy: 'inàd.
obstinate: 'anîd.
obstruct: (hinder) mena', yimna'; (block) sedd, yasidd.
obstruction: see **obstacle**.
obtain: ḥaṣṣal, yuḥaṣṣil; nàl, yanàl.
obtainable: *v.* to be obtainable, ḥaṣal, yaḥṣal.
obvious: wâdhih, bêyyen.
obviously: wâdhiḥan.
occasion: *v.* sebbeb, yusebbib; *n.* (cause) sebeb, *pl.* asbàb; (time) marra, *pl.* marràt; (appropriate time) munàsaba; there is no occasion for, la ḥàja ila.
occasional: aḥyànan (*adv.*)
occasionally: aḥyànan.
occident: gharb.
occidental: gharbî.
occupancy: iqâma.
occupant: qâ'id.
occupation: (work) shughl, wadhîfa; military occupation, iḥtilàl.
occupy: (possess) qa'ad fî, yaq'ad; (hold) dhabaṭ, yadhbaṭ; (occupy country), iḥtell, yaḥtell; occupy time, akhadh waqt, yakhadh.
occur: (happen) ṣâr, yaṣîr; jara, yijrî; ḥadath, yaḥdath; occur to mind, khaṭar fîl bàl, yakhṭar.
occurrence: (event) ḥâditha, *pl.* ḥawâdith; (happening) wuqû'.
ocean: baḥr, oqiyânôs.
o'clock: es sâ'a.
October: tishrîn awwal.
odd: (strange) gharîb; (uneven,

of number) ferd, tek; £5 odd, khams lîrat wa kusûr.
odious: karîh.
odium: 'âr.
odour: rîḥa.
of: (possession; see p. 48 f.) màl (see p. 49); (about) 'an; min jehet; min ṭarf; man of wealth, ṣâḥib flûs (see further, p. 49).
off: (generally implied in verb); (to a distance) ba'îd; off and on, aḥyànan; bâ'dh el awqât; I am off, ana râyiḥ.
offence: (trespass) ta'addî; (crime) dheneb; give offence, kedder, yukeddir; take offence, ishma-azz, yashma-izz.
offend: see **offence**.
offended: mutekedder.
offender: mudhnib, muta'addi.
offensive: *adj.* (annoying) muz-'ij; (foul) karîh; *n.* (attack) hujûm.
offer: *v.* (present) qaddam, yuqaddim; (propose) 'aradh, ya'radh; offer to do, ràd yusawwî, yarîd; *n.* 'arîdha.
office: *n.* (position) wadhîfa, mâ-murîya; (place of business) idâra, hâfîs; post office, posṭakhâna.
officer: (military) dhâbiṭ, *pl.* dhubbâṭ; (civil) mâ-mûr, *pl.* mâ-mûrîn.
official: *adj.* resmî; *n.* ma-mûr.
officially: resman.
officiate: qâm bil wadhîfa, yaqûm.
officious: fudhûlî, mutafâdhil.
offspring: dhurrîya.
often: kathîr; kathîr marràt; wàjid.
oil: dihn; (petroleum) gàz, nafadh; castor-oil, dihn kharwa; olive oil, dihn zêt; *v.* dehen, yidhan; dehhen, yudehhin.
oilcloth: mushemma'.
oily: dahîn, mudehhen.
ointment: marham, dihn.
oke: ($2\frac{3}{4}$ lb.) hugga, *pl.* hugag.
okra: bâmia.
old: (of person) kabîr, *pl.* kibâr; musinn; old man, shâyib, *pl.* shiyàb; old woman, 'ajûz, *pl.* 'ajâyiz; (of thing) 'atîq, *pl.* 'utuq; (ancient) qadîm; 12 years old, 'amruh thnâsh sena (cp. **age**); get old (of person) shêyyeb, yushêyyib; get old (of thing) 'ataq, ya'taq.
old age: shêb.
oleander: difla.
olive: zêtûn; see also **oil**.
omelet: omlêt, 'ajja.
omen: ishâra, *pl.* ishâràt.
ominous: naḥas.
omission: (oversight) sehu; (leaving out) ḥadhf.
omit: (leave out) terek, yitrak; ḥadhaf, yaḥdhaf; (omit by mistake) seha, yes-ha.
omnipotent: qâdir.
omnipresent: ḥâdhir fî kull makàn.
omniscient: 'ârif bi kull shê.
on: (upon) 'ala; on the occasion of, 'and; on the way, bid darb; (forward) ila qadàm; (continually) dhall (with 2nd person present of verb); off and on, aḥyànan.
once: ferd marra; at once, hessa, ḥâlan; all at once, ferd marra; once upon a time, ferd marra, ferd yôm.
one: *adj.* wâḥid, *fem.* wâḥida, ferd; one night, ferd lêla; one by one, wâḥid wâḥid; *n.* el insàn; no one, maḥad; not

one, la wâhid; every one, kull wâḥid.
one-eyed: a'war.
onion: başla, *pl.* başal.
only: *adj.* wâḥid; *adv.* faqaṭ, bes.
onward: ila qadàm.
open: *v.* feteḥ, yiftaḥ; fekk, yafukk; *v. intrans.* infeteḥ, yenfetiḥ; iftekk, yeftekk; *adj.* maftûḥ, mafkûk.
opening: (aperture) fetḥa; (beginning) iftitâḥ.
openly: (publicly) 'alanan, jihâran.
operate: *v. trans.* shaghghal, yushaghghil; *v. intrans.* ishtaghal, yashtaghil; perform operation, sawwa 'amalîya, yusawwî.
operation: (military) ḥaraka, *pl.* ḥarakàt; (surgical) 'amalîya, *pl.* 'amalîyàt.
operator: (telegraph) têlchî, *pl.* têlchîya.
opiate: munawwim, muraqqid.
opinion: rai, *pl.* ârâ; fikr; *pl.* afkâr.
opium: ofyûn, tiryàk.
opponent: muqâwim.
opportune: munàsib.
opportunity: furṣa, *pl.* furaṣ.
oppose: qâwam, yuqâwim; dhâdad, yudhâdid.
opposite: (over against) muqâbil, qubàl; (opposed to) dhudd.
opposition: muqâwama, mudhâdada.
oppress: dhalam, yadhlam.
oppression: dhulm.
oppressive: (tyrannous) dhâlim; (of heat) thaqîl.
oppressor: dhâlim, *pl.* dhâlimîn.
option: khiyâr, ikhtiyâr.
optional: ikhtiyârî.
or: aw; yô.
oral: shafàhî.
orally: shifàhan.
orange: portugâla, *pl.* portugâl.
oration: khuṭba, khiṭâb.
orator: khaṭîb.
orbit: madàr.
ordain: (prescribe) amar, yamur; (confer holy orders upon) resem, yersem.
ordained: (predisposed) maktûb; (to holy orders) marsûm.
order: *v.* (command) amar, yamur; *n.* (command) amr, *pl.* awâmir; (system) nidhâm, tertîb; money order, ḥawàla posṭa; *conj.* in order that, ḥatta; put in order, retteb, yurettib; put in order (repair) ṣallaḥ, yuṣalliḥ; out of order, kharâb.
orderly: *adj.* muntadhim; *n.* (officer) yâwar.
ordinance: ḥukm, *pl.* aḥkàm.
ordinarily: 'âdatan.
ordinary: 'âdî.
ordnance: jubakhâna.
organ: (member of body) 'adhu, *pl.* a'dhâ; (musical instrument) muzîqa; (medium) wâsiṭa.
organization: tandhîm, nidhâm.
organize: nadhdham, yunadhdhim.
organized: muretteb, muntadham.
orient: sharq.
oriental: sharqî.
origin: mebda, aṣl.
original: *adj.* awwal, aṣlî; *n.* aṣl.
originality: faṭna.

originally: aṣlan.
originate: *v.trans.* awjad, yûjid; *v. intrans.* ibteda, yebtedi.
ornament: *v.* zêyyen, yuzêyyin; *n.* zîna.
ornamented: muzêyyen.
orphan: yatîm, *pl.* yatàma, îtàm.
ostensible: muṭadhâhir.
ostensibly: dhâhiran.
ostentation: fakhfakha.
ostracize: ṭarad, yaṭrad.
other: âkhar, *f.* ukhra, *pl.* ukhar, akhirîn; ghair. See also **each**.
otherwise: (if not) wa illa; (another way) 'ala ghair ṭarîqa.
Ottoman: 'othmànî, osmanlî; Ottoman Empire, ed dawlat el 'othmànîya.
ought: (physical necessity) làzm, làzim; (moral obligation) wàjib; he ought to have gone, kàn làzm yarûḥ (cp. p. 109).
ounce: ons, *pl.* onsàt.
our: *pron. suffix*, na; màluna (after noun).
ourselves: anfusuna.
out: barra, khârij.
outbreak: (riot) thôra; (of disease) bidàya.
outcast: maṭrûd.
outcome: natîja.
outcry: ṣiyâḥ, ṣêḥa.
outdo: ghalab, yaghlab.
outdone: maghlûb.
outdoors: see **out**.
outer: barrânî.
outfit: lawàzim.
outgoing: râyiḥ.
outing: nuzha.
outlaw: *n.* manfî.
outlay: maṣraf.
outlet: makhraj.
outline: *v.* sawwa jedwal, yusawwî; *n.* (abridgement) mukhtaṣar.
outlook: mustaqbil.
outlying: khârijî.
outpost: ṭalî'a, *pl.* ṭalâyi'.
outrage: *n.* qabîḥa.
outrageous: khârij.
outright: (at once) ḥâlan.
outrun: sebeq, yisbaq.
outside: *adv.* barra, khârij; *n.* barrât, khârij.
outstanding: (of debt) bâqî; (prominent) bêyyen.
outstretched: mamdûd.
outward: ila khârij.
outwit: ghalab, yaghlab.
oval: bêdhî.
oven: furn, tannûr.
over: (above) 'ala, fôq; (more than) ekther min; (ended) khalaṣ; all over (wholly), kullish, kulluh; over and over, amrâr; over and above, fadhlan 'ala; over again, tekrâr.
overboard: bil mai.
overcharge: ṭalab zàyid, yaṭlab.
overcome: ghalab, yaghlab.
overdue: (of note) fàyit istiḥqâq; (of ship) fàyit waqtuh.
overeat: akal zàyid, ya-kul.
overestimate: qaddar zàyid, yuqaddir.
overfeed: *v.trans.* ṭa''am zàyid, yuṭa''im.
overflow: *v.* fâdh, yafîdh; *n.* zôd, fêdh, fêyadhân.
overhanging: bàriz.
overhaul: (examine) keshef, yikshaf; (catch up) laḥaq, yilḥaq.
overhead: fôq; fôq er râs.
overland: barran.
overlay: ghashsha, yughashshi

(lit. counterfeit); lebbes, yulebbis (lit. clothe).
overload: ḥammal zàyid, yuḥammil.
overlook: (neglect) ghafal 'an, yaghfal; (excuse) 'adhdhar, yu'adhdhir; (superintend) nâdhar, yunâdhir.
overlooking: mushrif 'ala.
overpay: a'ṭa zàyid, yu'ṭî.
overrule: (quash) baṭṭal, yubaṭṭil.
oversee: nâdhar, yunâdhir.
overseer: nâdhir, *pl.* nudhdhâr.
oversight: (mistake) sehu; (superintendence) nadhâra.
overtake: laḥaq, yilḥaq.
overthrow: *v.* qalab, yaqlab; *n.* inqilâb.
overturn: qalab, yaqlab.
overweight: wazn zàyid.
overwork: *v.* ṭa'ab zàyid, yiṭ'ab.
owe: expressed by madyûn, 'ala, or maṭlûb; e.g. I owe you, lek 'alêyya; ana maṭlûb illek; ana madyûn lek.
owing: maṭlûb ila; owing to (on account of), min sebeb.
owl: bûma.
own: *v.* (possess) melek, yimlak; (admit) qarr, yaqurr, *adj.* màl, with *pron. suffix*; khâṣa.
owner: ṣâḥib; àbû (before *gen.*).
ox: thôr, *pl.* thîràn.

P

pace: *v.* mesha, yimshî; *n.* khaṭwa, *pl.* khaṭwàt.
pacific: hàdi, salîm.
Pacific Ocean: el baḥr el pàsifîkî.
pacify: hedda, yuheddi; sekken, yusekkin.
pack: *v.* lemm, yalimm; (press) kebes (chebes), yikbas; *n.* (bundle) ḥazma, *pl.* ḥuzam; (load) ḥiml; pack of cards, desta.
package: amàna, *pl.* amàyin.
pack-horse: kadîsh, *pl.* kiddesh; dâba, *pl.* dawàb.
pack-saddle: jilàl.
pad: *v.* (stuff) ḥasha, yaḥshu; *n.* spinal pad, libàdat edh dhahr.
paddle: *v.* gharraf, yugharrif; *n.* gharrâfa, *pl.* gharârîf.
paddle-wheel: parwâna, *pl.* parwânàt.
padlock: qufl, *pl.* qufûl.
page: wajh, *pl.* wajhàt; ṣaḥîfa, *pl.* ṣaḥâyif.
paid: *pass. part.* mûfì.
pail: baldi, *pl.* baldiyàt; saṭl, *pl.* suṭûl; (large) piyàla, *pl.* piyàlàt.
pain: *v. intrans.* waja', yûja' *n.* waj'.
painful: yûja'.
pains: (care) daqqa.
painstaking: kaddûd.
paint: ṣabagh, yaṣbagh; dharab bôya, yadhrab; *n.* ṣabagh, bôya.
painter: ṣabbâgh, *pl.* ṣabbâghîn; (artist) muṣawwir.
pair: zôj, *pl.* azwàj.
palace: qaṣr, *pl.* quṣûr.
palatable: ladhîdh.
palate: saqf el ḥalq.
pale: *adj.* (from fear) aṣfar; (light in colour) kàshif, âchiq.
palm: (of hand) keff; (tree) nakhla, *pl.* nakhl; palm leaf, ṣa'f.
palpitation: khafaqân.
palsy: fàlij.
paltry: denî.

pamphlet: karràsa, *pl.* karàrîs.
pan: diset; (frying-pan) ṭâwa.
pane: (of glass) jàma, *pl.* jàmàt.
panic: ru'ba.
pannier: sella, *pl.* eslàl.
panorama: mandhar.
pant: *v.* leheth, yilheth.
pantaloons: pantalôn.
papal: papâwî.
paper: (material) kàghid, qarṭâs; (document) warqa, *pl.* awrâq; (newspaper), jarîda, *pl.* jaràyid: blotting-paper, kàghid nashshàf; *adj.* min kàghid.
par: (equality) musâwàt; at par, 'alal qîmat el aṣalîya.
parable: methel, *pl.* emthàl.
parade: *v.* sâr, yasîr; *n.* (manœuvre) manâwara.
paradise: firdaws.
paraffin: gàz.
paragraph: faṣl.
parallel: *adj.* muwàzin, mutasàwî; parallel lines, khuṭûṭ mutasâwia.
paralysis: fàlij.
paralytic: maflûj.
parapet: supêr, *pl.* supêràt.
parasite: muta'alliq.
parasol: shemsîya, *pl.* shamàsî.
parcel: amàna, *pl.* amàyin.
parched: (dry) yàbis, maḥrûq.
pardon: *v.* 'afa 'an, ya'fu; sàmaḥ, yusàmiḥ: *n.* 'afu, musàmaḥa; I beg your pardon, el 'afu.
pare: see **peel**.
parent: (father) wàlid; (mother) wàlida; parents (*dual*), wàlidên.
parentage: aṣl.
parenthesis: hilàlên.
paring: *n.* gishr, *pl.* gishûr.
Paris: pàrîs.
park: (garden) bustàn, *pl.* basàtîn; (field park) markaz.
parley: *v.* tadhàkar, yatadhàkar; *n.* mudhàkara.
parliament: mejlis nawàb; parlament.
parole: *n.* kalàm sharf; on parole, taḥt esh sharf.
parrot: bîbî metto.
parse: 'arrab, yu'arrib.
Parsee: fârsî, *pl.* furs.
parsimonious: bakhîl, mumsik
parsley: krafs.
parson: qass, *pl.* qassàn.
part: *v. trans.* (separate) farraq, yufarriq; *v. intrans.* (be separated) fâraq, yufâriq; part with (do without), jàz min, yajûz; *n.* (portion) qasm, *pl.* aqsàm; juz, *pl.* ajzà; (share) ḥuṣṣa, *pl.* ḥuṣaṣ; (side) jànib, ṣafḥa, ṣôb; (some) bâ'dh; for the most part, el aghlab; on the part of, min qibl.
partake: *v.* (as of food) tanàwal, yatanàwal.
partial: (not general) juz-î; (biased) bi maḥâbàt.
partiality: maḥâbàt.
partially: (in part) qasman.
participant: mushterik, *pl.* mushterikîn.
participate: ishterek, yeshterik.
participle: active participle, ism fâ'il; passive participle, ism maf'ûl.
particular: (special) khaṣûṣî; (exacting) mudaqqiq; in particular, khaṣûṣan.
particulars: tafâṣîl; cp. **detail**.
parting: (separation) firâq; (as of roads) mafraq.

partition: (dividing) taqsîm; (as wall) ḥâjiz; *v.* qassam, yuqassim.
partly: bâʻdh; shê.
partner: sharîk, *pl.* shurakâ.
partnership: shiràka, sherika, shirka.
partridge: ḥajal, *pl.* ḥajlàn.
parts: (region) dîra, nawâḥî.
party: (assembly) jamâʻa; (political) ḥazb, *pl.* aḥzàb; (dinner-party) ʻazîma, walîma; (litigant) ṭarf, *pl.* aṭrâf; be a party to, ishterek fî, yeshterik.
pasha: pâsha, *pl.* pâshawàt.
pass: *v. intrans.* fàt, yafût; marr, yamurr; *v. trans.* (to hand) nawwash, yunawwish; (to pass resolution) qarrar, yuqarrir; to let pass, fawwat, yufawwit; to pass time, fawwat waqt, yufawwit; to come to pass, ḥadath, yaḥdath; *n.* (permission) pâs, *pl.* pâsàt; (defile) madhîq.
passage: (act of passing) murûr; (passage way) majàz; (passage in book) ʻabâra; (journey) sefer; passage money, nôl.
passenger: ʻabri, *pl.* ʻabrîya.
passion: (strong emotion) ḥammîya; to be in a passion, zaʻal, yizʻal.
passive: (not resisting) sàkin; passive voice, majhûl.
passport: pasaport; teskera murûr.
past: *adj.* mâdhî, fàyit; *n.* mâdhî.
paste: *v.* lezzeq, yulezziq; *n.* ʻajîn, ṣamagh.
pasteboard: muqawwa.
pastime: inshirâḥ.
pastor: (clergyman) qass, *pl.* qassàn.
pastry: shoghl ʻajîn.
pasturage: marʻa.
pat: *v.* ṭabṭab, yuṭabṭab.
patch: *v.* raqqaʻ, yuraqqiʻ; *n.* raqʻa, *pl.* ruqaʻ.
patent: *v. trans.* ḥaṣṣal imtiyàz, yuhaṣṣil; *n.* imtiyàz.
patented: mumtàz, maḥṣûr.
paternal: abawî; min ṭarf el àb.
path: sikka, *pl.* sikek; darb, *pl.* durûb.
pathetic: mu-eththir.
patience: ṣabr; to have patience, ṣabar, yaṣbar; iṣṭabar, yaṣṭabir.
patient: ṣabûr, *pl.* ṣabûrîn; to be patient, see **patience**.
patiently: bi ṣabr.
patriarch: shêkh, *pl.* shuyûkh; Chaldaean patriarch, petrak.
patriarchal: shêkhî.
patriot: muḥibb lil waṭn.
patriotic: see **patriot**.
patriotism: ghîra waṭnîya.
patrol: *n.* dawwarîya.
patronize: (help) sâʻad, yusâʻid; (stoop to) tedenna ila, yetedenna.
pattern: namûna, *pl.* namàyin.
paucity: qilla.
Paul: bûlus.
pauper: faqîr, *pl.* fuqarâ.
pauperize: faqqar, yufaqqir.
pause: *v.* wagaf, yogaf; *n.* wagfa.
pave: ṭabbaq, yuṭabbiq.
paw: *n.* fore-paw, îd, *dual* îdên; hind-paw, rijl, *dual* rijlên.
pawn: *v.* rahan, yarhan.
pay: *v.* wafa, yûfî; (to be worth doing) ṣarraf, yuṣarrif; *n.* maʻâsh.
payable: yûfa.
payment: (act of paying) defʻ; (instalment) qasṭ, *pl.* aqsâṭ.

pea: ḥummuṣ.
peace: salàm; (after war) ṣulḥ; to make peace, taṣâlaḥ, yataṣâlah.
peaceable: salîm.
peaceful: hàdî.
peach: khôkha, *pl.* khôkh.
peacock: ṭâwûs.
pear: armôṭ.
pearl: lûlû.
pearl-diver: ghawwâṣ, *pl.* ghawâwîṣ.
pearl-diving: ghôṣ.
peasant: fallâḥ, *pl.* falàlîḥ, filḥ.
pebble: ḥaṣwa, *pl.* ḥaṣu.
peck: *v.* naqqar, yunaqqir.
peculiar: (strange) gharîb; peculiar to (belonging to) khâṣṣ ila.
peculiarly: (especially) khaṣûṣan.
pecuniary: màlî.
pedal: (of bicycle) paidàn.
peddle: *v. trans.* dâr bi, yadûr bi.
peddler: (hawker) dawwâr.
pedestrian: màshî, *pl.* màshiyîn.
pedigree: aṣl, resn.
peel: *v.* gashshar, yugashshir; *n.* gishr, *pl.* gishûr.
peerage: (rank) ritbat amîr.
peg: (small stake) thabàt.
pell-mell: shadhr madhr.
pen: (for writing) qalm, *pl.* aqlàm; (for animals) yâkhûr, ḥadhra.
penal: jazà-î.
penalty: qaṣâṣ.
pence: pensàt.
pencil: qalm raṣâṣ, *pl.* aqlàm raṣâṣ.
pending: *adj.* mutawaqqif; *prep.* mutawaqqif ʻala.
pendulum: raqqâṣ.
penetrate: *v. trans.* deshshesh, yudeshshish; *v. intrans.* deshsh, yadishsh.
penetrating: (intelligent) faṭîn; (of cold) qâriṣ.
peninsula: shibh jazîra.
pen-knife: qalm ṭrâsh.
penman: khaṭṭâṭ.
penmanship: ḥusn khaṭṭ.
penniless: muflis.
penny: peni, *pl.* pensàt.
pent up: maḥṣûr.
people: *n.* nàs, unàs; the people, el ahàlî; a people, shaʻb; umma, *pl.* umam; the common people, el ʻâmma.
peopled: maskûn.
pepper: filfil.
peppermint: naʻnâʻ.
perceive: shàf, yashûf.
per cent: bil mîa.
percentage: (rate) bil mîa; (proportion) qasm.
perceptible: mubêyyen.
percolate: naqaṭ, yanqaṭ; nezz yanizz.
percussion cap: kapsûn.
peremptory: qaṭʻî.
perennial: ṭûl es sena.
perfect: *v.* kemmel, yukemmil; qadha, yaqdhî; temmem, yutemmim; *adj.* kàmil, tàmm.
perfected: mukemmel, tamàm.
perfection: kamàl.
perfectly: tamàman, kullish.
perforate: naqab, yinqab.
perforce: jabran.
perform: *v. trans.* qadha, yaqdhî.
performance: (doing) iqdhâ, ijrâ; (act) qadhîya; (musical performance) ḥafla.
perfume: *v.* ʻaṭṭar, yuʻaṭṭir; *n.* ʻaṭr.

perfumer: 'aṭṭâr, *pl.* 'aṭâṭîr.
perfunctory: dôhàn.
perhaps: yimkin, rubbama, bilki.
peril: khaṭr, *pl.* akhṭâr.
perilous: mukhṭir.
period: of (time) mudda, zamàn, dôr; (full-stop) nuqṭa.
periodical: *adj.* min waqt ila waqt; *n.* (paper) jarîda, *pl.* jaràyid.
periodically: min waqt ila waqt.
perish: helek, yihlak.
perjury: shahàdat zûr.
permanence: dawàm.
permanent: dàyim; yadûm.
permanently: 'ala dawàm.
permissible: ma-dhûn, jàyiz, mubâḥ.
permission: rukhṣa.
permit: *v.* rakhkhaṣ, yurakhkhiṣ; khalla, yukhallî; *n.* rukhṣa, ma-dhûnîya.
pernicious: mu-edhdhî.
perpendicular: qâyim, wâgif, 'amûdî.
perpetrate: fa'al, yif'al.
perpetrator: mudhnib.
perpetual: dàyimî.
perpetually: daiman; 'ala dawàm.
perpetuate: adàm, yudîm.
perplex: ḥayyar, yuḥayyir.
perplexed: mutaḥayyir.
perplexity: ḥîra.
perquisite: mulḥiqàt.
persecute: idhṭahad, yadhṭahid.
persecution: idhṭihâd.
perseverance: thabàt, mudàwama.
persevere: thebet, yithbat.
persevering: thàbit, mudâwim.
Persia: îrân; bilàd el 'ajem.
Persian: 'ajemî, *pl.* 'ajem; îrânî, *pl.* îrâniyîn; (language) fârsî.
persistence: iṣrâr.
persistent: mudmin.
person: shakhṣ, *pl.* ashkhâṣ; (in grammar) first person, mutekellim; second person, mukhâṭab; third person, ghâyib.
personal: shakhshî.
personally: shakhshan.
perspiration: 'araq.
perspire: 'araq, ya'raq.
persuade: qanna', yuqanni'.
persuasion: taqnî'; (creed) medh-heb, i'tiqâd.
persuasive: muqni'.
pertain: khaṣṣ, yakhuṣṣ.
pertinent: munàsib.
perturb: az'aj, yuz'ij.
perturbation: inzi'âj, qalq.
pervade: 'amm, ya'umm.
perverse: 'aqsi, muta'ânid.
perverseness: 'inàd.
pervert: 'awwaj, yu'awwij.
pessimist: sodâwî.
pest: waba.
pester: àdha, yu-àdhi.
pestle: hâwan; (for rice) jâwan.
pet: *n.* maḥbûb, mudellel; *v.* lâṭaf, yulâṭif.
petition: *n.* (request) istid'â; *v.* istad'a, yastad'i.
petitioner: musted'i.
petroleum: gàz, nafadh.
petty: juz-î.
pharmacist: ejzàchî, *pl.* ejzàchîya.
pharmacy: (science) ṣêdalîya.
phase: (condition) ḥâla, dôr.
pheasant: durrâj, *pl.* darârîj.
phenomenal: 'ajîb, khâriq.

phenomenon: ḥâditha, *pl.* ḥawâdith.
philanthropic: khairî.
philanthropist: rejul khairî.
philanthropy: khairîya.
philologist: loghawî.
philology: 'ilm el loghàt.
philosopher: fêlosôf, *pl.* falâsifa.
philosophical: felsefî.
philosophy: felsefa.
phlegm: belgham.
phlegmatic: bàrid.
phonograph: fônoghrâf, ḥâkî.
photograph: *v.* ṣawwar, yuṣawwir; jarr 'aks, yajurr; akhadh resm, ya-khudh; *n.* 'aks, *pl.* 'ukûs; resm, *pl.* rusûm.
photographer: muṣawwir, fôtoghrâfchî.
photography: taṣwîr.
phrase: 'ibâra, *pl.* 'ibârât; jumla, *pl.* jumal.
phraseology: 'ibârât.
physic: (laxative) mus-hil.
physical: jesedîya.
physically: jesedîyan.
physician: ṭabîb, *pl.* aṭibbâ.
physics: 'ilm eṭ ṭabî'iyàt.
piano: piyânô.
piastre: qursh, *pl.* qurûsh.
pick: *v.* (choose) istanqa, yastanqî; (gather) lemm, yalimm; jena, yijnî; pick up, laqaṭ, yilqaṭ; pick up (improve) ta'addal, yata'addal; pick at, dhajjar, yudhajjir; *n.* (tool) ṭabr, ḥîb.
picked: (selected) mustenqa.
picket: *n.* ṭali'a, *pl.* ṭalâyi'.
pickle: *n.* ṭurshî.
picnic: *n.* nuzha.
picture: *n.* ṣûra, *pl.* ṣuwar; resm, *pl.* rusûm; *v.* ṣawwar, yuṣawwir.

pie: barma.
piebald: abqa', *fem.* baq'a, *pl.* buq'.
piece: *v.* raqqa', yuraqqi'; *n.* waṣla, *pl.* waṣl; qaṭ'a, *pl.* quṭa'; in pieces, waṣla waṣla.
piecemeal: *adv.* shê fashê.
pier: eskela.
pierce: *v.* (make hole in) thaqab, yithqab; naqab, yinqab.
piercing: *adj.* ḥâdd.
piety: taqwa.
pig: khanzîr, *pl.* khanâzîr.
pigeon: ḥamâma, *pl.* ḥamâm.
pile: *v.* kawwam, yukawwim; *n.* (heap) kôma, *pl.* kûwam; (stake) tikma, *pl.* tikem.
pilfer: ikhteles, yakhtelis.
pilgrim: (to Mecca) ḥajjî, *pl.* ḥujàj; (to Kerbela) zàyir, *pl.* zuwwâr.
pilgrimage: (to Mecca) ḥijj, ḥajj; (to Kerbela) ziyâra; to go on pilgrimage, ḥajj, yaḥijj.
pill: ḥabb, *pl.* ḥubûb; ḥabbâya, *pl.* ḥabbâyàt.
pillage: *v.* neheb, yinhab; *n.* neheb.
pillar: 'âmûd, *pl.* 'awâmîd.
pillow: makhadda, *pl.* makhâdît.
pillow-case: wajh makhadda.
pilot: *n.* rabbân; *v.* sêyyer, yusêyyir.
pilotage: ujrat rabbân.
pimple: ḥabba.
pin: dembûs, *pl.* danâbîs.
pincers: kilâbatên.
pinch: *v.* qaraṣ, yaqraṣ; at a pinch, 'and el ḥâja.
pine: *n.* (wood) chàm.
pineapple: ananàs.
pink: *adj.* (rose-coloured) wardî.
pin-money: kharjîya.
pioneer: *n.* el awwal.

pious: khâyif Allâh; taqî, *pl.* atqiyà.
pip: *n.* (seed) bizra, *pl.* bizr.
pipe: *n.* (tube) bamba, ambûba; (for smoking) sabîl.
piracy: qarṣânîya.
pirate: qarṣân.
pistachio: fistiq.
pistol: warwar, *pl.* warâwir.
piston: mîl, *pl.* emyàl.
pit: *n.* bîr, ḥafra.
pitch: *v. trans.* (smear with pitch) gêyyer, yugêyyir; (pitch tent) naṣab, yanṣab; dharab, yadhrab; (throw) debb, yadibb; *v. intrans.* (on waves) la'ab, yil'ab; *n.* (substance) gîr.
pitcher: (for water) ibrîq, *pl.* abârîq; (for milk) jak; (Arab water ewer) meskhena, *pl.* masâkhin.
pith: *n.* (in plants) libb.
pitiful: muḥzin.
pitiless: min dûn raḥma.
pity: *v.* shefeq 'ala, yishfaq; taḥannan 'ala, yataḥannan; *n.* shefeqa, ḥanu, raḥma; what a pity, yâ lil esef; it is a pity, yûjib el esef.
pivot: *n.* madâr.
placard: i'làn, *pl.* i'lânàt.
placate: sekken, yusekkin.
place: *v.* ḥaṭṭ, yaḥuṭṭ; wadha', yodha'; *n.* makàn, *pl.* amàkin; maḥall, *pl.* maḥallàt; take place, ḥadath, yaḥdath; jara, yijrî; take place of, akhadh makàn, ya-khudh; in place of, 'iwadh; (with verb) 'iwadhma.
placid: hàdî.
plague: *v.* (tease) kedder, yukeddir; *n.* (disease) ṭâ'ûn, waba; (affliction) dharba, *pl.* dharabàt.
plain: *n.* barrîya, chôl; *adj.* (evident) wâdhiḥ; (unornamented) sàda.
plainly: (evidently) wâdhiḥan; (sincerely) khâliṣ.
plaintiff: mudda'î.
plan: *v.* (scheme) debber, yudebbir; (draw) resem, yirsam; *n.* (scheme) fikr, *pl.* afkâr; tadbîr, *pl.* tadàbîr; (drawing) resm, plân.
plane: *n.* (surface) saṭḥ; (tool) randa; *v.* (to plane) dharab randa, yadhrab.
planet: kôkab, *pl.* kawâkib.
plank: lôḥa, *pl.* lôḥ, lôḥàt.
plant: *v.* (seed) zara', yizra'; (trees) shetel, yishtal; (set up) naṣab, yanṣab; *n.* nabàt, *pl.* nabàtàt.
plantain: môza, *pl.* môz.
plaster: *v.* (wall) jaṣṣas, yujaṣṣiṣ; *n.* (for walls) juṣṣ; (adhesive) lezga.
plastering: tajṣîṣ.
plastic: lêyyin.
plate: *v.* lebbes, yulebbis; *n.* (dish) ṣaḥn, *pl.* ṣuḥûn, ṣuḥûna; (of sheet iron) sâch.
platform: takhta.
plausible: ma'qûl.
play: *v.* la'ab, yil'ab; (play music) daqq, yadiqq; *n.* la'b; (dramatic) tashkhîs.
player: (in sport) lâ'ib, *pl.* lâ'ibîn; (actor) mushakhkhis.
playfully: fil la'b.
playground: mal'ab.
playing: *n.* (music) dharb muzîqa; (acting) tashkhîs.
plaything: la'ba, la'bâya.
plea: ḥijja.
plead: (supplicate) iltemes, yeltemis; terejja, yeterejja; (in court) ḥâma, yuḥâmî.

pleader: (advocate) muḥâmî; see also **advocate**.

pleasant: (of person, or weather) laṭîf.

please: (give pleasure) 'ajjab, yu'ajjib; (satisfy) radhdha, yuradhdhî; if you please, min fadhlek.

pleased: (happy) farḥân, mukêyyif; (willing) râdhî.

pleasure: (delight) farḥ, surûr; (amusement) wunsa; (enjoyment) kêf; it gives me pleasure, yasirrnî; with pleasure, mimnûn; at pleasure, 'alal kêf; take pleasure in, teledhdhedh fî, yeteledhdhedh.

pledge: *v.* (promise) wâ'ad, yuwâ'id; (pawn) rahan, yarhan; *n.* (promise) wa'd; (pawn) rahn; (guarantee) kafàla; (deposit) 'arabûn.

Pleiades: thurêya.

plentiful: mabdhûl, wâfir.

plenty: (enough) kifàya, kàfi; (opulence) ni'ma.

pleurisy: dhàt el jenb.

pliable: lêyyin.

pliers: kilàbatên.

plight: (condition) ḥâla.

plod: *v.* kedd, yakidd.

plot: *v.* (conspire) desses, yudessis; (draw) resem, yirsam; *n.* (conspiracy) dasîsa, *pl.* dasàyis.

plough: *v.* karab, yikrab; *n.* faddàn.

ploughing: karâb.

pluck: *v.* qala', yaqla'; (gather flowers) qaṭaf, yaqṭaf.

plug: *v.* sedd, yasidd; *n.* sedàd.

plum: anjâṣ.

plumage: rîsh.

plumb-line: shàhûl, shàqûl.

plump: *adj.* samîn, *pl.* samàn.

plunder: *v.* neheb, yinhab; *n.* nahîba, kesb.

plunge: *v. trans.* ṭammas, yuṭammis; *v. intrans.* ṭamas, yaṭmas.

pluperfect: mâdhî fîl mâdhî.

plural: jum'.

plus: wa.

plush: qadîfa.

ply: (go to and fro) taraddad, yataraddad.

pneumatic: hawâ-î.

pneumonia: dhàt er rîya.

poached: (of eggs, known by cooks as *pûch*).

pocket: *n.* jêb, *pl.* juyûb.

pocket-book: jôzdàn.

pocket-knife: châkûch; qalm ṭrâsh.

poem: qaṣîda.

poet: shâ'ir, *pl.* shu'arâ.

poetry: shi'r.

point: *v.* (aim) nêshen, yunêshin; point at, ashâr ila, yushîr; point to (direct to) dell ila, yadill; *n.* (sharp end) râs; (dot) nuqṭa, *pl.* nuqaṭ; (subject) mawdhû'; (question) mesela; on point of, ràd, yarîd (see p. 108); to the point, mukhṭaṣar, mufîd.

pointed: musenn.

poison: *v.* semmem, yusemmim; *n.* semm.

poisonous: musimm, masmûm.

poker: maghrafa.

Poland: polônia.

polar: qaṭbî.

pole: *v.* (as boat) defa', yidfa'; *n.* (end of axis) quṭb; (of wood) 'âmud, *pl.* 'awâmîd; (for bellum) murdî, *pl.* marâdî.

police: *n.* polîs; police station, markaz polîs.

policy: (course of action) siyàsa.
polish: *v.* ṣaqqal, yuṣaqqil; *n.* ṣabgh; (gloss) lem'a.
polished: maṣqûl; (cultured) adîb.
polite: adîb, *pl.* udabà, adîbîn.
politeness: àdàb.
political: siyàsî; political officer, ḥâkim siyàsî.
politically: siyàsatan.
politics: siyàsiyàt.
poll: *v.* (register) qayyad nufûs, yuqayyid; *n.* (register) defter nufûs.
pollen: laqâḥ; *v.* scatter pollen, laqqaḥ, yulaqqiḥ.
poll-tax: wergo shakhṣî.
pollute: nejjes, yunejjis.
polluted: nejis.
polygamy: tekthîr en nisa.
polytheist: mushrik.
pomegranate: rummâna, *pl.* rummân.
pommel: *v.* basaṭ, yabsaṭ; *n.* (of saddle) kerfûz.
pomp: fakhfakha.
pond: birka.
ponder: ifteker, yeftekir; teemmel, yete-emmel.
pontoon: dûba, *pl.* dûwab.
poop: akhîr el markab.
poor: (not rich) faqîr, *pl.* fuqarâ; (lean) dha'îf, *pl.* dhu'âf; (unfortunate) meskîn, *pl.* masàkîn; (not good) dûnî.
pope: pâpa.
populace: el ahàlî.
popular: (beloved) maḥbûb; (prevailing) jàrî, 'âmm.
popularly: 'and el 'awâm.
populated: maskûn.
population: (people) el ahàlî; (number of people) 'adad en nufûs.
populous: muḥashshad.
porcupine: qanfadh, *pl.* qanâfidh.
pore: *n.* masàmm, *pl.* masàmmàt.
pork: laḥm khanzîr.
porous: nâdhiḥ.
porridge: ḥarîsa.
port: (harbour) bandar, *pl.* banàdir; mîna; (side) yisâr.
portable: yanshàl.
Porte: Sublime Porte, el bàb el 'âlî.
portend: dell ila, yadill.
porter: (gate-keeper) bawwàb, *pl.* bawwàbîn; qâpuchî; (carrier) ḥammàl, *pl.* ḥamàmîl.
portfolio: (case for papers) maḥfadha, janta; (office) nadhâra.
portion: (share) ḥaṣṣa, *pl.* ḥaṣaṣ; (part) qasm, *pl.* aqsàm; juz, *pl.* ajzà.
portmanteau: janta, *pl.* jantàt.
portrait: ṣûra, *pl.* ṣûwar.
portray: ṣawwar, yuṣawwir; (describe) waṣaf, yoṣaf.
Portugal: portugâl.
Portuguese: portugêzî.
position: (place) mawqa', *pl.* mawâqi'; makàn, *pl.* amàkin; (office) mâ-mûrîya; (state) ḥâla; to be in a position to, lahu ṭâqa an.
positive: (certain) akîd; (confident) mutayaqqin; (absolute) qaṭ'î; (opposite negative) 'ijàbî.
positively: (certainly) akîd, yaqîn; (absolutely) qaṭ'an.
possess: melek, yimlak.
possessed by: (owned by) ràji' ila.
possession: (owning) temelluk; (property) mulk, *pl.* amlàk;

ḥalàl; take possession of, dhabaṭ, yadhbaṭ.
possessive case: (in grammar) el mudhâf ilêhî.
possibility: imkàn.
possible: mumkin; yimkin; as —as possible, bigadr el imkàn; bigadma yimkin.
possibly: yimkin.
post: *v.* ba'ath bil posṭa, yib'ath; *n.* (mail) posṭa; post office, posṭakhâna; (position) mâmûrîya; (of wood) khashba.
postage: ujrat el posṭa; posṭa.
posterity: dhurrîya.
postman: posṭachî.
postmaster: mudîr posṭa.
postpone: akhkhar, yu-akhkhir.
postponement: ta-khîr.
postscript: mulḥiq.
postulate: faradh, yafradh.
posture: hê-a.
pot: (cooking) jidr, *pl.* jidûr; (for water, very large) ḥibb, *pl.* ḥibûb; (medium) habbàna; (small) tinqa, *pl.* tineg; sharba, *pl.* sharâbi.
potato: patêta.
potter: kawwàz, *pl.* kawàwîz.
pottery: fakhâra.
pouch: kîs, *pl.* akyàs.
poultice: labîkha, *pl.* labàyikh.
poultry: ṭuyûr el bêt.
pounce: ṭafar 'ala, yaṭfar.
pound: *v.* daqq, yaduqq; *n.* (weight) raṭl; (money) pâwn, *pl.* pâwnàt; lîra, *pl.* lîràt.
pour: *v. trans.* ṣabb, yaṣubb.
poverty: fuqr.
powder: *n.* (fine dust) ṭôz; gunpowder, bârûd.
power: (strength) quwa; (legal authority) ḥaqq; (government) dawla, *pl.* duwal; (influence) nufûdh.
powerful: qawî, *pl.* aqwiyâ, quwai.
powerless: 'âjiz.
pox: small-pox, jidrî.
practicable: yaṣîr.
practical: 'amalî.
practically: bil ḥaqîqa.
practice: (habit) 'âda, *pl.* 'awâyid; (action) temrîn, isti'màl, mumârasa, pratîk; (performance) ijrâ.
practise: *v. trans.* mâras, yumâris; merren, yumerrin; *v. intrans.* tamâras, yatamâras; temerren, yetemerren.
praise: *n.* (to God) ḥamd; (to man) medḥ; *v.* ḥamad, yaḥmad; medeḥ, yimdaḥ.
prawn: rubyàn.
pray: (worship) ṣalla, yuṣallî; (entreat) iltemes, yeltemis; istarḥam, yastarḥim.
prayer: ṣala, *pl.* ṣalawàt.
preach: wa'adh, yo'adh; khaṭab, yakhṭab.
preacher: wâ'idh, khaṭîb.
preaching: wa'dh, khiṭâba.
precarious: mudrik.
precaution: tenbîh.
precede: sebeq, yisbaq.
precedence: afdhalîya.
precedent: sàbiqa, *pl.* sawàbiq.
preceding: sàbiq.
precept: waṣîya, *pl.* waṣâyâ.
precious: thamîn, 'azîz.
precipitate: *v.* (hasten) 'ajjal, yu'ajjil.
precise: mudaqqiq (active); mudaqqaq (passive).
precision: daqqa.
preclude: mena', yimna'.
predestination: qadha wa qadr

predicate: *n.* khabr.
predict: tenebba, yetenebba.
predominant: mustawlî.
pre-eminent: mumtàz.
prefer: fadhdhal, yufadhdhil.
preferable: awla, akhair.
preference: (choice) ikhtiyâr.
preferment: taraqqî.
pregnant: ḥâmil.
prejudice: *v.* neffer, yuneffir; *n.* ghill; nufûr.
prejudiced: muteneffer.
prejudicial: mudhirr.
preliminary: (preparatory) isti'dàdan ila; *n.* isti'dàd.
premature: qabl el waqt.
premeditate: ta'ammad, yata'ammad.
premeditated: muta'ammad.
premier: (minister) ṣadr.
prepaid: jawàbli.
preparation: isti'dàd.
preparatory: isti'dàdî.
prepare: *v. trans.* ḥadhdhar, yuḥadhdhir; *v. intrans.* taḥadhdhar, yataḥadhdhar; ista'add, yasta'idd.
prepared: ḥâdhir, musta'add.
preposition: ḥarf jarr.
prepossessing: qâbil.
preposterous: muḥâll; khilàf el 'aql.
prerogative: ḥaqq, imtiyàz.
prescribe: waṣṣa, yuwaṣṣî.
prescription: (medical) racheta.
presence: (being present) ḥudhûr; (existence) wujûd; in presence of, fî ḥudhûr.
present: *adj.* (at hand) ḥâdhir; (existing) mawjûd; to be present, ḥadhar, yaḥdhar; at present, el ḥîn, fîl ḥâdhir; for the present, muwaqqatan; *n.* (gift) hadîya, *pl.* hadàyà.
present: *v.* qaddam, yuqaddim.
presentation: taqdîm, idhhâr.
presently: hessa; bâ'ad shwêya.
preservation: ḥafdh.
preserve: *v.* ḥafadh, yaḥfadh; *n.* (fruit) murabba.
preside: tarâ-as, yatarâ-as.
presidency: riyàsa.
president: ra-îs, *pl.* ru-asâ.
press: *v.* (squeeze) 'aṣar, ya'ṣar: (squeeze fruit) kebes, yikbes; (crowd) zaḥam, yizḥam; (urge) laḥḥ, yaiuḥḥ; (compel) sakhkhar, yusakhkhir; *n.* (printing press) maṭba'a; (mechanical press) ma'ṣara; (urgency) dharûra.
pressing: (urgent) dharûrî.
pressure: (weight) thuql; (urgency) dharûra.
prestige: nufûdh, saṭwa.
presume: faradh, yafradh.
presumption: (supposition) fardh, iftirâdh; (arrogance) tajàsur.
presumptuous: jasûr.
presuppose: faradh, yafradh.
pretence: ḥijja.
pretend: idda'a, yadda'î; sawwa ka-innahu, yusawwî.
pretext: ḥijja.
pretty: laṭîf, ḥulû, jamîl.
prevail: (overcome) ghalab, yaghlab; (predominate) 'amm, ya'umm.
prevailing: ghâlib.
prevalence: kuthra.
prevent: mena', yimna'.
prevention: men'.
previous: sàbiq, qabl.
previously: qabl, sàbiqan.
prey: *v.* ifteres, yefteris; beast of prey, ḥaiwân mufteris.
price: qîma, *pl.* aqyàm; si'r, *pl.* as'âr.

prick: *v.* naghaz, yanghaz; prick up ears, shenher, yushenhir.
pride: tekebbur; (laudable satisfaction) iftikhâr.
priest: qass, *pl.* qassàn.
primarily: aṣalîyan.
primary: (school) ibtidà-î.
prime minister: ṣadr a'dham.
primer: (reading-book) mabàdî qirâya.
primitive: (original) aṣalî; (simple) basîṭ.
primogeniture: bukûra.
prince: (ruling) amîr, *pl.* umarâ; (son of king) ibn el melk; (crown prince) welî 'ahd.
princess: (ruling) amîra; (daughter of king) bint el melk.
principal: *adj.* kabîr, ra-îsî; *n.* (of school) mudîr; (of money) râs màl; sarmâya.
principally: khaṣûṣan; el ekther.
principle: (simple truth) mebda, *pl.* mabàdî; (tenet) 'aqîda, *pl.* 'aqâyid; (rule) qâ'ida, *pl.* qawâ'id.
print: *v.* ṭaba', yaṭba'; *n.* ṭab'; (cloth) chît.
printer: maṭba'achî.
prison: ḥabs; in prison, maḥbûs.
prisoner: (prisoner of war) asîr, *pl.* usarâ; take prisoner, esser, yu-essir; be taken prisoner, te-esser, yete-esser.
private: *adj.* (personal) shakhṣî; (secret) sirrî; *n.* (soldier) nefer, *pl.* neferàt.
privately: 'ala infirâd.
privation: (want) mashaqqa.
privilege: (permission) rukhṣa; (chance) furṣa; (advantage) imtiyàz.
prize: *v.* themmen, yuthemmin; qaddar, yuqaddir; *n.* jà-iza, *pl.* jawà-iz.
probable: muḥtemil, mumkin.
probably: yimkin, bilkî.
probate: maḥkama waṣâya.
probation: tejruba.
probationer: taḥt et tejruba.
probe: *v.* dharab mîl, yadhrab; *n.* mîl.
problem: mes-ela, *pl.* masàyil.
problematical: mushkil.
procedure: mu'âmala; civil procedure, muḥâkamat el ḥuqûq; criminal procedure, muḥâkamat jinà-îya.
proceed: (go) râḥ, yarûḥ; (begin) qâm, yaqûm; gâm, yagûm; (issue) ṣadar, yaṣdar; proceed against, aqâm da'wa, yuqîm.
proceeding: *n.* mu'âmala; (legal proceeding) muḥâkama.
proceeds: ḥâṣil, maḥṣûl.
process: (method) nasaq, ṭarîqa.
proclaim: a'lan, yu'lin.
proclamation: i'làn.
procurable: yaḥṣal.
procure: ḥaṣṣal, yuḥaṣṣil.
prodigal: mubedhdhir, musrif.
prodigious: 'adhîm.
produce: *v.* (bring forward) jàb, yajîb; (cause) sebbeb, yusebbib; entej, yuntij; *n.* ḥâṣil, wàridàt.
product: (result) natîja; (fruit) ḥâṣil.
production: (act of production) tawlîd.
productive: (of soil) mukhṣib; productive of (causing) musebbib.
profane: profane language, teshtûm; masebba.

profess: (claim) idda'a, yadda'î; (declare) ṣarraḥ, yuṣarriḥ; (profess religion) i'taqad, ya'taqid.
professedly: dhâhiran.
profession: (vocation) wadhîfa; (declaration) iqrâr; profession of faith, shahàda; i'tiqâd.
professor: (teacher) istàdh, *pl.* asàtidha.
proficient: musta'idd.
profit: *v.* fàd, yafîd; nefa' yinfa'; *v. intrans.* istafàd, yastafîd: *n.* maḥṣûl, mekseb, ribḥ.
profitable: râbiḥ, murbiḥ.
profligate: safîh.
profound: 'amîq.
profuse: fàyiq, khârij.
profusion: kuthra.
programme: barnàmaj.
progress: *v.* taqaddam, yataqaddam; taraqqa, yataraqqa; *n.* taqaddum, taraqqî.
progressive: mujidd.
prohibit: mena', yimna'.
prohibited: mamnû'.
prohibition: men'.
project: *v.* (jut out) ṭala', yiṭla'; berez, yibraz; *v* (plan) 'azam, ya'zam; *n.* fikr, rai.
projectile: qanbala, *pl.* qanàbil; gulla, *pl.* gulel.
projection: bàriz.
prolific: (human) muwellid; (of woman) jayyàba.
prolong: ṭawwal, yuṭawwil.
prolongation: taṭwîl, iṭàla.
promenade: *v.* temeshsha, yetemeshsha; *n.* temeshshî.
prominent: (conspicuous) mubêyyen, bêyyen; (important) mu'tebir.
promise: *v.* wâ'ad, yuwâ'id; *n.* wa'd.
promissory note: kampiyàla *pl.* kampiyàlàt.
promote: (facilitate) sehhel, yusehhil; (promote in rank) rafa', yarfa'; (cause) sebbeb, yusebbib.
promotion: tarfî'.
prompt: *v.* (incite) ḥarrak, yuḥarrik; *adj.* (punctual) 'ala waqt; (ready) musta'idd.
promptly: 'alal waqt.
promulgate: aṣdar, yuṣdir.
prone: (liable) qâbil.
pronoun: dhamîr, *pl.* dhamâyir.
pronounce: lafadh yalfadh; (declare) ṣarraḥ, yuṣarriḥ.
pronunciation: talaffudh.
proof: (trial) tajruba; (evidence) barhân, *pl.* barâhîn; dalîl, *pl.* adilla.
prop: *v.* sened, yisnad; *n.* watad.
propagate: (generate) wallad, yuwallid; (spread) nesher, yinshar.
propagation: (act of) tawlîd; (spreading) intishâr.
propel: defa', yidfa'.
propeller: parwâna.
proper: (fitting) lâyiq; (own) khâṣṣ, khaṣûṣî; proper noun, ism khâṣṣ.
property: (estate) mulk, *pl.* amlàk; màl, *pl.* amwàl; (quality) ṣifa.
prophecy: *n.* nubûwa.
prophesy: *v.* tenebba, yetenebba.
prophet: nebi, *pl.* anbiyà.
prophetic: nebawî.
propitiate: radhdha, yuradhdhî.
propitious: (of time) musâ'id.

proportion: (relation) nisba; (share) ḥaṣṣa, *pl.* ḥaṣaṣ; in proportion to, bi nisba ila; in proportion as, bigadrma, bigadma.
proportionally: bi nisba.
proposal: ʿarîdha; (scheme) fikr, *pl.* afkâr.
propose: (put forward) ʿaradh, yaʿradh; (intend) qaṣad, yaqṣad.
proposition: (proposal) ʿarîdha; (demand) ṭalba, *pl.* ṭalabàt; ṭalâba.
proprietor: (of house, &c.) ṣâḥib; (of garden) mellàk, *pl.* mellàka.
propriety: munàsaba.
prose: nether.
prosecute: (claim) sâq daʿwa, yasûq; (person) aqâm daʿwa, yuqîm.
prosecutor: muddaʿî.
proselyte: dâkhil, *pl.* dukhalâ.
prospect: (view) mandhar; (hope) eml.
prosper: *v. intrans.* nejjaḥ, yunejjiḥ; waffaq, yuwaffiq.
prosperity: najâḥ.
prosperous: nàjiḥ, muwaffaq.
prostitute: *n.* fâḥisha, *pl.* fawâḥish; gaḥba, *pl.* gaḥâb.
prostrate: *v. trans.* waqqaʿ, yuwaqqiʿ, *adj.* mutemedded.
protect: ḥâfadh, yuḥâfidh; ḥâma, yuḥâmi.
protection: muḥâfadha; (of government) ḥimàya.
protectorate: taḥt ḥimàya.
protest: *v.* iʿtaradh, yaʿtaridh; sawwa protesto, yusawwî; *n.* iʿtirâdh, protesto.
protestant: protestânî; *pl.* protestân.
protrude: ṭalaʿ, yiṭlaʿ.
proud: (vain) mutekebbir; proud of (taking pride in) muftakhir.
prove: *v.* (test) jarrab, yujarrib; (establish) barhan, yubarhin; thebbet, yuthebbit.
provender: ʿilfa.
proverb: methel, *pl.* amthàl.
provide: (prepare) ḥadhdhar, yuḥadhdhir; (supply) jehhez, yujehhiz.
provided that: bi sharṭ an.
providence: (divine) ʿinàya ilàhîya.
provident: mudebbir.
province: wilàya, *pl.* wilàyàt.
provision: (stipulation) sharṭ, *pl.* shurûṭ.
provisions: arzâq.
provisional: waqtî, mashrûṭ.
provisionally: muwaqqatan.
provoke: (excite) hêyyej, yuhêyyij; (annoy) kedder, yukeddir.
prow: ṣadr.
proxy: by proxy, niyàbatan.
prudent: ḥâzib, mudebbir.
prune: *v.* zebber, yuzebbir; *n.* (fruit) ʿalûcha.
Prussia: prûsia.
Prussian: prûsî.
psalm: mazmûr, *pl.* mazàmîr.
puberty: sinn el bulûgh.
public: *adj.* (common) ʿumûmî; (belonging to state) amîrî, mîrî; make public, aʿlan, yuʿlin; *n.* el ʿâmma, el ʿawâm.
publication: (act of) neshr; (thing published) tà-lîf, *pl.* ta-àlîf.
publicity: shuhra.
publicly: jihâran.
publish: ṭabaʿ, yaṭbaʿ; nesher, yinshar.
publisher: nàshir.
pudding: pûdink.

pull: *v.* (draw) jarr, yajurr; pull down, hedem, yihdam; *n.* jarr, jarâra.
pulley: bakara.
pulpit: manbar, *pl.* manâbir.
pulse: (at wrist) nabdh.
pulverize: daqq, yaduqq; saḥaq, yisḥaq.
pump: *v.* jarr bi ṭramba, yajurr; *n.* ṭramba.
pumpkin: yaqtîn.
punctual: 'alal waqt.
punctually: tamàman 'alal waqt.
punctuation: fàriz, *pl.* fawàriz.
puncture: *v.* inbaṭṭ, yanbaṭṭ; *n.* zarf.
punish: qâṣaṣ, yuqâṣiṣ.
punishable: yuqâṣaṣ.
punishment: qiṣâṣ.
punitive: ta'qîbî.
punt: *v.* defa', yidfa'.
pupil: telmîdh, *pl.* talàmîdh; (of eye) bîbî.
puppy: juru, *pl.* jarâwî.
purchase: see **buy**.
purchaser: mushterî.
pure: (clear) ṣâfî; (not defiled) ṭâhir; (unmixed) khâliṣ.
purgatory: maṭ-har.
purge: *v.* (cleanse) ṭahhar, yuṭahhir; (relax) sehhel, yusehhil; *n.* mus-hil.
purify: ṭahhar, yuṭahhir; naqqa, yunaqqî.
purity: (cleanness) ṭahâra; (chastity) 'iffa.
purple: arjuwànî.
purpose: *v.* qaṣad, yaqṣad; nawa, yinwî; 'azam, ya'zam; *n.* qaṣd, ghâya.
purposely: 'amdan, qaṣdan.
purse: *n.* kîs, jôzdàn.
pursuance: in pursuance of, ittibâ'an ila.
pursue: teba', yitba'.
pursuit: (following) muṭârada; (vocation) wadhîfa, shoghl.
pus: mudd.
push: *v. trans.* defa', yidfa'; *v. intrans.* (advance) taqaddam, yataqaddam; *n.* def'a.
put: (place) ḥaṭṭ, yaḥuṭṭ; put off (postpone) akhkhar, yuakhkhir; put on (wear) lebes, yilbas; put out (light) ṭaffa, yuṭaffî.
putty: sharîs, ghara.
puzzle: *v.* ḥayyar, yuḥayyir; *n.* ḥîra; (be puzzled) taḥayyar, yataḥayyar.
puzzling: muḥayyir.
pyramid: herem, *pl.* ihrâm.

Q

quadruped: ḥaiwân àbû arba'.
quaint: gharîb, tuḥâf.
qualify: *v. trans.* (render fit) ḥadhdhar, yuḥadhdhir; (limit) ḥaddad, yuḥaddid; (describe) waṣaf, yoṣaf; *v. intrans.* ista'add, yasta'idd.
quality: (kind) jins, shikl; (attribute) ṣifa, *pl.* ṣifât; ṭabî'a.
quandary: ḥîra.
quantity: miqdâr, kemmîya.
quarantine: karantîna.
quarrel: *v.* takhâṣam, yatakhâṣam; tanàza', yatanàza'; *n.* nizâ'.
quarrelsome: munàzi', mashhûr.
quarry: *n.* maḥjar.
quarter: *v.* (lodge) nezzel, yunezzil; (divide into four) qas-

sam ila arba'; *n.* (fourth part) rub', *pl.* arbâ'; chàrik, *pl.* chawàrîk (T.); (direction) jiha; (of town) maḥalla; (of year) thalàthat ishhur; (mercy) raḥma.
quarters: (lodgings) menzel; head-quarters, markaz.
quarter-master: mâ-mûr arzâq; quarter-master-general, mâ-mûr el i'âsha.
quash: (annul) baṭṭal, yubaṭṭil.
quay: eskela.
queen: melika, *pl.* melikàt.
queer: *adj.* (strange) gharîb.
quell: (subdue) sekken, yusekkin.
quench: ṭaffa, yuṭaffî.
question: *v.* (ask) se-el, yes-el; (doubt) shekk, yashikk; *n.* suwàl, *pl.* suwàlàt, esela; (matter discussed) mes-ela, *pl.* masàyil; (doubt) shekk; out of the question, muḥâll.
questionable: meshkûk.
quick: (fast) khafîf, sarî'; (clever) dhekî, *pl.* edhkiyà
quickly: bil 'âjl.
quickness: sur'a, khiffa.
quicksilver: zîbaq.
quiet: *v.* sekken, yusekkin; sekket, yusekkit; *adj.* hàdî, sàkin; *imper.* keep quiet, iskat; *n.* sukût, hudu.
quietly: bi sukût.
quill: rîsha.
quilt: lahâf, *pl.* lahâfàt.
quince: safarjil.
quinine: kînakîna; sulfâta.
quit: (leave) terek, yitrak.
quite: kullish; bil kullîa.
quotation: iqtibàs; (price) si'r.
quote: iqtebes, yaqtebis.

R

rabbit: arnab, *pl.* arânib.
rabies: inkilàb.
race: *v. intrans.* tasàbaq, yatasàbaq; *n.* (horse race) sharṭ, musàbaqa; (among men) musàbaqa, sabâq; (kind of men) jins, *pl.* ajnàs; (a people) umma, *pl.* umam.
race-course: mêdàn.
radiate: tasha''ab, yatasha''ab.
radical: *adj.* (original) aṣalî; *n.* (letter in root of word) aṣl.
radically: (entirely) bil kullîa.
radish: fijl.
radius: nuṣf el quṭr.
raft: kelek, *pl.* aklàk.
rafter: jisr.
rag: *n.* khirqa, *pl.* khiraq; waṣla, *pl.* waṣlàt.
rage: (anger) zâ'l.
ragged: mushaqqaq.
raid: *v.* ghaza, yaghzu; *n.* ghazu.
rail: *n.* (of ship) maḥajjil.
railway: sikkat ḥadîd; rêl; see also **station**.
raiment: hudûm, libs.
rain: *n.* maṭr; it rains, tamṭar.
rainbow: qôs qadaḥ (qazaḥ).
rainy: mumṭir, maṭrî.
raise: rafa', yarfa'; shàl, yashîl; (cause) sebbeb, yusebbib; (raise army) jama', yijma'; (raise grain) zara', yizra'; (raise animals) rabba, yurabbî.
raisin: zabîb.
rake: *v.* reshsh, yarishsh.
rally: *v. trans.* lemm, yalimm; *v. intrans.* iltemm, yeltemm.
ram: (sheep) kebsh, *pl.* kubûsh; *v.* ṣadam, yaṣdam.
ramble: *n.* meshya, siyâḥa; *v.* temeshsha, yetemeshsha.

rancid: zenekh.
random: at random, bil hawa.
range: *v.* (place in order) ṣaffat, yuṣaffit; *n.* (of mountains) silsala.
rank: *v.* (estimate) ḥasab, yaḥsab; (arrange) ṣaffat, yuṣaffit; *n.* (position) ritba, *pl.* ritab; from the ranks, alailî.
ransack: dawwar, yudawwir; fettesh, yufettish.
ransom: *v.* efda, yufdî; *n.* fidwa, fidya.
rap: *v.* (strike) daqq, yaduqq; *n.* daqqa.
rapid: khafîf, sarî'.
rapidity: sur'a.
rapidly: bi sur'a; khafîf; bil 'âjl.
rare: (scarce) nàdir; (curious) gharîb, 'antîqa; (underdone) nî; 'ala nuṣṣ.
rarefied: (of air) khafîf.
rarely: nàdir; bi nàdir; qalîl.
rascal: khabîth.
rash: *v.* to be rash; da'am, yid'am.
rat: jurêdî, *pl.* jurêdîya.
rate: *v.* ḥasab, yaḥsab; *n.* (price) si'r, *pl.* as'âr; (proportion) nisba; (degree) dereja; (of speed) sur'a; at any rate, 'ala kull ḥâl.
rather: (undoubtedly) ma'lûm, belli; (to some extent) no'an mâ; shwêya; he would rather go, yarîd yarûḥ wa là yadhull.
ratification: taṣdîq.
ratify: ṣaddaq, yuṣaddiq.
ratio: nisba.
ration: ta'yîn.
rational: (endowed with reason) dhû 'aql; (reasonable) ma'qûl.
rationally: 'aqlîyan.
ravage: kharrab, yukharrib.
rave: hedhrem, yuhedhrim.
ravel: *v. intrans.* inḥall, yanḥall.
ravine: wâdî.
raw: (uncooked) nî; (without knowledge) ghashîm.
raze: hedem, yehdem.
reach: waṣal, yoṣal; out of reach, mâ yannàsh.
react: radd, yarudd.
read: qara, yaqra.
readily: (easily) bi suhûla; (quickly) bi sur'a.
readiness: isti'dàd; (willingness) ridha.
reading: qirâya, qirâ-a; reading-book, kitàb qirâya.
ready: ḥâdhir, zàhib; (quick) sarî'; make ready, ḥadhdhar, yuḥadhdhir.
real: (true) ṣaḥîḥ, ḥaqîqî; (actual) nefs el (followed by noun).
reality: ḥaqîqa.
realize: (understand) derek, yidrak; sha'ar, yish'ar; (earn) ḥaṣṣal, yuḥaṣṣil.
really: bil ḥaqîqa; ḥaqîqatan.
realm: memleka, *pl.* mamàlik.
reap: ḥaṣad, yaḥṣad.
reaper: ḥâṣid, *pl.* ḥâṣidîn.
reaping: ḥuṣâd.
rear: *v. trans.* (train) rabba, yurabbî; *v. intrans.* (as horse) jefel, yijfel; *n.* akhîr; to the rear, ila wara.
rearguard: dhuwêl; sâqa.
reason: *n.* (faculty) 'aql; (cause) sebeb, *pl.* asbàb; *v.* (discuss) tabâḥath, yatabâḥath.
reasonable: (sensible) ma'qûl; (moderate) mutawassiṭ.
reasoning: mubâḥatha.
reassure: emmen, yu-emmin.
rebate: *n.* isqâṭ, isqonto.

rebel: *v.* 'aṣa, ya'ṣî; *n.* 'âṣî, *pl.* 'aṣiyîn.
rebellion: thôra, 'aṣyân.
rebound: radd, yarudd.
rebuff: *v.* radd, yarudd; *n.* rafdh, radd.
rebuild: 'ammar, yu'ammir.
rebuke: *v.* wabbakh, yuwabbikh; *n.* tawbîkh.
recall: *v.* (remember) tedhekker, yetedhekker; (call back) istarja', yastarji'; (annul) baṭṭal, yubaṭṭil.
recapture: istarja', yastarji'.
recede: radd, yarudd.
receipt: (act of receiving) qabdh, wuṣûl; (voucher) wuṣûl; 'ilmwakhabr.
receive: akhadh, ya-khudh; (receive money) qabadh, yaqbadh.
recent: jadîd.
recently: fî hel qurb.
receptacle: mâ'ûn, *pl.* muwâ'în.
recess: (short vacation) farâgha, ta'ṭîl; (in wall) râzûna, *pl.* ruwâzîn.
recipient: âkhidh.
reciprocal: mutabàdil.
reciprocate: 'âwadh, yu'âwidh.
recitation: tekrîr.
recite: kerrer, yukerrir; tela, yetlu.
reckless: da'am, yid'am.
reckon: (count) ḥasab, yaḥsab; (esteem) ḥasab, yaḥsab; reckon on, i'temed 'ala, ya'temid.
reclaim: istaradd, yastaridd.
reclamation: istirjâ'.
recline: itteka, yetteki; temedded, yetemedded.
recognition: i'tirâf.
recognize: 'araf, ya'raf; (acknowledge) qarr, yaqurr.
recoil: *v.* (of gun) refes, yirfas; *n.* (of gun) refsa.
recollect: tedhekker, yetedhekker.
recommend: (commend) waṣṣa, yuwaṣṣî; naṣaḥ, yanṣaḥ; (praise) medeḥ, yimdaḥ.
recommendation: letter of recommendation, tawṣia.
recompense: jàza, yujàzî; *n.* thawàb.
reconcile: ṣâlaḥ, yuṣâliḥ.
reconciliation: muṣâlaḥa, ṣulḥ.
reconnoitre: jesses, yujessis; khamm, yakhumm.
record: *v.* qayyad, yuqayyid; *n.* qaid.
recourse: muràja'a.
recover (regain) ḥaṣṣal, yuḥaṣṣil; (regain health) ta'addal, yata'addal.
recovery: (regaining) taḥsîl; (in health) ta'âfa.
recreation: lehwa.
recruit: *v.* recruit troops, lebbes 'asker, yulebbis; *n.* (new soldier) 'asker jadîd.
rectangle: mustaṭîl.
rectify: ṣallaḥ, yuṣalliḥ; 'addal, yu'addil.
rectum: maq'ad.
recur: radd, yarudd; tekerrer, yetekerrer.
red: *m.* aḥmar, *f.* ḥamra, *pl.* ḥumr.
redeem: (ransom) fekk, yafukk; (in religious sense) feda, yifdî.
redeemer: fàdî.
redness: ḥamra.
redoubt: istiḥkàm.
redress: anṣaf, yunṣif; *n.* inṣâf, ta'wîdh.

reduce: (lessen) nezzel, yunezzil; (make fewer) qallal, yuqallil; reduce to (change to) ḥawwal, yuḥawwil; reduce price of, naqqaṣ, yunaqqiṣ.
reduction: (in number) tanqîṣ; (in size) taṣghîr; (in price) isqonto, isqâṭ.
reed: qaṣba, *pl.* qaṣab; bardî.
reef: *v.* (reef sail) khanaq, yakhnaq; *n.* (of rock) fisht.
re-enforce: see **reinforce.**
refer to: (send to) ḥawwal ila, yuḥawwil; (allude to) ashâr ila, yushîr.
reference: (sending to) taḥwîl ila; (allusion) ishâra; letter of reference, tawṣiya; with reference to, min jehet; fî khuṣûṣ; min ṭarf.
refine: (clean) ṣaffa, yuṣaffî; (educate) hedhdheb, yuhedhdhib.
refinement: (cleaning) taṣfia; (of manner) tehedhdhub.
refit: jehhez, yujehhiz.
reflect: *v. trans.* ʽakkas, yuʽakkis; *v. intrans.* inʽakas, yanʽakis; (think) te-emmel, yete-emmel.
reflection: (of light) inʽikâs; (thought) te-emmul; (blame) madhemma.
reform: *v. trans.* ṣallaḥ, yuṣalliḥ; *v. intrans.* taṣallaḥ, yataṣallaḥ.
reformation: iṣlâḥ.
refract: kesser, yukessir.
refraction: inkisâr.
refrain: *v.* imtenaʽ, yemteniʽ; tejenneb, yetejenneb.
refresh: (make cool) berred, yuberrid; (revive) jeddded, yujeddid; (strengthen) qawwa, yuqawwî.
refreshing: muberrid.
refreshments: muberridât; refreshment-room, ṣufrakhâna.
refuge: melja; take refuge, ilteja, yelteji.
refugee: shârid, multeji.
refund: *v.* rejjaʽ, yurejjiʽ.
refusal: rafdh.
refuse: *v.* rafadh, yarfadh; *n.* (garbage) zabâla.
refute: radd, yarudd.
regain: istarjaʽ, yastarjiʽ.
regard: *v.* (pay attention to) bâla bi, yubâlî; (esteem) iʽtabar, yaʽtabir; (think) ḥasab, yaḥsab; *n.* (attention) intibâh; (respect) iʽtibâr; with regard to, min jehet, min ṭarf; out of regard to, iḥtirâman ila; regards, taḥyiyât.
régime: dôr, ḥukm.
regiment: ṭâbûr, *pl.* ṭawâbîr.
regimental: ṭâbûrî.
region: qaṭʽa; ṭarf, *pl.* aṭrâf.
register: *v. trans.* qayyad, yuqayyid; (letter) ʽahhad, yuʽahhid; *v. intrans.* taqayyad, yataqayyad; *n.* (book) defter.
registered: (recorded) muqayyad; (of letter) mutaʽahhad; taʽahhudlî (T.).
registration: (recording) taqyîd.
regret: *v.* te-essef, yute-essif; *n.* esef.
regular: (according to rule) qânûnî; (according to time) muʽayyan; (orderly) munṭadham; regular soldier, nidhâmî, *pl.* nidhâmîya.
regularity: nidhâm, tertîb.
regularly: ḥasab el qânûn.
regulate: nadhdham, yunadhdhim; retteb, yurettib.

regulator: mîzàn.
reign: *v.* ḥakam, yaḥkam; melek, yimlak; *n.* ḥukm.
reinforce: (strengthen) qawwa, yuqawwî; sened, yisnad; (with troops) a'ṭa imdàd, ya'ṭî.
reinforcements: imdàd.
reins: suyûr.
reinstate: rejja', yurejji'; ḥaṭṭ tekrâr, yaḥuṭṭ.
reject: rafadh, yarfadh.
rejoice: *v. trans.* farraḥ, yufarriḥ; *v. intrans.* faraḥ, yifraḥ.
rejoicing: farḥ.
relapse: *v.* irtadd, yartadd; *n.* (illness) neksa.
relate: *v.* (tell) ḥaka, yaḥkî; qaṣṣ, yaquṣṣ.
related: *v.* be related to, yakhuṣṣ (with *object* or *pron. suffix*).
relation: (connexion) nisba; (kindred) qarîb, *pl.* qarâyib.
relationship: qarâba.
relative: (having connexion) nisbî; (kindred), see **relation**.
relatively: bi nisba.
relax: rakhkha, yurakhkhî.
relaxation: (lessening) tarakhkhî.
release: fekk, yafukk; seyyeb, yuseyyib; fellet, yufellit; *n.* fekkàn.
relent: làn, yalîn.
reliable: yu'temed 'alêh.
reliance: i'timàd.
relic: ether, *pl.* àthàr; 'antîqa, *pl.* 'antîqàt.
relief: (help) musâ'ada; (as from pain) istirâḥa; (to poor) i'âna.
relieve: (make easy) khaffaf, yukhaffif; (help) sâ'ad, yusâ'id; (take turn) beddel wîya, yubeddil; (from siege) khallaṣ, yukhalliṣ.
religion: diyàna, dîn.
religious: dînî.
relinquish: jàz min, yajûz.
relish: (enjoy) teledhdhedh bi, yeteledhdhedh.
reluctant: mû râdhi.
rely: i'temed, ya'temid; ittekel, yettekil.
remain: baqa, yibqa; dhall, yadhull.
remainder: baqîya, *pl.* baqâyâ; fadhla, *pl.* fadhlàt.
remaining: bâqî.
remains: fadhla, bâqî; (corpse) jinàza.
remark: *v.* lâḥadh, yulâḥidh; *n.* mulâḥadha.
remarkable: 'ajîb.
remarkably: 'ajîb.
remedy: 'ilàj.
remember: tedhekker, yetedhekker; dheker, yidhkar; dhall fîl bàl, yadhull.
remind: dhekker, yudhekkir.
remit: (send) ḥawwal, yuḥawwil.
remittance: (act of sending) taḥwîl; (sum of money) ḥawàla.
remnant: baqîya.
remonstrate: i'taradh, ya'taridh.
remote: ba'îd.
remove: shàl, yashîl; naqal, yanqal.
remuneration: bakhshîsh.
remunerate: bakhshash, yubakhshish.
remunerative: muksib.
render: (give) a'ṭa, ya'ṭî; (present) qaddam, yuqaddim.
renew: jedded, yujeddid.

renewal: tajdîd.
renounce: neker, yankar.
renovate: see **renew.**
renown: shuhra.
renowned: mashhûr.
rent: *v.* ejjer, yu-ejjir; istà-jar, yastà-jir; kera, yikrî; *n.* îjâr, karwa.
rental: îjâr, karwa.
reorganize: nadhdham tekrâr, yunadhdhim.
repair: 'ammar, yu'ammir; ṣallaḥ, yuṣalliḥ.
repairs: ta'mîràt.
repeal: nesakh, yinsakh.
repeat: kerrer, yukerrir.
repeatedly: mirâran.
repel: defa', yidfa'.
repent: (from sin) tàb, yatûb; (regret) teneddem, yeteneddem.
repentance: tôba.
repetition: tekrîr.
replace: (restore) radd, yarudd; (substitute) 'awwadh, yu'awwidh.
reply: *v.* jàwab, yujàwib; *n.* jawàb.
report: *v.* (inform) akhbar, yukhbir; (as committee) qarrar, yuqarrir; *n.* (rumour) shàya'; (of gun) ḥiss; (of committee) râpôrt, ṭaqrîr.
reprehensible: yulàm.
represent: (stand in place of) nàb 'an, yanûb; (indicate to) dell ila, yadill; (show) 'aradh, ya'radh; (describe) waṣaf, yoṣaf.
representation: (showing) beyàn, idhhâr; representation for another, niyàba, wakàla.
representative: *adj.* niyàbî; *n.* (person) nàyib.
repress: saḥaq, yisḥaq.
reprimand: *v.* wabbakh, yuwabbikh; *n.* tôbîkh.
reproach: 'ayyar, yu'ayyir; *n.* ta'yîr.
reprove: wabbakh, yuwabbikh.
republic: jamhûrîya.
republican: jamhûrî.
repudiate: neker, yankar; rafadh, yarfadh.
repugnant: makrûh.
repulse: *v.* radd, yarudd; *n.* difâ'.
repulsive: qabîḥ.
reputation: ism, sharf.
request: *v.* ṭalab, yaṭlab; *n.* ṭalba, *pl.* ṭalabàt.
require: (demand) ṭalab, yaṭlab; (need) iḥtàj, yahtàj; lezem, yilzam (with pron. suff. of person requiring), e.g. yilzamni, I need.
requirement: (need) ḥàja, *pl.* ḥàjàt; (demand) ṭalba, *pl.* ṭalabàt.
requisite: *adj.* làzm, làzim, dharûrî; *n.* lawàzim.
requisition: *v.* dhabaṭ, yadhbaṭ.
rescind: fesekh, yifsakh.
rescue: *v.* khallaṣ, yukhalliṣ; *n.* khalâṣ.
research: *n.* teftîsh.
resemble: shebeh, yishbah; shàbah, yushâbih.
resemblance: mushàbaha.
resent: istaṣ'ab, yastaṣ'ib.
reservation: (condition) sharṭ, *pl.* shurûṭ.
reserve: *v.* ḥafadh, yaḥfadh; *n.* iḥtiyâṭ; (caution) taḥaffudh.
reservoir: ḥôdh.
reside: seken, yiskan.
residence: (house) mesken; (sojourn) sikna.

resident: *n.* sàkin, *pl.* sukkàn; political resident, nàyib.
resign: (give up office) ista'fa, yasta'fi; (yield) sellem, yusellim.
resignation: (from office) isti'fâ.
resist: qâwam, yuqâwim; dhâdad, yudhâdid.
resistance: muqâwama.
resolute: 'âzim, muṣirr.
resolutely: muṣirr.
resolution: (firmness) iṣrâr; (a decision) qarâr.
resolve: (determine) 'azam, ya'zam.
resourceful: mudebbir.
resources: tharwa; râs màl.
respect: i'tabar, ya'tabir; iḥtaram, yaḥtarim; *n.* i'tibâr, iḥtirâm; *n.* (relation) jeha, *pl.* jehàt; with respect to, min jehet; min ṭarf; fî khuṣûṣ; in every respect, min kull jeha.
respectable: mu'tabar.
respectful: muḥterim.
respective: khâṣṣ.
respectively: kull men wâḥid.
respiration: teneffus.
respire: teneffes, yeteneffes.
respite: muhla.
respond: jàwab, yujàwib.
respondent: (legal) mudda'a 'alêh.
response: jawàb.
responsibility: mas-ûlîya.
responsible: mas-ûl; (dependable) yu'tamad 'alêh.
rest: *n.* (from toil) râḥa, istirâḥa; (remainder) baqîya, bâqî; (support) mesned; *v. intrans.* istarâḥ, yastarîḥ; *v. trans.* (support) sened, yisnad.
restaurant: loqanda.
restless: râḥatsiz.
restoration: tarjî'.
restore: rejja', yurejji'.
restrain: mena', yimna'.
restraint: (act) men'; (thing) màni'.
restrict: ḥaddad, yuḥaddid.
restriction: taḥdîd.
result: *v.* netej, yintaj; *n.* natîja, *pl.* natàyij.
resume: reja' ila, yarja'.
resurrection: qiyàma.
retail: *adj.* bi mufridàt.
retailer: mayàzchî.
retain: ḥafadh, yaḥfadh; dhamm, yadhumm.
retaliate: intaqam, yantaqim.
retard: 'awwaq, yu'awwiq.
retinue: ma'îya.
retire: (retreat) insaḥab, yansaḥib; (go to sleep) nàm, yanàm; (from service) taqa''ad, yataqa''ad.
retired: bi taqa''ud.
retirement: (retreat) insiḥâb; (seclusion) infirâd; (from office) taqa''ud.
retreat: *v.* (withdraw) insaḥab, yansaḥib; *n.* (withdrawal) insiḥâb.
retrench: (cut down expenses) naqqaṣ, yunaqqiṣ.
retrieve: istarja' yastarji'.
retrograde: ila wara.
return: *v. trans.* rejja', yurejji'; *v. intrans.* raja', yarja'; *n.* (coming back) ruju'; (profit) maḥṣûl.
reveal: keshef, yikshaf; bêyyen, yubêyyin.
reveille: yât burasî (T.).
revenge: *v.* take revenge upon, intaqam min, yantaqim; *n.* intiqâm.
revenue: (income) wàridàt; revenue department, idâra

màlîya; revenue commissioner, mudîr màlîya.
reverse: *v.* 'akkas, yu'akkis; reverse decision, fesekh, yifsakh; *n.* 'aks.
revert: raja', yarja'; 'âd, ya'ûd.
review: *v.* (reconsider) ràja', yuràji'; review troops, nâdhar, yunâdhir; *n.* (reconsideration) muràja'a: (of troops) munâdhara; (periodical) majella.
revile: shettem, yushettim.
revise: ṣallaḥ, yuṣalliḥ.
revision: taṣlîh.
revive: *v. intrans.* iḥtaya, yaḥtaya.
revoke: fesekh, yifsakh.
revolt: *v.* 'aṣa, ya'ṣî; *n.* 'aṣyân, thôra.
revolution: (motion) dawarân; (political) inqilâb.
revolve: *v. trans.* adâr, yudîr; *v. intrans.* dâr, yadûr; iftarr, yaftarr.
revolver: warwar, *pl.* warâwir.
reward: *v.* jàza, yujàzî; *n.* mujàza.
rheumatism: rîḥ.
rhyme: *v. intrans.* jà 'alal qâfia, yîjî; *n.* qâfia.
rib: (of person) dhal', *pl.* dhulû'; (of boat) shêlmàn.
ribbon: sharîṭ, *pl.* sharâyiṭ.
rice: timmen; (unhulled) shileb.
rich: (wealthy) ghani, *pl.* aghnia; zengîn, *pl.* zengînîn; (fertile) mukhṣib; (of food) dahîn.
riches: ghina, tharwa.
richness: (wealth) ghina; (fertility) khuṣb.
rid: (to free from) fekk, yafukk; khallaṣ, yukhalliṣ; to get rid of (to be free from) takhallaṣ min, yatakhallaṣ.
ride: rekeb, yirkab.
rider: (horseback) khayyàl, *pl.* khayyàla.
ridge: (of land) 'alwa.
ridicule: *v.* qashmar, yuqashmir; dhaḥak 'ala, yidhḥak; *n.* qashmara, istihzà.
ridiculous: (laughable) mudhḥik; (preposterous) muḥâll; khilàf el 'aql.
rife: sàrî.
riffraff: ḥabarbesh.
rifle: *v.* neheb, yinhab; *n.* (gun) tufka, *pl.* tufek; (Martini) mâtlî, *pl.* mâtliyàt.
rifleman: tuffâk, *pl.* tuffâka.
right: *v.* (set straight) 'addal, yu'addil; (right a wrong) anṣaf, yunṣif; *adj.* (correct) tamàm, ṣawâb; (proper) munàsib, làyiq; (opposite of left) yamîn; right hand, yimna; *n.* (justice) 'adàla; (just claim) inṣâf; to be in the right, el ḥaqq fî yed; to the right, ilal yamîn.
righteousness: ṣalâḥ.
rightful: ḥaqîqî.
rightfully: bi ḥaqq.
rightly: bil ḥaqq.
rigid: (stiff) jàmid; (strict) ṣârim.
rigorous: shadîd.
rigour: shidda.
rim: ḥâfa, ṭarf.
rind: gishr, *pl.* gishûr.
ring: *v. trans. and intrans.* (ring bell) daqq, yaduqq; *n.* (circular object) ḥalaqa; (finger ring) maḥbas; (sound) ranîn.
ringleader: 'agîd; glît.
rinse: fêyya', yufêyyi'.
riot: *n.* thôra.
rip: *v. trans.* fetek, yiftak;

v. intrans., rip up, infetek, yenfetik.
ripe: mustawî.
ripen: *v. intrans.* istawa, yastawî.
rise: *v.* (stand up) gâm, yagûm; (from bed) qa'ad, yaq'ad; (ascend) ṣa'ad, yaṣ'ad; (rise, of sun) ṭala', yiṭla'; (rise, of wind) 'ala, ya'lû; (rise, of price) zàd, yazîd; *n.* (ascent) ṣu'ûd; (appearance) dhuhûr; sunrise, ṭulû' esh shems.
risk: *v.* takhâṭar bi, yatakhâṭar; *n.* mukhâṭara.
rites: furûdh, ṭuqûs.
ritual: *n.* ṭaqs.
rival: *v.* dhâdad, yudhâdid; *n.* mudhâdid.
river: (large) shaṭṭ, *pl.* shuṭûṭ; (smaller) nahr, *pl.* anhur.
rivet: *v.* perchem, yuperchim; *n.* mismâr, *pl.* masàmîr.
road: darb, *pl.* durûb; ṭarîq, *pl.* ṭurq.
roast: *v.* shawa, yashwî; *n.* rôsto; laḥm mushwî.
rob: seleb, yislab; (rob house) saraq, yasraq.
robber: ḥarâmî, *pl.* ḥarâmîya.
robbery: sirqa, teslîb, nehb.
robe: 'aba, *pl.* 'ubi; (priest's robe) bedla; (imam's robe) jubba.
robust: matîn.
rock: *v. trans.* (e.g. boat) la''ab, yula''ib; (e.g. cradle) hezz, yahizz; *v. intrans.* (of boat) la'ab, yil'ab; (of cradle) ihtezz, yehtezz; *n.* ṣakhra, *pl.* ṣakhr.
rocket: ṣa'âda.
rocky: muṣakhkhar.
rod: (stick) 'ûda.
rogue: khabîth, shêṭân.
roll: *v. trans.* qalab, yaqlab; (wrap) leff, yaliff; *v. intrans.* inqalab, yanqalib; *n.* (round bundle) leffa; (of bread) ṣâmûna, *pl.* ṣâmûnàt; (list) jedwal, qaima.
roller: (for roads) menderûna.
roof: *n.* saṭḥ, *pl.* suṭûḥ; roof of mouth, saqf el ḥalq.
room: (chamber) gubba, *pl.* gubab; ghurfa, *pl.* ghuraf; ḥujra, *pl.* ḥujar; ôdha, *pl.* ûwadh; (space) makàn.
roomy: wâsi'.
root: *n.* (of plant) 'irq, *pl.* 'urûq; (origin) aṣl.
rope: ḥabl, *pl.* ḥibàl.
rosary: sibḥa.
rose: jumbut, ward.
rosewater: mai ward.
rot: khâs, yakhîs.
rotary: dawwâr.
rotation: dawarân.
rotten: khâyis, fàsid.
rough: (not smooth) khashn.
roughly: (as estimate) takhmînan.
round: *adj.* (circular) mudawwar; all round, min kull jeha.
rouse: *v.* (from sleep) qa''d, yuqa''id; (excite) hêyyej, yuhêyyij.
rout: *v. trans.* kesser, yukessir; *n.* kesra.
route: ṭarîq.
row: *v. trans.* (boat) jedhef, yijdhaf; *n.* (file) ṣaff, *pl.* ṣufûf; (quarrel) 'arka.
royal: sulṭânî.
rub: ferek, yifrak; rub out, maḥa, yimḥî.
rubber: (elastic) làstîk.
rubbish: zabàla.
rubble: kankrî, ḥashu.

rudder: sukkàn.
rude: (uncultured) waḥshî; (ill-mannered) ghair adîb; (rough) khashan.
rudiments: mabàdî.
ruffle: *n.* (plait) keshkesh.
rug: (carpet) zûlîya, *pl.* zawàlî; prayer-rug, sajàda.
ruin: *v. trans.* kharrab, yukharrib; demmer, yudemmir; to be ruined, telef, yitlaf; *n.* (of building) kharâba; (loss) khasâra, kesr; ruins, àthàr qadîma.
rule: *v.* (govern) ḥakam 'ala, yaḥkam; (with lines) saṭṭar, yusaṭṭir; *n.* (canon) qânûn, *pl.* qawânîn; destûr; (principle) qâ'ida, *pl.* qawâ'id; (government) ḥukm.
ruled: (with lines) musaṭṭar.
ruler: (governor) ḥâkim, *pl.* ḥukkàm; (for lines) masṭara.
rumble: *v.* qarqar, yuqarqir.
rumour: shàyi'.
run: *v. intrans.* (move fast) rekedh, yirkadh; (flow) jara, yijrî; (extend) imtedd, yemtedd; *v. trans.* (as ship) meshsha, yumeshshî.
running: *n.* rakâdh; *adj.* (of water) jàrî; (in succession) mutatàbi'.
rupee: rubîya (rubîa), *pl.* rubîyàt (rubiàt).
ruse: ḥîla, *pl.* ḥiyal.
Russia: rûsia.
Russian: muskôfî, rûsî.
rust: *v. trans.* zenjer, yuzenjir; *v. intrans.* tezenjer, yetezenjer; *n.* zinjàr.
rusty: muzenjer.
ruthless: qâsî; min dûn raḥma

S

Sabaean: ṣubbi, *pl.* ṣubba.
sabbath: sebt.
sack: (small) kîs, *pl.* akyàs; (large) gonîya, *pl.* gawânî; *v.* (pillage) neheb, yinhab; ferhed, yuferhid; (discharge) baṭṭal, yubaṭṭil; 'azzal, yu'azzil; *v.* (be discharged) in'azal, yan'azil.
sacrament: sirr muqaddas.
sacred: muqaddas.
sacrifice: *v.* (give up) jàz min, yajûz; *n.* (offering) dhabîḥa; (loss) khasâra.
sacrilege: hetk.
sacrilegious: muhtik.
sad: (sorrowful) ḥazîn, *pl.* ḥazînîn, ḥazàna; (causing sadness), muḥzin; to be sad, ḥazan, yaḥzan.
saddle: *v.* serej, yisraj; *n.* sarj, *pl.* surûj; camel saddle (for riding), shadàd; camel saddle (for load), ḥadàja.
saddle-bag: khurj, *pl.* khuraj.
saddle-cloth: shaplagh, maṭraḥa.
saddle-girth: ḥizàm.
saddler: sarràj.
sadness: ḥuzn.
safe: *adj.* (secure) amîn, sàlim; *v.* to be safe, selem, yislam; *n.* money safe, ṣandûq ḥadîd.
safeguard: *v.* ḥâfadh, yuḥâfidh; *n.* muḥâfadha.
safely: bi salàma.
safety: amàn, salàma.
safety-valve: gubbàn bukhâr.
sag: *v.* taqawwas, yataqawwas.
sagacity: dhekà.
sail: *v.* (leave) mesha, yimshî; *n.* (of cloth) shrâ', *pl.* shuru'.

sailor: (of sailing-boat) mellâḥ, *pl.* melàlîḥ; (of steamer) khalâṣî; *pl.* khalâṣîya.
saint: qadîs, *pl.* qadîsîn.
sake: khâṭir, ejel; for the sake of, khâṭir; min ejel, li ejel.
sal ammoniac: milḥ shanàdir.
salad: salâṭa.
salary: ma'âsh, *pl.* ma'âsht.
sale: bî'; for sale, lil bî'.
saliva: rîq.
sallow: aṣfar.
salmon: sàmon fîs.
saloon: (of ship) sâlon.
salt: milḥ.
salted: mumelleḥ.
salt-cellar: memlaḥa.
saltness: mulûḥa.
salty: màliḥ.
salubrious: nàfi'.
salutary: mufîd.
salutation: salàm.
salute: *v.* akhadh temennî, yakhudh; *n.* temennî.
salvation: khalâṣ.
same: the same thing, nefs esh shê; the same as that, mithl hadhàk; mithl dhàk; all the same, kulluh wâḥid.
sample: namûna, *pl.* namàyin.
sanction: *v.* (allow) rakhkhaṣ, yurakhkhiṣ; *n.* (permission) rukhṣa.
sand: raml.
sandal: na'al, *pl.* na'âl.
sand-fly: barghash.
sand-grouse: gaṭâ.
sand-paper: kàghid zimpâra.
sandy: ramalî.
sane: ṣaḥîḥ el 'aql.
sanitary: (conducive to health) mufîd liṣ ṣaḥḥa; sanitary department, ṣaḥîya.
sash: ḥizàm.
satan: shêṭân, iblîs.
satchel: janṭa.
satin: aṭlas.
satisfaction: (pleasure) surûr.
satisfactorily: ḥasab el muràd; 'alal kêf.
satisfactory: ḥasab el muràd; 'alal kêf.
satisfied: râdhi, muktefi; (with food) sheb'ân.
satisfy: (make content) radhdha, yuradhdhi; (make replete) shebba', yushebbi'.
saturate: naqqa', yunaqqi'.
saturated: munaqqa'.
Saturday: yôm es sebt; Saturday night, lêlat el aḥad.
sauce: marq, sâs.
sauce-pan: ṭâwa.
saucer: mâ'ûn, *pl.* mawâ'în; ṣaḥn.
saucy: lisàn ṭawîl.
sausage: basṭârma.
savage: waḥshî, *pl.* wuḥûsh.
save: (rescue) khallaṣ, yukhalliṣ; (lay up) dhamm, yadhumm; (avoid expense) iqtaṣad, yaqtaṣid.
saviour: mukhalliṣ.
saw: *n.* (implement) minshâr, *pl.* manâshîr.
saw-dust: nushâra.
say: qâl, yaqûl; gâl, yagûl.
saying: qawl, *pl.* aqwâl; gawl, *pl.* agwâl.
scab: gishr.
scaffold: (for workmen) skella.
scale: *n.* (balance) mîzàn; (thin layer) teklis; (of map) miqyàs; (gradation) mîzànîya.
scamp: khabîth.
scant: *adj.* qalîl.
scar: *n.* kedema.
scarce: nàdir; qalîl yalteqî.
scarcely: bil kàd.
scarcity: qilla.

scare: *v. trans.* khawwaf, yukhawwif; *n.* khôf.
scarf: ghitra.
scatter: bedhdher, yubedhdhir; shettet, yushettit.
scattered: mushettet.
scavenger: zabbàl.
scene: (spectacle) mandhar.
scenery: (landscape) mandhar.
scent: *v.* ishtemm, yeshtemm; *n.* rîḥa, raiḥa.
scented: mu'aṭṭar.
sceptical: shakûk.
schedule: qaima, jedwal.
scheme: *v.* debber, yudebbir; *n.* fikr, *pl.* afkâr; see also **plan**.
schism: inshiqâq.
scholar: (pupil) telmîdh, *pl.* talàmîdh; (sage) 'âlim, *pl.* 'ulemâ.
school: medresa, *pl.* madàris; maktab (mekteb), *pl.* makàtib.
schoolmaster: mu'allim, *pl.* mu'allimîn.
science: 'ilm, *pl.* 'ulùm; natural science, 'ilm ṭabî'î.
scientific: 'ilmî.
scientifically: 'ilmîyan.
scissors: maqaṣṣ.
scold: *v.* zejer, yizjar.
scope: (for action) mêdàn; (content) iḥtiwâ.
scorch: ḥaraq, yaḥraq.
score: *n.* (twenty) 'ashrîn; (result of play) maḥṣûl.
scorn: *v.* iḥtaqar, yaḥtaqir; *n.* iḥtiqâr, ihàna.
scornful: muzderî, muhîn.
scorpion: 'aqrab, *pl.* 'aqârib.
Scotch: iskotlandî.
Scotland: iskotlanda.
scoundrel: sharîr, *pl.* ashrâr.
scour: *v.* (clean) ḥakk, yaḥukk; (search) dawwar, yudawwir.
scout: *v.* jesses, yujessis, keshshef; *n.* jàsûs, *pl.* jawàsîs.
scowl: *v.* 'abbas, yu'abbis.
scrap: *n.* (morsel) waṣla, *pl.* waṣal.
scrape: *v.* ḥakk, yaḥukk; *n.* (difficulty) mushkil, ṣa'ûba.
scratch: *v.* kharmash, yukharmish; ḥakk, yaḥukk.
scream: *v.* ṣêyyeḥ, yuṣêyyiḥ; ṣâḥ, yaṣîḥ; *n.* ṣiyâḥ.
screen: *v.* (hide) setter, yusettir; *n.* (partition) ḥâjiz; (protection from insects) khashm bulbul.
screening: (material for protection from insects) khashm bulbul; (of grain) nakhâla.
screw: burghî, *pl.* barâghi; *v.* shedd bi burghî, yashidd.
scribble: shakhkhaṭ, yushakhkhiṭ.
scribe: kàtib, *pl.* kuttàb.
scriptures: el kitàb el muqaddas.
scrub: *v.* jela, yijlî.
scruples: *v.* to have scruples, irtàb, yartàb.
scrupulous: (exact) mudaqqiq.
scrutinize: daqqaq, yudaqqiq.
scrutiny: tadqîq.
scum: waghaf, zebed.
scythe: menjel.
sea: baḥr, *pl.* abḥur, buḥûr.
seal: *v.* (with seal) mahar, yamhar; *n.* (stamp) muhr, *pl.* muhûr.
sealing-wax: lukk.
seam: *n.* (of garment) kafàfa, khiyâṭa.
seaman: mellâḥ, *pl.* malàlîh.
seamstress: khayyâṭa.
search: *v.* (look for) dawwar, yudawwir; (examine) fettesh, yufettish; *n.* teftîsh.

sea-shore: sâḥil el baḥr.
sea-sick: dàyikh.
sea-sickness: dôkha.
season: *v.* (e.g. wood) jeffef, yujeffif; (accustom) ʿawwad, yuʿawwid; *n.* (time) mûsim; (of year, e.g. summer) faṣl.
seat: *v. trans.* qaʿʿad, yuqaʿʿid; *n.* (chair) kursî, *pl.* karàsî; skamlî, *pl.* skamliyàt.
secede: infaṣal, yanfaṣil.
seclusion: infirâd, waḥda.
second: *adj.* thànî; *n.* (part of minute) thània, *pl.* thawànî.
secondary: (unimportant) mâ muhimm.
second-hand: mustaʿmal.
secondly: thàniyan.
second-rate: ʿâdî, dûnî.
secret: *adj.* sirrî, khafî; *n.* sirr, *pl.* asrâr.
secretary: kàtib, *pl.* kuttàb; secretary for foreign affairs, nâdhir khârijîya; secretary for home affairs, nâdhir dâkhilîya; secretary for war; nâdhir ḥarbîya; secretary for education, nâdhir muʿârif.
secrete: *v.* (hide) akhfa, yukhfî; ketem, yiktam.
secretly: khufyatan, sirran.
sect: firqa, *pl.* firaq; (religious) medhheb, *pl.* madhàhib.
section: (portion) qasm, *pl.* aqsâm; (division) firqa.
secular: ʿalimî.
secure: *v.* (obtain) ḥassal, yuḥassil; (make safe) emmen, yu-emmin; (guarantee) keffel, yukeffil; *adj.* amîn, ma-mûn.
security: (safety) emnîya; (pledge) kafàla; give security, keffel, yukeffil.
sediment: dihla.
sedition: fitna.
seditious: muftin.
see: shàf, yashûf.
seed: bizr, *pl.* buzûr.
seedy: (ill) wajʿân, marîdh, kêfsiz.
seek: (search for) dawwar ʿala, yudawwir; (try) ijtehed, yejtehid; ràd, yarîd.
seem: bêyyen, yubêyyen; bàn, yabàn.
seemingly: ḥasab edh dhâhir.
segregate: efrez, yufriz.
seize: (grasp) mesek, yimsak; kadhdh, yakudhdh; jawwad, yujawwid; lezem, yilzam; (seize legally) dhabaṭ, yadhbaṭ.
seizure: dhabṭ.
seldom: nàdir, qalîl.
select: *v.* istanqa, yastanqî; *adj.* mustanqa.
selection: ikhtiyâr.
self: nefs, *pl.* anfus, enfus.
self-denial: inkâr en nefs.
self-esteem: iʿtibâr en nefs; shîma.
selfish: nefsànî.
selfishness: nefsànîya.
sell: bâʿ, yabîʿ.
seller: bâyiʿ, bayyâʿ.
selling: bîʿ.
selves: anfus; see **self**.
semi: nuṣṣ, nuṣf.
semitic: sàmî.
senator: min el aʿyàn.
send: baʿath, yibʿath; arsal, yursil; send for, baʿath ʿala, yibʿath.
senior: el akbar.
sensation: (feeling) iḥsàs.
sense: (faculty) ḥass, *pl.* ḥawàs; (meaning) maʿna; (understanding) ʿaql.
senseless: (foolish) bila maʿna; (unconscious) ghâbat ruḥuh.

sensible: (discerning) 'âqil, *pl.* 'uqqâl; (wise) ma'qûl.
sentence: *v.* ḥakam, yaḥkam; *n.* (judgement) ḥukm; (in grammar) jumla, *pl.* jumal; 'ibâra, *pl.* 'ibâràt.
sentiment: (thought) fikr, *pl.* afkâr; (feeling) 'âṭif, *pl.* 'awâṭif.
sentinel: nôbachî, *pl.* nôbachîya.
separate: *v.* farraq, yufarriq; *v. intrans.* iftaraq, yaftariq; iftekk, yeftekk; *adj.* 'airî, munferid.
separately: 'airî; kull men wâḥid.
sepoy: sipâhî, *pl.* sipâhîya; 'asker hindî, *pl.* 'asker hinûd.
September: êlûl.
sequence: tatàbu'.
sequestrate: ḥajaz, yaḥjaz.
sequestration: ḥajz.
sergeant: châwûsh, *pl.* chawâwîsh; sergeant-major, bâsh châwûsh.
serious: (important) muhimm; (dangerous) mukhṭir; (of illness) thaqîl.
seriously: (earnestly) bi ahemmîya.
seriousness: ahemmîya.
sermon: wa'dh, khuṭba.
serpent: ḥayya, *pl.* ḥayâya.
servant: khâdim, *pl.* khuddàm; khizmachî, *pl.* khizmachîya.
serve: khadam, yakhdam; (serve purpose of) nefa', yinfa'.
service: khidma; (use) fàida.
serviceable: mufîd.
sesame: simsim.
session: jelsa.
set: *v. trans.* ḥaṭṭ, yaḥuṭṭ; khalla, yukhallî; set (e.g. clock) 'addal, yu'addil; set aside (single out) 'ayyan, yu'ayyin; set aside (abrogate) baṭṭal, yubaṭṭil; set free, fakk, yafukk; seyyeb, yuseyyib; set up, naṣab, yanṣab; *v. intrans.* set (of the sun) ghâb, yaghîb; set out on journey, sàfar, yusàfir; *n.* (combination) ṭaqm, ṭakhm.
settee: takhat, *pl.* tukhût.
settle: *v. trans.* (cause to live) sekken, yusekkin; qa''d; yuqa''id; (settle a matter) debber, yudebbir; qadha, yaqdhî; (settle an account) sedd, yasidd; ṣaffa, yuṣaffî; *v. intrans.* (become clear) ṣufi, yuṣfa.
settlement: (place) mesken; (payment) def', defâ'; marriage settlement, wahbîya.
seven: (*with masc.*) seb'a; (*with fem.*) seb'.
seventeen: sebatâsh.
seventeenth: sàbi' 'asher.
seventh: *n.* sub', *pl.* asbâ'; *adj.* sàbi'.
seventieth: es seb'în.
seventy: seb'în.
sever: qaṭa', yaqṭa'; gaṭa', yagṭa'.
several: kathîr, 'adîd.
severe: (strict) ṣârim, qâsî; (excessive) shadîd.
severity: ṣarâma.
sewage: khiyàs.
sewer: (for sewage) bàlû'a, *pl.* balàlî'.
sex: jins.
shackle: *v.* ḥaddad, yuḥaddid; *n.* pringa.
shad: sabûr.
shade: fê.
shadow: khayàl.

shady: fê, mudhill.
shaft: (in machinery) shàf, 'âmûd.
shah: shâh.
shake: *v. trans.* hezz, yahizz; ḥarrak, yuḥarrik; (e.g. carpet) nafadh, yanfadh; shake hands, a'ṭa yed, ya'ṭî; *v. intrans.* ihtezz, yehtezz; taḥarrak, yataḥarrak.
shallow: mai qalîl; gêsh.
shame: *v. trans.* khajjal, yukhajjil; 'ayyar, yu'ayyir; *n.* (disgrace) 'âr, 'aib.
shameful: 'aib.
shameless: min dûn ḥaya; mâ yesteḥî.
shape: *v. trans.* shekkel, yushekkil; *n.* (form) shikl, *pl.* ashkàl; (mould) qâlib, *pl.* qawâlib.
share: *v. trans.* shàrak, yushàrik; *v. intrans.* ishterek, yeshterik; *n.* ḥaṣṣa, *pl.* ḥaṣaṣ; sehm, *pl.* esham (*pron.* es-ham).
shareholder: shàrik, *pl.* shurakâ.
shark: kôsech.
sharp: ḥâdd.
sharpen: senn, yasinn; ḥaddad, yuḥaddid.
sharpness: ḥidda.
shatter: kesser, yukessir.
shave: *v.* zêyyen, yuzêyyin.
shaving: zayàn.
she: hîya.
shed: *v.* (e.g. blood) sefek, yisfak; (e. g. feathers) tenessel, yetenessel.
sheep: (general term) ghanam; (male sheep) kebsh, khâruf; (female sheep) na'ja.
sheet: (of bed) charchaf, *pl.* charàchif; sheet of paper, warqa.
sheeting: khâm.
shelf: raff, *pl.* rufûf.
shell: *v. trans.* (take off shell) gashshar, yugashshir; (bombard) dharab bi ṭôp, yadhrab; *n.* (covering) gishr, *pl.* gishûr; (of oysters, &c.) maḥâr; (explosive) gulla, *pl.* gulal, gulel; dàna *pl.* danàt.
shelter: *v. trans.* setter, yusettir; *v. intrans.* ilteja, yelteji; *n.* (protection) melja.
shepherd: râ'î ghanam.
shield: *v. trans.* ḥâma, yuḥâmî.
shift: *v. trans.* ḥawwal, yuḥawwil; *v. intrans.* taḥawwal, yataḥawwal; *n.* (change) taḥwîl, tabdîl.
shilling: shilin, *pl.* shilinàt.
shine: dhawa, yadhwî.
shiny: làmi'.
ship: *n.* (steam-ship) markab, *pl.* maràkib; (sailing ship) safîna, *pl.* sufn, safàyin; *v. trans.* ba'ath, yib'ath; ḥammal, yuḥammil.
shipment: taḥmîl.
shirt: (over-shirt) thôb; (under-shirt) fànîla, qamîṣ.
shiver: *v. intrans.* (shake) rejef, yarjaf.
shoal: (shallow place) shelha, *pl.* shelhàt.
shock: *v. trans.* ra''d, yura''id; *n.* ṣadma.
shoe: *v. trans.* na''al, yuna''il; *n.* qandara, *pl.* qanàdir, qandaràt.
shoemaker: qandarachî, *pl.* qandarachîya.
shoot: *v.* rama, yarmî; *n.* (date-shoot) farkh, *pl.* furûkh.
shooting: *n.* (firing) ramî.

shop: *n.* dukkàn, *pl.* dukàkîn.
shopkeeper: dukkànchî, *pl.* dukkànchîya ; àbû dukkàn.
shore: (of sea) sâḥil.
short: qaṣîr, *pl.* qiṣâr ; (lacking) nâqiṣ ; *v.* fall short, qaṣṣar, yuqaṣṣir.
shortcomings: quṣûr.
shorten: qaṣṣar, yuqaṣṣir.
shorthand: khaṭṭ = ikhtizàlî.
shortly: (soon) 'an qarîb ; (briefly) mukhtaṣar.
shortsighted: (myopic) qaṣîr en nadhr.
shot: *n.* (act) ramya, chêla ; (small bullets) sechem ; (marksman) tuffâk, nêshenchî. See also **cannon-ball, shell.**
should: (ought) kàn làzm (see p. 109).
shoulder: kitf, *pl.* aktàf ; 'âtiq, *pl.* 'awàtiq ; *v.* akhadh 'alal kitf ('âtiq), ya-khadh.
shoulder-blade: deffa.
shout: *v.* ṣâḥ, yaṣîḥ ; ṣêyyeḥ, yuṣêyyiḥ ; *n.* ṣiyâḥ, ṣêḥa.
shove: *v. trans.* defa', yidfa' ; da'am, yid'am.
shovel: shibl.
show: *v. trans.* rawwa, yurawwî ; shawwaf, yushawwif ; (demonstrate) bêyyen, yubêyyen ; (direct) dell, yadill ; *v. intrans.* bêyyen, yubêyyen ; dhahar, yadhhar ; *n.* (exhibition) ma'radh.
shower: zakhkha.
shrewd: shêṭân, ḥâdhiq.
shrewdness: shêṭana, ḥadhâqa.
shrine: mazâr.
shrink: *v. intrans.* (become short) qaṣar, yaqṣar ; shrink from (recoil from) ishma-azz min, yashma-izz.
shudder: *v.* rejef, yarjaf.
shun: (avoid) tejenneb 'an, yetejenneb.
shut: *v. trans.* sedd, yasidd ; *v. intrans.* insedd, yensedd.
shuttle: mankûk.
shy: musteḥî, maḥjûb.
sick: marîdh, *pl.* mardha ; waj'ân, *pl.* waj'ânîn ; sea-sick, dàyikh ; *v.* become sick, tamarradh, yatamarradh.
sicken: *v. trans.* la''ab, en nefs, yula''ib.
sickle: menjel.
sickly: (often ill) 'alîl, *pl.* 'alîlîn.
sickness: mardh, *pl.* amrâdh ; waj', *pl.* awjâ'.
side: *v.* side with, màl ila, yamîl ; *n.* (of object) jànib, *pl.* jawànib ; ṣafḥa, *pl.* ṣafḥàt ; (direction) jeha ; (party) firqa, ḥazb ; right side (front), wajh ; wrong side (back), dhahr ; by the side of, bijànib, yem.
sideways: 'ardh.
siege: muḥâṣara.
siesta: gêlûla.
sieve: *n.* mankhal, gharbâl.
sift: gharbal, yugharbil.
sigh: *v.* taḥaṣṣar, yataḥaṣṣar ; *n.* ḥaṣra.
sight: (seeing) nadhr ; (view) mandhar ; (of gun) nêshénga ; at sight, ḥîn en nadhr ; *v.* come in sight, bêyyen, yubêyyen ; lose sight of, dheyya', yudheyyi'.
sign: *v.* (sign name) amdha, yumdhî ; *n.* 'alàma, *pl.* 'alàmàt.
signal: ishâra, *pl.* ishâràt ; *v.* ashâr, yushîr.
signature: imdhâ.
significance: (importance) ahemmîya ; (meaning) ma'na.

significant: muhimm.
signify: ʿana, yaʿnî.
silence: *v. trans.* sekket, yusekkit; keep silence, seket, yiskat; *n.* sukût.
silent: sàkit, hàdî.
silently: bi sukût.
silk: ibrîsam, ḥarîr.
silken: min ibrîsam.
silk-worm: dûd ḥarîr.
sill: ʿataba.
silly: saqîʿ, jàhil.
silt: *n.* dihla.
silver: *n.* fidhdha; *adj.* min fidhdha.
silversmith: ṣâyigh, *pl.* ṣâgha.
similar: mithl, yishbah.
similarity: mushàbaha.
similarly: bil mithl.
simple: (not complicated) basîṭ; (ignorant) ghashîm.
simplicity: basâṭa.
simplify: sehhel, yusehhil.
simply: (only) faqaṭ; (plainly) basîṭ; bi basâṭa.
simulate: sawwa ka-innahu, yusawwî.
simultaneously: fî dhîk es sâʿa; fî dhàk el waqt.
sin: *v.* akhṭa, yukhṭî; *n.* khaṭîya, *pl.* khaṭâyâ.
since: (from the time of) min; (inasmuch as) mà dàm.
sincere: mukhliṣ; bi qalb ṣâfî.
sincerely: bi khulûṣ.
sincerity: ikhlâṣ.
sinful: khâṭî, mukhṭî.
sing: ghanna, yughannî; rettel, yurettil.
singing: *n.* ghana.
single: (one only) ferd wâḥid; (unmarried) ʿazab.
singly: wâḥid wâḥid.
singular: (strange) gharîb; (opposite to plural) mufrid.
sink: *v. trans.* nezzel, yunezzil; (of ship) gharraq, yugharriq; *v. intrans.* nezel, yinzal; (of ship) gharaq, yaghraq; *n.* bàlûʿa.
sinless: bila khaṭîya.
sinner: khâṭi, *pl.* khuṭât.
sip: *v.* tereshshef, yetereshshef; *n.* reshfa.
siphon: ambûba.
sir: (to native) effendim; (to knight) sêr.
sister: ûkht, *pl.* khawàt.
sit: qaʿad, yaqʿad; jeles, yijlas.
site: mawqaʿ.
situated: ṣâyir, wâqiʿ.
situation: (site) mawqaʿ; (condition) ḥâl, *pl.* aḥwâl; (employment) mâ-mûrîya, wadhîfa.
six: (*with masc.*) sitta, (*with fem.*) sitt.
sixteen: sittâsh.
sixteenth: sàdis ʿasher.
sixth: *n.* suds, *pl.* asdàs; *adj.* sàdis, sàt.
sixthly: sàdisan.
sixtieth: es sittîn.
sixty: sittîn.
size: kubr, ḥajm.
skeleton: hêkal.
sketch: *v.* resem, yirsam (yersem).
skewer: shîsh, *pl.* ashyàsh.
skilful: mâhir, mustaʿidd.
skilfully: bi mahâra; mâhir.
skill: mahâra, istiʿdàd.
skilled: mustaʿidd.
skillet: ṭâwa.
skim: *v. trans.* (of milk) gêmer, yugêmir; *v.* (go over lightly) marr el ʿain, yamurr.
skin: *v. trans.* ṣallakh, yuṣal-

likh; *n.* jiled, *pl.* jilûd; water-skin, garba, *pl.* gurab; (of fruit) gishr, *pl.* gishûr.
skip: gamaz, yagmaz; (omit) terek, yitrak.
skipper: (captain) qapṭân, *pl.* qapâṭîn.
skirmish: *v.* tanâwash, yatanâwash; *n.* munâwasha.
skirt: *n.* tanûra.
skull: jumjuma.
skull-cap: ʻaraqchîn.
sky: sema.
slack: *adj.* rakhu; (lax) ghâfil.
slacken: *v. trans.* rakhkha, yurakhkhî; *v. intrans.* (become less) khaff, yakhuff.
slander: *v.* iftera, yefterî; *n.* iftirà.
slant: *v. intrans.* màl, yamîl; *n.* mêl.
slanting: màyil.
slap: kefekh, yikfakh.
slate: *n.* (for writing) lôḥ ḥajar.
slaughter: *v.* dhebeḥ, yidhbaḥ; *n.* dhibḥ.
slaughter-house: maṣlakh.
Slav: slâfî; slaw.
slave: ʻabd, *pl.* ʻabîd.
slavery: ʻabûdîya.
sleek: emles.
sleep: *v.* nàm, yanàm; *n.* nôm.
sleepy: naʻsân.
sleeve: rudn, *pl.* ardàn.
slender: rafîʻ, dhaʻîf.
slice: (of bread) waṣla, *pl.* waṣl.
slide: *v.* zeleq, yizlaq.
slight: *adj.* (little) qalîl; (thin) rafîʻ, dhaʻîf; *v.* istahàn, yastahîn.
slightly: qalîl.
slim: rafîʻ.
sling: *n.* (weapon) miqlâʻ; (of ship) slink; (for arm) shedda.
slip: *v.* zeleq, yizlaq; *n.* (error) sehu.
slipper: bâbûch, *pl.* bawâbîch.
slippery: zelek.
slipshod: khabbâṣ.
slit: *v.* shaqq, yashuqq; *n.* shaqq.
slope: *v.* slope up, ṣaʻad, yaṣʻad; slope down, inḥadar, yunḥadir; *n.* ṣuʻûd; inḥidâr.
sloping: màyil.
sloppy: wasikh.
slovenly: khabbâṣ.
slow: *adj.* baṭi, thaqîl; (of watch) muta-akhkhir.
slowly: yawâsh.
sly: ḥayyàl, *pl.* ḥayyàlîn; on the sly, bil bôqa.
small: ṣaghîr, *pl.* ṣighâr.
smallness: ṣughr.
small pox: jidrî.
smart: *v.* wajaʻ, yojaʻ; *adj.* (quick) khafîf; (clever) shâṭir, *pl.* shuṭṭâr.
smash: *v.* kesser, yukessir; *v. intrans.* tekesser, yetekesser.
smattering: qalîl.
smear: lawwath, yulawwith.
smell: *v. trans.* ishtemm, yeshtemm; *v.* (emit odour (bihrîḥa; *n.* (odour) rîḥa; *n.* (sense) shemm.
smile: *v.* tebessem, yetebessem; *n.* besma.
smilingly: bashûsh; bi bashàsha.
smith: blacksmith, ḥaddàd, *pl.* ḥaddàdîn; gold and silver smith, ṣâyigh; copper smith, ṣaffar.
smoke: *v. trans.* (fumigate) dakhkhan, yudakhkhin; smoke tobacco, sharab titen, yishrab; dakhkhan, yudakhkhin; *n.* dukhân.

smoky: mudakhkhan.
smooth: *adj.* (not rough) màlis; (level) 'âdil; (of the sea) hàdî.
smother: *v. trans.* khanaq, yakhnaq; *v. intrans.* ikhtanaq, yakhtaniq.
smuggle: herreb, yuherrib.
smuggler: muherrib.
smuggling: tehrîb.
snake: ḥayya, *pl.* ḥayâya.
snatch: khaṭaf, yakhṭaf.
sneeze: 'aṭas, ya'ṭas; *n.* 'aṭsa.
snore: *v.* shakhar, yashkhar; *n.* shakhîr.
snow: *n.* thelej.
snuff: *n.* enfîya, burnûṭi.
snug: muretteb.
so: (thus) hîchî, hàkadha; so and so, fulàn; so much so that, ila hed dereja ḥatta; so so, bên wa bên; and so on (&c.), ila âkhirihi; wa enta râyiḥ.
soak: *v. trans.* nagga', yunaggi'.
soap: ṣâbûn.
sober: (serious) razîn; (not intoxicated) ṣâḥî.
so-called: el musemma.
sociability: 'ishra.
sociable: mu'âshir.
socialism: ishtirâkîya.
socialist: ishtirâkî.
socially: bên unàs.
society: (collection of people) jam'îya; (companionship) mu'âshara, 'ishra; human society, el ḥeyat el ijtimâ'îya.
sock: jôrib, *pl.* juwârib.
soda: (soda-water) ṣôda, gâzôz; (chemical) mîna.
sodden: (of ground) nazîz.
sofa: qanapa, *pl.* qanapàt.
soft: lêyyin.
soften: lêyyen, yulêyyin.
softly: (quietly) yawâsh; bi sukût.
softness: lîna.
soil: *v.* (make dirty) wassakh, yuwassikh; la'was, yula'wis; *n.* (earth) turâb, trâb.
sojourn: *v.* istaqâm, yastaqîm; *n.* istiqâma.
solar: shemsî.
solder: *v. trans.* laḥam, yilḥam; *n.* liḥâm.
soldier: *sing. and pl.* 'askar, 'asker. See also **military**.
sole: *n.* (of foot) keff; (of shoe) na'l; *n.* (fish) mezleq, mezlàq; *adj.* waḥîd.
solely: faqaṭ.
solemn: (impressive) khaṭîr; (serious) razîn.
solicit: iltemes, yeltemis.
solicitor: wakîl dâ'wa; muḥâmî.
solicitous: bil fikr.
solid: *adj.* (firm) qawî, thàbit; (not liquid) jàmid.
solidify: *v. trans.* jemmed, yujemmid; *v. intrans.* jemed, yijmad.
solitary: munferid, munqaṭa', mutawaḥḥish.
solitude: inqitâ', waḥsha.
solution: (explanation) ḥall; (liquid) maḥlûl.
solve: ḥall, yaḥull.
some: bâ'dh, shê; (a little) shwêya, qalîl; some of, el bâ'dh min.
somebody: ferd wâḥid.
something: ferd shê; shê.
sometime: ferd yôm.
sometimes: bâ'dh el awqât; bâ'dh waqt.
somewhat: shwêya.
somewhere: ferd makàn.

son: ibn, *pl.* benîn (banîn); *pl.* (racial sense) ibnà; *pl.* (before *gen.*) benî.
son-in-law: zoj bint; khatn.
song: naghma; pesta.
soon: bil ʿâjel (ʿajal); bis sâʿa; ḥâlan; as soon as, awwalma; ḥâlama; as soon as possible, fî awwal waqt.
sooner: qabl.
soothe: sekken, yusekkin.
sordid: denî.
sore: *n.* dumla; *v.* to be sore (painful) wajaʿ, yûjaʿ.
sorrel: *adj.* ashgar.
sorrow: ḥuzn.
sorrowful: ḥazîn.
sorry: mute-essif.
sort: *v. trans.* istanqa, yastanqî; *n.* jins, *pl.* ajnàs; shikl, *pl.* ashkàl.
sortie: hujma.
soul: (immortal) rûḥ, *pl.* arwâḥ; nefs; (individual) nefer, *pl.* neferàt; nefs, *pl.* anfus, enfus.
sound: *v.* (try depth) khaṭar, yakhṭar; *n.* (noise) ḥiss, ṣawt; *adj.* (whole) ṣaḥîḥ; (healthy) ṣâhî; (strong) qawî; sound sleep, thaqîl.
soundings: ghumq, ʿumq.
soundness: ṣaḥḥa.
soup: shorba, sûp.
sour: ḥâmidh.
source: (of river) menbaʿ; (origin) aṣl, menbaʿ, maṣdar.
sourness: ḥumûdha.
south: jinûb; south wind, sharqî; *adv.* jinûban.
south-east: jinûb sharq.
southern: jinûbî.
southward: lil jinûb.
south-west: jinûb gharb.
souvenir: tidhkâr, yadigâr.
sovereign: *n.* (ruler) sulṭân, *pl.* salâṭîn; (coin) lîra anglêzîya; *adj.* sulṭânî.
sovereignty: salṭa.
sow: *v.* zaraʿ, yizraʿ.
sower: zarrâʿ.
sowing: zarʿ.
space: (of time) mudda; (place) makàn; (distance) masàfa.
spacious: wâsiʿ, wasîʿ.
spade: misḥa.
Spain: ispanya.
span: *v.* (extend over) ʿabar, yaʿbar; *n.* (handbreadth) shibr, *pl.* ashbâr.
Spanish: ispanyôlî.
spanner: spana, miftâḥ.
spare: *v.* (do without) khalla, yukhallî; (not punish) terek, yitrak; *adj.* (little) qalîl; (thin) dhaʿîf; spare time, fârigh.
spark: sharâra, *pl.* sharâràt.
sparkle: lemaʿ, yilmaʿ; *n.* lemʿa.
sparkling: làmiʿ.
sparrow: ʿaṣfûr, pl. ʿaṣâfîr.
spatter: *v. trans.* rashsh, yarishsh.
speak: ḥaka, yaḥkî (ḥacha, yaḥchî); tekellem, yetekellem.
speaker: mutekellem.
speaking: kalàm, ḥakî.
spear: ramḥ, *pl.* armâḥ; fish-spear, fàla.
special: khaṣûṣî, makhṣûṣ.
specially: makhṣûṣ, khaṣûṣan.
specie: nuqûd; maskûkàt.
species: jins, *pl.* ajnàs.
specific: khaṣûṣî.
specifically: makhṣûṣ, khaṣûṣan, khâṣatan.
specification: taʿrîfa.
specify: *v.* (state definitely) khaṣṣaṣ, yukhaṣṣiṣ.
specimen: namûna, *pl.* namàyin.
speck: laṭkha.

speckled : argash, munaqqaṭ.
spectacle : mandhar.
spectacles : mandhara, *pl.* mandharàt, manâdhir; güzlik (T.).
spectacular : mudhish (mudhish).
spectator : mutafarrij, *pl.* mutafarrijîn.
speculate : taṣawwar, yataṣawwar.
speech : (faculty of) nuṭq; (language) kalàm, ḥakî; (discourse) khiṭâb, khuṭba.
speed : *n.* 'ajala, sur'a.
speedily : bil 'âjel ('ajal).
speedy : sarî', khafîf.
spell : *v.* tehejja, yetehejja.
spelling : tehjia, tehejjî.
spend : ṣaraf, yaṣraf.
spendthrift : mubedhdhir.
sphere : (globe) kurra.
spherical : mudawwar.
sphinx : abul hôl.
spices : bahâràt.
spider : 'ankabût, *pl.* 'anâkîb.
spigot : ḥanafîya, muzembela.
spill : *v. trans.* kebb, yakibb (chebb, yachibb); *v. intrans.* inkebb, yenkebb.
spin : *v. trans.* (e.g. thread) ghazal, yaghzal; (whirl) farr, yafurr; *v. intrans.* (turn) iftarr, yaftarr.
spindle : mighzal.
spine : sansûr.
spirit : (soul) rûḥ, nefs; (vigour) qûwa, ḥidda.
spirited : nashîṭ; hibb rîḥ.
spirits : (alcoholic) muskiràt; (methylated) spirito.
spiritual : rûḥânî; rûḥî.
spiritually : rûḥîyan.
spit : *v. intrans.* (expectorate) tefel, yitfal; *n.* (iron prong) shîsh; (of land) lisàn.
spite : *v. trans.* 'ânad, yu'ânid; *n.* 'anàd; in spite of, ghaṣban 'an; raghman 'an.
spittle : (saliva) rîq.
spleen : ṭaḥâl.
splendid : fâkhir, 'âl.
splice : baram, yabram.
splint : ṣaffâga.
splinter : *v. trans.* feshsheq, yufeshshiq; *n.* feshqa.
split : *v. trans.* shaqq, yashuqq; *v. intrans.* inshaqq, yanshaqq; *n.* shaqq.
spoil : *v. trans.* kharrab, yukharrib; *v. intrans.* kharab, yakhrab; *n.* (plunder) nehb, kesb.
spoke : (of wheel) barmagh.
sponge : sangar.
sponsor : kafîl.
spontaneous : min nefsuh; minuh bih.
spontaneously : min nefsuh; minuh bih.
spoon : khâshûga, *pl.* khawâshîg.
spoonful : see **spoon.**
sport : *v. intrans.* la'ab, yil'ab; *n.* (play) la'b.
spot : *v.* (for target) raṣad, yarṣad; *n.* (stain) lekka, *pl.* lekek; laṭkha; (place) makàn, *pl.* amàkin.
spout : *n.* khashm.
sprain : *v.* fesekh, yifsakh; *n.* feskh.
spread : *v. trans.* (extend) medd, yamudd; (e.g. news) nesher, yanshar; sheyya', yusheyyi'; (e.g. bed) farash, yafrash; *v. intrans.* imtedd, yemtedd; (of news) intashar, yantashir; shâ', yashî'.
spring : *v. intrans.* (leap) ṭafar, yatfar: (originate) ṣadar,

yasdar; spring up (of plant) nebet, yinbat; *n.* (season) rabî'; (leap) ṭafra; (of water) 'ain, *pl.* 'uyûn; (of carriage) gôs; zambrak; (of watch) zambrak.

sprinkle: *v.* reshsh, yarishsh.

sprout: *v.* nebet, yinbat; *n.* warga.

spry: nashîṭ.

spur: *v.* leked, yilkad; *n.* (for horse) shâbûr; (of mountain) râs; on spur of moment, 'alal fôr.

spurious: kidhb, muzawwar.

spurn: rafadh, yarfadh.

spurt: *v.* fâr, yafûr; *n.* fôra.

spy: *v.* jesses, yujessis; *n.* jàsûs, *pl.* jawàsîs.

spy-glass: darbîn, *pl.* darâbîn.

squabble: *v.* tanàza', yatanàza'; *n.* niza'.

squad: ṭakhm.

squadron: (of fleet) firqa.

squalid: ta'îs, ḥaqîr.

squall: *n.* dharba.

squalor: ta'âsa.

squander: bedhdher, yubedhdhir.

square: *v. trans.* rabba', yurabbi'; (square accounts) ṣaffa, yuṣaffî; *n.* (geometrical figure) murabba'; (open place) mêdàn; (carpenter's) gônia; (space drawn, as on chess-board) khâna.

squash: *v.* saḥaq, yisḥaq; *n.* (vegetable) yaqṭîn.

squeak: *v.* waswas, yuwaswis; *n.* waswasa.

squeeze: 'aṣar, ya'ṣar.

squinting: *adj.* aḥwal.

stab: *v.* ta'an, yaṭ'an.

stability: thabàt.

stable: *n.* ṭôla; *adj.* thàbit.

stack: *v.* kawwam, yukawwim; *n.* kôma.

staff: (stick) 'aṣa; (of army) arkàn ḥarb; staff officer, dhâbiṭ arkàn ḥarb.

stage: (raised place) dekka; (of journey) kônâgh, *pl.* kowânîgh.

stagger: *v. intrans.* tamàyal, yatamàyal.

stagnant: (of water) khâyis, wâgif.

stain: *v. trans.* lawwath, yulawwith; *n.* lekka.

stair: derej.

stake: *v. trans.* (e.g. honour) khâṭar, yukhâṭir; (wager) râhan, yurâhin; *n.* (pledge) rahn; (stick) ithbàt; at stake, taḥt el khaṭr.

stale: *adj.* 'atîq.

stalk: *n.* (of plant) sâq.

stall: (for animal) ma'laf; (in bazaar) basṭa; chember.

stallion: ḥuṣân shabûwa.

stammer: *v.* eltegh, yultigh.

stamp: *v.* (with foot) daqq rijl, yaduqq; (stamp letters) ṭamagh, yaṭmagh; *n.* (postage stamp) pûl, *pl.* apwàl; (postage mark) ṭamgha, istampa.

stand: *v. trans.* waggaf, yuwaggif; *v. intrans.* wagaf, yogaf; stand up for, dàfa' 'an, yudàfi'; stand up, qâm, yaqûm; *n.* (pedestal) rijl; (defence) mudàfa'a.

standard: (flag) bêraq, *pl.* bayâriq; ṣanjaq, *pl.* ṣanàjiq; (criterion) qiyàs, qânûn.

standing: (rank) maqâm, ritba.

star: nejma, *pl.* nujûm.

starboard: yamîn.

starch: nisha.

stare: daḥḥaq, yudaḥḥiq.
start: *v. trans.* meshsha, yumeshshî; *v. intrans.* (move) mesha, yimshî; (begin) ibteda, yebtedi; (be alarmed) fezz, yafizz; *n.* (beginning) bidàya, ibtidà; (alarm) fezza; get start of, sabaq, yasbaq.
startle: fezzez, yufezziz.
startling: mur'ib.
starvation: môt (mawt) jû'.
starve: *v. trans.* mawwat jû', yumawwit; *v. intrans.* màt jû', yamût.
state: *v.* 'aradh, ya'radh; ṣarraḥ, yuṣarriḥ; *n.* (condition) ḥâla; (governed community) ḥakûma, memleka; United States of America, el wilàyàt el muttaḥida.
stated: (regular) mu'ayyan.
statement: 'aridha, taqrîr.
state-room: qamâra, *pl.* qamâyir.
statesman: siyàsî, *pl.* siyàsiyîn.
statesmanship: siyàsa.
station: *v.* ḥaṭṭ, yaḥuṭṭ; *n.* railway station, maḥaṭṭa, *pl.* maḥaṭṭàt; police station, markaz polîs.
stationary: wâgif.
stationery: qarṭâsîya.
statistics: tafâṣîl.
statue: timthàl, *pl.* tamàthîl.
stature: qâma.
status quo: al ḥâla kema hîya.
statute: qânûn, *pl.* qawânîn.
statutory: qânûnî, nidhâmî.
stave: *v.* stave in, naqab, yanqab; stave off, akhkhar, yu-akhkhir.
stay: *v. trans.* (support) sened, yisnad; *v. intrans.* (remain) baqa, yibqa; dhall, yadhull; *n.* baqâ, iqâma, istiqâma.
stead: instead of, fî makàn (with *pron. suffix*); 'iwadh (with *pron. suffix*); bidàl (with *pron. suffix*). See also **instead of.**
steadfast: thàbit, râsikh.
steadfastness: thabàt.
steadily: dhall, yadhull (with pres. of verb).
steadiness: thabàt.
steady: thàbit, ḥudâr.
steal: bâq, yabûq; saraq, yasraq.
stealing: bôqa, sirqa.
stealthily: bil bôqa; bi sukût.
steam: *n.* bukhâr, ishtîm.
steam-boat: markab bukhâr; markab dukhân; **bâkhira,** *pl.* bawâkhir.
steel: *n.* fûlàdh.
steep: *adj.* shàmikh.
steer: *v.* dâr, yadîr.
steersman: sukkànchî.
stench: rîḥa.
stenographer: mukhtazil.
stenography: khaṭṭ ikhtizàlî; ikhtizàl.
step: *v.* mesha, yimshî; khaṭa, yakhṭu; step aside, wakhkhar, yuwakhkhir; *n.* (pace) khaṭwa, *pl.* khaṭawàt; (sound of feet) dôsa; (degree) dereja; (course of action) wâsiṭa, *pl.* wasâyiṭ; chàra.
step-brother: ibn el àb *or* ibn el umm.
step-daughter: rabîba.
step-father: rejul el umm.
step-mother: marat el àb.
step-sister: bint marat el àb *or* bint rejul el umm.
step-son: rabîb.
sterile: (of woman) 'âqir; (of

soil) ghabra; (disinfected) naqî, mâhil.
sterilize: ṭahhar, yuṭahhir; naqqa, yunaqqi.
sterling: *adj.* (of English money) anglêzî.
stern: *n.* (of ship) akhîr; *adj.* 'abûs, mu'abbas.
stew: *v.* ṭabakh, yaṭbakh; *n.* (food) yakhna, ishtû.
stick: *v. trans.* (make adhere) lazzaq, yulazziq; *v. intrans.* lazaq, yalzaq; (become immovable) chelleb, yuchellib; stick out (protrude) berez, yibraz; *n.* (of wood) 'aṣa, *pl.* 'uṣî; 'ûda, *pl.* 'uwad.
sticky: lezej, lezeq.
stiff: (not pliable) ṣalb; (formal) ṣa'ab.
stiffness: ṣalâba.
stigma: (disgrace) 'âr.
still: *adj.* (calm) hàdî; (motionless) wâgif; (silent) sàkit; *v.* keep still, seket, yiskat; *adv.* (nevertheless) mâ' hâdha; (till now) ila hessa; ilalàn; (not having stopped) bâ'ad; là zàl; *n.* (for spirits) enbîq.
stimulate: *v.* nebbeh, yunebbih.
stimulus: taḥrîdh.
sting: *v.* ladagh, yaldagh.
stinginess: bukhl.
stingy: bakhîl, khasîs.
stink: *v.* jâyif (*adj.*); *n.* jîfa, rîḥa.
stinking: jàyif.
stint: *v. trans.* ḥaddad, yuḥaddid; ḥaṣar, yaḥṣar.
stipend: ma'âsh.
stipulate: sharaṭ, yashraṭ.
stipulation: sharṭ, *pl.* shurûṭ.
stir: *v. trans.* ḥarrak, yuḥarrik; *v. intrans.* taḥarrak, yataḥarrak.
stirrup: rakàb.
stitch: *v.* khayyaṭ, yukhayyiṭ; *n.* nefdha.
stock: *v.* (have on hand) 'and (see p. 13); *n.* (race) aṣl, dhahr; (capital) râs màl; (share) ḥaṣṣa, *pl.* ḥaṣaṣ; sehm, *pl.* es-ham; (of goods) bidhâ'a.
stomach: ma'da.
stone: *v. trans.* throw stones, rama ḥijâr, yarmî; rejem, yarjam; *n.* (mineral) ḥajar, *pl.* hijâr; (of ring) faṣṣ; (of fruit) nawâya; (for grinding) raḥa: (for whetting) charkh.
stony: muḥajjar, ḥajarî.
stool: (low chair) skamli, takhta.
stoop: dennech, yudennich; inḥana, yanḥanî.
stop: *v. trans.* waggaf, yuwaggif; (close hole) sedd, yasidd; (prevent) mena', yimna'; *v. intrans.* wagaf, yogaf; (cease) baṭṭal, yubaṭṭil; (lodge) nezel, yinzal; *n.* wagfa; (punctuation) nuqṭa.
stoppage: towqîf; (obstruction) sadàda.
stopper: (of bottle) sadàda.
storage: (keeping in store) dhamm; (store charges) ardhîya.
store: *v.* (preserve) ḥâfadh, yuḥâfidh; *n.* (quantity) miqdâr; (stock) râs màl; mûna; (shop) makhzan.
store-room: makhzan, *pl.* makhâzin.
stores: arzâq, dhakhâyir.
stork: legleg, *pl.* lagàlig.
storm: *n.* dharba, *pl.* dharbàt; forṭona; *v.* take by storm, dhabaṭ, yadhbaṭ.
stormy: 'ajàj.

story: ḥikàya, *pl.* ḥikàyàt; qaṣṣa, *pl.* qaṣaṣ; (of house) ṭabaqa, *pl.* ṭabaqàt; qâṭ, *pl.* qu-ûṭ.
stout: matîn, *pl.* matàn.
stove: bukhâri; ṣôpa (T.).
stow: *v.* dhamm, yadhumm.
straggle: ta-akhkhar, yata-akkhar.
straggler: muta-akhkhir.
straight: 'âdil; (directly) râsan; ferd râs; straight ahead, gûbal; ila gadàm.
straighten: 'addal, yu'addil.
straightforward: ashkarà (P.).
strain: *v.* (test severely) khalkhal, yukhalkhil; (sprain) fesekh, yifsakh; (filter) ṣaffa, yuṣaffì; strain effort, (do one's best), bedhel jehd, yibdhal; *n.* (severe test) khalkhala; (sprain) fesekh.
strait: (sea-passage, or pass) madhîq.
strand: (sea-shore) sâḥil, shâṭî; (of rope) bisla; *v.* (run aground) sheleh, yishlah.
stranded: shelhàn.
strange: 'ajîb, gharîb.
stranger: gharîb, *pl.* ghurabà.
strangle: *v.* *trans.* khanaq, yakhnaq; *v.* *intrans.* ikhtanaq, yakhtaniq.
strap: *n.* sêr, *pl.* suyûr.
stratagem: ḥîla, *pl.* ḥiyal.
strategic: muhimm, markazî.
strategy: ḥîla ḥarbîya.
stratum: ṭabaqa, *pl.* ṭabaqàt.
straw: tibn.
strawberry: chilek (T.); frez.
stray: *v.* tàh, yatîh.
streak: *v.* khaṭṭaṭ, yukhaṭṭiṭ; *n.* khaṭṭ, *pl.* khuṭûṭ.
streaked: mukhaṭṭaṭ.
stream: *v.* *intrans.* jara, yijrî; *n.* (small river) nahr, *pl.* anhur.
street: darb, *pl.* durûb; ṭarîq, *pl.* ṭurq; shâri', *pl.* shawâri'.
strength: qûwa.
strengthen: qawwa, yuqawwî.
strenuous: shadîd, ḥàdd, ḥâmî.
strenuously: bi shidda; ḥâmî.
stress: (*n.* strain) thuql; (accent) quwat eṣ ṣawt; lay stress on, el muhimm (literally, the important thing is).
stretch: *v.* *trans.* medd, yamudd; *v.* *intrans.* imtedd, yemtedd; *n.* (distance) masàfa.
stretcher: *n.* sedya, na'sh.
stretcher-bearer: shayyàl, *pl.* shayyàlîn.
strew: ṭashshar, yuṭashshir.
strict: ḥàdd.
strictly: bi tadqîq; strictly speaking, el ḥaqîqa.
strictness: shidda.
stride: *v.* shabbakh, yushabbikh; *n.* shabkha.
strife: 'arka.
strike: *v.* dharab, yadhrab; daqq, yaduqq; (of clock) daqq, yaduqq; (from work) baṭṭal, yubaṭṭil.
striking: *adj.* (impressive) 'ajîb mudhish (mud-hish).
string: *n.* (cord) khaiṭ, *pl.* khuyûṭ; sûtlî; (for musical instrument, of gut) watr; (do., of wire) sîm.
stringent: shadîd, keskîn.
stringy: lîfî.
strip: *v.* (make naked) ṣallakh, yuṣallikh; (peel) gashshar, yugashshir; *n.* medda, *pl.* emdàd.
stripe: *n.* (line) khaṭṭ, *pl.* khuṭûṭ; (with whip) sôwṭ.

striped: mukhaṭṭaṭ.
strive: ijtehed, yejtehid.
stroke: *v.* (with hand) mesaḥ, yimsaḥ; *n.* (blow) ṣawâb, râshdi, dharba; (of pen) shakhṭa.
stroll: *v.* temeshsha, yetemeshsha; *n.* temeshshî.
strong: qawî (qawi), *pl.* quwai; guwi, *pl.* guwai.
structure: (building) bunyàn; (arrangement) tertîb.
struggle: *v.* (try) ijtehed, yejtehid; (resist) dàfa', yudafi'; (as in agony) tamarghal, yatamarghal; *n.* (strong effort) jehd; (fight) 'arka.
stubborn: 'anîd.
student: (in school) telmîdh, *pl.* talàmîdh; ṭâlib, *pl.* ṭalaba.
studiously: (purposely) 'amdan.
study: *v.* deres, yidras; ṭâla', yuṭâli'; *n.* ders, *pl.* durûs; *n.* (act of) muṭâla'a,
stuff: *v. trans.* ḥasha, yaḥshû; *n.* (material) màdda, *pl.* mawàd; (goods) aghrâdh.
stuffing: ḥashu.
stumble: *v.* 'athar, ya'thar.
stumbling-block: 'athra.
stump: (of tree) burṣ.
stun: dawwakh, yudawwikh.
stupefy: khaddar, yukhaddir.
stupendous: 'adhîm.
stupid: thaqîl, *pl.* thaqâl.
stupidity: ḥamâqa, jahàla.
stupor: khumûl.
sturdy: ḥudâr.
stutter: *v.* eltegh, yultigh.
style: *n.* (manner) ṭarîqa; (fashion) môda; (kind) shikl, *pl.* ashkàl; nô', *pl.* anwâ'; (form of writing) naṣṣ.
subaltern: mulàzim, *pl.* mulazimîn.
subdue: ṭêyya', yuṭêyyi'.
subject: *v.* (subdue) ṭêyya, yuṭêyyi'; subject to (make to undergo) ḥaṭṭ taḥt, yaḥuṭṭ; *n.* (matter discussed) mawdhû'; (subject of sentence) mubteda; (subject of government) teb'a, *pl.* teb'a; ra'îya; *adj.* subject to (under) taḥt; (liable to) qâbil.
subjection: iṭâ'a.
sublime: sàmî.
submarine: ghawwâṣa, *pl.* ghawwâṣàt.
submerge: *v. intrans.* ghâṣ, yaghûṣ.
submission: teslîm, ṭâ'a.
submissive: ṭâyi'.
submit: (yield) ṭâ', yaṭî'; sellem, yusellim; (offer) 'aradh, ya'radh.
subordinate: *adj.* dûn; *n.* taḥt îd.
subordination: (subjection) ṭâ'a.
subpœna: iḥdhârîya.
subscribe: (to periodical) ishterek fî, yeshterik; (agree to) wâfaq, yuwâfiq; (give to) tabarra', yatabarra'.
subscriber: mushterik.
subscription: (to paper) ishtirâk; (amount given) i'âna.
subsequent: tàlî.
subsequently: fîma bâ'ad.
subside: heda, yehdî.
subsidiary: dûn, far'î.
subsidize: a'ân, yu'în.
subsidy: i'âna.
substance: (material) màdda; (essential part) zibda, khulâṣa.
substantial: (actual) ḥaqîqî.

substantially: bil ḥaqîqa.
substantiate: ḥaqqaq, yuḥaqqiq.
substitute: *v. trans.* beddel, yubeddil; ʻawwadh, yuʻawwidh *n.* bedel; (person) nàyib.
substitution: taʻwîdh.
subtract: ṭaraḥ, yaṭraḥ; nezzel, yunezzil.
subtraction: ṭarh.
suburb: nâḥiya, *pl.* nawâḥî.
succeed: (follow) tebaʻ, yitbaʻ, (follow in office) khalaf, yakhlaf; (be successful) nejaḥ, yinjaḥ.
succeeding: see **subsequent**.
success: najâḥ, tôfîq.
successful: nàjiḥ, muwaffaq.
successfully: nàjiḥ.
succession: (series) tawàtur; (to throne) khalàfa; (in succession) wara bâʻadhuh; bi tatàbuʻ.
successive: mutatàbiʻ.
successively: wara bâʻadhuh; bi tatàbuʻ.
successor: khalf.
succinct: mukhtaṣir.
succinctly: bil ikhtiṣâr.
succumb: sellem, yusellim.
such: mithl (after noun).
suck: maṣṣ, yamuṣṣ.
suckle: radhdhaʻ, yuradhdhiʻ.
suction: maṣṣ.
sudden: fujâ-î.
suddenly: fuj-atan, defʻatan.
sue: ishteka ʻala, yeshtekî.
suet: shaḥm.
suffer: te-ellem, yete-ellem.
suffering: elem.
suffice: kefa, yikfî.
sufficient: kàfi.
sufficiently: kàfi; bi kafàya.
suffocate: *v. trans.* khanaq, yakhnaq; *v. intrans.* ikhtanaq, yakhtaniq.
sugar: sheker.
suggest: aʻṭa rai, yaʻṭî.
suggestion: rai, *pl.* ârâ.
suicide: *n.* intiḥâr; *v.* commit suicide, intaḥar, yantaḥir.
suit: *v.* qaṭaʻ ʻaql, yaqṭaʻ; wâfaq, yuwâfiq; *n.* (of clothes) qâṭ, bedla; (lawsuit) daʻwa.
suitable: muwâfiq, munàsib.
sulphur: kibrît.
sultan: sulṭân, *pl.* salâṭîn.
sultry: wakhîm.
sum: *n.* (total) majmûʻ; (of money) miblagh.
summarily: fî waqtuh; dhîk es sâʻa.
summary: mukhtaṣar.
summer: gêdh, ṣêf; *v.* pass summer, gêyyedh, yugêyyidh.
summit: râs.
summon: daʻâ, yadʻû.
summons: (subpœna) iḥdhârîya.
sun: shems.
sun-burned: maḥrûq min esh shems.
Sunday: yôm el aḥad; el aḥad; Sunday evening, mesa el aḥad.
sun-flower: shems wa qamr.
sun-light: shems.
Sunnite: sunnî, *pl.* sunna.
sunny: bih shems.
sunrise: ṭulûʻ esh shems.
sunset: maghrib; ghurûb esh shems.
sunshine: shems.
sup: taʻashsha, yatʻashsha.
superb: fâkhir.
supererogation: thawàb, ejer.
superficial: dhâhirî, saṭḥî.
superficially: dhâhiran.
superfluous: zàyid.

superintend: nâdhar, yunâdhir.
superintendence: nadhâra.
superintendent: nâdhir.
superior: *n.* ra-îs, *pl.* ru-asâ; *adj.* (better) aḥsan; (higher) a'la; (more) ekther.
superlative: (grammatical term) ism tafdhîl.
supernatural: fôq eṭ ṭabî'a.
supersede: (take office of) khalaf, yakhlaf; (take place of) baṭṭal, yubaṭṭil.
superstition: 'aqîda fàsida.
superstitious: 'aqaiduh fàsida.
supervise: nâdhar, yunâdhir.
supervision: nadhâra.
supervisor: nâdhir, murâqib.
supper: 'ashâ.
supple: lêyyin.
supplement: *v.* alḥaq, yulḥiq; *n.* mulḥiq.
supplementary: mulḥiq.
suppliant: multemis.
supplies: arzâq, muhimmàt.
supply: *v.* jehhez, yujehhiz; *n.* mûna, miqdâr.
support: *v.* (hold up) sened, yisnad; (maintain) 'ayyash, yu'ayyish; *n.* (prop) mesned; (maintenance) ma'îsha; (backing) ta-yîd.
suppose: (make hypothesis) faradh, yafradh; (think) dhann, yadhunn.
supposing: fardhan idha.
supposition: fardh.
suppress: (destroy) saḥaq, yisḥaq; (prevent) mena', yimna'.
supreme: awwal, a'la
supremely: ila a'la dereja
sure: (certain) akîd, mu-ekked; (confident) mutayaqqin; (safe) amîn.
surely: là budd.
surety: (person) kafîl; (bond) kafàla.
surface: wajh.
surgeon: jarrâḥ.
surgery: jirâḥa.
surgical: jarâḥi.
surmise: *v.* dhann, yadhunn.
surmount: ghalab, yaghlab.
surname: ism 'âyila ('â-ila).
surpass: fâq, yafûq.
surplus: fadhla.
surprise: *v. trans.* dehhesh, yudehhish; be surprised, ta'ajjab, yata'ajjab; *n.* ta'ajjub.
surprising: 'ajîb.
surrender: *v.* sellem, yusellim; *n.* teslîm.
surround: ḥawwaṭ, yuḥawwiṭ.
survey: *v.* (measure) qâs, yaqîs; hendes, yuhendis; *n.* hendesa, qiyàs.
surveying: *n.* misâḥa, hendesa.
surveyor: messâḥ, *pl.* messâḥîn.
survive: baqa, yibqa.
survivor: bâqî, *pl.* bâqîn.
susceptible: ḥassàs.
suspect: *v.* shekk, yashikk.
suspected: mashbûh.
suspend: (hang) 'allaq, yu'alliq; (stop) waggaf, yuwaggif; baṭṭal, yubaṭṭil.
suspender: âsqî (T.).
suspense: bil fikr, ḥîra.
suspension: towqîf.
suspicion: shekk, shubha; under suspicion, taḥt esh shekk.
suspicious: muwaswis, mushtebih.
sustain: (endure) taḥammal, yataḥammal; (support) 'ayyash, yu'ayyish; sened, yisnad.

sustenance: (food) qût.
swaddle: qammaṭ, yuqammiṭ.
swagger: *v.* tabakhtar, yatabakhtar.
swallow: *v.* bela', yibla'; *n.* (bird) khaṭṭaf.
swamp: *n.* hôr, *pl.* ahwâr.
swampy: hôr.
swarm: *v.* tahàfat, yatahàfat.
swarthy: esmer, *pl.* sumr.
swathe: *v.* leff, yaliff.
sway: *v.* (move) ihtezz, yehtezz; *n.* (rule) ḥukm.
swear: *v.* (take oath) ḥalaf, yaḥlaf; (curse) sebb, yasibb.
swearing: (taking oath) ḥalf yamîn: (cursing) teshtûm, masebba.
sweat: *v.* 'araq, ya'raq; *n.* 'arq.
sweaty: 'arqân.
Sweden: asûj.
sweep: *v.* kenes, yiknas.
sweeper: kennàs, *pl.* kanànîs.
sweeping: kunàsa.
sweet: ḥulu.
sweets: ḥalâwa, ḥalâwiyàt.
sweetness: ḥalâwa, ḥalâ.
swell: *v.* waram, yoram.
swelling: *n.* wurûm, warm.
swerve: *v.* màl, yamîl.
swift: *adj.* khafîf, sarî'.
swiftly: khafîf; bi sur'a.
swim: *v.* sebeḥ, yisbaḥ.
swimming: *n.* sibḥ.
swindle: ghashsh, yaghishsh.
swine: khanzîr, *pl.* khanâzîr.
swing: *v. intrans.* ihtezz, yahtezz.
switch: *n.* (of railway) maqaṣṣ.
swollen: wârim.
swoon: *v.* ghâbat er rûḥ, taghîb; *n.* ghashî.
sword: sêf, *pl.* suyûf.
syllable: maqṭa'.
symbol: remz, *pl.* rumûz.
symbolical: remzî.
symmetrical: mu'tedil.
sympathize: e.g. I sympathize with you, khâṭirî yenkesir 'alêk ('my heart is broken on your account').
sympathy: 'awâṭif; fil khâṭir.
symptom: 'alàma.
synagogue: torât.
synonym: mutaràdif.
syntax: naḥu.
syphilis: frengî.
Syria: sûrîya, shàm.
Syriac: sûriyànî.
Syrian: sûrî.
syringe: *n.* shranqa, ḥaqna; *v.* dharab shranqa, yadhrab.
syrup: dibes.
system: nidhâm, ṭarz, nasq, tertîb.
systematic: muntadham.
systematically: muntadham.
systematize: nadhdham, yunadhdhim.

T

table: (furniture) mêz, *pl.* mêzàt, muyûz; (list) jedwal, *pl.* jadàwil.
tablet: (of medicine) qarṣa, *pl.* quraṣ.
tack: *n.* (small nail) mismâr ṣaghîr; (of boat) khayûr; *v.* (of boat) khâyar, yukhâyir.
tackle: *v.* (undertake) qâm 'ala, yaqûm; *n.* (equipment) 'idda.
tact: faràsa.
tactics: ḥarakàt, tadàbir.
tail: dhêl, *pl.* dhuyûl; (of sheep) lîya.
tailor: khayyâṭ, *pl.* khayyâyîṭ.
take: akhadh, ya-khadh (yakhudh); take away, wadda, yuwaddî; take care, dâr bàl,

yadîr; take hold of, lezem, yilzam; qadhdh, yaqudhdh; take part, ishterek, yeshterik; take place, ṣâr, yaṣîr; jara, yijrî; take leave, tawâda', yatawâda'; take after (resemble), shebeh, yishbah.

tale: (story) ḥikàya', *pl.* ḥikàyàt.

tale-bearer: nammàm.

tale-bearing: namîma.

talent: (gift) môhaba.

talk: *v.* ḥaka, yaḥkî; *n.* ḥakî, kalàm.

tall: (of person) ṭawîl, *pl.* ṭawâl; (of thing) 'âli.

tallow: shaḥm.

tally: *v. trans.* ḥasab, yaḥsab; *v. intrans.* ṭâbaq, yuṭâbiq.

tamarind: tamr hind.

tambourine: deff.

tame: *v.* rabba, yurabbî; *adj.* alîf.

tamper: taḥarrash, yataḥarrash.

tan: *v. trans.* (of leather) dabbagh, yudabbigh.

tangible: qadàm el 'ain.

tangle: *v. trans.* kharbaṭ, yukharbiṭ; *v. intrans.* takharbaṭ, yatakharbaṭ; *n.* kharbaṭa.

tank: ḥôdh, tenka.

tanner: dabbâgh.

tanning: dibàgha.

tantalize: 'adhdhab, yu'adhdhib

tantamount: 'abâra 'an.

tap: *v.* daqq, yaduqq; *n.* daqqa.

taper: *v.* taraffa', yataraffa'.

tar: *v* gêyyer, yugêyyir; *n.* gîr.

tardy: baṭi, muta-akhkhir.

target: nîshàn.

tariff: resm, ta'rîf.

tarnish: *v. trans.* sawwad, yusawwid; *v. intrans.* eswedd, yeswedd.

tarpaulin: mushemma'.

tart: *n.* halâwa ma'jûn; *adj.* ḥâmidh.

task: *n.* shughl (shoghl), *pl.* ashghâl.

tassel: (of fez) peskûl; (of robe, &c.) kerkusha, *pl.* karâkish.

taste: *v.* dhâq, yadhûq; *n.* dhôq, ṭa'âm.

tasteless: bila ṭa'âm; fàhî.

tasty: (of food) ladhîdh.

tattered: mushaqqaq.

tattoo: *v.* daqq, yaduqq; degg, yadigg; *n.* degga.

taunt: *v.* 'ayyar, yu'ayyir; 'ayyab, yu'ayyib; *n.* ta'yîr.

tax: *v.* ḥaṭṭ resm, yaḥuṭṭ; *n.* resm, mîrî.

taxable: 'alêh resm.

taxation: resm.

tax-gatherer: taḥṣîldâr, *pl.* taḥṣîldârîya.

tea: chai.

teach: 'allam, yu'allim.

teacher: mu'allim, *pl.* mu'allimîn.

tea-cup: finjàn, *pl.* fanàjîn.

team: zôj khêl.

tea-pot: kûrî.

tear: *v.* shaqq, yashuqq; *n.* (rent) shaqq; *n.* (from eye) dem'a, *pl.* dumû'.

tease: kedder, yukeddir; 'adhdhab, yu'adhdhib.

tea-spoon: khâshûga màlat chai.

technical: iṣṭilâḥî.

technicality: (small point) far'.

technically: qânûnan.

tedious: mut'ib, thaqîl.

teetotaller: mumteni'.

telegram: teleghrâf, *pl.* teleghrâfât.
telegraph: *v.* têyyel, yutêyyil; daqq teleghrâf, yaduqq; *n.* teleghrâf.
telegraphic: barqî, teleghrâfî.
telephone: *v.* ḥaka bi têlfôn, yaḥkî; *n.* têlfôn.
telescope: darbîn, *pl.* darâbîn.
tell: (relate) ḥaka, yaḥkî; (inform) khabbar, yukhabbir; (say) qâl, yaqûl; gâl, yagûl.
temper: *v.* (temper iron) saqa, yasqî; (soften) lêyyen, yulêyyin; *n.* (disposition) akhlâq; (anger) za'l.
tempered: good tempered, ṭayyib el akhlâq; bad tempered, redi el akhlâq.
temperament: akhlâq, ṭabî'a.
temperance: 'iffa, i'tidàl.
temperate: mu'tedil.
temperature: derejat el ḥarâra.
temple: hêkal, *pl.* hayàkil.
temporal: dunyàwî, waqtî.
temporary: muwaqqat.
tempt: (entice) jedheb, yijdhab; tempt to evil, shawwaq ila sharr, yushawwiq.
temptation: tajriba, *pl.* tajârib.
tempting: mushawwiq.
ten: (*with masc.*) 'ashera; (*with fem.*) 'asher.
tenable: yandhabiṭ.
tenacious: muṣirr.
tenacity: iṣrâr.
tenant: mustà-jir.
tend: *v. trans.* (care for) dàra, yudàrî; (incline to) màl ila, yamîl; qâbil (*part.*).
tendency: mêl.
tender: *v.* (offer) 'aradh, ya'radh; qaddam, yuqaddim; *adj.* (soft) lêyyin; (at heart) raqîq; (sensitive) raqîq.
tenet: 'aqîda, *pl.* 'aqâyid.
tennis: tenis; la'b ṭôpa.
tense: *n.* zamàn; *adj.* (strained mushedded.
tent: khêma, *pl.* khiyam; chàdir (T.), *pl.* chawàdir.
tentative: lit tajriba.
tenth: *n.* 'ushr, *pl.* a'shâr; *adj.* 'âshir.
tenure: (holding) iltizàm.
tepid: fàtir, dàfî.
term: *v.* semma, yusemmi; *n.* (time) mudda; (name) ism, *pl.* asàmi, ismà; (condition) sharṭ, *pl.* shurûṭ; on good terms, zên wîya; on bad terms, mû zên wîya.
terminate: *v. trans.* (end) khatam, yakhtam; *v. intrans.* inteha, yentehi.
termination: nihàya.
terminology: iṣṭilâḥât.
terminus: ḥadd.
terrible: (causing fear) mukhawwif.
terrify: khawwaf, yukhawwif.
territorial: *n.* (soldier) mutaṭawwi'.
territory: mulk, bilàd.
terror: khôf, ru'b.
terse: mukhtaṣir.
test: *v.* imtaḥan, yamtaḥin; jarrab, yujarrib; *n.* imtiḥân, tajriba.
testament: (will) waṣîya; Old Testament, el 'ahd el qadîm; New Testament, el 'ahd el jadid.
testator: muwaṣṣi.
testify: shehed, yishhad.
testimonial: shahàda, *pl.* shahàdàt.
tether: *v.* shebbeḥ, yushebbiḥ; *n.* shabâḥ.
Teutonic: alemânî.

text: (original text) metn, aṣl; (of Scripture) àya, *pl.* àyàt.
texture: terkîb.
than: (after comparative) min (takes *pron. suffixes*); (before verb) min an.
thank: sheker, yishkar; teshekker li, yeteshekker; thank you, mimnûn; muteshekker; kethther khairek.
thankful: muteshekker, mimnûn.
thanks: *n.* teshekkur, shukr.
that: (*dem. pron.*) *masc.* hadhàk (*or* dhàk) el; *fem.* hadhîk (*or* hadhîch) el; (*rel. pron.*, who, which) *sing.* elledhî, *pl.* elledhîn; *conj.* ann (with *pron. suff.*) in order that, ḥatta.
that is: ya'nî.
the: el.
theatre: tiyàtro, *pl.* tiyàtrowàt.
theft: bôqa, sirqa.
their: *pron. suffix*, hum; màlehum (after noun).
theirs: màlehum.
them: *pron. suffix*, hum (see pp. 13, 18 f., 69).
themselves: anfusuhum, nefeshum.
then: (at that time) hadhàk el waqt; (in that case) fa idhan; (after which) thumma; now and then, bâ'dh el awqât.
theology: 'ilm el làhût.
theoretically: fikran, 'aqlan.
theory: fikr, takhayyul.
there: hinàk; there is, are, âkû; there was, were, kàn âkû; here and there, minna minnàk.
thereafter: bâ'ad dhàlik.
thereby: bi hel wâṣiṭa.
therefore: lidhàlik; min hes sebeb; li hes sebeb; khâṭir hàdha.
thereof: min dhàk; (concerning that) 'an dhàk.
thereupon: 'ala hàdha.
these: (with persons) hadhôl; (with things) hel, hàdhîl.
they: hûm, hûmma.
thick: (of board) matîn; (of paper) thakhîn; (of stick) ghalîdh; (of liquid) thakhîn; (of smoke) kathîf, mutakàthif; (dense, of grass) thakhîn.
thicken: thakhkhan, yuthakhkhin.
thickness: mutn, thukhn, ghuldh (cp. **thick**).
thief: (robber) ḥarâmî, *pl.* ḥarâmîya; (sneak) bawwâq, *pl.* bawwâqîn; sâriq, *pl.* sâriqîn.
thievery: bôqa, sirqa.
thigh: fakhdh.
thimble: kishtibàn.
thin: *v.* raqq, yaruqq; khaffaf, yukhaffif; *adj.* (of paper) raqîq; (of rope) rafî'; (of person) dha'îf; (of horse) hazîl, dha'îf; (of liquid) khafîf; (of vegetation) khafîf.
thing: shê, *pl.* eshyà.
think: (exercise thought) iftekar, yeftekir; (suppose) dhann, yadhunn.
thinly: khafîf.
thinness: riqqa, ruf', dhu'f, hezl, khuffa (cp. **thin**).
third: *n.* thulth, *pl.* athlàth; *adj.* thàlith.
thirst: *v.* 'aṭash, ya'ṭash; *n.* 'aṭash.
thirsty: 'aṭshân, *pl.* 'atshânîn.
thirteen: thalathatâsh.
thirteenth: thàlith 'asher (*masc.*); thàlitha 'ashra (*fem.*).
thirtieth: eth thalàthîn.
thirty: thalàthîn.

this: hàdha (*masc.*), hàdhi (*fem.*); (before noun) hàdhel (*masc.*), hàdhil (*fem.*), hel.
thistle: shôk.
thither: ila hinàk; hinàk.
thorn: shôk; (camel thorn) 'âgûl.
thorough: (in work) mudaqqiq; (complete) tamàm.
thoroughfare: darb, ṭarîq.
thoroughly: tamàman.
those: (with persons) hadhôlàk; (with things) hadhìk; those who, elledhìn.
though: wa law, ma' ann; as though, ka inn.
thought: *n.* (faculty) tefekkur; (idea) fikr, *pl.* afkâr.
thoughtful: (pensive) mutefekkir; (considerate) muftekir, mubàlî.
thoughtless: bila fikr.
thoughtlessly: bila fikr.
thousand: elf; *pl.* ulûf; *pl.* (with number) àlàf.
thousandth: el elf.
thread: khaiṭ, *pl.* khuyûṭ.
threadbare: munḥass.
threat: tehdîd.
threaten: hedded, yuheddid.
threatening: muheddid; (imminent) qarîb.
three: (*with masc.*) thalàtha; (*with fem.*) thalàth.
thresh: dàs, yadûs.
threshing: *n.* dôs.
threshold: 'ataba.
thrifty: mudebbir.
thrive: (prosper) nejaḥ, yinjaḥ.
throat: ḥalq.
throb: daqq, yaduqq; khafaq, yakhfaq.
throbbing: *n.* khafaqân.
throne: takhat, 'arsh.
throng: *v.* izdaḥam, yazdaḥim; *n.* izdiḥâm, khalq.
through: (from end to end) min ras ila ras; mâ bên; fî; (by means of) bi wâṣiṭat; (finished) khalaṣ.
throughout: fî kull; *adv.* bil kullîa.
throw: *v.* (fling) rama, yarmî; throw away, debb, yadibb; throw down, ṭaraḥ, yaṭraḥ.
thrust: *v.* thrust in, dakhkhal, yudakhkhil; thrust out, ṭalla', yuṭalli'; thrust through, ṭa'an, yaṭ'an.
thumb: ibhàm.
thunder: *n.* ra'd, qarâqî'; it thunders, tar'ad.
Thursday: yôm el khamîs.
thus: hîchî, hàkadha, kedha.
thwart: *v.* 'akkas, yu'akkis.
tick: *n.* (insect) qarâd: (of clock), taqtaqa; *v.* ṭaqq, yaṭuqq.
ticket: teskera, *pl.* tasàkir.
tickle: daghdagh, yudaghdigh.
ticklish: (critical) mukhṭir.
tide: *n.* medd wa jizr; flood tide, medda; ebb tide, jizr.
tidings: khabr, *pl.* akhbâr; good tidings, bashâra.
tidy: muretteb.
tie: *v.* shedd, yashidd; rabaṭ, yarbaṭ; *n.* (cravat) boyunbâgh (T.); (bond) rabâṭ; (equal result) musâwa.
tier: ṣaff, *pl.* ṣufûf; ṭabaqa, *pl.* ṭabaqât.
tiger: nimr, *pl.* numûr.
tight: (of rope) mashdûd; watertight, masdûd.
tighten: shedded, yusheddid.
tightly: ḥêl.
Tigris: ed dijla.
tile: (flat) qarmîd; (cylindrical) barbakh, *pl.* barâbikh.

till: *v.* felaḥ, yiflaḥ; 'ammar, yu'ammir; *prep.* (until) ḥatta, ila; (before verb) lîmâ.

tiller: (farmer) fellâḥ, *pl.* felàlîḥ; (rudder) sukkàn.

tilt: *v. trans.* (incline) mêyyel, yumêyyil; *v. intrans.* màl, yamîl; *n.* (inclination) mêl.

timber: khashab, *pl.* akhshàb.

time: waqt; (period of time) mudda; (season) zamàn; (fois) marra, *pl.* marràt; dôra, *pl.* doràt; nôba, *pl.* nobàt; def'a, *pl.* def'àt; (leisure) farâgha; in the meantime, fî dhàk el ithnà; by the time that, 'ala ma; for a time, ila mudda; for the time being, fîl ḥâdhir; for a long time (past), min zamàn; in the course of time, mâ' murûr ez zamàn; what time is it? es sâ'a kem; bêsh es sâ'a.

timely: fî waqtuh.

timid: khawwâf.

tin: *n.* tenek; *v.* bêyyedh, yubeyyidh.

tinge: lawwan, yulawwin; *n.* lôn, *pl.* alwàn.

tinker: *n.* tenekchî, *pl.* tenekchîya.

tiny: ṣughairûn.

tip: *v. trans.* (overturn) qalab, yaqlab; *v. intrans.* (tip over) inqalab, yanqalib; *v.* (give tip) a'ṭa bakhshîsh, ya'ṭî; *n.* (gift) bakhshîsh; (top) râs.

tire: *v. trans.* ta''b, yuta''ib; *v. intrans.* ta'ab, yit'ab; *n.* (of bicycle, &c.) jiled, lastik; (of wagon) dabàn.

tired: tâ'bân, *pl.* tâ'bânîn.

tiresome: (wearying) mut'ib; (boring) mudhawwij.

tithe: *v.* 'ashshar, yu'ashshir; *n.* 'ushr, *pl.* 'ushûr.

title: (heading) 'anwàn; (of rank) ritba, *pl.* ritab; (title deed, ḥijja; (addition to name, by-name, nickname) laqab, alqâb.

to: ila, li (with pron. suffix).

toadstool: fuṭar.

toast: *n.* (toasted bread) tôs.

tobacco: titen.

tobacconist: tattàn, *pl.* tattàna; tittenchî, *pl.* tittenchîya.

to-day: belyôm, elyôm.

toe: *n.* uṣbu' er rijl, *pl.* aṣâbi'; ṣub' er rijl.

together: wîya bâ'dh (followed by pron. suffix); *v.* put together, rekkeb, yurekkib.

toil: *v.* ta'ab, yit'ab; *n.* ta'b.

token: 'alàma, *pl.* 'alàmàt.

tolerable: (bearable) yataḥammal; (medium) mutawassiṭ.

tolerably: bên wa bên.

tolerate: taḥammal, yataḥammal.

toleration: taḥammul, lîna.

toll: *n.* (fee) resm.

tomato: *sing. and pl.* ṭamâṭa.

tomb: qabr, *pl.* qubûr.

to-morrow: bàkir, bàcher, ghada, bukra; day after to-morrow, bâ'ad bàcher; ogub bàcher.

ton: ton, *pl.* tunûn.

tone: (sound) ṣawt: (of letter, &c.) kêfîya.

tongs: màsha, minqâsh.

tongue: (organ) lisàn; (language) logha, *pl.* loghàt; lisàn, *pl.* elsina.

tonic: muqawwî.

tonnage: (capacity) míḥmal.
too: (also) aidhan, hum, humêna; too much, kathîr, zàyid (see p. 108).
tool: àla, *pl.* àlàt; 'idda.
tooth: sinn, *pl.* isnàn, sinûn; (molar) dhirṣ, *pl.* dhurûṣ.
toothache: waj' sinn.
toothpick: miswâk.
top: *n.* (highest part) râs; (surface) saṭḥ; (spinning-top) misrâ'.
topic: mawdhû', *pl.* mawâdhî'.
torment: *v.* 'adhdhab, yu'adhdhib; *n.* 'adhàb.
torpedo: *n.* torpîdo; *v.* dharab torpîdo, yadhrab; torpedo-boat, torpîdîya; torpedo-boat destroyer, mudemmira.
torrid: ḥârr.
toss: *v. trans.* (throw) rama, yarmî; shemmer, yushemmir; *v. intrans.* (as on sea) inqalab, yanqalib.
total: *n.* majmû'; el yakûn; *adj.* kullî.
totally: kullish, bil kullîa.
toto: in toto, kullîyan.
touch: *v.* jàs, yajîs; mess, yamiss; lemes, yilmas; *n.* (sense of touch) lems.
touching: *adj.* (pathetic) mueththir.
tough: qawî.
tour: *v. intrans.* sâḥ, yasîḥ; dharab siyâḥa, yadhrab; *n.* siyâḥa.
tourist: sayyâḥ, *pl.* sayyâḥîn.
tow: *v.* galaṣ, yaglaṣ.
toward: ila; ila ṭarf; naḥu.
towel: peshkir, *pl.* pashàkîr.
tower: (of church) burj; (Arab watch-tower) maftûl, *pl.* mafàtîl.
towering: shàmikh.
town: beled, *pl.* bilàd, buldàn.
toy: *n.* la'bàya, *pl.* la'bàyàt.
trace: *v.* (draw) resem, yirsam; (follow) gâf, yagîf; teba', yitba'; *n.* ether, *pl.* àthàr.
track: *v.* gâf, yagîf; *n.* (path) sikka; railway track, sikka; (trace) ether, *pl.* àthàr.
tract: (space of ground) masâḥa, qaṭ'a; (leaflet) karràza, *pl.* karàrîz.
trade: *v. trans.* (barter) beddel, yubeddil; *v. intrans.* (exchange) tabàdal, yatabàdal; (do commerce) tàjar, yutàjir; *n.* (commerce) tajâra; (occupation) ṣan'a, shughl; *n.* (exchange) tabàdul.
trader: tàjir, *pl.* tujjâr; bayyâ' sharrai.
tradition: (religious) ḥadîth, *pl.* aḥâdîth; ruwâya, *pl.* ruwâyàt.
traditional: naqlî.
traffic: *v.* tàjar, yutàjir; *n.* (trade) tajâra; (passing to and fro) râyiḥ jai.
train: *v.* (teach) rabba, yurabbî; 'allam, yu'allim; *n.* (railway train) qaṭr, trên.
trait: (characteristic) sajîya, *pl.* sajàyà.
traitor: khâyin.
tramp: *v.* (with the foot) dàs, yadûs; (march) mesha, yimshî; *n.* (vagabond) serserî.
trample: dàs, yadûs.
tramway: tramwê, trâm.
tranquil: hàdî, sàkin.
tranquillity: hudu.
transact: qadha, yaqdhî.
transaction: mu'âmala, *pl.* mu'âmalàt.
transcend: fâq, yafûq.
transcribe: naqal, yanqal.

transfer: ḥawwal, yuḥawwil; *n.* taḥwîl.
transform: ghayyar, yughayyir.
transformation: taghyîr.
transgress: ta'adda, yata'adda.
transgression: ta'addî.
transient: fàyit.
transit: murûr.
transition: intiqâl.
transitive: muta'addi.
translate: tarjam, yutarjim.
translation: tarjama.
translator: mutarjim.
transmission: taḥwîl.
transmit: ḥawwal, yuḥawwil; ba'ath, yib'ath.
transparent: (to sight) shaffàf; (to understanding) bêyyen.
transpire: jara, yijrî.
transplant: shetel, yishtal.
transport: *v.* naqal, yanqal; *n.* (carrying) naqlîya.
transportation: naqlîya.
trap: *v.* ṣâd, yaṣîd; (ambush) dharab kamîn, yadhrab; *n.* (for animals) miṣyada; (for birds) shibcha.
travel: sàfar, yusàfir; *n.* sefer, siyâḥa.
traveller: musàfir, *pl.* musàfirîn.
tray: ṣînîya, *pl.* ṣawànî.
treacherous: (person) khâyin.
treachery: khiyàna.
tread: *v.* dàs, yadûs.
treason: khiyàna.
treasure: *v.* qaddar, yuqaddir; *n.* khazna, kenz.
treasurer: amîn eṣ ṣandûq.
treasury: khazna.
treat: *v.* (act towards) 'âmal, yu'âmil; treat with (negotiate) tadhàkar, yatadhàkar; treat medically, 'âlaj, yu'âlij; treat of, baḥath 'an, yibḥath; *n.* lidhdha.
treatment: mu'âmala; (medical) mu'âlaja.
treaty: mu'âhada, *pl.* mu'âhadàt.
tree: shejera, *pl.* ashjâr, shejer.
tremble: rejef, yarjaf.
tremendous: 'adhîm.
trench: *n.* khandaq, *pl.* khanâdiq.
trespass: *v.* ta'adda, yata'adda; *n.* ta'addî.
trial: (test) tajriba; (legal) muḥâkama; (affliction) balîya, *pl.* balàyà.
triangle: muthelleth.
tribe: 'ashîra, *pl.* 'ashâyir; qabîla, *pl.* qabâyil; sub-tribe, ṭaifa, *pl.* ṭawâyif.
tribunal: maḥkama.
tributary: *adj.* (subject) tàbi'; *n.* (stream) shâkha, *pl.* shawâyikh.
tribute: (tax) khirâj; (of praise) medḥ.
trick: *v.* ghashsh, yaghishsh; *n.* ḥîla, *pl.* ḥiyal.
trickle: *v.* sàl, yasîl; *n.* sêyalàn.
trifle: *v.* izdera, yezderi; *n.* (small matter) shê juz-î.
trifling: *adj.* juz-î.
trigger: zanàd.
trim: *v.* (decorate) zêyyen, yuzêyyin.
Trinity: thàlûth, tathlîth.
trip: *v. trans.* 'aththar, yu'aththir; *v. intrans.* 'athar, ya'thar; *n.* (excursion) sefra, siyâḥa.
triple: thalàth qu-ûṭ.
Tripoli: ṭrâblis el gharb.
triumph: *v.* intaṣar, yantaṣir; ghalab, yaghlab; *n.* ghalba, nuṣra.

triumphant: muntaṣir, ghâlib.
trivial: juz-î.
troop: *n.* (soldiers) jêsh, qôm; (cavalry) firqa.
tropical: ḥârr.
tropics: el bilàd el ḥârra.
trot: *v.* hedheb, yehdheb; *n.* hedhb.
trouble: *v.* kedder, yukeddir; dawwakh, yudawwikh; az'aj, yuz'ij; *n.* (disturbance) kedr, kalûfa; (affliction) balîya, *pl.* balàyà; take trouble, kellef, yukellif.
troublesome: (annoying) mudhajjir, mukeddir.
trough: (for water) ḥôdh.
trousers: (European) pantalôn; (Oriental) sirwâl.
trowel: màlich.
truce: hudna, 'aṭla.
true: (genuine) ḥaqîqî; (not false) ṣaḥîḥ, ṣadq; (not treacherous) amîn; (straight) 'âdil.
truffles: chimma, kimma.
truly: (indeed) bil ḥaqîqa; (not falsely) bi ṣadq.
trunk: (of tree) jidh', *pl.* jidhû'; (chest) ṣandûq, *pl.* ṣanâdîq; (of elephant) kharṭûm.
trust: *v. trans.* emmen min, yuemmin min; thaqq bi, yathiqq; *n.* (confidence) thiqqa; (confidence in) i'timàd 'ala; thing in trust, amàna.
trustee: wakîl.
trustworthy: amîn.
truth: (opposite to falsehood) ḥaqîqa, ṣadq, ṣaḥîḥ; (abstract truth) ḥaqq; (truth of a matter) ṣaḥḥa.
truthful: ṣâdiq.
truthfulness: (of person) ṣadq; (of a matter) ṣaḥḥa.
try: (endeavour) jarrab, yujarrib; ijtehed, yejtehid; (test) jarrab, yujarrib; (try legally), sawwa muḥâkama, yusawwî; try on (clothing), lebes, yilbas.
trying: (troublesome) mushkil, zaḥma.
tub: (bath) ḥôdh, ḥamàm.
tube: (of metal, &c.) lûla; (of water-pipe) marpîch.
tuberculosis: daqq, ṣull.
Tuesday: yôm eth thalàthà.
tug: *v.* jarr, yajurr; *n.* (tug-bat) markab jarrâr.
tuition: (school) ḥaqq et tedrîs.
tumble: *v. trans.* waqqa', yuwaqqi'; *v. intrans.* waqa', yoqa'.
tumbler: (for drinking) glâs, *pl.* glasàt.
tumour: dumla.
tumult: dhajja.
tune: (song) naghma; (air) maqâm.
tunic: dishdàsha.
tunnel: sirb, *pl.* esrâb.
turban: 'imàma, *pl.* 'amàyim; leffa, *pl.* leffàt.
turbid: khâbiṭ.
turbulent: mushawwash.
Turk: turkî, 'osmanlî, 'othmànî; the Turks, et turk; el 'osmanlî.
turkey: (fowl) dijàj el hind.
Turkey: (country) turkîya.
Turkish: (language) turkî; (people) 'osmanlî, 'othmànî.
turmoil: teshwîsh.
turn: *v. trans.* turn round, dàr, yadîr; (twist) farr, yafurr; turn over, qalab, yaqlab; turn back, radd, yarudd; turn into (change into) ḥawwal, yuḥawwil; *v. intrans.* turn round, dâr, yadûr; (twist)

iftarr, yaftarr; turn over, inqalab, yanqalib; turn into (become), ṣâr, yaṣîr; turn back, radd, yarudd; turn up, bêyyen, yubêyyin; turn sour (of milk), ḥamadh, yaḥmadh.

turn: *n.* (of wheel) dawarân, tadwîr; (chance to act) dôr, nôba; by turn, bi dôr. See **turning**.

turner: charrâkh.

turning: (in road) dôra, *pl.* dôràt; 'ôja, *pl.* 'ôjàt.

turning-point: fâṣil.

turnip: shalgham.

turpentine: terpenten.

turtle: ragga, rafsh.

turtle-dove: ṭêr qamrî.

tutelage: ḥimàya.

tutor: *v.* derres, yuderris; *n.* mu'allim, muderris.

twaddle: *n.* (vain talk) ḥakî fârigh; ṭarahàt.

twelfth: thànî 'asher (*masc.*); thània 'ashra (*fem.*).

twelve: ithnâsh, thnâsh.

twentieth: el 'ashrîn.

twenty: 'ashrîn.

twin: tôm.

twine: *v. trans.* fetel, yiftal; *v. intrans.* tefettel, yetefettel; *n.* (cord) sûtlî.

twinkle: lema', yilma'.

twinkling: *n.* (of eye) laḥdhat 'ain.

twirl: *v. trans.* baram, yabram; *v. intrans.* iftarr, yaftarr.

twist: *v. trans.* fetel, yiftal; baram, yabram; *v. intrans.* (e.g. river) dâr, yadûr; *n.* fetla.

two: ithnên (*masc.*); thentên (*fem.*); (for nouns) use dual ending *ên*.

twofold: mudhâ'af.

type: *n.* (model) namûna, *pl.* namàyin; (kind) jins, *pl.* ajnàs; (printing) ḥarf, *pl.* ḥurûf.

typewriter: makîna màlat kitàba.

typhoid: tîfo.

tyrannical: dhâlim, *pl.* dhâlimîn.

tyrannize: dhalam, yadhlam.

tyranny: dhulm.

tyrant: dhâlim.

U

udder: dhar'.

ugly: bish', qabîḥ.

ulcer: dumla.

ulterior: akhîr.

ultimately: akhîran.

ultimatum: qarâr akhîr.

ultimo: esh shahr el mâdhî.

un-: generally expressed by prefixing *mâ*, *mû* or *ghair* before adj. or participle, *'adm* before nouns.

umpire: 'ârfa, *pl.* 'awârif.

unable: mâ muqtedir.

unacceptable: mû qubûl; mâ maqbûl.

unaccustomed: mâ muta'awwid.

unaided: waḥduh.

unanimous: muttefiq.

unanimously: bi ṣawt wâḥid.

unassuming: mutawâdhi'.

unavailable: bila fàyida.

unawares: see **unguarded**.

unbelief: kufr.

unbeliever: kàfir, *pl.* kuffâr.

unbounded: khârij.

unbroken: (successive) muttaṣil.

unbutton: ḥall, yaḥull; **fekk**, yafukk.

unceasing: bila inqiṭâ'.
uncertain: (thing) mashkûk; (person) mâ mutayaqqin; ma'lûm.
uncertainty: shekk.
uncivilized: waḥshî.
uncle: (paternal) 'amm, *pl.* a'màm; (maternal) khâl, *pl.* akhwâl, khawâl.
unclean: (ceremonially) nejis.
uncleanness: najàsa.
unclouded: ṣâḥî.
uncoil: ḥall, yaḥull; fekk, yafukk.
uncomfortable: mâ mustarîḥ.
uncommon: (rare) nàdir.
uncomplaining: ṣabûr.
uncompromising: ṣa'ab el mirâs.
unconnected: munfaṣil.
unconscious: mâ yaḥiss.
unconsciously: min dûn ma'-rifa.
uncontrolled: mâ madhbûṭ; min dûn dhabṭ.
uncouth: khashn.
uncover: keshef, yikshaf.
uncultivated: kharâb.
undeniable: muḥaqqaq, akîd.
undecided: ḥâyir.
under: (below) taḥt, ḥadr, jôa; (less than) aqall min; *adj.* taḥtânî.
undergo: jara 'ala, yijrî; kàbad, yukàbid; taḥammal, yataḥammal.
underground: taḥt el gâ'.
underhanded: khafî.
underling: ḥadr el îd.
underneath: taḥt, ḥadr, jôa.
underrate: istakhaff, yastakhiff.
underscore: shakhkhat ḥadr, yushakhkhit.
undersell: bâ' arkhaṣ min, yabî'.
understand: iftehem, yefte-him; fehem, yifham.
understanding: (faculty) fehm, idrâk; (agreement) ittifâq.
undertake: (set to work on) bàshar bi, yubàshir; (take on one's self) akhadh 'ala nefsuh, ya-khudh; (promise) ta'ahhad, yata'ahhad.
undertaking: (enterprise) mes-ela.
undesigned: bi ittifâq.
undesirable: mâ yanràd; mâ maryûd.
undivided: kàmil, tàmm.
undo: (untie) ḥall, yaḥull; (reverse) baṭṭal, yubaṭṭil.
undoubtedly: bila shekk; ma'lûm.
undress: *v. intrans.* neza' hudûm, yinza'.
undue: (excessive) zàyid.
unduly: zàyid, khârij.
uneasiness: qalq.
uneasy: (worried) mutashaw-wish.
unequivocal: qaṭ'î.
uneven: (e.g. of road) wa'ar.
unexpectedly: 'ala ghafla.
unfaithful: khâyin.
unfasten: (e.g. rope) ḥall, ya-ḥull; (e.g. door) fekk, yafukk.
unfeigned: khâliṣ.
unfit: *v.* 'aṭṭal, yu'aṭṭil; *adj.* (incapable) mâ muqtedir.
unfitness: 'adm iqtidâr.
unfold: basaṭ, yabsaṭ; keshef, yikshaf.
unforseen: mâ muntadhar.
unfortunate: (man) ḥadhdh mû zên; (thing) manḥûs.
unfortunately: min sû el ḥadhdh.
unfounded: bila aṣl.
unfrequented: mâ bih rijl.

unfriendly: (expressed by noun and preposition) 'adâwa wîya (cp. **hostility, with**).
ungainly: thaqîl.
ungovernable: 'anîd.
ungratefulness: 'adm mimnûnîya.
ungrounded: bila aṣl.
unguarded: min dûn muḥâfadha; at a moment (unawares), ghaflatan.
unhappy: maghmûm.
unharness: fekk, yafukk.
unhealthful: mudharr liṣ ṣaḥa.
unhealthy: munḥarif el mizàj.
unhurt: sàlim.
uniform: *n.* hudûm resmîya; *adj.* musâwa, mutasâwî.
uniformity: (sameness) iṭṭirâd; (regularity) intidhâm.
uniformly: muṭṭarid.
unimportant: mâ muhimm; zahîd.
uninhabitable: mâ yensekin.
unintentionally: sehwan.
uninterrupted: muttaṣil.
uninterruptedly: ferd râs.
union: (joining) tawḥîd, jam'; (concord) ittifâq, ittiḥâd; (society) jam'îya.
unique: farîd, waḥîd.
unison: bi ṣawt wâḥid; suwa.
unit: ferd, *pl.* afrâd.
unite: *v. trans.* waḥḥad, yuwaḥḥid; *v. intrans.* ittefeq, yettefiq; ittaḥad, yattaḥid.
united: mattaḥad, muttefeq; (things) muttaṣal; United States, el wilàyàt el muttaḥida.
unitedly: suwa.
unity: ittiḥâd; unity of God, waḥdânîya.
universal: 'umûmî, 'âm.
universally: 'umûman.
universe: kawn.
university: kullîa jàmi'a.
unjust: dhâlim.
unjustly: min dûn ḥaqq.
unkind: qâsî.
unkindly: bi qasâwa.
unknown: (person) mâ ma'rûf; (thing) majhûl.
unlawful: khilàf el qânûn; mâ yajûz; (religiously) muḥarram, ḥarâm.
unlawfully: bila ḥaqq.
unleavened: faṭîr.
unless: idha mâ.
unlike: *adj.* mû mithl; mukhâlif ila.
unlikely: no exact equivalent. Expressed by *mâ adhunn* (I don't think so), or by *ba'îd* (far).
unload: nafadh, yanfadh.
unlock: fekk, yafukk.
unlucky: mashûm, naḥs.
unmanageable: (of mare) wakîḥa, *pl.* wukâḥ, wukkâḥ; (of horse) 'abath.
unmarried: 'azib.
unmerciful: qâsî.
unmindful of: ghâfil 'an.
unmingled: khâliṣ.
unnecessary: mû làzim.
unoccupied: fârigh.
unofficial: ghair resmî.
unpaid: maṭlûb.
unprincipled: munàfiq.
unquestionable: akîd.
unravel: ḥall, yaḥull.
unremitting: mustamirr,
unripe: akhdhar.
unroll: nesher, yinshar.
unruly: mutamarrid.
unsafe: mukhṭir.
unseen: khafî.
unsettle: shawwash, yushawwish.

unsheathe: sell, yasill.
unshod: ḥâfî.
unsightly: bish'.
unsound: of unsound mind, mukhtell esh shu'ûr.
unspent: bâqî.
unstable: (fickle) mutaqallib.
unsteady: mutala''ib.
unsurpassed: khârij, fàyiq.
unsystematic: mukharbaṭ, makhbûs.
unthinking: ghâfil.
untie: ḥall, yaḥull.
untied: maḥlûl.
until: ḥatta; lîmâ; ila an.
untrue: mû ṣaḥîḥ; kidhb.
untruth: kidhb.
unusual: (rare) nàdir; (exceptional) khârij.
unusually: kullish, khârij.
unvarying: dàyim.
unwell: munḥarif el mizàj; mâ luh kêf.
unwholesome: mudhirr.
unwieldly: thaqîl.
unwilling: mû râdhî.
unwillingly: min dûn ridhâ.
unwillingness: 'adm ridhâ.
unwind: ḥall, yaḥull.
unwise: jàhil.
unwisely: bi jahàla.
unwittingly: sehwan.
unyielding: (to argument) 'anîd.
up: (above) fôq; (not abed) qâ'id; (of the sun) ṭâli'a; upstairs, fôq; hard up, îduh dhayyiqa.
upbraid: wabbakh, yuwabbikh; rezzel, yurezzil.
uphill: ṣu'ûd.
uphold: (support) sened, yisnad; (maintain) eyyed, yueyyid.
uplift: rafa', yarfa'.
upon: (of place) 'ala, fôq; (of time) 'ala.
upper: fôqânî.
upperhand: tasalluṭ.
upright: *n.* (perpendicular post) qâyim; *adj.* mustaqîm.
uprightness: istiqâma.
uproar: ṣêḥa, dhajîj.
uproot: qala', yaqla'.
upset: *v.* qalab, yaqlab; be upset, inqalab, yanqalib.
upshot: (result) natîja.
upsidedown: maqlûb.
upward: ila fôq.
urge: laḥḥ 'ala, yaluḥḥ.
urgency: dharûra.
urgent: (pressing) dharûrî; (insistent) muliḥḥ.
urgently: dharûrî.
urinate: *v.* bàl, yabûl.
urine: bôl.
ursa: (astron.) ed dibb.
us: *pron. suffix* na (see pp. 13, 18 f., 69).
usage: (treatment) mu'âmala; (use) isti'màl; (custom) 'âda.
use: *v.* ista'mal, yasta'mil, (treat) 'âmal, yu'âmil; *n.* isti'màl; (benefit) fàyida, *pl.* fawàyid; in use, musta'mal; to be of no use, mâ yafîs.
used: (employed) musta'mal; used up, khalaṣ; used to (accustomed to), muta'awwid; used to (formerly), kàn *with pres. of verb.*
useful: mufîd; nefa', yinfa'.
usefulness: fàyida.
useless: bila fàyida; 'abath.
uselessly: bila fàyida; 'abathan.
usual: 'âdî.
usually: ekther el awqât; 'âdatan.

usurp: ightaṣab, yaghtaṣib.
usury: riba; to practise usury, ya-kul riba.
utensil: (dish) ma'ûn, *pl.* mawâ'în; (tool) àla, *pl.* àlàt.
utility: fàyida.
utmost: ghâya, nihàya; do one's utmost, bedhel kull jehd, yibdhal.
utter: *v.* naṭaq, yanṭaq; lafadh, yalfadh; *adj.* (absolute, complete), kullî.
utterly: bil kullîa.

V

vacancy: (post) makàn fârigh; firâgha.
vacant: fârigh, khâlî.
vacate: farragh, yufarrigh; akhla, yukhlî.
vacation: (school-vacation) ta'ṭîl, tabṭîl, furṣa; (holiday) furṣa, rukhṣa.
vaccinate: laqqaḥ, yulaqqiḥ; (for smallpox) daqq jidrî, yaduqq.
vaccination: talqîḥ.
vaccine: laqâḥ.
vacillate: teredded, yeteredded; taqallab, yataqallab.
vacillating: muteredded, mutaqallab.
vacillation: tereddud.
vacuum: khalâ.
vagabond: serseri, *pl.* serseriya.
vague: mubham.
vain: (proud) râs kabîr; mutekebbir; (ineffectual) 'abath; in vain, 'abath; 'abathan; bila fàyida.
vainly: 'abath, 'abathan, suda.
valiant: shujâ'.
valid: saḥîḥ, jêyyid.
validity: saḥḥa.
valise: janta, *pl.* jantàt.
valley: wâdî, *pl.* awdia.
valour: jasâra, shajâ'a.
valuable: (precious) thamîn, 'azîz; (beneficial) mufîd.
valuation: tathmîn.
value: *v.* (estimate) themmen, yuthemmin; (prize) aziz 'and *with suff.*; *n.* (worth) themen; (price) qîma, *pl.* aqyàm; (importance) i'tibâr.
valve: wàlf.
van: (advance part) muqaddama; (van-guard) rawâd; (vehicle for transport) 'arabâna màlat ḥiml.
vanish: ghâb, yaghîb.
vanity: (pride) tekebbur, kubriya; (emptiness) buṭl.
vanquish: ghalab, yaghlab.
vapour: bukhâr.
variable: mukhtelif.
variance: ikhtilàf.
variation: ikhtilàf, taghayyur.
variety: ashkàl (lit. 'kinds').
various: mukhtelif.
varnish: dharab warnîs, yadhrab; *n.* warnîs.
vary: *v. trans.* ghayyar, yughayyir; *v. intrans.* taghayyar, yataghayyar; ikhtelef, yakhtelif.
vassal: tàbi'.
vast: 'adhîm.
vastness: 'adhama.
vat: (large) ḥôdh; (small) jarra.
vaulted: ma'qûd, 'aqàda.
veal: laḥm 'ijl.
vegetable: khadhra, *pl.* khadhrawàt; *adj.* nabàtî.
vegetate: nebet, yinbat.
vegetation: 'ushb, khadhâr.
vehement: (of speech) qawî, ḥàdd.

vehicle: (carriage, wagon) 'arabâna, *pl.* 'arabâyin.
veil: *v. trans.* setter, yusettir; *v. intrans.* seter, yistar; *n.* (for women) pûshî.
vein: 'irq, *pl.* 'urûq; damâr, *pl.* damâràt.
velocity: khiffa, sur'a.
velvet: qadîfa.
venerable: mu'tabar, muwaqqar.
venerate: iḥtaram, yaḥtarim.
veneration: iḥtirâm.
vent: *v.* ṭalla', yuṭalli'; give vent to, adhhar, yudhhir.
ventilate: fekk lil hawa, yafukk.
ventilation: tarwîḥ.
ventilator: bâdgîr (P.).
venture: *v.* tajàsar, yatajàsar; (risk) mukhâṭara.
Venus: (planet) zuhra.
veranda: ṭârma, *pl.* ṭârmàt.
verb: fi'l, *pl.* af'âl.
verbatim: ḥarfîyan.
verdict: ḥukm, fetwa.
verge: *v.* qârab, yuqârib; *n.* (edge) ḥadd; on the verge of, fî ḥâl el.
verify: ḥaqqaq, yuḥaqqiq.
vermicelli: sha'rîya.
vermin: qaml.
vernacular: loghat el bilàd.
verse: (in poetry line) bêt, *pl.* abyàt; (in sacred book) àya, *pl.* àyàt; (opposite of prose) shi'r.
versed: (informed) mukhtebir.
version: (of story) ruwàya.
vertical: qâyim, wâgif, 'amûdi.
vertically: wâgif; fôq ḥadr.
very: *adj.* (same) nefs el; *adv.* kathîr, kullish, wàjid, hwâyi.
vessel: (for cooking) jidr, *pl.* jidûr; (for drinking) dolka; (ship) markab, *pl.* maràkib; blood-vessel, damâr, *pl.* damâràt.
vest: (waistcoat) yelek, ṣadrîya; (singlet) fànîla; *v.* dhamman, yudhammin; be vested in, tadhamman fî, yatadhamman.
vested: (fixed, of rights) mamlûk.
vestibule: majàz.
vestige: ether, *pl.* àthàr.
veteran: mutadarrib.
veterinary surgeon: bêṭâr.
veto: *v.* mena', yimna'; enha 'an, yunhî; *n.* men', nehî.
vex: kedder, yukeddir.
vexatious: mukeddir, mudawwikh.
viaduct: qanṭara, *pl.* qanâṭir.
vibrate: ihtezz, yehtezz.
vibration: ihtizàz.
vice: *n.* (in general) fasàd, sharr; (in particular) radhîla, *pl.* radhàyil; *adj.* wakîl.
viceroy: nàyib el melk.
vice versa: bil 'aks.
vicious: (morally) sharîr, fàsid; (of horse) 'abath; (intense) shadîd.
vicissitudes: taqallabàt.
victor: ghâlib, *pl.* ghâlibîn.
victorious: muntaṣir, manṣûr.
victory: ghalba, nuṣra.
victual: *v.* jehhez, yujehhiz; *n.* ṭa'âm, *pl.* aṭ'ima.
vie with: taghâlab wîya, yataghâlab.
view: *v.* shàf, yashûf; *n.* (scene) mandhar; (opinion) rai, *pl.* ârâ; have in view, nawa, yinwî; point of view, jeha.
vigilant: muntebih.
vigorous: (strong) qawî, nashîṭ; (healthy) muta'âfî.
vigorously: ḥêl.

vigour: qûwa, nashâṭ; (health) 'âfia.
vile: (dirty) wasikh; (unclean) nejis; (repulsive) karîh.
villa: qaṣr, *pl.* quṣûr.
village: qarya, *pl.* qura; koi, *pl.* koyàt; dhêy'a, *pl.* dhiyâ'; (of huts) jamâ'a, *pl.* jamâ'àt.
villain: khabîth.
vindicate: (clear a person) barrar, yubarrir; (prove a thing) thebbet, yuthebbit.
vindication: (of person) tabrîr; (of thing) ithbàt.
vine: (grape-vine) tislâqa.
vinegar: khall.
vineyard: karm, *pl.* kurûm.
violate: (break law) keser, yiksar; (trespass) ta'adda, yata'adda.
violation: kesr, ta'addî.
violence: (strength) qûwa, shidda; (vehemence) ḥidda.
violent: (strong) qawî, shadîd, ḥêl; (excessive) khârij.
violet: *n.* benefsha; *adj.* benefshî.
violin: (European) sinakamana; (Bedouin) rabàba.
virgin: 'adhra, *pl.* 'adhâra; virgin soil, gâ' bikr.
virtual: ḥaqîqî.
virtually: bil ḥaqîqa.
virtue: (in general) ṣalâh, zênîya; (in particular) fadhîla, *pl.* fadhâyil; in virtue of, binà-an 'ala.
virtuous: fâdhil; (pure) 'afîf.
virulence: shidda.
virulent: shadîd.
vis-à-vis: muqâbil; (face to face) wajh ila wajh.
visé: *v.* ṣaddaq, yuṣaddiq; *n.* taṣdîq.
visible: yanshàf, bêyyen.
vision: (eyesight) shôf, baṣr; (apparition) khayàl.
visionary: (imaginary) taṣawwurî; (unreal) bila asàs.
visit: *v.* zâr, yazûr; *n.* ziyâra, *pl.* ziyâràt.
visitor: khaṭṭâr (*s.* and *pl.*).
vital: (important) muhimm.
vitality: (life) ḥayàt; (strength) qûwa.
vivacious: nashîṭ.
viz.: ya'nî.
vizier: wazîr, *pl.* wuzarâ.
vocabulary: (book) qâmûs, *pl.* qawâmîs; (words available) kalimàt.
vocation: shughl (shoghl), *pl.* ashghâl.
vogue: 'âda; in vogue, musta'mal.
voice: *n.* ṣawt, *pl.* aṣwât; ḥiss; (opinion, choice) ṣawt, ikhtiyâr.
void: *adj.* fârigh, khâlî; null and void, baṭṭâl; *n.* firâgha.
volatile: ṭâyir; yaṭîr.
volcano: barkân; jebel nâr.
volley: ramya.
volume: (book) kitàb, *pl.* kutub; (tome) mujelled, *pl.* mujelledàt; (size) ḥajm.
voluntarily: bil ikhtiyâr; min kêfuh.
voluntary: ikhtiyârî.
volunteer: *v. trans.* qaddam min nefsuh, yuqaddim; *v. intrans.* (as soldier) taṭawwa', yataṭawwa'; *n.* mutaṭawwa', *pl.* mutaṭawwa'în.
vomit: *v.* zâ', yazû'; debb min ḥalquh, yadibb; istafragh, yastafrigh; taqayya, yataqayya.
vote: *v.* intakhab, yantakhib; debb ṣawt, yadibb; *n.* ṣawt, *pl.* aṣwât.

voter: muntakhib.
voting: intikhâb.
voucher: (receipt) wuṣûl, sened.
vouch for: (guarantee) tekeffel bi, yetekeffel.
vow: *v.* nedher, yindhar; *n.* nidhr.
vowel: *v.* (point with vowel) ḥarrak, yuḥarrik; *n.* ḥarf 'illa *pl.* ḥurûf.
voyage: *n.* sefra, sefer.
vulgar: (common) dàrij; (mean) denî, ḥaqîr.
vulgarly: (commonly) 'and el 'awâm.

W

wadded: mulebbed.
wade: khâdh, yakhûdh.
wag: *v. trans.* hezz, yahizz. See also **shake**.
wage: *v.* wage war, taḥârab, yataḥârab; *n.* (daily) yômîya; (monthly) shahrîya.
wager: *v.* tarâhan, yatarâhan; *n.* ruhn.
wages: see **wage**.
wagon: 'arabâna mâlat ḥiml.
wail: *v.* ṣêyyeḥ, yuṣêyyiḥ.
wailing: *n.* ṣiyâḥ.
waist: (of body) ḥizàm; (of clothing) polka.
waistcoat: yelek, ṣadrîya.
wait: *v.* istandhar, yastandhir; wait on, khadam, yakhdam.
waiter: (at table) sufrachî.
waive: jâz min, yajûz.
wake: *v. trans.* wa''a, yuwa''î; qa''ad, yuqa''id (ga''ad, yuga''id); *v. intrans.* ḥass, yaḥiss.
wakeful: sàhir, sahrân.
waken: see **wake**.
walk: *v.* mesha, yimshî; *n.* (gait) meshî; (distance) memsha; take a walk, temeshsha, yetemeshsha.
wall: ḥâyiṭ, *pl.* hîṭân; (of garden) ṭôf.
walnut: jôz.
wander: (stroll) temeshsha, yetemeshsha; (stray) tàh, yatîh; (talk nonsense) kharbaṭ, yukharbiṭ.
wanderer: seyyâḥ.
wane: *v.* (of moon) naqaṣ, yanqaṣ.
want: *v.* (desire) ràd, yarîd; (need) iḥtàj, yaḥtàj; 'âz, ya'ûz (with pron. suff. of person wanting); *n.* (need) ḥàja, *pl.* hàjàt; in want, muḥtàj.
wanting: *adj.* (missing) nâqiṣ.
war: ḥarb, *pl.* ḥurûb; muḥâraba, *pl.* muḥârabàt; *v. trans.* to wage war with, ḥârab, yuḥârib; *v. intrans.* to make war, taḥârab, yataḥârab.
ward: *n.* (person under guardian, minor) qâṣir, *pl.* quṣṣar; *v.* ward off, defa', yidfa'; in ward, taḥt muḥâfadha.
warder: ghurdyân, muḥâfidh.
ward-robe: (clothing) elbisa; (cupboard) dûlàb.
warehouse: 'anbâr, *pl.* 'anâbîr.
warfare: muḥâraba, ḥarb.
warlike: ḥarbî.
warm: (moderately hot) dàfî: (do., of water) fàtir; *v. trans.* (heat) ḥamma, yuḥammî; (heat the body) deffa, yudeffî; *v. intrans.* taḥamma, yataḥamma; tedeffa, yetedeffa.
warmth: (moderate heat) defu.
warn: nebbeh, yunebbih; khaṭṭar, yukhaṭṭir.
warning: *n.* tenbîh, taḥdhîr,
warp: *v. trans.* 'awwaj, yu'awwij; lawa, yilwî; *v. intrans.*

inḥana, yanḥanî; *n.* (in loom) sida.
warrant: *v.* (give right to) fawwadh, yufawwidh; (guarantee) ta'âhad, yata'âhad; *n.* (authority) tafwîdh.
warrior: 'arrâk, *pl.* 'arrâka.
wart: fàlûl.
wary: muntebih.
wash: *v. trans.* ghasal, yaghsal; ghassal, yughassil; *v. intrans.* ightasal, yaghtasil.
washer: (ring) sadàda.
washerwoman: ghassàla.
wasp: zambûr, *pl.* zanàbîr.
waste: *v.* (squander) etlef, yutlif; waste time, dhêyya', yudhêyyi'; lay waste, kharrab, yukharrib; *n.* (loss) khasâra.
watch: *v.* naṭar, yanṭar; (keep eye on) 'ain 'ala; (keep awake) seher, yis-har; watch for, intadhar, yantadhir; taraqqab, yataraqqab; *n.* (time-piece) sâ'a, *pl.* sâ'àt.
watchful: muntebih.
watchmaker: sâ'achî, *pl.* sâ'achîya.
watchman: nâṭûr, *pl.* nawâṭîr.
watch-tower: mafıûl, *pl.* mafàtîl.
water: *v.* (irrigate) saqa, yisqî; (water animals) saqa, yisqî; *n.* mai.
water-bottle: (army) maṭrîya.
water-carrier: saqqa, *pl.* saqâqî.
water-closet: edeb, edebkhâna, ebdestkhâna.
water-course: sâqia, *pl.* sawâqî.
water-melon: reggî.
waterpot: (used by Arab women) meskhena, *pl.* masâkhin.
water-tight: mâ yadishsh bih el mai. See also **tight**.
water-wheel: (for irrigation) nâ'ûr, *pl.* nawâ'îr.
wave: *v.* (as grain) tamawwaj, yatamawwaj; *v. trans.* (as flag) eshsher, yu-eshshir; *n.* (of the sea) môj, *pl.* amwàj; rôj.
waver: tereddad, yeteredded.
wax: *n.* shem'; sealing-wax, lukk.
waxed: (of oilcloth) mushemma'.
way: (road) darb, *pl.* durûb; ṭarîq, *pl.* ṭurq; (manner) ṭarîqa, jûra; (direction) jeha, ṭarf; one way or another, shlôn mâ kàn; in the way, fid darb; *v.* get out of way, wakhkhar, yuwakhkhir.
we: eḥna, naḥen, naḥnu.
weak: dha'îf, *pl.* dhu'âf.
weaken: *v. trans.* dha''f, yudha''if.
weakly: rakhu.
weakness: dhu'f; (failing) 'aib.
wealth: tharwa.
wealthy: ghani, *pl.* aghniâ; zengîn, *pl.* zengînîn.
wean: faṭam, yafṭam.
weapon: silâḥ, *pl.* esliḥa.
wear: *v. trans.* (put on) lebes, yilbas; wear out, etlef, yutlif; *v. intrans.* (last) dàm, yadûm; wear out, telef, yitlaf; wear out (of clothes) taqaṭṭa'; yataqaṭṭa'; *n.* telf; (use) fàyida.
weariness: ta'b.
wearisome: muta''ib.
weary: *adj.* (fatigued) ta'bân; (tiresome) muta''ib; *v. trans.* ta''b, yuta''ib.
weather: hawa; (climate) manâkh.

weave: ḥâk, yaḥûk.
weaver: ḥâyik.
weaving: ḥiyàka.
web-footed: makfûf.
wed: *v. trans.* zawwaj, yuzawwij; *v. intrans.* tazawwaj, yatazawwaj.
wedding: (occasion) 'urs; (ceremony) nikâḥ, zawàj, barrâkh.
wedge: *n.* gîna.
Wednesday: yôm el arba'â.
week: usbû' (isbû'), *pl.* asàbî', sabâya'.
weekly: *adj.* usbû'i; *adv.* usbû'îyan; kull usbû'.
weep: beka, yibkî.
weeping: *n.* bukâ, buchâ.
weigh: *v. trans.* wazan, yozan; 'ayyar, yu'ayyir; *v. intrans.* waznuh (lit. 'its weight is').
weight: *n.* (heavy thing) thuql, *pl.* athqâl; (heaviness) wazn; (disk for weighing) 'ayâr; (importance) ahemmîya.
weighty: (heavy) thaqîl, *pl.* thaqâl; (importance) ahemmîya.
welcome: *v.* taraḥḥab bi, yataraḥḥab; *n.* tarḥâb; (exclamation) marḥaba; ehlen wa sehlen; *adj.* (acceptable) maqbûl.
weld: laḥam, yalḥam; to be welded, iltaḥam, yaltaḥim.
welfare: khair.
well: *n.* bîr, *pl.* abyâr; *adj.* (healthy) muta'âfi; kêfuh zên; *adv.* (Fr. bien) ṭayyib, zên; as well as (also) kema aidhan; hum; (exclamation) well done, âferin (T.), brâwo; well off, ḥâluh zên.
well-bred: adîb, *pl.* adîbîn, udabâ.
west: *n.* gharb; *adj.* gharbî; *adv.* gharban, gharbî.
wet: *adj.* (soaked) mubellel; (damp) murṭib, nedî; *v. trans.* bellel, yubellil.
wharf: eskela, *pl.* eskelàt.
wharfage: ardhîya.
what: *interr. pron.* (alone) shinû, shlôn; (after verb or prep.) êsh; e.g. what do you want? êsh tarîd; what book? yâ kitàb; ê kitàb; what is the name of...? shism; what a large house, shlôn bêt kabîr.
whatever: kullemâ, kullmâ, êshmâ.
wheat: ḥanṭa.
wheel: *n.* charkh, *pl.* churûkh; dûlàb, *pl.* dawàlîb; (steering-wheel) sukkàn; paddle-wheel, parwâna, *pl.* parwânàt.
wheelbarrow: 'arabâna màlat îd.
when: *interr.* yimta, metta; *rel.* lemma.
whence: min ên.
whenever: yimtamâ, metamâ.
where: (*interr.*) wên, ên; (at the place in which) wên, ên.
whereabouts: *n.* makàn.
whereas: (inasmuch as) mà dàm; bima ann; (as a matter of fact) wal ḥàl.
whereby: elledhî bi.
wherefore: (for which reason) lidhàlik.
whereupon: 'ala hàdha.
whereto: ila wên; ila ên.
wherever: wênma, ênma.
whet: senn, yasinn.
whetstone: masinn.
whether: e.g. I don't know whether he will go or not, ana mâ a'rif idha yarûḥ yô la;

I like both, whether this or that; aḥibb el ithnên idha kàn hàdha aw dhàk.
which: *interr. pron.* yâhû, yâ; (before noun) ê, yâ; *rel. pron.* elledhî.
whichever: yâ.
while: *adv.* (as long as) ṭûlma; ma dàm; (when) fî ithnà; lemma; bênama; *n.* (time) mudda; long while, mudda ṭawîla; mudda; short while, mudda qaṣîra; all the while, min el awwal; all the while (as long as) ṭûlmâ; worth while, yiswa; *v.* while away time, dhêyya' el waqt, yudhêyyi'.
whine: *v.* nawwaṣ, yunawwiṣ.
whip: *v.* basaṭ, yabsaṭ; *n.* qâmchî.
whipping: basṭa.
whirl: *v. trans.* farr, yafurr; *v. intrans.* iftarr, yaftarr.
whirlpool: khôra.
whisky: wiskî.
whisper: *v.* washwash, yuwashwish; *n.* washwasha,
whistle: *v.* ṣôfar, yuṣôfir; *n.* (implement) didik.
white: *masc.* abyadh; *fem.* bêdha, *pl.* bîdh; *n.* bayâdh.
whiten: bêyyedh, yubêyyidh.
whiteness: bayâdh.
whitewash: *v.* bêyyedh, yubêyyidh; dharab mai al'âb, yadhrab; *n.* mai al'âb.
whither: wên, liwên, ila wên.
who: *interr.* men; who is there? menu; *rel. sing.* (*masc.*) elledhî, ellî, (*fem.*) elletî, *pl.* elledhîn.
whoever: kull men; whoever it be, kàyin men kàn.
whole: (all) kull, kull el; (sound) ṣaḥîḥ; on the whole, 'ala wajh el 'umûm.
wholesale: bil jumla.
wholesome: mufîd.
wholly: bil kullîa.
whooping-cough: àbû ḥumêra.
whose: *interr.* màl men; *rel.* elledhî *foll. by suff. to noun.*
why: *interr.* lêsh; *rel.* lêsh; that is why, li hes sebeb.
wick: fatîla, *pl.* fatàyil.
wicked: sharîr, *pl.* ashrâr.
wickedness: sharr, fasàd.
wicker: rôṭ.
wide: (broad) 'arîdh, *pl.* 'arâdh; (capacious) wasî'; (remote) ba'îd.
widely: (much) kathîr.
widen: wassa', yuwassi'; **ar**radh, yu'arridh.
wideness: wus'a.
widespread: muntashar.
widow: armala, *pl.* arâmil.
widower: expressed by: maratuh mêyyita.
width: 'ardh.
wield: shaghghal, yushaghghil; ista'mal, yasta'mil.
wife: (Arab) ḥarma, *pl.* ḥarîm, niswàn; (European) zôja, *pl.* zôjàt; madâma, *pl.* madâmàt.
wild: (not tame) waḥshî; (of country) waḥshî; (of fruit) barrî.
wilderness: qifâr.
wildly: see **uncontrolled**.
wilful: 'anîd.
will: *v.* (desire) ràd, yarîd; (bequeath) waṣṣa, yuwaṣṣî; *n.* (faculty, purpose) iràda.
willing: râdhî.
willingly: min kêfuh; bi ridhâh.

willingness: ridhâ.
willow: ṣafṣâf.
wily: ḥayyàl.
win: (gain) ḥaṣṣal, yuḥaṣṣil; rabaḥ, yarbaḥ; (overcome) intaṣar, yantaṣir; ghalab, yaghlab.
wind: *v. trans.* (of rope) leff, yaliff; (of watch) naṣab, yanṣab; *v. intrans.* (as river) dâr, yadûr; *n.* (moving air) hawa.
winding: yadûr.
window: shubbàk, *pl.* shabàbik.
window-pane: jàma, *pl.* jàmàt.
windy: bih hawa.
wine: sharâb.
wing: janâḥ, *pl.* janâḥ; *pl.* (literary) ejniḥa.
wink: *v.* ramash, yarmash; *n.* ramsha.
winnow: *v.* darra, yudarri.
winter: *v.* qadha esh shita, yaqdhî; *n.* shita; *adj.* shitwî.
wipe: mesaḥ, yimsaḥ.
wire: têl, sîm.
wiry: (as person) ledun.
wisdom: ḥikma, idrâk.
wise: fahîm, 'âqil, ḥakîm.
wisely: bi ḥikma.
wish: *v.* (desire) ràd, yarîd; aràd, yurîd; wish for, ishteha, yeshtehî; ishtâq ila, yashtâq; I wish you, etemenna lek; *n.* marâm.
wit: (wittiness) sur'at jawàb; (sagacity) dhekà. faṭna; at one's wit's end, mutaḥayyir.
with: mâ', wîya; (by means of) bi; (as result of) min.
withdraw: *v. trans.* jarr, yajurr; *v. intrans.* injarr, yanjarr; insaḥab, yansaḥib.
withdrawal: istirjâ'; (military) insiḥâb.
wither: *v. intrans.* yebes, yêbes.
withhold: dhamm, yadhumm; dhabaṭ, yadhbaṭ.
within: dâkhil.
without: (outside) khârij; (not possessing) bi dûn (bidûn); min dûn (mindûn); bila.
withstand: qâwam, yuqâwim; (endure) taḥammal, yataḥammal.
witness: *n.* (person) shàhid, *pl.* shuhûd; (testimony) shahàda; *v.* shehed, yishhad.
wittingly: 'amdan.
witty: ḥâdhir el jawàb.
woe: (trouble) balîya, belwa; (exclamation) wêl.
wolf: dhîb, *pl.* dhiyàb.
woman: ḥarma, mara, *pl.* ḥarîm, niswàn, nisa.
wonder: *v.* ta'ajjab, yata'ajjab; *n.* 'ajab, ta'ajjub; (a wonder) 'ajîba; no wonder, hel bett; ma'lûm.
wonderful: 'ajîb.
wonderfully: 'ajîb; 'ala ṣûra 'ajîba.
wood: (substance) khashab; (fuel) ḥaṭab; (clump of trees) zôr.
word: kalima, *pl.* kalimàt.
work: *v.* ishtaghal, yashtaghil; *n.* shughl (shoghl).
worship: *v.* 'abad, ya'bad; sejed, yisjad; *n.* 'abàda, sujûd; (divine service) ṣala.
worshipper: 'âbid, *pl.* 'âbidîn.
worst: *v.* (overcome) keser, yiksar; to be worsted, inkeser, yenkesir; *adj.* akhrab, enges, arda.
worth: qîma, themen; *adj.* yiswa; a rupee's worth, bi rubîa.

worthiness: istiḥqâq.
worthless: mâ yiswa shê.
worthy: mustaḥiqq, mustaḥaqq, mustehil.
would: (should) see p. 106.
wound: *v.* jarraḥ, yujarriḥ; *n.* jurḥ, *pl.* jurûḥ.
wounded: majrûḥ, *pl.* majàrîḥ; jarîḥ, *pl.* jarḥa.
wrangle: *v.* ta'ârak, yata'ârak; tanàza', yatanàza'; *n.* munàza'a.
wrap: leff, yaliff; *v. intrans.* wrap up, ilteff, yelteff.
wrapper: leffàf.
wrapping: lifàfa.
wrath: za'l, ghadhb.
wreak: wreak vengeance, intaqam min, yantaqim.
wreck: *v.* (e.g. ship) keser, yiksar; gharraq, yugharriq; (ruin) kharrab, yukharrib; demmer, yudemmir; *n.* (thing wrecked) ḥaṭâm; (act of being wrecked) kesra.
wrench: *v.* lawa, yilwi; *n.* miftâḥ.
wrest: *v.* (take forcibly) ightaṣab, yaghtaṣib; (change meaning) 'awwaj, yu'awwij.
wrestle: tamâṭal, yatamâṭal.
wrestler: pehlawànchi.
wrestling: maṭâl, pehlawàn.
wretched: sê-î; mû zên (e.g. house) ta'îs, ḥaqîr.
wretchedness: ta'âsa.
wring: (e.g. clothes) 'aṣar, ya'ṣar; (twist) baram, yabram.
wrinkle: *v. trans.* 'afas, ya'fas; *v. intrans.* ta'affas, yata'affas; *n.* ṭarqa.
wrist: khaṣr.
write: keteb, yiktab.
writer: kàtib, *pl.* kuttàb; (penman) khaṭṭâṭ.
writhe: lawa, yilwî.
writing: kitàba, kitba.
wrong: *n.* (injustice) dhulm; (sin) khaṭîya; *adj.* (incorrect) ghalaṭ, ghalṭân; (unjust) dhulm; *v.* ta'adda 'ala, yata'adda.
wrongfully: (mistakenly) sehwan; (unjustly) bi dhulm.

Y

yard: dhrâ', *pl.* udhru'; (enclosure) sâḥa.
yarn: (thread) ghazal; (story) ḥikàya, *pl.* ḥikàyàt; sàlifa, *pl.* sawàlif; tell yarn, sawlaf, yusawlif.
yawn: *v.* tathàwab, yatathàwab.
year: sena, *pl.* (three to ten) senawàt, *pl.* senîn; last year, el 'âm; year before last, awwal el 'âm.
yearly: *adj.* senawî; *adv.* senawîyan.
yearn: ishtâq, yashtâq.
yearning: shôq, ishtiyâq.
yeast: khamra, khamîra.
yell: *v.* 'ayyaṭ, yu'ayyiṭ; *n.* 'ayâṭ.
yellow: aṣfar, *fem.* ṣafra, *pl.* ṣufr.
yellowish: aṣfarânî.
yellowness: ṣafâr.
yelp: *v.* 'awwa, yu'awwî.
yes: ê, nâ'am, ênâ'am, belli.
yesterday: embârḥa, ems; day before yesterday, awwal embarḥa; awwal ems.
yet: (still) bâ'ad; (nevertheless) ma' hàdha; (not yet) bâ'ad *with negative.*
yield: *v.* (produce) debb, yadibb; (give in) sellem, yusellim.
yoke: *n.* cheteb.

yolk: ṣafâr el bêdh.
yonder: ghâdî.
you: (pers. pron.) *sing. masc.* enta; *sing. fem.* enti; *pl.* entu, entum; (after verb or preposition) pron. suffix, *sing. masc.* k *after vowel*, ek *after consonant*; *sing. fem.* ch *after vowel*, ech, eki *after consonant*; *pl.* kum *after vowel*, ekum *after consonant* (see pp. 13, 18 f., 69).
young: *adj.* ṣaghîr, *pl.* ṣighâr; *n.* (of animal) farkh, *pl.* furûkh.
youngster: (boy) ṣabai, *pl.* ṣabyàn.
your: pron. suffix, *sing. masc.* k *after vowel*, ek *after consonant*; *sing. fem.* ch *after vowel*, ech *after consonant*; *pl.* kum *after vowel*, ekum *after consonant*.
yours: màlek, màlech, màlekum.
yourself: nefsek.
youth: (period) ṣughr; (young man) shàb, *pl.* shabbàn.
youthful: ṣaghîr, genj (T.).
youthfulness: shabàb.

Z

zeal: ghîra.
zealous: ghayûr, *pl.* ghayûrîn.
zephyr: nesma.
zest: shôq.
zig-zag: munḥanî.
zinc: tûtya.
zone: (of earth) manṭaqa; zone of fire, khaṭṭ el ḥarb.
zoology: ʿilm el ḥaiwânàt.
zoological: ḥaiwânî.

REVISED AND ADDITIONAL VOCABULARY

[The asterisk indicates changes in the previous vocabulary.]

A

***accident:** add 'âridh *pl.* 'awâridh.
***account:** add (to a. of) li ḥisàb.
***accuse:** add et-hem, yut-him.
acquittal: barâ-a, tebriya.
***actually:** add fi'lan.
actor: mumeththil; mushakhkhiṣ.
adenoids: rudhêdàt.
***adequate:** add (he is a. to) bihi el kifà-a.
adjourn: ejjel (session) jelsa; (case) da'wa.
adjournment: tà-jîl.
adjutant: musâ'id.
administrator: mudîr.
adolescent: murâhiq.
adopt: (motion) qarrar; *v. intrans.* taqarrar.
ad valorem: ḥasab el qîma.
***advance:** add *v. trans.* (money) selef; *n.* selfa: selef.
***advantage:** (take a. of opportunity), intehez el furṣa.
adviser: mustashâr.
adze: ṭabr.
aerated: (water) mai ghâzî.
aerial: (radio) silk hawâ-î.
aerodrome: maṭâr.
affidavit: ifàda.
***agéd:** add musinn.
aggregate: *n.* majmû'.
aggressor: muta'addi.
agitate: (pol.) shâghab, yushâghib.
agitation: mushâghaba.
agitator: mushâghib.
agreement: ittifâq; muwâfaqa.
***aim:** add (gun) *v.* ṣawwab 'ala.
air-force: qûwa jôwîyya.
airport: mîna jôwî.
alarm: (warning) indhâr.
***alcohol:** add el kuḥûl.
***allegiance:** add (oath of a.) yamîn eṭ ṭâ'a.
allotment: takhṣîṣ.
allowances: mukhaṣṣaṣàt.
***altogether:** delete (ensemble) suwa read bil kulliya.
amalgamate: *v.* intrans. indemej.
amalgamation: indimàj.
ambassador: add mufawwadh.
ambition: ṭamûḥ.
ambitious: ṭâmiḥ.
ambulance: naqqâla.
amend: dheyyel 'ala; 'addal.
amendment: tadhyîl.
amicable: wuddî.
ammonia: shanàdir; nashàdir.
ammunition: 'itàd.
analyse: ḥall, yaḥull.
analysis: taḥlîl.
***anchor:** add *v.* ersa, yursî.
***angle:** add (right) zâwiya qâ-ima; (acute) zâwiya ḥâdda; (obtuse) zâwiya munferija.
announcement: inbà.

annul: add algha, yulghî.
antiseptic: mu'aqqim.
***anxious:** (disturbed) add muqlaq.
apoplexy: sekta qalbîya.
apparatus: 'idda.
appeal: *v.* ista-naf; n. isti-nâf.
appendicitis: iltihàb ez zàyidet ed dûdîya.
***appendix:** (book) tadhyîl (anat.) zàyida dûdîya.
applaud: ṣaffaq.
applause: taṣfîq.
appliance: 'idda; àla.
apply: (put) ḥaṭṭ, yaḥuṭṭ; wadha'; (for position) istad'a.
***appointment:** (e.g. prof.) mu'âyada; 'iyàda.
appraise: themmen; khamman; qaddar.
appropriation: takhṣîṣ; i'timàd.
***Arabic:** add el 'arabîya.
arbitration: taḥkîm.
arbitrator: ḥakam
archaeologist: 'âlim etherî.
archaeology: 'ilm el àthàr; 'ilm el 'âdiàt.
area: (size) masâḥa.
***arm:** add *v.* selleḥ.
armistice: hudna.
armoured car: sayyâra muderra'a.
arrears: baqâyâ.
arrest: *v.* alqa qabdh 'ala, yulqî; waqqaf; *n.* ilqâ qabdh; towqîf.
***arsenal:** delete tereskhâna; read makhzan el 'itàd.
artillery: delete tôpchîa; read medfa'îya.
***ascent:** add ṣu'ûd.
***ascertain:** add istefser.
assassinate: ightàl, yaghtàl
assassination: ightiyàl.
***assembly:** add mejlis, pl. majàlis.
assess: khamman; themmen.
assessment: takhṣîṣ; taqdîr.
assessor: mukhammin.
assets: mawjûdàt; (cash) m. naqdîya; (current) m. jawàla; (fixed) m. thàbita.
assyrian: 'ashûrî; athûrî.
asthma: tenk nefes.
at all: batàtan.
athletic: riyâdhî.
***athletics:** add al'âb riyâdhîya.
atmospherics: aḥdàth jôwîya; muzâḥama.
attaché: mulḥaq.
audit: *v.* daqqaq; *n.* tadqîq.
auditor: mudaqqiq.
authorization: takhwîl; tafwîdh.
authorize: khawwal; fawwadh.
autonomy: ḥukm dhàtî.

B

Babylon: bàbil.
***bachelor:** add 'azab, pl. a'zàb; (b. of arts) 'azab el funûn.
badge: wisàm.
bail: *n.* kafàla.
bait: ṭa'âm.
***balance:** add *v.* (bal. acct.) raṣad el ḥisàb; *n.* (bal. sheet) warqat el ḥâl; bayàn el hâl (cash bal.) raṣîd naqdî.
***bale:** add bàla.
***ball:** add kurra, *pl.* kurràt.
ballast: ṭa'ân.
ballot: warqat el intikhâb.
bandage: add dhamàd; *v.* leff; shedd; dhammad.
***bank:** add (for money) maṣ-

raf, *pl.* maṣârif; (river) ḥâfa; dhifa, *pl.* dhifàf.
***banker**: add ṣâḥib maṣraf.
***bank-note**: add warqa naqdîya.
bankruptcy: iflàs.
***banner**: add 'alam, *pl.* a'làm; liwa, *pl.* elwiya; ra-ya, *pl.* ra-yàt.
barbed wire: têl munebbel; silk shôwkî.
***barber**: add ḥallâq.
bare-foot: add *pl.* ḥufàt.
bare-headed: muferra'.
barely: bil kàd.
***barracks**: add thekena.
***barrel**: add (gun): sabaṭâna.
barricade: mitràs.
basket ball: kurrat es sella.
battalion: fôwj, *pl.* afwàj.
***battle**: add ma'raka; wâqi'a; waq'a.
***bayonet** delete singi; read ḥarba.
beacon: minâra.
***bearer**: add (e.g. letter) ḥâmil.
bearing: (geo.) ittijàh; (mech.) kursî; (relationship) nisba.
***beggar**: add musta'ṭî; shâḥidh.
***bell**: add (large) nâqûs, *pl.* nawâqîs.
***belong to**: add khâṣṣ li; 'âyid li.
belt: hizàm; (mech.) qâyish.
***bench**: add maq'ad, *pl.* maqa'id; raḥla.
bequest: (will): waṣîya.
***bet**: add *n.* rahn; *v.* tarâhan.
***betroth**: add khaṭab.
betrothed: (fem.) makhṭûba; khaṭîba.
***beware of**: taḥaffadh min.
***bill**: add (Parl.) làyiha; (b. of lading) setemî; warqat esh shaḥn.
***birth**: add *v.* (give b. to) walad, yalad; jàb, yajîb.
bladder: (anat.) mathàna.
***blanket**: add ḥrâm, *pl.* ḥrâmàt.
***bleed**: add dema, yidmî,
blister: *n.* baṭbaṭa.
block house: makhfar.
blonde: ashkar.
***board**: add (b. of) mejlis; (date b.) lejnat et tumûr.
boarding school: medresa lêlîya.
***boil**: add *n.* (Baghdad b.) ukhet; nebdha.
bolshevism: bolshefikîya; shuyû'îya.
***bomb**: add *v.* qaṣaf, yaqṣaf.
bombardment: qaṣf.
bona fide: bi ḥusn nîya.
***bond**: *v.* add (give b.) a'ṭa kafàla.
book case: dûlàb kutub.
***book keeper**: add dhâbiṭ ed dafàtir.
***boot**: add ḥidhà, *pl.* eḥdhiya.
bore: *v. trans.* (e.g. socially) az'aj; ṣadda'; *n.* muz'ij; muṣaddi'; *v.* (hole) zaraf; thaqab.
***born**: add (be born): wulid, yûlad.
***bottom**: add qa'r.
boundary: ḥadd, *pl.* ḥudûd.
***bow**: add *v.* inḥana.
***bowels**: add im'â.
boxer: mulàkim.
boxing: mulàkama.
boycott: *v.* qâṭa' *n.* muqâṭa'a
brake: muwaqqif; dhâbiṭa.
***branch**: add (office): shu'ba.
brand: mârka; (camel) wesm.
***brass**: add naḥâs aṣfar.

breakage: makàsir.
brigade: (mil.) liwa; (fire b.) firqa iṭfâ-îya.
brigadier: amîr liwa.
broadcasting: idhâ'a.
broadcasting station: markaz idhâ'a.
***bruise**: add *v.* radhdh, yarudhdh; *n.* radhdha.
budget: (gov't) mîzànîya.
***bugle**: delete bûri; burazan; read bûq, *pl.* abwâq.
***build**: add sheyyed.
bulb: (elec.): miṣbâḥ.
bulge: *v. intrans.* taqawwas
bulk: (in b.): sà-ib.
***butt**: naṭaḥ.

C

cabinet: (pol.) wizâra.
cactus: ṣabr.
Cairo: el qâhira.
calk: qallaf.
camera: àlat et taṣwîr.
***camp**: *n.* add mukhêyyem.
campaign: *n.* ḥamla.
cancel: abṭal, yubṭil.
cancer: àkila.
candidate: mureshsheḥ.
canteen: maṭ'am.
cantonment: ḥâmiya.
***cap**: add (Iraqi) sidâra, *pl.* sidàyir.
***capacity**: add si'a.
***capital**: delete paitakht; add (money) râs màl.
capitalism: râs màliya.
capitalist: râs màlî, *pl.* râs màliyîn.
***captain**: delete (mil.) yozbashi; read ra-îs.
carbolic acid: asîd fenîk; ḥâmidh fenîk.
***card**: add baṭâqa.
cards: (play) *v.* la'ab waraq.
caretaker: ḥâris, *pl.* ḥurrâs nâṭûr, *pl.* nawâṭîr.
***cargo**: add shaḥna.
carnation: qranfil.
***carriage**: add 'ajala.
***cartridge**: add kharṭûsh; bindiqa; ṭalqa; c. belt: 'itàd.
***case**: (e.g. small-pox) iṣâba, *pl.* iṣâbàt.
cashier: amîn eṣ ṣandûq.
castrate: khaṣa, yakhṣî.
castration: khaṣî.
casualty: khasâra, *pl.* khasâyir.
catarrh: zukàm.
***catch**: add (fish): ṣâd, yaṣîd.
***cavalry**: add khayyàla.
celebration: ḥafâwa; iḥtifàl; ḥafla.
cell: (plant) khullîya, *pl.* khullîyàt; khulàyà.
censor: murâqib.
censorship: raqâba.
***ceremony**: add ḥafla.
cess-pool: bàlû'a, *pl.* balàlî'.
chairman: ra-îs el kursî.
challenge: *v.* nàzal, yunàzil.
chamberlain: qâ-im el balâṭ.
champion: *n.* baṭal, *pl.* abṭâl.
***channel**: add (small) mashrûb; *pl.* mashàrib.
chaplain: qass; qasîs.
***charcoal**: delete faḥm Karachi.
***charge**: add (battery) teres, yitras; *n.* (legal) tuhma.
chargé: qâ-im bil a'màl.
***cheat**: delete ghishsh, read ghashsh.
***cheque**: add ṣakk, *pl.* ṣukuk, (crossed c.) ṣakk musaṭṭar.
chilblain: dalghûth.
chloroform: benj; muraqqid.
choice: ikhtiyâr; (give c.) khayyar.

***cholera**: add ḥedha.
***choose**: add *v.* intakhab; delete khayyar.
chrysanthemum: dâ-ûdî.
***cigarette**: add sigâra, *pl.* sigâyir.
***circular**: add *n.* manshûr, *pl.* manàshîr.
circulation: (of blood) jaryàn.
circumference: dà-ira; muḥîṭ.
citizen: teb'a.
***civil**: (not mil.) add medenî; (c. court): maḥkama medenîya.
class: add (social) ṭabaqa.
clinic: maḥall 'iyàda.
clogged: masdûd.
***closet**: add marḥâdh.
clue: ether, *pl.* àthàr.
clumsy: thaqîl.
c.o.d.: ed def' 'and et teslîm.
code: (secret) shufra; (penal): qânùn el 'aqûbàt.
codliver oil: dihn semek.
coeducation: ta'lîm muzdawij.
coinage: maskûkàt.
colic: makhṣa.
***collar**: add (dog) ṭôwq.
colleague: zamîl, *pl.* zumalâ.
collector: (customs) mudîr; (tax) jàbî, *pl.* jubàt.
collide: isṭadam.
collision: isṭidâm.
colloquial: ed dàrija; el 'âmmîya.
***colonel**: delete mir alai; qaimaqàm; read za'îm; (lt.-col.) 'aqîd.
colonize: ista'mar.
colony: musta'mara.
comedy: riwàya hezelîya.
comical: mudhḥik.
***command**: add *v.* a'waz ila; *n.* i'âz.
commissariat: i'âsha.
commission: (fee) ḥaqq es sa'i.
committee: lejna, *pl.* lujàn; wafd, *pl.* wufûd.
communism: shuyû'îya.
communist: shuyû'î.
community: (e.g. Eur.) jàliya.
***company**: (mil.) delete buluk; read serrîya, *pl.* serràyà.
***compass**: (mariner's) add bûṣala.
competition: (e.g. sports) mubàràt.
***composition**: add (literary) inshà.
compound: (interest) fàyidh murekkeb.
compromise: tarâdha, *n.* tarâdhî.
compulsory: ijbârî.
concession: imtiyàz.
***conduct**: *v. trans.* add râfaq.
conference: mudhàkara; muàmara; mu-tamar.
***confidence**: read thiqa.
***confident**: read mûthiq.
***confirm**: add eyyed, yu-eyyid; ekked, yu-ekkid.
confirmed: (be c. in) tethebbet fî.
***confiscate**: add ḥajaz.
***confiscation**: add ḥajz.
***confusion**: (of mind) irtibàk; (noise) dhôwdhâ.
***connexion**: add *n.* (elec.) îṣâl.
conscription: tejnîd.
consignee: mursal ilêhi.
consignment: irsàlîya.
consignor: mursil.
constipation: qabûdhîya.
***consul**: delete balyoz; add (c. gen.) qunṣal 'am; (vice c.) nàyib qunṣal.
consume: istehlek.
consumer: mustehlik.

consumption: istīhlàk; (tub.) da es sull.
contact: tamàss.
contents: muḥtawiyàt.
contest: (ath.) mubàràt.
***contract**: add (become smaller): taqallaṣ.
contraction: taqalluṣ; (lit.) ikhtiṣâr.
contractor: muqâwil; multezim.
***contradict**: add nâqadh.
cooperation: ta'âwun.
corn: (maize) arnûs; (on foot) mismâr.
coronation: tetwîj.
corporal: nàyib 'arîf; (lance c.) jundî awwal.
corps: (mil.) fêlaq.
corrugated iron: chinko.
costs: takàlîf.
***counterfeit**: delete sakhta; read *n.* tezwîr; taqlîd; adj. muqallad; muzawwar.
***court**: add (royal) balâṭ; (c. of appeal) maḥkamet el isti-nàf; (crim. c.) maḥkamet el jiza; (civil c.) maḥkama medeniya; (com c.) maḥkama tujjârîya.
covenant: mîthâq.
***coward**: read jabàn.
cracked: maftûr.
credentials: awrâq el i'timàd.
***credit**: add (to c. of) li ḥisàb; (assets) i'timàd.
***creditor**: add dàyin.
crew: khalâṣîya.
criticism: intiqâd.
criticize: intaqad.
***crop**: add (grain) ghalla; (tree) ḥiml.
cross-eyed: ajqal.
crow-bar: hîb; mi'wal.
crown: add *v.* tawwaj.
cultivated: (agric.) ma'mûr; mu'ammar.
culture: thaqâfa.
cultured: muthaqqaf.
culvert: qanṭara.
***cup**: add kûb, *pl.* akwàb; (tin) dôwlka.
curator: mudîr el mat-ḥaf.
curly: mu'anqash; mukenkel.
currency: 'umla.
***current**: add *n.* (elec.) tayâr; qûwa; (direct c.) qûwa muta'âqiba; (alt. c.) qûwa mutabàdila.
curriculum: minhaj et tedrîs.
***curtain**: add sitâr.
curve: *v. trans.* kawwas; aḥna; *v. intrans.* takawwas; inḥana; *n.* kàws; inḥinâ.
cylinder: osṭawâna.

D

dairy: mejbena; melbena.
dam: sedda.
Damascus: esh shàm; dimishq.
***date**: add (fruit) green: chimrî; yellow: khalâl; ripe: ruṭub; dry: tamr.
***deadly**: add qâtil; mumit.
deal in: ta'âṭa fî.
debit: *n.* ṭalab.
debtor: maṭlub.
***decide**: add (determine) qarrar.
decision: qarâr.
declaration: taṣrîh; (d. of war) i'làn ḥarb.
decorate: zeyyen; zakhraf.
decoration: add wisàm.
decrease: *v. trans.* naqqaṣ; *v. intrans.* naqaṣ; *n.* tanqîṣ.
decree: add (royal) iràda melekîya.
***deed**: (act) 'aml, *pl.* a'màl.

***defence:** add (Min. of D.); wizâret ed difâʿ.
deficit: ʿajz.
***delay:** add *n.* mumâṭala.
delegate: nàyib, *pl.* nawwàb.
delegation: wafd.
deliberate: *v.* tadàwal fi; tadhàkar fi; (adj. slow) muteennî.
deliberately: (purposely) taʿammudan; ʿamdan.
delirious: hàdhì.
demonstrate: *v.* (prove) barhan, yubarhin.
demonstration: barhân; (public) mudhâhara.
demurrage: ḥaqq et taʿṭîl.
***dentist:** ṭabîb asnàn.
denture: ṣafîḥa.
department: qasm; dà-ira, *pl.* dawâ-ir.
depend on: (person) iʿtamad ʿala; (thing) tawaqqaf ʿala.
dependent: *n.* muʿâl.
***deposed:** add *pp.* makhlûʿ.
***deposit:** add *v.* waddaʿ; *n.* wadîʿa, *pl.* wadâyiʿ.
depot: mustawdaʿ.
depreciation: telf; istihlàk.
depression: maḥall nâṣi; (financial) ezema.
deputation: wafd.
***deride:** add istehza fî.
***derision:** add istihzà.
derivation: ishtiqâq.
derived from: mushtaqq min.
***descent:** add (act of) nuzûl.
destination: maqṣad.
detachment: mufraza.
***detail:** add (in d.) bi tafṣîl.
deteriorate: bela, yibla.
determine: (make up mind) ʿazam; (discover) istefser.
determined: (decided) ʿâzim ʿala.

detour: fetla; ʿarràja.
develop: *v. intrans.* taraqqa.
development: ruqî; taraqqî; tarqiya.
diabetes: bôwl sukkarî.
diagnose: shakhkhaṣ.
diagnosis: tashkhîṣ.
diagonal: *n.* watr.
dialect: lehja.
dialogue: muḥâwara.
dictate: *v.* (lit.) emla, yumlî.
dictation: imlà.
dictator: diktâtôr.
dictatorship: diktâtôrîya.
diet: pehrîz (P.).
dinar: dînâr, *pl.* danànîr.
***dining room:** add ghurfet et ṭaʿâm.
dinner jacket: smôkinkh.
dip: ghaṭṭas.
diplomacy: siyàsa.
diplomatic: (service) khidma khârijîya; (corps) hêy-a siyàsîya ejnebîya.
dipping: taghṭîs.
disability: ʿajz.
disarm: nezaʿ silâḥ.
disarmament: nezʿ silâḥ.
disbursements: maṣârîf.
***discharge:** add (gun) *v.* aṭlaq
***discipline:** add *n.* tedrîb.
discount: *n.* khaṣm; (rate of d.) siʿr el khaṣm; siʿr el qaṭʿ.
discrepancy: khalal.
discretion: (judgement) baṣîra; (at your d.) ʿala hawâk.
discuss: nâqash fì; bâḥath fì.
discussion: munâqasha; mubâḥatha.
disembark: nezel, yinzel.
***disgrace:** add *v.* ḥaqqar.
dishonest: ghashshàsh.
disinfect: ʿaqqam.
disinfectant: muʿaqqim.

dispensary: mustawṣaf.
dispense with: istaghna 'an.
disposal: (at your d.) taḥt amrek.
dispose of: takhalla 'an.
distil: qaṭṭar, yuqaṭṭir.
distillation: taqṭîr.
***distress**: add balîya.
ditch: add sâqia, *pl.* sawâqî; mashrûb, *pl.* mashàrîb.
division: (math.) qasma; taqsîm; (mil.) firqa, *pl.* firaq.
dock: *n.* raṣîf, *pl.* arṣifa; (dry d.) gûdî.
document: wathîqa, *pl.* wathàyiq; sened, *pl.* senedàt.
doll: la'ba.
domestic: (animal) dàjin, *pl.* dawàjin; (politics) dâkhilî; (house) bêtî.
draft: ḥawàla, *pl.* ḥawàyil.
drain: *n.* (from roof) mirzàb, *pl.* maràzîb; (cess-pool) bàlû'a, *pl.* balàlî'.
drainage: (system) balàlî'.
draught: (of air) tayâr.
***draughts**: add dàman.
draw-back: (money) istirdàd; (hindrance) màni'.
dredge: *v.* ḥafar.
dredger: ḥaffâr.
***dress**: for hudûm yilbas, read yilbas hudûm; add irteda.
***drill**: add (mil.) temrîn; *v.* (mech.) zaraf; *n.* mizraf.
***driver**: (car, loc.) sàyiq.
dromedary: dhalûl, *pl.* dhilel.
drop: *v. trans.* fellet; *n.* (liq.) qaṭra.
dropsy: istisqâ.
dry-dock: gùdî.
due: (payable) mustaḥaqq.
dues: (customs) resm, *pl.* rusûmàt; (fees) ujra, *pl.* ujûr.
***dull**: (uninteresting) mumill; (not sharp) a'ma (lit. blind).
dusty: mughabbar.
dutiable: ma'rûdh li resm.
***duty**: add (on duty) bi nôba; (e.g. doctor on duty); ṭabîb el khafr.

E

***early**: add bàkiran; mubekkiran.
earn: rabaḥ; ḥaṣṣal.
earnings: maḥṣûl *pl.* maḥâṣil.
earthquake: zelzela ardhîya.
ebb-tide: jizr.
eclipse: (sun) kusûf; (moon) khusûf.
economic: iqtiṣâdî.
economical: muqtaṣid.
economics: iqtiṣâdiyàt.
economize: iqtaṣad.
***education**: add (Min. of E.) wazîr el ma'ârif; (Dir. of E.) mudîr el m.
***effect**: add *v.* ejra, yujrî; *n.* tà-thîr.
effective: nàfidh.
Egypt: miṣr; maṣr.
elective: ikhtiyârî.
electric: delete lektrîkî; read kahrabâ-î.
element: (first prin.) mebda, *pl.* mabàdî; (nat.) 'anṣar, *pl.* 'anâṣir.
eloquence: faṣâḥa; balâgha.
***eloquent**: for faṣih read faṣîḥ.
embezzle: ikhteles.
embezzlement: ikhtilàs.
emigrate: hàjar.
employé: mustakhdam.
employer: mustakhdim.
encourage: shejja'.
encouragement: tashjî'.
endeavour: *v.* add ḥâwal; *n.* muḥâwala.

endorse: (note) dhahhar; jêyyer.
endorsement: tadhhîr; tejyîr.
***endure:** add *v. intrans.* dàm, yadûm.
enforce: neffedh.
engage: (labour) istakhdam; (e.g. seat) lezem; ḥajaz.
***engine:** add àla, *pl.* àlàt.
***English:** add (lang.) el anglêzîya.
***enjoy:** add temeṭṭa' bi.
***enjoyment:** temeṭṭu'.
***enlist:** delete keteb fil 'askariya; read *v. trans.* jenned; *v. intrans.* tejenned.
enlistment: tejnîd.
***entire:** add adj. kullî.
***envelope:** add *n.* mughallaf.
epidemic: waba.
Epsom salts: milḥ frangî.
equality: musàwàt.
equip: jehhez.
***equipment:** add mujehhezàt.
***error:** add ghalṭa.
***escape:** *v.* add hereb, yihrab.
escort: *v.* râfaq; *n.* muḥâfadha; ma'îya.
essential: dharûrî.
essentials: jôwhariyât.
establishment: mu-essesa.
estate: (by will) terika.
***estimate:** add *n.* takhmîn.
evacuate: akhla, yukhlî.
evaporate: *v. trans.* bakhkhar; *v. trans.* tabakhkhar.
***even:** add (number) zôwj.
***ever:** delete (not used); read use participle; e.g. have you ever seen; enta shàyif?
exactly: tamàman.
excavation: tanqîb.
excavator: munaqqib.
***exchange:** add (rate of) si'r et tabàdul.
excise: *n.* makûs.
executive: adj. ijrâ-î; idârî.
exempt: mu'fa.
exemption: i'fà.
exhibition: ma'radh.
***exist:** for wajad, yojad read wujid, yûjad.
expand: temedded.
expansion: temeddud.
expedient: *n.* wasîla, *pl.* wasà-il.
expedition: (mil.) ḥamla.
expenditures: maṣrûfàt.
***expense:** add nefeqa, *pl.* nefeqât; (at my e.) 'ala ḥisàbi; 'ala nefeqatî.
expert: *n.* and *adj.* khabîr, *pl.* khabîrîn.
expiration: intihà.
explode: infejer.
explosion: infijâr.
***export:** delete ba'ath, read aṣdar; (e. duty) resm el ikhrâj.
exports: ṣâdiràt.
extension: (time) imdàd.
external: khârijî.
extra: zàyid; idhâfî.
extract: *n.* (e.g. from newspaper) nubdha; *v.* (tooth) shala'; *v.* (draw out) istakhraj.
extradition: istirdàd.
extravagant: musrif; mubedhdhir.

F

face: add *v.* wàjah.
faction: ḥazb, *pl.* aḥzàb.
factory: delete karkhana, fabrika; read ma'mal, *pl.* ma'âmil.
fail: (exam.) reseb; (bank) inkeser; (not succeed) khâb, yakhîb.

failure: (exam.) rusûb; (bank) inkisàr; iflàs; (general) khêba.
fair: (weather) ṣâfì; (complexion) ashkar; (medium) mutawassiṭ; (equitable) inṣâf (*n.*).
fall through: *v.* (fail) baṭal, yabṭal.
***false**: add (counterfeit) muzawwar; (witness) shàhid zûr.
***falsehood**: add tezwîr.
familiar with: mukhtebir.
***family**: add (circle of relatives); usra.
fan: add mirwaḥa.
fare: (e.g. railway) ujra; (bill of f.) qâ-imet et ṭa'âm; mànû.
farewell: add adj. widâ'î.
fascism: fashîstîya.
fashion: zê *pl.* ezyà; môda.
fashionable: ḥasab ez zê.
***fatal**: add qâtil.
***father-in-law**: ḥamu; (Moslem) 'amm.
fathom: *n.* bâ', *pl.* bâ'àt.
***fault**: add *v.* (find f. with) intaqad; qadaḥ.
***favour**: (ask f. of) ista'ṭaf; (do f.) 'amal ma'rûf.
favoured: (most-f. nation) ekther el umam khaṭwatan.
favouritism: muḥâbàt.
***feast**: add walîma, *pl.* walàyim.
features: (of face) malàmiḥ.
fee: resm; ujra.
***feel**: add sha'ar, yash'ar.
***feeling**: add shu'ûr.
***feelings**: ḥâssiyàt.
felt: *n.* jôwkh; màhûd.
***female**: add (pers. or animal); untha, *pl.* unàth.
fence: muḥajjil; siyàj.
fender: jinâḥ.
fertilize: (soil) semmed: (date-tree) laqqaḥ.
***fever**: add ḥumma; (adj.) maḥmûm.
***file**: add (paper) mandham; maḥfadh.
film: sharîṭ; film, *pl.* aflàm.
filter: *v.* ṣaffa; *n.* maṣfì; maṣfa.
final: nihà-î.
finance: (Min. of F.) wazîr el màliya.
financial: màlî; (f. year) sena màlîya.
***fine**: *v.* add gharram; *n.* add gharâma.
***finish**: add temmem; enha, yunhî.
***finished**: add mutemmem.
***fire**: add *v.* (gun) aṭlaq nâr; (f. brigade) firqa iṭfâ-îya.
***fire-place**: add mawqad.
fit: add *v. trans.* rehhem; *v. intrans.* rehem, yarham.
fitter: barrâd; musawwî; fiter.
***flag**: delete beraq; sanjaq; bandera; read 'alam, *pl.* a'làm.
flank: (of animal) fakhdh; (of army) jinâḥ.
flare: mish'al.
flask: (thermos) zemzemîya.
***flat**: add (f. rate) si'r qaṭ'î.
flatter: melleq.
flattery: tamlîq.
flaw: 'aib, *pl.* 'uyûb.
fleet: *n.* asṭôl.
flexible: merin.
float: *v. intrans.* ṭâf, yaṭûf, âm, ya'ûm.
***flog**: add jeled.
***flood**: add feyadhân.
floor: gâ'a; ardhîya.

***flow**: add (overflow) fâdh, yafîdh.
flying: *n*. ṭeyarân.
foggy: mudhabbab.
following: adj. (e.g. day) tàlî.
foot-ball: kurrat el qadam.
forbear: imtena'.
***forbidden**: delete yasaq.
ford: *v*. khâdh, yakhûdh, *n*. makhâdha.
foreclose: ḥajaz er rahn.
forefather: jidd, *pl*. ajdàd; selef, *pl*. aslàf.
***forehead**: read jabîn.
forenoon: add dhaḥa.
forest: ghâba.
***forgery**: delete sakhatâr loghîa; read tezwîr.
formal: resmî.
formula: qâ'ida, *pl*. qawâ'id.
fortunately: min ḥusn el ḥadhdh.
fraction: (common) kesr 'âdi; (decimal) kesr 'ushrî.
***frame**: add iṭâr.
franc: frank, *pl*. frankàt.
fraud: tadlîs.
***free**: delete serbest.
***free-mason**: delete farmasòni; read màsônî.
***freight**: add (charges) ujûr esh shaḥn.
fresh: add (air) naqî.
***friction**: add (after tafrik) iḥtikàk.
friendly: add bashùsh.
frock: nefnûf.
frock-coat: bonzhûr (F.); *v*. (wear a f.) tabanzhar.
frost: ṣaqî'; jaḥîl.
***frozen**: add mujemmed.
***fuel**: add wuqûd.
***funnel**: (instrument) add maṣabb.
***furlough**: add ijàza.
***furnish**: (supply) add jehhez.
***furrow**: add thelem.
***fuse**: add (elec.) fyûz.

G

gallon: gàlon, *pl*. gàlonàt.
***gambler**: add muqâmir.
***gang**: add 'uṣâba.
***gangrene**: add ghanghrîn.
***gardener**: add bustànî.
***garrison**: add ḥâmiya.
garter: 'âsqi.
***gasp**: add tenehhed.
***gauge**: *v*. qâs, yaqîs; *n*. miqyàs.
***gazette**: add (gov't) majella el waqâyi' el ḥukûmîya.
***gendarme**: add derek.
***gendarmerie**: add derek.
***general**: read (Gen.) 'amîd (Lt.-Gen.) farîq awwal; (Maj.-Gen.) farîq thànî; (Brig.-Gen.) amîr liwa.
generator: muwallid.
***genius**: add (prodigy) nàbigha, *pl*. nawàbigh.
gentleman: sharîf, *pl*. ashrâf.
***gently**: add bi huda.
***Germany**: add jarmanîya.
***girder**: shêlmàn, *pl*. shêlmànàt.
***give**: add (charity) tabarra'.
***gladden**: add asarr, yusirr.
***gladness**: add surûr.
***glance**: add *n*. lemḥa.
gland: ghadda, *pl*. ghadad.
***glass**: add zujàj.
***glasses**: add (field) nadhâra.
glaucoma: mai aswad.
gnat: barghash.
goal: (in game) add hedef; gôwl, *pl*. gôwlàt.
go back on: insaḥab min.
go on with: dàwam 'ala, yudàwim.

go through with: kemmel; enjez, yunjiz.
***governmental**: ḥukûmî.
***graduate**: *v.* (from school) add *intrans.* takharraj; *n.* kharîj.
***grandmother**: add bîbîya.
***grate**: (fire-place) add mawqad.
***grateful**: add wafî.
***gratitude**: add (quality) wafâ.
gratuity: ikrâmîya.
***graze**: add saraḥ.
grazing-rights: ḥuqûq el mar'a.
greaser: zayyàt.
***grouse**: add (bird) qaṭā; add *v.* taqamqam.
***guarantee**: add *n.* dhamàn.
***guard**: *v.* add khafar, yakhfar; *n.* (sentinel) add khafar; ḥâris.
guard-house: makhfar.
***guide**: *v.* add ershed, yurshid.
***gun**: (rifle) add bunduqîya.
***gun-boat**: add bârija, *pl.* bawârij.
***gunner**: add medfa'î.
***gunsmith**: add bunduqî.
gunny: jinfâṣ.
gunny-bag: gôwnîya, *pl.* gawânî.

H

***half-pay**: add nuṣf ràtib.
***halt**: (command) qif, *pl.* qifû.
hangar: ḥadhîra; wakr; saqîfa.
***harbour master**: delete mir bahr; read mudîr marfa.
***harness**: *n.* add 'idda.
haversack: mizwada; khurj, *pl.* khuraj.
***helmet**: add khûdha, *pl.* khuwadh.
***help**: add *v. trans.* as'af, yus'if; add (it cannot be helped) mâ lahu 'ilàj.
***hide**: (self) ikhteba; ikhtefa
***hinge**: add mafṣala.
***holiday**: (vacation) add ijàza; (festival) add 'aṭla.
***horizontal**: ufuqî.
***horn**: (musical) add bûq.
***hose**: add (after anbûb) ôwj.
***hospital**: delete khastakhâna; read musteshfa, *pl.* musteshfiyàt.
***hotel**: add fandaq.
***house**: add dâr, *pl.* dûr.
hub: (of vehicle) baṭikha, jurlâq.
humane: shafûq.
humaneness: shefeqa; insànîya.
humanity: (mankind) besherîya; besher.
hydrant: ḥanafîya.
hyena: dhab'.

I

***ideal**: add (high i.) el methel el a'la.
***identity**: add hûwîya.
***ill**: delete kêfsiz; khasta.
***ill-bred**: delete tarbietsiz.
***ill-fated**: delete ogharsiz.
***immunity**: add (from sickness) manâ'a.
***imports**: add idkhâlàt.
***importer**: add mûrid; mustawrid.
***impregnable**: add ḥaṣîn.
***incinerator**: delete dogha, *pl.* duwagh; read miḥraqa.
***income**: dakhl.
income tax: dharîbat ed dakhl.

***incorrect**: delete yaghnish.
***indeterminate**: read ghair mu'ayyan.
***indigestion**: delete jali; read sû hadhm.
***individual**: (adj.) add ferdî; (*n.*) add ferd, *pl.* afràd.
***indorsement**: add tadhhîr.
***ineligible**: read ghair munàsib.
***inevitable**: add la maḥâla.
***infantry**: delete piyada, read meshàt.
infection: tesemmum.
influenza: influenza.
***inform**: add aṭla' 'ala, yuṭli'.
***information**: add iṭṭilâ'.
initiate: *v.* (begin) ibteker; (into lodge) kerres.
***initiation**: add (into lodge) tekrîs.
***initiative**: add ibtikàr; (take the *i.*) ibteker.
***inn-keeper**: add ṣâḥib el khân, ṣâḥib el fandaq.
***inquiry**: add (investigation) taḥqîq.
***inside**: add dhimn.
installation: (e.g. elec.) terkîb.
***institution**: (society) add ma'had; mu-essesa.
***insulate**: add a'zal.
***insulation**: add i'zàl.
***insure**: add dhaman, yadhman.
insured: mu-emmen; madhmûn.
integral part: juz'la yetejezza.
***intelligence department**: add dà-iret el istikhbâràt.
***interference**: (radio) tadâkhul; tazâḥum.
international: add (i. law) el qânûn ed duwalî.
***interval**: add (after mudda) fetra.
***invade**: add ghaza, yaghzû.
***invasion**: add ghazu.
***investment**: tashghîl.
Iranian: îrânî.
***iron**: (flat) add mikwàt.
isolation hospital: musteshfa el 'azl.

J

jack: (for car) râfi'; bazzûn; 'aqrabiya.
***jail**: add sijn; (in j.) masjûn.
***jailor**: delete urdiyàn.
jamboree: mihrjàn.
***jaundice**: add dà es ṣafâr.
***jointed**: murfaq.
***joist**: delete zanzibar.
judge: (civil) add ḥâkim, *pl.* ḥukkàm.
***jurisdiction**: add ṣalâḥîya.
***jut**: add berez, yibraz.
jutting: bàriz.

K

***kit**: (soldier's) add 'idda.
***knapsack**: add khurj, *pl.* khuraj.
knit: (with thread) add ḥâk, yaḥûk.

L

***laboratory**: add mukhteber.
labourer: 'âmil, *pl.* 'ummâl.
***lady**: add sêyyida.
***lamp**: add siràj; miṣbâḥ.
***lance-corporal**: delete wakîl ôn bâshî; read jundî awwal.
***lash**: *n.* (whip) add sawṭ.
***latch**: delete chekelek; read ghalaq.
***lathe**: add tûrna.
latrine: marḥâdh; edeb; bêt el khala.

***launch**: add *n.* rafàṣa; rafàṣ.
lavatory: bêt el khala.
lawn: (grass) marj.
***lawyer**: add muḥâmî.
League of Nations: ʿuṣbat el umam.
***leak**: *v.* add teserreb; *n.* add teserrub; tenfîṣ.
leash: (dog) resn.
***leave**: *v. trans.* add (depart) ghâdar.
***leave**: *n.* (permission) add ijàza; (on leave) add bil ijàza.
Lebanon: libnàn.
***leg**: add (of triangle) dhalʿ, *pl.* dhulûʿ.
***legation**: add mufawwadhiya.
***legislation**: add tashrîʿ.
***lens**: add ʿadasa.
***leper**: add majdhum; mujardam.
***leprosy**: add judhàm; jurdàm.
levies: shabàna.
liabilities: duyûn; khuṣûm.
***liability**: add (responsibility) khudhûʿ.
liaison: ʿalâqa; irtibâṭ.
***license**: add *n.* (permission) ijàza.
***lift**: *n.* (elevator) add râfiʿa.
lighting: tenwîr.
***limp**: *v.* add dhalaʿ, yadhlaʿ; adj. rakhu.
lineman: (elec.) mâ-mûr aslàk.
***load**: (load gun) add mela, yimlî; *n.* add (elec.) ḥamûla.
***loan**: add *v.* qaradh, yaqradh.
lodge: read *v. intrans.* bàt, yabît, add *n.* (masonic) maḥfal.
***loop-hole**: add maghzal.
lorry: sayyàret ḥiml.
***low**: (after nâṣî) read wâṭî.
***loyal**: add mukhliṣ
***loyalty**: add ikhlâṣ.
***lurk**: add tarabbaṣ; telebbed.

M

***machine**: add àla, *pl.* àlàt.
mad: adj. majnûn; (dog) maklûb; *v.* go mad (dog) keleb, yiklab.
***magazine**: (paper) add majella.
***mail**: delete posta, read barîd.
***maintenance**: (preservation) add ṣiyâna.
***major**: (officer) muqaddam; (maj. gen.) farîq thànî; (serg. maj.) ra-îs urafâ; (adj. of age) bàligh; (the greater) el ekther; el aghlab.
***majority**: (rank of m.) read ritba muqaddam.
***malaria**: add ḥumma malâria.
***male**: read dheker.
mandate: intidàb.
mandated: muntedeb.
mange: ḥaṣaf.
manger: maʿlaf.
mango: ʿamba.
manifest: (shipping) setemî, *pl.* setemiyàt.
***manual**: add yedawî.
***manufactory**: delete kirkhana; read maʿmal.
***manufacturer**: add ṣâḥib maʿmal.
***marauder**: add luṣṣ, *pl.* luṣûṣ.
***marble**: add rukhâm.
***marksman**: add haddàf.
***mason**: delete farmasônî, read màsônî.
***massage**: *v.* add delek, yidlak.
matriculate: *v. trans.* add sejjel; *v. intrans.* add tesejjel.

matriculation: add tesjîl; delete qaid.
matron: (hospital) ra-îsat el mumarridhàt.
***measure:** add (safety m.) wasà-il el wiqâya; (temporary m.) wasà-il waqtîya.
***mechanical:** read mîkàníkî.
***mechanics:** read mîkàníkî-yàt.
***medal:** add wisàm.
***meeting:** (athletic) mubà-ràt.
***mend:** *v. trans.* add (darn) rawwaf.
***menial:** read (low) denî, *pl.* edniyà.
***merchandise:** add bidhâ'a, *pl.* badhâyi'.
***metre:** add (elec.) miqyàs.
***microbe:** add jarthûma, *pl.* jaràthîm.
midwife: jidda; qâbila, *pl.* qawâbil.
***milky:** add ḥalîbî.
***mine:** (of minerals) add manjam, *pl.* manàjim.
***minister:** (diplomatic) add mufawwadh; (prime m.) delete ṣadr; read ra-îs wuzarâ; add (m. resident) mufaw-wadh muqîm.
***mint:** (place of coinage) add madhrab en nuqûd.
minutes: (of meeting) maḥ-dhar.
misprint: *n.* ghalṭa maṭba'îya.
***misrepresent:** add shawwah.
***misrule:** add sû idâra.
***missionary:** add mubeshshir.
***mistake:** *n.* add ghalṭa, *pl.* ghalṭàt.
***mister:** delete ṣâḥib.
***mode:** (fashion) add zê, *pl.* ezyà.
***mollify:** add ṭayyab khâṭir.
***moment:** add burha; laḥdha.
***monopoly:** add inḥiṣâr.
moon-lit: muqmir; qamarî.
***mortar:** add (implement) hâwan.
***mother-in-law:** add (Mos-lem) 'amma.
***motor:** read muḥarrik; (m. boat) rafàṣ; rafàṣa; (m car) sayyâra; (m. cycle) motorsai-kel; darràja bukhârîya.
***mouldy:** add muqaṭṭan.
***moult:** read beddel rîsh; tenessel.
***mount:** (mount guard) delete ḥaṭṭ nôbachî; read akhfar, yukhfir.
mumps: nakkâf.
***munitions:** delete jubakhâna; read dhakhâyir.
***muscular:** add dhalî'.
***musician:** add musikâr.

N

***nape:** (of neck) read gafa; delete 'ilba.
***napkin:** add mendîl, *pl.* manàdîl.
***navigable:** ṣâliḥ li sêr es sufun.
nazism: nâtziya.
N.C.O.: dhâbiṭ ṣaff.
***necktie:** add rabṭa.
***needlessly:** for sadan read sudan.
***negotiation:** add mufâwadhâ.
nestorian: athûrî; 'ashûrî.
***neutral:** add (zone) minṭaqat el ḥiyàd.
***noise:** (uproar) add dhôwdhâ.
nomadic tribes: 'ashâyir ruḥ-ḥal.
***nominate:** add reshsheḥ.
***nomination:** tershîḥ.

***nose**: (person) add enf.
***notary**: add kàtib el 'adl.
***note**: (bank note): add warqa naqdîya.
notification: balâgh; teblîgh.
***nourish**: add ghadhdha.
***nourishing**: add mughadhdhî.
***nourishment**: add ghadha.
numeral: raqam, *pl.* arqâm.
nun: râhiba, *pl.* râhibàt.
***nurse**: *n.* add (hospital) mumarridha.

O

***oasis**: add daghl, *pl.* adghâl.
objective: *n.* (purpose) hedef.
***obligatory**: add ijbârî.
obnoxious: makrûh; karîh.
observatory: marṣad.
observer: râṣid.
***offence**: (crime) read dhenb, *pl.* dhunûb.
***office**: (post o.) delete posṭakhâna; read dàiret el barîd; add (place of business) maḥall 'iyàda.
***operator**: (telegraph) read mâ-mûr barq.
opine: irte-e, yerte-î.
***opinion**: add (public o.) er rai el 'âm.
***opportunity**: add (seize o.) intehez el furṣa.
optimist: mutafà-il.
***order**: (money o.) read ḥawàla barîd.
***orderly**: delete yawar; read murâfiq.
***ordinance**: add farîdha, *pl.* faràyidh.
***ordnance**: delete jubakhâna; read 'îna.
organic: 'adhalî.
***outbreak**: (of disease) delete bidaya; read ifshà; (of war) nushûb.
***outline**: add *n.* (e.g. of speech) ru-ûs aqlàm.
***overhaul**: add *n.* termîm.
***overhead**: add *n.* (costs) takàlîf idârîya.
overlap: inṭawa 'ala; iktenef.

P

pact: mîthâq.
***paid**: add mûfa.
***pail**: delete (large) piyala, *pl.* piyalàt.
***pain**: add *v.* ellem, yu-ellim; *n.* elem, *pl.* àlàm.
***painful**: add mu-lim.
***painstaking**: add mudaqqiq.
***parade**: add (drill) meshîya; (cerem.) isti'râdh.
***paraffin**: add nafdh.
***paragraph**: add faqra.
***parapet**: delete super, *pl.* superat; read istiḥkàm.
***parasite**: add 'âla.
***parcel**: add ruzma, *pl.* ruzam; ṭard, *pl.* ṭurûd.
***park**: (garden) add ḥadîqa, *pl.* ḥadàyiq.
***partridge**: add darràj.
***passport**: delete pasaport; teskera murûr; read jawàz sefr.
***patent**: add *n.* barà-et ikhtirâ'.
pave: add ballaṭ; 'abbad.
pavement: (sidewalk) mamarr; memsha; (road) raṣîf; balâṭ.
paving: tablîṭ.
***pay**: *n.* add ràtib, *pl.* rawàtîb.
peculiarity: khaṣîṣa, *pl.* khaṣâyiṣ.

peer: *v.* daḥḥaq; shakhaṣ; ḥadaq.
pension: taqâ'ud; (on p.) mutaqâ'ad.
perambulator: 'arabet el walad.
***perceive**: add sha'ar.
***percentage**: add (rate) nisba mîyawîya.
***perforate**: read yanqab.
***periodical**: (paper) add majella.
permit: *v.* add edhen, ya-dhen.
Persian: delete 'ajemi, *pl.* 'ajem.
***pessimist**: add mutashà-im.
***pharmacist**: delete ejzáchî, read ṣêdali, *pl.* ṣayâdila.
***pharmacy**: add (place) ṣêdala.
***phenomenon**: add dhâhira, *pl.* dhawâhir.
***photograph**: *n.* add ṣûra shemsiya.
***physical**: read jesedî.
physiology: fesleja.
***pick**: (tool) add mi'wal.
***pilot**: *n.* add (air) sàyiq.
***pioneer**: add fettâḥ ṭarìq.
***pistol**: add museddes.
***piston**: add medechcha; kabàs.
***placard**: add manshûr, *pl.* manàshîr.
***platform**: add dekka; (large) marsaḥ; masraḥ.
platoon: faṣîl, *pl.* faṣâyil.
platter: ṣaḥn.
plebiscite: istiftà esh sha'b.
***plug**: add (elec.) miftâḥ; pluk.
pock-marked: munebbed; muneqresh.
***police**: read shuraṭî, *pl.* shuraṭa (p. station) markaz shuraṭa.
***policy**: add (insurance) wathîqa et ta-mîn; (course of action) khiṭṭa; minhaj.
poppy: khashkhàsh.
***portmanteau**: add maḥfadh.
***position**: add (state of affairs) wadh'îya; (cash p.) wadh'îya naqdîya.
***post**: read *v.* ersel bil barîd, yursil; *n.* (mail) barid; posṭa; (p. office) dàiret el barîd; (position) wadhîfa, *pl.* wadhâyif; (wood) khashba.
***postage**: read ujrat el barîd.
***postman**: add muwazzi' barîd.
***postmaster**: read mudîr el barîd.
***postpone**: add ejjel, yu-ejjil.
Posts and Telegraphs: (Dep't of) dàiret el barq wal barîd.
***postscript**: read mulḥaq.
***preclude**: add ḥâl dûn, yaḥûl.
***preliminary**: add (adj.) temhîdî.
premium: (insurance) qasṭ, *pl.* aqsâṭ.
***prepaid**: delete jawabli; read madfû' selfan.
prepay: defa' selfan.
***prescription**: delete racheta; read waṣf.
***pressure**: (weight) add dhaghṭ.
prickly heat: ḥaṣaf.
***prime minister**: delete sadr a'dham; read ra-îs wuzarâ.
***printer**: delete maṭba'achî; read ṭabbâ'.
***prison**: add sijn; (in p.) masjûn.
private: *n.* (soldier) add jundî.
***probably**: delete bilki.
proceedings: ijrâ-àt.
procession: mawkab.

***produce**: *n.* add maḥṣûl.
***project**: *n.* add mashrû' *pl.* mashàrî'.
projector: (cinema) 'adasa.
***programme**: add minhaj.
propaganda: beththda-âya.
***proposal**: add iqtirâḥ.
***prosper**: for *intrans.* read *trans*; add *v. intrans.* nejaḥ yinjaḥ.
protectorate: add maḥmîya.
***protestant**: add injîlî.
***province**: add (Iraq) liwa, *pl.* elwiya.
***provision**: (budget allowance) i'timàd.
***provisional**: temhîdî.
puddle: birka.
***pump**: add *v.* dhakhkh; *n.* madhakhkha; (cent.p.) khanzîra.
pumping station: maḥaṭṭet edh dhakhkh.
purr: shakhar, yashkhar.
***pus**: add jarâḥa.

Q

quack: *v.* baṭbaṭ.
quake: (earth) zelzela ardhîya.
qualifications: istishhàdàt.
qualified: kefu ila (obj.)
***quarantine**: add 'azl muṣabîn.
***quarrelsome**: delete mashhur, add 'arîk.
***quarry**: *n.* add miqla'.
***quay**: add raṣîf.
***quell**: add akhmad.
***question**: add (pol. q.) qadhîya, *pl.* qadhâyâ.
quibble: ràdagh, yuràdigh.
quilted: mulebbed.
***quit**: add (leave) ghâdar, yughâdir.
***quorum**: niṣâb.
quota: 'adad maḥdûd.
quotient: khârij

R

rabid: sherish.
rabies: keleb.
radio: râdio; idhâ'a jôwiya; (instr.) midhyâ'.
raft: add remeth.
***raid**: add *n.* ghâra.
***rake**: delete rashsh, yarishsh, read meshsheṭ.
rank: (from the r.) delete alailî; read nàshî min el jund.
rash: delete da'am, yid'am; read (adj.) ṭâyish; *n.* (disease) ḥarâra; ṭafaḥ jildî.
***ratification**: add muṣâdaqa 'ala; ibrâm.
***ratify**: add abram.
rattle: *n.* qarqa'a; kharkhasha.
***raw**: add (materials) mawàd awwalîya.
ray: shu'â', *pl.* eshi'a; (X-rays) eshi'a runtjenîya.
razor: mûs, *pl.* amwàs.
rebellious: mushâghib; thàyir; 'âṣî.
receipts: maqbûdhàt; iràdàt.
***receive**: add tesellem; (r. salary) taqâdha.
receiver: (telephone) simâ'a.
***recent**: add ḥadîth.
***recently**: add ḥadîthan.
***receptacle**: add inà.
reception: (social) mà-daba.
recipe: waṣf.
reciprocity: muqâbala bil mithl.
***reckless**: delete da'am; read ṭâyish.
reconnaissance: istiṭlâ'.
***reconnoitre**: istaṭla'.
***record**: add sijl.
***recover**: add (regain) istarja'.

***recruit:** read *v.* jenned, *n.* mustajidd.
***rectum:** add ist.
***redness:** add ḥamâr.
***reduction:** (in price) add tenzîl.
refinery: maṣfa; maṣaffa.
***refreshment room:** add ghurfat eṭ ṭa'âm.
refrigerator: muberrida.
***refund:** *v.* add istarja'; *n.* istirdàd; istirjâ'.
***regiment:** delete tâbûr, *pl.* tawâbir; read katîba, *pl.* katàyib, fôwj, *pl.* afwàj.
***regimental:** delete ṭâbûrî; read katîbî.
***region:** add qaṭr, *pl.* aqṭâr.
***register:** read *v. trans.* add sejjel; (letter) sejjel; *v. intrans.* read tesejjel, *n.* (book) defter; sijl.
***registered:** (of letter) read musejjel; delete ta'ahhudlî.
***registration:** read tesjîl.
regulation: (rule) nidhâm, *pl.* andhima.
***regulator:** add (irrig.) sedda; (fan) munadhdhim.
***relief:** (to poor) add is'âf.
***relinquish:** add (e.g. post) takhalla 'an; 'adal 'an.
remand: *v.* awqaf.
***remuneration:** delete bakhshîsh; read mukàfà.
***renounce:** add (disown) teberra min.
***repeat:** add a'âd, yu'îd.
***repetition:** add i'âda.
***representative:** *n.* add mumeththil.
reproduction: (anat.) tanàsul.
reptile: zuḥḥâfa.
***reserve:** *v.* add ḥajaz, yaḥjaz.
reserved: (seat) maḥjûz.
reservoir: add khazàn.
residency: safâra.
residue: rusûb.
***resign:** (give up office) istaqâl, yastaqîl.
***resignation:** (from office) istiqâla.
resort: *n.* (summer) maṣîf, *pl.* maṣâyif.
***restaurant:** add maṭ'am, *pl.* maṭâ'im.
***restless:** delete râḥatsiz; read muqlaq.
***resume:** add 'âd ila, ya'ûd.
résumé: khulâṣa; mulakhkhaṣ.
***retired:** add mutaqâ'id.
retract: (e.g. words) saḥab, yisḥab.
***reveille:** delete yât burasî (T.); read bûq er ruqâd.
***revolver:** add museddes.
riddle: (conundrum) hazûra.
***rifle:** (gun) add bunduqîya.
***ripe:** add nâdhij.
***robber:** add luṣṣ, *pl.* luṣûṣ.
***robust:** add dhalî'.
***rocky:** add ṣakharî.
***roller:** add mekbes.
***rotation:** add (in r.) bi dôwr.
***round:** add (prep.) ḥawl.
roundness: kurrawîya.
***royal:** add melekî; mulûkî.
***rubber:** add maṭâṭ.
rupture: *n.* (anat.) fetek; (of relations) inqiṭâ'.
***rust:** add *n.* ṣada.

S

***salary:** add ràtib, *pl.* rawàtib.
***salutation:** add taḥîyya.
***salute:** delete akhadh temennî; read ḥayya, yuḥayyî.
salve: *n.* marham.

sanction: *n*. add (boycott) ʿaqûba, *pl*. ʿaqûbàt.
sarcasm: tehekkum.
sarcastic: mutehekkim.
***scale**: add *n*. (balance) gubbàn.
***scar**: *n*. add nadba.
***scheme**: *n*. add mashrûʿ.
screw-driver: mafell; dernafîs (F.).
***secretary**: *n*. add sekertàr; (Sec. for Educ.) read nâdhir maʿârif.
***section**: (of document) bend, *pl*. bunûd.
***sediment**: add rusûb.
senate: mejlis aʿyàn.
***senator**: add ʿain, *pl*. aʿyàn.
***send**: add dezz, yadizz.
sensation: (e.g. bodily) ḥâssa.
sensitive: ḥassàs.
***sentinel**: add khafîr.
septic: masmûm.
sequel: mulḥaq.
***sergeant**: read ʿarîf, *pl*. ʿurafâ; (s. maj.) ra-îs ʿurafâ; (q. mast. s.) ʿarîf iʿâsha.
series: teselsul.
***serious**: (temperament) jiddî.
***seriously**: bi jiddîya.
***seriousness**: jiddîya.
***settlement**: (after discussion) ḥall.
sexton: bawwàb.
shade: *n*. add (window) parda; sitâr; (lamp) madhalla.
***shake**: (hand) add taṣâfaḥ.
***shallow**: add dhaḥal.
***share-holder**: add musàhim.
shear: *v*. (sheep) jezz, yajuzz.
***shed**: add *n*. makhzan.
shell: (bombard) add qaṣaf, yaqṣaf.
***shepherd**: add shàwi, *pl*. shawai; shawâwî.
***ship**: (steamship) add bâkhira, *pl*. bawâkhir.
***shoe**: add ḥidhà, *pl*. eḥdhiya.
***shop**: add ḥânût, *pl*. ḥawânît.
short-hand: khaṭṭ ikhtizàlî.
***shot**: (act) add ṭilqa nârîya.
***shovel**: add mijrafa.
***shrapnel**: minthâr.
***sight**: (of gun) add sadàda.
***sign**: *v*. (sign name) add waqqaʿ, yuwaqqiʿ.
signaller: mukhâbir.
***signature**: add towqîʿ.
***silken**: add ḥarîrî.
***silver**: adj. add fidhdhî.
sinewy: dhaliʿ.
***sir**: delete (to native) effendim; read sêyyidi.
siren: ṣâfira.
***situation**: add (state of affairs) wadhʿîya.
skilled: add (s. labourers) ʿummàl màhirin.
***slipshod**: add mutahàmil.
***slovenly**: add mutahàmil.
***slowly**: add baṭi.
***smith**: (copper smith) read ṣaffâr.
***soft**: add (pliable) merin.
***soil**: *n*. (earth) add turba.
***soldier**: add jundî, *pl*. jundiyyîn.
***sour**: add *v*. râb, yarûb (adj. milk) râyib.
***sovereign**: add *n*. (ruler) melek, *pl*. mulûk.
***sovereignty**: siyàda.
***spare**: (spare time) add farâgh; (e.g. tire) iḥtiyâṭ.
***spatter**: add laṭṭakh.
***speaker**: add (loud s.) ḥâkî.
specialist: ikhtiṣâṣî.
specialize: takhaṣṣaṣ.
***spend**: add enfed, yunfid.

spent: *v. intrans.* (be spent); nefed, yinfed.
*__spit__: *v. intrans.* (expectorate) add baṣaq, yabṣaq; *n.* add baṣâq.
*__spoke__: add fermel, *pl.* faràmil.
*__spontaneously__: add min tilqâ nefsihi.
spool: bekera.
*__spoon__: add mal'aqa.
*__squad__: delete ṭakhm; read rahṭ, *pl.* arhâṭ.
*__squadron__: (air force) serrîya; *pl.* serràya.
*__stage__: (raised place) add mersaḥ; (of journey) meshya.
*__stagger__: add tarannaḥ.
*__stamp__: (postage s.) delete pul; read ṭâbi', *pl.* ṭâwâbi'.
*__standard__: (flag) delete beraq, sanjaq; read 'alam, *pl.* a'làm; liwa, *pl.* elwiya; râya, *pl.* râ-yàt.
*__stare__: shakhaṣ fi, yashkhaṣ.
*__statement__: read 'arîdha.
*__station__: (police s.) read markaz shuraṭa; (s. master) mudîr maḥaṭṭa.
*__statistics__: add iḥṣâ-iyàt.
*__stay__: *n.* add (for pole) mesned.
*__steersman__: add sukkànî.
stem: *n.* (of plant) sâq.
*__sterile__: (disinfected) mu'aqqam.
sterilization: ta'qîm.
*__sterilize__: add 'aqqam.
*__stipend__: add ràtib, *pl.* rawàtib.
stoker: waqqâd.
*__stop__: (close hole) add ḥasha, yaḥshu.
*__stove__: add mawqad.
*__straightforward__: delete ashkara (P.); read jihâran.
*__street__: add jàda, *pl.* jàdàt.
*__stress__: (accent) add nubra.
*__stretcher__: add naqqâla.
*__strike__: (from work) add adhrab, yudhrib; *n.* idhrâb.
*__string__: *v.* (s. beads) ladham, yaldham.
*__stripe__: (with whip) add jelda.
*__structure__: (building) add binà, *pl.* ebniya.
*__style__: (fashion) add zê, *pl.* ezyà.
*__subdue__: add akhdha', yukhdhi'.
*__subject__: (liable to) add ma'rûdh ila.
*__subordinate__: *n.* add mustakhdam.
*__succeed__: add (to throne); tabawwa el 'arsh.
*__succession__: (to throne) tabawwu.
*__successor__: add (to throne) khalîfa.
*__such__: add kedha with *n.* or *adj.*
*__suction__: add imtiṣâṣ.
*__sugar__: add sukkar.
sulk: add ḥarad, yaḥrad; ta'abbas.
sulky: ḥardàn.
*__summer__: *v.* add ṣeyyef.
*__summit__: add qimma, *pl.* qimam.
*__summon__: add nàda, yunàdî.
sundry: shetta.
*__sunny__: add mushmis.
*__supplementary__: add *adj.* idhâfî.
*__supply__: *n.* add tejhîz; (water s.) isàlet el mà.
*__suppress__: add (rebellion) akhmad, yukhmid.

***surely**: add muḥaqqaq.
surly: shekis.
***swagger**: add tarannaḥ.
***swamp**: add mustenqa'a.
***switch**: add (elec.) miftâḥ; (s. board) lôwḥat et taqsîm.
***syphilis**: delete frengi; read zuhrîya.
***syringe**: *n.* add ibra.

T

***table**: (furniture) mindhada.
***take**: add (takes time) yastaghriq waqt.
***tally**: add *n.* (t. clerk) kàtib ta'dàd.
***tangible**: add malmûs; maḥsûs.
***tank**: add khazàn; (mil. t.) dabbàba.
***tap**: *n.* add (water) ḥanafîya; mazembla.
***target**: add hedef.
***tariff**: add ta'rîfa.
***tasteless**: add màsikh.
***tax**: *n.* add dharîba, *pl.* dharâyib; (on animals) kôda.
***taxable**: ma'rûdh li resm.
***taxation**: add jibàya.
***tax gatherer**: delete tahsildar; read jàbi, *pl.* jubàt.
***team**: (athletic) firqa, *pl.* firaq.
***technically**: fennan.
***tedious**: mumill.
***telegram**: read barqîya.
***telegraph**: *v.* read abraq, yubriq; *n.* read barqîya.
***telephone**: *n.* add ḥàkî; maserra.
***telescope**: add mirqab.
***temple**: add (of head) ṣadgh, *pl.* aṣdâgh.
***tender**: add *n.* (financial) 'iṭâ; munâqasa; add (*adj.*) ṭarî.
***tentative**: add tajrîbî.
***theft**: add seriqa.
***theory**: add nadharîya.
thermos flask: zemzemîya.
***ticket**: add baṭâqa, *pl.* baṭâqàt.
***tight**: add (e.g. belt) adj. ḥazîq.
***tighten**: add ḥazzaq.
***tile**: (flat) delete qarmid; read kàshî.
***time**: add (European t.) zawàlì; add *v.* (takes t.) yastaghriq waqt.
toilet: (W.C.) marḥâdh, *pl.* marâḥîdh; bêt el khalâ.
***torpedo**: add nassàf.
torrent: sêl; tayâr.
tournament: mubàràt.
***towel**: add minshefa, *pl.* manàshif.
townsman: ḥadharî.
***tract**: (leaflet) karràsa, *pl.* karàrîs.
trade-mark: 'alàma fâriqa.
traffic: *n.* add (movement) naqlîya; naqlîyàt; (t. department) idâret en naqlîyàt.
***train**: *n.* (railway train) delete qaṭr; tren; read qaṭâr.
***treasury**: add khazîna.
***tribunal**: add hê-ya.
trigonometry: 'ilm el muthellethàt.
***Tripoli**: add (of Syria) ṭrablis esh shàm.
***tropics**: add el manâṭiq el ḥàrra.
truck: see lorry.
***trust**: *v. trans.* add wathaq bi, yathiq; *n.* (confidence) read thiqa.

***try**: (legally) ḥâkam, yuḥâkim.
***tube**: (of metal) read lûlab.
tuck: (in cloth) khubna.
***tunnel**: add nafaq.
twice: marratên; mudhâ''af.
twilight: (morning) fijr; (evening) shafaq.
***typewriter**: read àla ṭâbi'a.

U

***unanimously**: add bi ittifâq el aṣwât; bil ijma'.
***unbelief**: add ilḥâd.
***unbeliever**: add mulḥid.
***unconsciously**: add fâqid esh shu'ûr.
***underling**: add taḥt el amr.
***understanding**: (agreement) add tafàhum.
unemployment: baṭâla.
***union**: add (trade) naqâba.
***unnecessary**: add ghair dhurûrî.
unveil: keshef; sefer.
unveiling: (face) sufûr.
***use**: (to be of no use) read mâ yufîd.
***utensil**: (dish) add inà, *pl.* awàni.

V

***vacant**: add (position) shâghir.
***vaccinate**: (for small pox) add ṭa''am.
***vaccination**: add taṭ'îm.
***vacuum**: add farâgh.
***value**: *v.* (estimate) add khamman.
***valve**: add ṣimâma.
***vehicle**: add 'ajala; 'araba.
***veil**: *n.* add ḥijàb.
***ventilate**: add rawwaḥ.
***ventilator**: add marwaḥ.
***vice-versa**: read el 'aks bil 'aks.
***violation**: add tajàwuz.
***virgin**: add bint.
***visionary**: (unreal) wehmî.
***vocation**: add miḥna, *pl.* miḥan.
***volley ball**: el kurrat et ṭâyira.
volt: folt.
voltage: qûwat et tayâr.
***vote**: *v.* add ṣawwat.
***voting**: add taṣwît.

W

***wage**: *n.* add ujra.
***wait**: add (wait for) intadhar; te-enna.
***waive**: add takhalla 'an.
***wake**: *v. intrans.* add istêqadh, yastêqadh; qa'ad, yaq'ad.
***wall**: add jidâr, *pl.* judràn.
wallet: kîs; juzdàn.
***warder**: delete ghurdyan; add ḥâris.
***ware-house**: add mustawda'.
***warrant**: *n.* add (w. officer) nàyib dhâbiṭ.
***water-closet**: add khala; marḥâdh.
water-fall: shalàla.
***wave**: add *v. intrans.* (flag) khafaq.
wave-length: ṭûl el môwja.
***weather**: (climate) add ṭaqs.
weed: *v.* rebbesh.
***wharf**: add raṣîf, *pl.* erṣifa.
***whip**: add *v.* jeled, yijlad.
***whistle**: *n.* (implement) add ṣâfira; ṣafâra.
***window**: add menfedh, *pl.* manàfidh.
winner: ghâlib.
***wire**: add silk, *pl.* eslàk.

wireless: là silkî.
wool: ṣûf.
workshop: maṣna‘; ma‘mal.
world: (of people) dunya; ‘âlim.
worm: dûda, *pl.* dûd.
wormy: mudawwad.
worry: *v. intrans.* tekedder; *v. trans.* kedder; az‘aj; *n.* kedr; ghamm; hamm.
wreath: iklîl, *pl.* akàlîl.
***wrestle**: add taṣâra‘.
***wrestler**: muṣâri‘.

Z

zero: ṣifr.
zionism: ṣihyônîya.
zionist: ṣihyônî.